AMERICA'S
TEST KITCHEN

ALSO BY THE EDITORS AT AMERICA'S TEST KITCHEN

The Complete Vegetarian Cookbook
The America's Test Kitchen New Family Cookbook
The Complete Cooking for Two Cookbook
The America's Test Kitchen Cooking School Cookbook
The Cook's Illustrated Meat Book
The Cook's Illustrated Baking Book
The Cook's Illustrated Cookbook
The Science of Good Cooking
The America's Test Kitchen Menu Cookbook
The America's Test Kitchen Quick Family Cookbook
The America's Test Kitchen Healthy Family Cookbook
The America's Test Kitchen Family Baking Book

THE AMERICA'S TEST KITCHEN LIBRARY SERIES

The Best Mexican Recipes
The Make-Ahead Cook
The How Can It Be Gluten Free Cookbook
Healthy Slow Cooker Revolution
Slow Cooker Revolution Volume 2: The Easy-Prep Edition
Slow Cooker Revolution
The Six-Ingredient Solution
Pressure Cooker Perfection
Comfort Food Makeovers
The America's Test Kitchen D.I.Y. Cookbook
Pasta Revolution
Simple Weeknight Favorites
The Best Simple Recipes

THE TV COMPANION SERIES

The Complete Cook's Country TV Show Cookbook
The Complete America's Test Kitchen TV Show Cookbook 2001–2015
America's Test Kitchen: The TV Companion Cookbook (2009 and 2011–2015 Editions)

THE COOK'S COUNTRY SERIES

From Our Grandmothers' Kitchens
Cook's Country Blue Ribbon Desserts
Cook's Country Best Potluck Recipes
Cook's Country Best Lost Suppers
Cook's Country Best Grilling Recipes
The Cook's Country Cookbook
America's Best Lost Recipes

AMERICA'S TEST KITCHEN ANNUALS

The Best of America's Test Kitchen (2007–2015 Editions)
Cooking for Two (2010–2013 Editions)
Light & Healthy (2010–2012 Editions)

THE BEST RECIPE SERIES

The New Best Recipe
More Best Recipes
The Best One-Dish Suppers
Soups, Stews & Chilis
The Best Skillet Recipes
The Best Slow & Easy Recipes
The Best Chicken Recipes
The Best International Recipe
The Best Make-Ahead Recipe
The Best 30-Minute Recipe
The Best Light Recipe
The Cook's Illustrated Guide to Grilling and Barbecue
Best American Side Dishes
Cover & Bake
Steaks, Chops, Roasts & Ribs
Italian Classics
American Classics

FOR A FULL LISTING OF ALL OUR BOOKS OR TO ORDER TITLES

CooksCountry.com
CooksIllustrated.com
AmericasTestKitchen.com
or call 800-611-0759

PRAISE FOR OTHER AMERICA'S TEST KITCHEN TITLES

"The entire book is stuffed with recipes that will blow your dinner-table audience away like leaves from a sidewalk in November."
SAN FRANCISCO BOOK REVIEW ON *THE COMPLETE COOK'S COUNTRY TV SHOW COOKBOOK*

"The sum total of exhaustive experimentation . . . anyone interested in gluten-free cookery simply shouldn't be without it."
NIGELLA LAWSON ON *THE HOW CAN IT BE GLUTEN FREE COOKBOOK*

"Even ultra-experienced gluten-free cooks and bakers will learn something from this thoroughly researched, thoughtfully presented volume."
PUBLISHERS WEEKLY ON *THE HOW CAN IT BE GLUTEN FREE COOKBOOK*

"The 21st-century *Fannie Farmer Cookbook* or *The Joy of Cooking.* If you had to have one cookbook and that's all you could have, this one would do it."
CBS SAN FRANCISCO ON *THE NEW FAMILY COOKBOOK*

"This book upgrades slow cooking for discriminating, 21st-century palates—that is indeed revolutionary."
THE DALLAS MORNING NEWS ON *SLOW COOKER REVOLUTION*

"One bag, 3 meals? Get the biggest bang for your buck."
FOX NEWS ON *THE MAKE-AHEAD COOK*

"The go-to gift book for newlyweds, small families or empty nesters."
ORLANDO SENTINEL ON *THE COMPLETE COOKING FOR TWO COOKBOOK*

"Some 2,500 photos walk readers through 600 painstakingly tested recipes, leaving little room for error."
ASSOCIATED PRESS ON *THE AMERICA'S TEST KITCHEN COOKING SCHOOL COOKBOOK*

"Ideal as a reference for the bookshelf and as a book to curl up and get lost in, this volume will be turned to time and again for definitive instruction on just about any food-related matter."
PUBLISHERS WEEKLY ON *THE SCIENCE OF GOOD COOKING*

"A one-volume kitchen seminar, addressing in one smart chapter after another the sometimes surprising whys behind a cook's best practices. . . . You get the myth, the theory, the science and the proof, all rigorously interrogated as only America's Test Kitchen can do."
NPR ON *THE SCIENCE OF GOOD COOKING*

"This encyclopedia of meat cookery would feel completely overwhelming if it weren't so meticulously organized and artfully designed. This is Cook's Illustrated at its finest."
THE KITCHN ON *THE COOK'S ILLUSTRATED MEAT BOOK*

"Carnivores with an obsession for perfection will likely have found their new bible in this comprehensive collection."
PUBLISHERS WEEKLY (STARRED REVIEW) ON *THE COOK'S ILLUSTRATED MEAT BOOK*

"This book is a comprehensive, no-nonsense guide . . . a well-thought-out, clearly explained primer for every aspect of home baking."
THE WALL STREET JOURNAL ON *THE COOK'S ILLUSTRATED BAKING BOOK*

"Buy this gem for the foodie in your family, and spend the extra money to get yourself a copy too."
THE MISSOURIAN ON *THE BEST OF AMERICA'S TEST KITCHEN 2015*

"Cook-friendly and kitchen-oriented, illuminating the process of preparing food instead of mystifying it . . . . the perfect kitchen home companion."
THE WALL STREET JOURNAL ON *THE COOK'S ILLUSTRATED COOKBOOK*

"A wonderfully comprehensive guide for budding chefs. . . . Throughout are the helpful tips and exacting illustrations that make ATK a peerless source for culinary wisdom."
PUBLISHERS WEEKLY ON *THE COOK'S ILLUSTRATED COOKBOOK*

"If this were the only cookbook you owned, you would cook well, be everyone's favorite host, have a well-run kitchen, and eat happily every day."
THECITYCOOK.COM ON *THE AMERICA'S TEST KITCHEN MENU COOKBOOK*

"There are pasta books . . . and then there's this pasta book. Flip your carbohydrate dreams upside down and strain them through this sieve of revolutionary, creative, and also traditional recipes."
SAN FRANCISCO BOOK REVIEW ON *PASTA REVOLUTION*

"Further proof that practice makes perfect, if not transcendent. . . . If an intermediate cook follows the directions exactly, the results will be better than takeout or Mom's."
THE NEW YORK TIMES ON *THE NEW BEST RECIPE*

"Rely on this doorstopper for explicit and comprehensive takes on recipes from basic to sophisticated."
TOLEDO BLADE ON *THE COMPLETE AMERICA'S TEST KITCHEN TV SHOW COOKBOOK*

"America's Test Kitchen spent two years reimagining cooking for the 21st century. The result is an exhaustive collection offering a fresh approach to quick cooking."
THE DETROIT NEWS ON *THE AMERICA'S TEST KITCHEN QUICK FAMILY COOKBOOK*

Cook's Country
EATS LOCAL

150 REGIONAL RECIPES
YOU SHOULD BE MAKING
NO MATTER WHERE YOU LIVE

BY THE EDITORS AT AMERICA'S TEST KITCHEN

Copyright © 2015 by the Editors at America's Test Kitchen

All rights reserved. No part of this book may be reproduced or transmitted in any manner whatsoever without written permission from the publisher, except in the case of brief quotations embodied in critical articles or reviews.

America's Test Kitchen
17 Station Street
Brookline, MA 02445

Library of Congress Cataloging-in-Publication Data
Cook's Country eats local : 150 regional recipes you should be making no matter where you live / by the editors at America's Test Kitchen.
    pages cm
Includes bibliographical references and index.
 ISBN 978-1-936493-99-9 (alk. paper)
1. Cooking, American. I. Cook's country. II. America's test kitchen (Television program)
 TX715.C78535 2015
 641.5973--dc23

                    2015005574

ISBN: 978-1-936493-99-9
Paperback: $26.95 US

Manufactured in the United States of America
10 9 8 7 6 5 4 3 2 1

Distributed by
Penguin Random House Publisher Services
1745 Broadway
New York, NY 10019

AMERICA'S TEST KITCHEN
RECIPES THAT WORK®

CooksCountry.com
CooksCountryTV.com
AmericasTestKitchenTV.com
AmericasTestKitchenFeed.com

Editorial Director: Jack Bishop
Editorial Director, Books: Elizabeth Carduff
Executive Editor: Lori Galvin
Senior Editor: Debra Hudak
Assistant Editor: Melissa Herrick
Editorial Assistant: Samantha Ronan
Design Director: Amy Klee
Art Director: Greg Galvan
Designer: Jen Kanavos Hoffman
Maps: Michael Newhouse
Photography Director: Julie Cote
Associate Art Director, Photography: Steve Klise
Staff Photographer: Daniel J. van Ackere
Additional Photography: Keller + Keller and Carl Tremblay
Food Styling: Catrine Kelty and Marie Piraino
Photoshoot Kitchen Team:
        Associate Editor: Chris O'Connor
        Test Cook: Daniel Cellucci
        Assistant Test Cook: Matthew Fairman
Production Director: Guy Rochford
Senior Production Manager: Jessica Lindheimer Quirk
Production Management Specialist: Christine Walsh
Production and Imaging Specialists: Heather Dube, Dennis Noble, Lauren Robbins, and Jessica Voas
Project Manager: Britt Dresser
Copy Editor: Barbara Wood
Proofreader: Pat Jalbert-Levine
Indexer: Elizabeth Parson

Pictured opposite title page: Harvey House Chocolate Puffs (page 287)
Pictured above: Rhode Island Johnnycakes (page 47), Chicago-Style Italian Beef Sandwiches (page 187), Bee Sting Cake (page 65)
Pictured on contents page: Chicken Riggies (page 13), South Carolina Shrimp Burgers (page 115), Cheese Frenchees (page 173), Tick Tock Orange Sticky Rolls (page 285)

CONTENTS

CHAPTER 1

NEW ENGLAND AND
THE MID-ATLANTIC

1

CHAPTER 2

APPALACHIA
AND THE SOUTH

77

CHAPTER 3

THE MIDWEST AND
GREAT PLAINS

171

CHAPTER 4

TEXAS AND
THE WEST

235

WELCOME
VIII

PREFACE
IX

DINING
DESTINATIONS
294

CONVERSIONS &
EQUIVALENTS
296

INDEX
298

WELCOME TO AMERICA'S TEST KITCHEN

This book has been tested, written, and edited by the folks at America's Test Kitchen, a very real 2,500-square-foot kitchen located just outside of Boston. It is the home of *Cook's Illustrated* magazine and *Cook's Country* magazine and is the Monday-through-Friday destination for more than four dozen test cooks, editors, food scientists, tasters, and cookware specialists. Our mission is to test recipes over and over again until we understand how and why they work and until we arrive at the "best" version.

We start the process of testing a recipe with a complete lack of preconceptions, which means that we accept no claim, no theory, no technique, and no recipe at face value. We simply assemble as many variations as possible, test a half-dozen of the most promising, and taste the results blind. We then construct our own hybrid recipe and continue to test it, varying ingredients, techniques, and cooking times until we reach a consensus. The result, we hope, is the best version of a particular recipe, but we realize that only you can be the final judge of our success (or failure). As we like to say in the test kitchen, "We make the mistakes, so you don't have to."

All of this would not be possible without a belief that good cooking, much like good music, is indeed based on a foundation of objective technique. Some people like spicy foods and others don't, but there is a right way to sauté, there is a best way to cook a pot roast, and there are measurable scientific principles involved in producing perfectly beaten, stable egg whites. This is our ultimate goal: to investigate the fundamental principles of cooking so that you become a better cook. It is as simple as that.

If you're curious to see what goes on behind the scenes at America's Test Kitchen, check out our daily blog, The Feed, at AmericasTestKitchenFeed.com, which features kitchen snapshots, exclusive recipes, video tips, and much more. You can watch us work (in our actual test kitchen) by tuning in to *America's Test Kitchen* (AmericasTestKitchen.com) or *Cook's Country from America's Test Kitchen* (CooksCountryTV.com) on public television. Tune in to *America's Test Kitchen Radio* (ATKradio.com) on public radio to listen to insights, tips, and techniques that illuminate the truth about real

home cooking. Want to hone your cooking skills or finally learn how to bake—from an America's Test Kitchen test cook? Enroll in a cooking class at our online cooking school at OnlineCookingSchool.com. And find information about subscribing to *Cook's Illustrated* magazine at CooksIllustrated.com or *Cook's Country* magazine at CooksCountry.com. Both magazines are published every other month. However you choose to visit us, we welcome you into our kitchen, where you can stand by our side as we test our way to the best recipes in America.

f FACEBOOK.COM/AMERICASTESTKITCHEN

y TWITTER.COM/TESTKITCHEN

▶ YOUTUBE.COM/AMERICASTESTKITCHEN

◉ INSTAGRAM.COM/TESTKITCHEN

℗ PINTEREST.COM/TESTKITCHEN

t AMERICASTESTKITCHEN.TUMBLR.COM

g+ GOOGLE.COM/+AMERICASTESTKITCHEN

PREFACE

Back in the 1970s, I drove across America on three different occasions, stopping in Tennessee diners, truck stops in Oklahoma, and local eateries from the Deep South to the Texas Panhandle to the fast-food haunts of Southern California. Not all of the food was brilliant, but once in a while I came across a recipe that was so special that it told the story of that particular place—it couldn't have been served anywhere else.

Yes, I was familiar with most of what New England has to offer, like Connecticut Steamed Cheeseburgers and Chicken Riggies, and I knew something about Muffulettas and Oyster Po' Boys from New Orleans as well as Cheddar Beer Soup from Wisconsin, but I had never tasted Moravian Sugar Cake, Sweet Potato Sonker from the Carolinas, Iowa Loose Meat Sandwiches (these sound awful and don't look so good but they are fabulous), Millionaire Pie, Texas Caviar, or Tick Tock Orange Sticky Rolls.

For half a century, local American regional specialties have been relegated to the back burner—community cookbook recipes that few of us took seriously. The food scene was all about the hottest New York, LA, or San Francisco chefs, the "new" American cuisine rather than the cooking of our past. And, to be fair, much of the older repertoire did need a fresh look to make it vital and modern without losing its essence. (That's where our test kitchen can help out—we rebuild recipes as if they are old cars, fixing the transmissions and restoring body work to new condition!) Plus, many recipes depend on hard-to-find local ingredients, and we work hard to make these recipes accessible to a national audience.

Cook's Country Eats Local is the result of almost a decade of investigation by the editors of *Cook's Country* magazine who have scoured the country looking for local specialties. We attend local food festivals, interview local restaurateurs and cooks, and spend weeks at a time on the road, the "Blue Highways" (small two-lane roads) that many writers have found so inspirational. What we have discovered is a whole new world of American cooking, recipes that have flown beneath the national radar for generations only to come back into the spotlight in time to honor our own culinary history.

Who wouldn't want a recipe for Thoroughbred Pie, made with butter, bourbon, and a layer of melted chocolate on the bottom? Or Iron Range Porketta, which is packed with the flavor of fennel (fresh and seeds), or Knoephla Soup, made with chicken and tiny dumplings (just squeeze the batter out of a zipper-lock bag that has one corner cut off)? Bierocks (also called Runsas) are more than tasty beef buns filled with beef, cabbage, and cheese. And, one of my favorites, Bee Sting Cake is made with lush vanilla custard filling, and the cake itself is a brioche-style cake with a honey-almond crust. I'll take that dessert over a French tart any day.

Plus, *Cook's Country Eats Local* provides regional maps with information about where to go to eat many of these recipes locally, from Maine to Southern California. And, of course, these recipes have been put through their paces at the Cook's Country test kitchen so you know that they will work the first time and every time.

When I was growing up, Marie Briggs, our town baker, was known for her hand-size molasses cookies that were soft, not hard, and had the salty tang of good blackstrap molasses. It was her signature recipe, although she also made top-notch biscuits and anadama bread as well. Just like Marie, there are thousands of cooks around the country who have their own local specialties, recipes that are tied to small towns and their history. This is the food of America's past and future, the recipes that make us who we are today.

Thanks for stopping by. We are proud of this collection of recipes and hope that many of these dishes become part of your culinary repertoire, no matter where you live.

CHRISTOPHER KIMBALL
Founder and Editor,
Cook's Illustrated and *Cook's Country*
Host, *America's Test Kitchen* and
Cook's Country from America's Test Kitchen

NEW ENGLAND AND THE MID-ATLANTIC

JOE BOOKER STEW
CENTRAL MAINE

MAPLE SYRUP PIE
VERMONT AND
NEW HAMPSHIRE

CANADA

UTICA GREENS
UTICA, NY

CHICKEN SPIEDIES
UPSTATE NEW YORK

MAINE

VT

NH

NEW YORK

MASS.

RI

CT

WELLESLEY
FUDGE CAKE
WELLESLEY, MA

PENNSYLVANIA

NJ

RHODE ISLAND
JOHNNYCAKES
RICHMOND, RI

BABKA
NEW YORK CITY, NY

PITTSBURGH
WEDDING SOUP
PITTSBURGH, PA

CITY CHICKEN
WESTERN
PENNSYLVANIA

ATLANTIC OCEAN

3 **Connecticut Steamed Cheeseburgers** ⭐

5 **Chicken Spiedies**

7 **Boneless Buffalo Chicken**

9 **Philadelphia Cheesesteaks** ⭐

11 **Chicken à la King**

   Toasted Italian Bread

13 **Chicken Riggies** ⭐

15 **Utica Greens**

17 **City Chicken**

19 **New England Bar Pizza** ⭐

21 **Corned Beef and Cabbage**

23 **Easy New England Clam Chowder**

23 **Common Crackers**

25 **Rhode Island Red Clam Chowder**

   Garlic Toasts

27 **New England Fish Chowder**

29 **Classic Corn Chowder**

   with Andouille and Bell Pepper

   with Chorizo and Chiles

   with Sweet Potatoes and Cayenne

   with Prosciutto and Sage

31 **Joe Booker Stew**

33 **Pittsburgh Wedding Soup**

35 **Waldorf Salad**

   with Dried Cherries and Pecans

   with Red Grapes and Almonds

   Curried Waldorf Salad with Green
     Grapes and Peanuts

37 **Cider-Glazed Root Vegetables**

   with Pomegranate and Cilantro

39 **Quicker Boston Baked Beans**

41 **Potato Knishes**

43 **Bialys**

45 **Ballpark Pretzels**

47 **Rhode Island Johnnycakes**

   Maple Butter

49 **Potato Biscuits with Chives**

   with Cheddar and Scallions

   with Bacon

51 **Garlic Knots**

53 **Anadama Bread**

55 **Babka**

57 **Hermit Cookies**

59 **Potato Chip Cookies**

   Chocolate-Dipped Potato
     Chip Cookies

61 **Boston Cream Cupcakes**

63 **Wellesley Fudge Cake**

65 **Bee Sting Cake**

67 **Cranberry Upside-Down Cake**

69 **Maple Syrup Pie**

   Crème Fraîche

71 **Marlborough Apple Pie**

73 **Summer Blueberry Crumble**

75 **Lemon Snow**

⭐ FIND A LOCAL HOT SPOT

✔ WHY THIS RECIPE WORKS

Connecticut's steamed burgers prove that medium-well beef need not be dry and gray. Taking a cue from the steam cabinets used by the state's burger pros, we created our own moist cooking environment with a Dutch oven and metal steamer basket. We pressed a small divot into the center of each patty to prevent the burgers from bulging upward while cooking. Our patties were steamed to a juicy medium-well in just 10 minutes; small amounts of savory tomato paste, soy sauce, and onion powder added to the ground beef before forming the patties kicked up their flavor. Placing the buns right in the pot and topping the burgers with shredded cheddar cheese allowed for soft, warm bread and gooey cheese that stayed put. After one bite, we were steamed burger converts. For burgers this juicy and flavorful, we were ready to forget the grill.

CONNECTICUT STEAMED CHEESEBURGERS

SERVES 4

We prefer these burgers cooked medium-well, but for medium burgers, steam them for 7 minutes before shutting off the heat and adding the cheese. Serve these burgers with the usual array of garnishes and condiments: lettuce, tomato, onion, ketchup, mayonnaise, and mustard.

1½	pounds 85 percent lean ground beef
2	teaspoons soy sauce
1	teaspoon onion powder
1	teaspoon tomato paste
¾	teaspoon salt
¾	teaspoon pepper
4	ounces sharp cheddar cheese, shredded (1 cup)
4	hamburger buns

1. Combine beef, soy sauce, onion powder, tomato paste, salt, and pepper in bowl. Divide beef into 4 balls. Gently flatten into patties ¾ inch thick and 4 inches wide. Press shallow divot into center of each patty. Bring 4 cups water to boil in covered Dutch oven over medium-high heat (water should not touch bottom of steamer basket).

2. Arrange patties in steamer basket. Set steamer basket inside Dutch oven, cover, and cook for 8 minutes. Remove Dutch oven from heat. Divide cheese evenly among burgers, cover, and let sit until cheese melts, about 2 minutes. Place bun tops on burgers and bun bottoms, cut side up, on top of bun tops. Cover and let sit until buns soften, about 30 seconds. Transfer bun bottoms to cutting board, add condiments, and top with burgers and bun tops. Serve.

EATING LOCAL ★ MERIDEN, CT

What do steamed cheeseburgers have to do with suburban Connecticut? These juicy burgers smothered in gooey cheese are said to descend from steamed beef-and-cheese sandwiches, which were sold from horse-drawn carts to construction workers in the Hartford area of central Connecticut in the 1920s. What were these construction workers building? Housing, retail shops, taverns—you name it—to accommodate an influx of residents from the city of Hartford to the suburbs. Horse-drawn trolley lines and later electric trolley lines made it possible for many of the city's residents to live in less crowded conditions, yet still be able to commute to work. The population of one suburb, West Hartford, grew from just 4,000 to more than 24,000 between 1910 and 1930. In 1959 in Meriden, Connecticut, **TED'S RESTAURANT** started steaming their first cheeseburgers—and they still make them today. The meat and cheese are cooked in separate molds in a custom-made steam cabinet; the burger browns and the cheese melts into a gooey mass. The two are combined into a fantastically messy but delicious burger you'll not soon forget.

TED'S RESTAURANT
1046 Broad St., Meriden, CT

✓ WHY THIS RECIPE WORKS

Traditionally, preparing chicken spiedies, upstate New York's juicy grilled chicken sandwiches, calls for up to a week of marinating before the meat ever hits the grill. We wanted to overrule this custom by creating a marinade that imparted tangy, bright flavor without the wait. Pricking the chicken with a fork before marinating allowed the flavor to penetrate the meat in only 30 minutes. A potent, oil-based marinade kept the chicken moist on the grill, and a drizzle of reserved marinade mixed with lemon, vinegar, and mayonnaise reinforced our spiedies' trademark flavors before serving. With these small changes, we had a zesty, full-flavored sandwich ready in time for dinner tonight.

CHICKEN SPIEDIES

SERVES 6

You will need six 12-inch metal skewers for this recipe.

½	**cup olive oil**
2	**tablespoons chopped fresh basil**
2	**garlic cloves, minced**
2	**teaspoons grated lemon zest plus 1 tablespoon juice**
1	**teaspoon salt**
½	**teaspoon pepper**
½	**teaspoon dried oregano**
¼	**teaspoon red pepper flakes**
3	**tablespoons mayonnaise**
1	**tablespoon red wine vinegar**
4	**(6-ounce) boneless, skinless chicken breasts, trimmed**
6	**(6-inch) sub rolls, partially split lengthwise, or 6 large slices Italian bread**

1. Combine oil, basil, garlic, lemon zest, salt, pepper, oregano, and pepper flakes in large bowl. Transfer 2 tablespoons oil mixture to separate bowl and whisk in mayonnaise, vinegar, and lemon juice; refrigerate until ready to serve. (Marinade and sauce can each be refrigerated, covered, for up to 2 days.)

2. Prick breasts all over with fork, cut into 1¼-inch chunks, and transfer to bowl with remaining oil mixture. Refrigerate, covered, for 30 minutes or up to 3 hours.

3. Remove chicken from marinade and thread chunks onto six 12-inch metal skewers.

4A. FOR A CHARCOAL GRILL: Open bottom vent completely. Light large chimney starter filled with charcoal briquettes (6 quarts). When top coals are partially covered with ash, pour evenly over grill. Set cooking grate in place, cover, and open lid vent completely. Heat grill until hot, about 5 minutes.

4B. FOR A GAS GRILL: Turn all burners to high, cover, and heat grill until hot, about 15 minutes. Leave all burners on high.

5. Clean and oil cooking grate. Place skewers on grill and cook (covered if using gas), turning frequently, until lightly charred and cooked through, 10 to 15 minutes.

6. Transfer chicken to rolls, remove skewers, and drizzle with mayonnaise mixture. Serve.

SPEEDY SPIEDIE PREP

For the most flavor in the least time, follow these quick steps.

1. To help marinade penetrate meat, prick chicken breasts all over with fork.

2. To expose more surface area to marinade, cut chicken into 1¼-inch chunks.

3. To build lots of flavor in only 30 minutes, combine chicken with highly seasoned marinade.

✔ WHY THIS RECIPE WORKS

For Buffalo chicken that could compete with the fiery finger food at our favorite sports bar, we wanted to create great flavor and texture from the inside out. These nuggets needed moist chicken, a crunchy coating, and just enough heat, plus a cool blue cheese dressing to keep the spicy burn in check. Taking a tip from fried chicken recipes, we soaked the chicken in a buttermilk brine to keep the meat juicy and seasoned before dredging it in a mixture of cornstarch, flour, baking soda, and a touch of hot sauce. This coating crisped beautifully, and our brilliant orange Buffalo sauce—thickened with cornstarch—clung to the crags nicely, ensuring a balanced dose of heat in every bite. Served with our homemade blue cheese dressing, this Buffalo chicken was game day–ready.

BONELESS BUFFALO CHICKEN SERVES 4 TO 6

In step 3, the fried chicken pieces can be held in a 200-degree oven for 30 minutes before being tossed with the sauce. A relatively mild cayenne pepper–based hot sauce, like Frank's, is essential; avoid hotter sauces like Tabasco. Stilton is an English blue cheese with a pungent, slightly sweet flavor. The dressing yields about 1½ cups.

CHICKEN

- 4 (6-ounce) boneless, skinless chicken breasts, trimmed and cut into 1½-inch chunks
- ½ cup buttermilk
- 1 teaspoon salt
- ¾ cup hot sauce
- ¼ cup water
- 1½ cups cornstarch
- 1 tablespoon unsalted butter
- ¼ teaspoon sugar
- 4 large egg whites
- ½ cup all-purpose flour
- ½ teaspoon baking soda
- 4 cups vegetable oil

DRESSING

- 3 ounces Stilton cheese, crumbled (¾ cup)
- ¾ cup mayonnaise
- 6 tablespoons sour cream
- 1½ tablespoons cider vinegar
- ¼ teaspoon pepper
- ⅛ teaspoon garlic powder

1. FOR THE CHICKEN: Combine chicken, buttermilk, and salt in large zipper-lock bag and refrigerate for 30 minutes or up to 2 hours. Combine hot sauce, water, 2 teaspoons cornstarch, butter, and sugar in small saucepan. Whisk over medium heat until thickened, about 5 minutes; set aside.

2. Whisk egg whites in shallow dish until foamy. Stir together flour, baking soda, remaining cornstarch, and 6 tablespoons hot sauce mixture in second shallow dish until mixture resembles coarse meal. Remove chicken from marinade and pat dry with paper towels. Coat half of chicken with egg whites, then dredge in cornstarch mixture. Transfer chicken to plate and repeat with remaining chicken.

3. Heat oil in Dutch oven over medium-high heat until oil registers 350 degrees. Fry half of chicken until golden brown, about 4 minutes, turning each piece halfway through cooking. Transfer chicken to paper towel–lined plate. Return oil to 350 degrees and repeat with remaining chicken.

4. Warm remaining hot sauce mixture over medium-low heat until simmering. Combine chicken and hot sauce mixture in large bowl and toss to coat.

5. FOR THE DRESSING: Process all ingredients in food processor until smooth, about 15 seconds, scraping down sides of bowl as needed. Serve with chicken. (Dressing can be refrigerated for up to 1 week.)

TO MAKE AHEAD: This dish freezes beautifully. In step 3, fry each batch of chicken until light golden brown, about 2 minutes. Drain and cool chicken on paper towel–lined plate, then transfer to freezer. Once chicken is completely frozen (this should take about 2 hours), transfer it to zipper-lock bag and freeze for up to 1 month. (Freeze sauce separately in airtight container for up to 1 month.) When ready to serve, heat 4 cups oil to 350 degrees and fry chicken in 2 batches until deep golden brown, about 2 minutes, turning each piece halfway through cooking. Reheat sauce in microwave or in saucepan over medium-low heat until warm. Toss chicken with sauce as directed. Serve.

✔ WHY THIS RECIPE WORKS

The best Philadelphia cheesesteaks are filled with tender, juicy meat tossed with just the right amount of cheese, but everything rides on the cut and thickness of the beef that fills those split sub rolls. For maximum flavor at a reasonable price, we turned to sirloin steak tips (though more expensive, rib-eye also works). To mimic the strips turned out by the professional meat slicers in Philly, we cut the tips into small chunks and pounded them into paper-thin, tender sheets of steak. Philadelphians like their cheesesteaks with provolone or American cheese or Cheez Whiz, and all three lend the perfect creamy finish to our homemade version. The lively debate over who serves the best cheesesteak in the city may never be resolved, but we were more than happy to serve up our full-flavored take on this classic sub.

PHILADELPHIA CHEESESTEAKS

SERVES 4

We prefer thin slices of provolone cheese cut to order at the deli counter for this recipe. (Packaged slices are too thick to melt quickly.) American cheese and Cheez Whiz are also traditional choices for cheesesteaks and can be used in place of the provolone here. If you're using Cheez Whiz, don't add it to the skillet with the beef in step 2. Instead, microwave ¾ cup in a bowl until warmed through and then spoon it over the assembled sandwiches.

- 1½ **pounds sirloin steak tips, trimmed and sliced with grain into 1-inch pieces**
- 2 **tablespoons vegetable oil**
- 2 **small onions, chopped**
  Salt and pepper
- 8 **thin slices deli provolone cheese (8 ounces), halved**
- 4 **(6-inch) sub rolls, partially split lengthwise**

1. Place beef pieces in single layer between 2 sheets of plastic wrap, spacing them 6 inches apart. Using meat pounder, pound beef until paper-thin (slices should be almost transparent). Heat 2 teaspoons oil in 12 inch nonstick skillet over medium-high heat until shimmering. Add onions and cook until softened and golden, about 5 minutes. Transfer to small bowl.

2. Heat 2 teaspoons oil in now-empty skillet over high heat until just smoking. Add half of beef to skillet (slices may overlap), season with salt and pepper, and cook until meat is no longer pink, about 1 minute per side. Off heat, layer 8 pieces of provolone over beef. Using spatula, pick up half of beef-provolone mixture and place it, beef side down, on top of other half of beef-provolone mixture. Cover skillet until provolone is melted, about 1 minute.

3. Divide beef-provolone mixture evenly between 2 rolls, evenly distribute half of onions over sandwiches, and pour any accumulated juices from skillet onto meat. Wrap each sandwich tightly in aluminum foil and set aside.

4. Wipe out skillet and repeat with remaining 2 teaspoons oil, remaining half of beef, remaining 8 pieces of provolone, remaining 2 rolls, and remaining half of onions. Wrap each sandwich tightly in foil and let sit for about 1 minute before serving.

EATING LOCAL ★ PHILADELPHIA, PA

The Philly cheesesteak sandwich was born in 1930 at **PAT'S KING OF STEAKS**, located in an Italian-American neighborhood in South Philadelphia. Today, there's a cheesesteak joint on nearly every corner in Philadelphia—even in Chinatown—and every place has its devoted followers. The tiny, bustling intersection where cheesesteak got its start is now home to two of the most famous cheesesteak joints in the city: **GENO'S STEAKS** and, of course, the original Pat's. We took a trip to Philly to see what all the hype was about. Even at 10:00 a.m., there were long lines at both establishments. At Pat's, Frank "Pat" Olivieri (the nephew of founder Pat Olivieri) showed us his custom-made German meat slicer as if it were a shiny new European sports car (the slicer, which cuts rib-eye steaks into those famously paper-thin slices, and the car would cost about the same). And at Geno's, Geno himself, whose father opened the restaurant in 1966, showed off his impeccably clean, sparkling kitchen. Both Pat and Geno made a killer cheesesteak that—loyalties aside—would do any Philadelphian proud.

PAT'S KING OF STEAKS 1237 E. Passyunk Ave., Philadelphia, PA
GENO'S STEAKS 1219 S. 9th St., Philadelphia, PA

♨ WHY THIS RECIPE WORKS

We wanted to restore this classic chicken dish to prominence while keeping the steps simple, so we started with its signature sauce. Rather than fiddle with egg yolks, we created depth of flavor by sautéing onions in oil before adding mushrooms, red bell pepper, and flour to create a robust roux. Once the cream, broth, and Madeira reduced, our updated sauce was as luxuriously silky as it was easy to prepare. To keep the chicken tender and moist, we soaked the breasts in cream, lemon, and salt. After reducing our sauce slightly, we added the brined chicken and poached it for only 10 minutes. One taste of our simplified chicken à la King, spooned over slices of crunchy toasted Italian bread, proved that this dish was ready for prime time.

CHICKEN À LA KING SERVES 4

An equal amount of brandy or dry Marsala can be substituted for the Madeira. Serve with Toasted Italian Bread (recipe follows).

¾ cup heavy cream
2 tablespoons lemon juice
Salt and pepper
4 (6-ounce) boneless, skinless chicken breasts, trimmed and cut into 1-inch pieces
1 tablespoon vegetable oil
1 onion, chopped fine
8 ounces white mushrooms, sliced thin
1 red bell pepper, seeded and chopped fine
3 tablespoons all-purpose flour
⅓ cup Madeira wine
1½ cups chicken broth
2 tablespoons minced fresh parsley

1. Whisk ½ cup cream, 1 tablespoon lemon juice, and 1 teaspoon salt together in bowl. Combine chicken and cream mixture in large zipper-lock bag; refrigerate for 30 minutes.

2. Heat oil in large skillet over medium-high heat until shimmering. Cook onion until golden, about 3 minutes. Add mushrooms, bell pepper, ¼ teaspoon salt, and ¼ teaspoon pepper and cook until vegetables have softened, about 5 minutes. Stir in flour and cook for 1 minute. Add Madeira, scraping up any browned bits, and cook until thickened, about 1 minute. Add broth and remaining ¼ cup cream and cook until sauce is very thick and spatula leaves trail when dragged through sauce, about 5 minutes.

3. Stir in chicken mixture and reduce heat to medium-low. Simmer, stirring frequently, until chicken is no longer pink, about 10 minutes. Off heat, stir in remaining 1 tablespoon lemon juice and parsley. Serve with Toasted Italian Bread.

TOASTED ITALIAN BREAD MAKES 8

Chicken à la King is typically served over toast, and we found the perfect match with supermarket Italian bread, whose soft texture toasted up into a crunchy, but still fork-friendly, slice.

8 (1-inch-thick) slices supermarket Italian bread
2 tablespoons unsalted butter, melted

1. Adjust oven rack to middle position and heat oven to 400 degrees. Arrange bread on baking sheet. Brush butter on both sides of bread slices.

2. Toast bread until golden brown, about 10 minutes, flipping slices halfway through cooking.

FIT FOR A KING?

Some say chicken à la King was created for the Kings—Mr. and Mrs. Clark King, the owners of the Brighton Beach Hotel in Brooklyn, New York—sometime around the turn of the century. The Brighton Beach Hotel was one of the 19th-century hotels created to cater to the upper class, who wanted to visit the seashore but didn't want to travel too far. There are at least a half dozen other theories—though none of them refer to royalty, as some might assume.

✔ WHY THIS RECIPE WORKS

"Riggies" aren't well known beyond Utica, New York, so we set out to make this hearty dish of rigatoni with spicy chicken and vegetables a new favorite on dinner tables coast to coast. Starting with the sauce, we developed rustic Italian flavor with crushed tomatoes, onion, garlic, oregano, bell pepper, and mushrooms. To inject riggies' signature spice, we stirred in chopped hot pickled cherry peppers and their brine before balancing out the sauce's acidity with cream. To infuse the meat with a little heat, we brined the chicken in cherry pepper brine and olive oil for just 30 minutes. With this much flavor in place, we could afford to simply poach the chicken in the sauce at the end. The sauce is stirred into al dente rigatoni (where "riggies" get their name) with a generous helping of Pecorino Romano.

CHICKEN RIGGIES SERVES 6

If you can find only sweet cherry peppers, add ¼ to ½ teaspoon red pepper flakes with the garlic in step 2. Parmesan cheese can be substituted for the Pecorino Romano.

4	**(6-ounce) boneless, skinless chicken breasts, trimmed and cut into 1-inch pieces**
¼	**cup finely chopped jarred sliced hot cherry peppers, plus 3 tablespoons cherry pepper brine**
3	**tablespoons olive oil**
	Salt and pepper
10	**ounces white mushrooms, trimmed and quartered**
2	**red bell peppers, stemmed, seeded, and cut into 1-inch pieces**
1	**onion, cut into 1-inch pieces**
5	**garlic cloves, minced**
1½	**teaspoons dried oregano**
1	**(28-ounce) can crushed tomatoes**
¾	**cup heavy cream**
¾	**cup pitted kalamata olives, halved lengthwise**
1	**pound rigatoni**
2½	**ounces Pecorino Romano cheese, grated (1¼ cups)**

1. Combine chicken, 2 tablespoons cherry pepper brine, 1 tablespoon oil, and 1 teaspoon salt in zipper-lock bag and refrigerate for at least 30 minutes or up to 1 hour.

2. Heat 1 tablespoon oil in Dutch oven over medium-high heat until shimmering. Stir in mushrooms, bell peppers, and ½ teaspoon salt and cook until browned, about 8 minutes. Transfer vegetables to bowl; set aside. Add remaining 1 tablespoon oil and onion to now-empty pot and cook over medium heat until softened, about 5 minutes. Stir in cherry peppers, garlic, and oregano and cook until fragrant, about 30 seconds. Add tomatoes, cream, and ½ teaspoon pepper and bring to boil. Reduce heat to medium and simmer, stirring occasionally, until sauce is very thick, 10 to 15 minutes. Stir in chicken and reserved vegetables and simmer, covered, until chicken is cooked through, 6 to 8 minutes. Add olives and remaining 1 tablespoon cherry pepper brine. Cover to keep warm.

3. Meanwhile, bring 4 quarts water to boil in large pot. Add rigatoni and 1 tablespoon salt and cook, stirring often, until al dente. Reserve ½ cup cooking water, then drain rigatoni and return it to pot. Add sauce and Pecorino and toss to combine, adding reserved cooking water as needed to adjust consistency. Season with salt and pepper to taste and serve.

EATING LOCAL ⭐ UTICA, NY

Around Utica, New York, the word "riggies" refers to the city's signature dish, rigatoni in a spicy, creamy tomato sauce with onions, peppers, and tender boneless chicken. Brimming with hometown pride for this Italian-American specialty, locals will advocate enthusiastically for their favorite versions, and anyone within earshot weighs in. Along the main drag, Genesee Street, we queried a woman in a gray business suit. "GEORGIO'S has the best," she responded, "hands down." A man in a stark white lab coat stopped short. "Georgio's is good," he said, "but CHESTERFIELD RESTAURANT has the original." That assertion caught the attention, or should we say contention, of a third guy, delivering FedEx packages. "Nah.... You really want to go to TEDDY'S, up in Rome. They won RiggieFest a few years running." RiggieFest? You read that right. It's an annual competition among restaurants and home cooks that fills the Utica Memorial Auditorium. The fest had come and gone for the year, but we spent 24 carbo-loaded hours running around Utica tasting and talking about riggies before developing our own version.

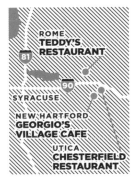

GEORGIO'S VILLAGE CAFÉ 60 Genesee St., New Hartford, NY

CHESTERFIELD RESTAURANT 1713 Bleeker St., Utica, NY

TEDDY'S RESTAURANT 851 Black River Blvd., Rome, NY

✓ WHY THIS RECIPE WORKS

Bitter greens can be a tough sell, but the tender, meaty escarole in this classic Chicken Riggies (page 13) side is irresistible. The winning flavor comes from capicola (also called coppa), an Italian dry-cured cold cut made from pork shoulder and neck meat; we found that both hot and sweet varieties put this dish on the right track. Browning the meat first established a savory base of flavor. After braising the escarole with the browned meat, onions, hot cherry peppers, and garlic, we stirred in homemade bread crumbs to absorb excess moisture. Grated Pecorino Romano along with another helping of bread crumbs contributed great crunchy texture to complement the greens' bold, hearty flavors.

UTICA GREENS   SERVES 6

You can use either hot or sweet capicola here. Whichever you choose, buy a ½-inch-thick slice (or use prosciutto) at the deli counter; avoid the prepackaged thin slices, as hearty cubes of meat are traditional for this dish. Do not use store-bought bread crumbs here. This dish is traditionally served with Chicken Riggies (page 13).

1   slice hearty white sandwich bread,
    torn into 1-inch pieces
3   tablespoons extra-virgin olive oil
4   ounces ½-inch-thick capicola,
    cut into ½-inch pieces
1   onion, chopped
¼   cup jarred sliced hot cherry peppers,
    chopped fine
4   garlic cloves, minced
2   large heads (2½ pounds) escarole,
    trimmed and chopped
½   cup chicken broth
¾   teaspoon salt
½   teaspoon pepper
1   ounce Pecorino Romano cheese, grated (½ cup)

1. Pulse bread and 1 tablespoon oil in food processor to coarse crumbs, about 5 pulses. Toast bread crumbs in Dutch oven over medium heat, stirring occasionally, until golden brown, about 5 minutes. Transfer crumbs to bowl; set aside. Wipe out pot with paper towels. Add remaining 2 tablespoons oil and capicola to now-empty pot and cook, stirring occasionally, until capicola begins to brown, 3 to 5 minutes. Stir in onion and cook until onion is softened and capicola is browned and crispy, about 5 minutes. Add cherry peppers and garlic and cook until fragrant, about 30 seconds.

2. Stir in half of escarole, broth, salt, and pepper. Cover and cook until greens are beginning to wilt, about 1 minute. Add remaining escarole, cover, and cook over medium-low heat, stirring occasionally, until stems are tender, about 10 minutes. Off heat, stir in Pecorino and ⅓ cup reserved bread crumbs. Top with remaining bread crumbs before serving.

GREENS WITH GUSTO

Utica Greens aren't any old pot of greens. They get their layers of flavor from these key ingredients.

CAPICOLA: Made from the shoulder and neck of a pig, capicola is seasoned with wine, garlic, herbs, and spices before it's cured and hung for several months. The process creates complex flavors that our tasters found "mustardy" and "cheesy." Buy sweet or hot and try it in sandwiches or calzones. The boys in the TV series *The Sopranos* pronounced it "gabagool." However you say it, it's delicious.

ESCAROLE: Escarole has a bitter, grassy flavor that takes well to assertive seasoning. It is commonly used in salads. Make sure to wash escarole well (we use a salad spinner), as the feathery leaves tend to hold a lot of soil.

SLICED HOT CHERRY PEPPERS: In the test kitchen, we're big fans of this convenience product. We use the pickled peppers to add robust flavor, heat, and texture to dishes, but we also often include the brine in sauces and marinades, as we did with our Chicken Riggies (page 13), to add brightness and piquant, vinegary notes.

✔ WHY THIS RECIPE WORKS

In Pennsylvania and farther afield, folks know they're getting pork (or veal) when they order city chicken, so we decided to embrace the pork's flavor for our modern take on this Depression-era classic. We selected a boneless butt roast as our base—its ideal fat-to-meat ratio lent itself well to the frying and baking this recipe required. A rub of garlic powder, thyme, and cayenne pepper on top of the standard salt and pepper seasoning gave the meat great flavor. After we cubed and skewered the seasoned meat, a roll in flour and panko bread crumbs created a perfectly crunchy outer coating. Frying in a Dutch oven contained the sizzling hot oil while the "chicken" fried, and an hour in the oven made the pork delectably tender. While the skewers cooled, we stirred together a creamy dill sauce for dipping.

CITY CHICKEN SERVES 6 TO 8

You will need eight 6-inch bamboo skewers for this recipe. If you can't find them, trim longer ones or the skewered meat won't fit in the pot for frying. Pork butt roast may be labeled "Boston butt." You can make the sauce and trim, season, and skewer the meat a day in advance.

CITY CHICKEN

1½	teaspoons salt
1½	teaspoons garlic powder
1	teaspoon pepper
¾	teaspoon dried thyme
¼	teaspoon cayenne pepper
1	(3-pound) boneless pork butt roast, trimmed and cut into 1-inch pieces
8	(6-inch) bamboo skewers
½	cup all-purpose flour
2	large eggs
2	tablespoons water
1¼	cups panko bread crumbs
2	cups vegetable oil

SOUR CREAM-DILL SAUCE

1	cup sour cream
1	tablespoon minced fresh dill
1½	teaspoons lemon juice
1	garlic clove, minced
	Salt and pepper

1. FOR THE CITY CHICKEN: Combine salt, garlic powder, pepper, thyme, and cayenne in medium bowl. Add pork and toss to coat thoroughly. Thread pork onto eight 6-inch bamboo skewers (6 to 8 pieces per skewer). (Skewers can be prepared up to 24 hours in advance.)

2. Adjust oven rack to middle position and heat oven to 325 degrees. Place wire rack inside rimmed baking sheet. Place flour in shallow dish. Whisk eggs and water together in second shallow dish. Place panko in third shallow dish. Working with 1 skewer at a time, dredge in flour, dip in egg, then coat with panko, pressing to adhere.

3. Heat oil in Dutch oven over medium heat to 350 degrees. Working with 4 skewers at a time, fry first side until golden brown, about 2 minutes. Flip skewers and continue to fry until golden brown on second side, about 2 minutes longer. Transfer to prepared wire rack. Repeat with remaining skewers. Transfer to oven and bake until pork is tender, about 1 hour. Place skewers on platter and let rest for 5 to 10 minutes.

4. FOR THE SOUR CREAM-DILL SAUCE: Meanwhile, whisk all ingredients together in bowl and season with salt and pepper to taste. Serve sauce with skewers.

PORK IN DISGUISE

City chicken may sound like a sophisticated chicken dish, but in fact, it's neither particularly fancy nor made with chicken. Instead, pork or veal cutlets are threaded onto skewers and made to resemble chicken drumsticks. The skewers are breaded, shallow-fried, then baked or braised for about an hour. City chicken came about during the Great Depression, when chicken was a pricey commodity, but it's part of a long-standing tradition of disguising foods to look like something else. In the mid-19th century, when supplies of flour, sugar, fresh fruit, and spices were cut off by blockade during the Civil War, clever Southern cooks created mock apple pie, said to smell and taste like real apples, from a "small bowl of crackers" combined with sweetener and tartaric acid (to replace the lemon juice) and, we suspect, a lot of imagination. Some 70 years later, hard times gave the pie a reprise: During the Depression, Ritz Crackers featured the recipe right on the box. Mock apple pie may have fallen out of favor, but city chicken is still popular in parts of Ohio, West Virginia, and Pennsylvania. Of course, it's no longer intended to fool diners: City chicken may have been born out of necessity, but it survived because it's delicious.

☑ WHY THIS RECIPE WORKS

Bar pizza, a New England creation, makes the perfect accompaniment to ice-cold beer (or the beverage of your choice). To re-create bar pizza's thin, crisp-yet-tender crust, crunchy raised edges, and bubbly, browned cheese at home, we used oiled cake pans as a stand-in for rimmed pizza pans. To reproduce its trademark edged crust, we made a lip of dough up the sides of the pan. For a simple uncooked sauce, we looked to canned diced tomatoes for our base. We processed the tomatoes with olive oil, dried oregano, sugar, salt, pepper, and pepper flakes into a smooth, tangy sauce in a snap. Spreading the sauce and cheese over the edges of the dough created the caramelized "laced" edges that these New England pizzas are known for. We found that baking the pizzas in a 500-degree oven on the bottom rack allowed the bottoms to crisp up while the cheese melted and browned gradually.

NEW ENGLAND BAR PIZZA SERVES 4

Clean the food processor in between making the dough and the pizza sauce. You will have some sauce left over; reserve it for another use. Use sharp cheddar cheese, not extra-sharp (which makes the pizzas too greasy).

DOUGH

1⅔	cups (8⅓ ounces) all-purpose flour
1	tablespoon sugar
1	teaspoon instant or rapid-rise yeast
⅔	cup water
1½	teaspoons extra-virgin olive oil
¾	teaspoon salt

SAUCE

1	(14.5-ounce) can diced tomatoes
1	teaspoon extra-virgin olive oil
½	teaspoon dried oregano
½	teaspoon sugar
¼	teaspoon salt
⅛	teaspoon pepper
⅛	teaspoon red pepper flakes

TOPPING

4	ounces sharp cheddar cheese, shredded (1 cup)
4	ounces whole-milk mozzarella cheese, shredded (1 cup)
1	tablespoon extra-virgin olive oil

1. FOR THE DOUGH: Process flour, sugar, and yeast in food processor until combined, about 3 seconds. With processor running, slowly add water; process dough until just combined and no dry flour remains, about 10 seconds. Let dough stand for 10 minutes. Add oil and salt to dough and process until dough forms satiny, sticky ball that clears sides of workbowl, 30 to 60 seconds.

2. Transfer dough to lightly oiled counter and knead until smooth, about 1 minute. Shape dough into tight ball and place in greased bowl. Cover with plastic wrap and let rise at room temperature until almost doubled in size, 2 to 2½ hours.

3. FOR THE SAUCE: Process all ingredients in clean, dry food processor until smooth, about 30 seconds; set sauce aside. (Sauce can be refrigerated for up to 2 days or frozen for up to 1 month.)

4. FOR THE TOPPING: Adjust oven rack to lowest position and heat oven to 500 degrees. Combine cheddar and mozzarella in bowl. Using pastry brush, grease bottom and sides of 2 dark-colored 9-inch round cake pans with 1½ teaspoons oil each.

5. Transfer dough to lightly floured counter, divide in half, and shape into balls. Gently flatten 1 dough ball into 6-inch disk using your fingertips. Using rolling pin, roll disk into 10-inch round. Transfer dough to prepared pan and press into corners, forcing ¼-inch lip of dough up sides of pan. Repeat with remaining dough ball.

6. Spread ⅓ cup sauce in thin layer over entire surface of 1 dough. Using pastry brush, brush sauce over lip of dough. Sprinkle 1 cup cheese mixture evenly over pizza, including lip. Repeat with remaining dough, ⅓ cup sauce, and remaining 1 cup cheese mixture.

7. Bake until crust is browned and cheese is bubbly and beginning to brown, about 12 minutes, switching and rotating pans halfway through baking. To remove pizzas from pans, run offset spatula along top edge of pizza crust. Once loosened, slide spatula underneath pizza and slide pizza onto wire rack. Let cool for 5 minutes. Slice and serve.

EATING LOCAL ★ RANDOLPH, MA

To research our recipe for bar pizza, we visited the **LYNWOOD CAFÉ** in Randolph, Massachusetts, housed in a stucco-and-clapboard building marked by neon Bud Light signs. The decor inside hasn't changed since the 1960s; wooden paneling, wooden booths, and Red Sox posters line the walls. The establishment has been around since the mid-1930s, Stephen Campanella, manager of the Lynwood, told us. "In 1935, right after Prohibition, this place was turned from a feed store into a bar. My great-grandfather Alfond purchased the place in 1949, and that's when we started serving pizza and operating the full bar." Having tasted their pizza, we hope they stay open for decades to come.

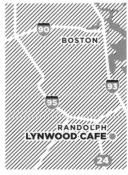

LYNWOOD CAFÉ
320 Center St., Randolph, MA

✓ WHY THIS RECIPE WORKS

We wanted to make this traditional New England spin on St. Patrick's Day dinner a meal that can be eaten—and thoroughly enjoyed—any day of the year. Starting with the corned beef, we bypassed boiling for a slow braise in the oven with chicken broth, vegetables, and spices. This turned out moist meat, made even better when we let it soak up 1 cup of the braising liquid as it rested. Moving to the stovetop, we simmered the potatoes in the cooking liquid for 10 minutes before adding the remaining vegetables to the pot, ensuring that they all finished cooking together without turning mushy. For a bit of sweetness, we included halved carrots, and butter added richness and silkiness. After only 30 minutes, our vegetables emerged flavorful and perfectly cooked, nicely complementing our corned beef.

CORNED BEEF AND CABBAGE SERVES 6 TO 8

Use flat-cut corned beef brisket, not point-cut; it's more uniform in shape and thus will cook more evenly. Use small red potatoes measuring 1 to 2 inches in diameter. When slicing the cabbage, leave the core intact or the cabbage will fall apart during cooking.

1	**(4- to 5-pound) corned beef brisket roast, rinsed, fat trimmed to ¼ inch**
4	**cups chicken broth**
4	**cups water**
12	**carrots, peeled (3 chopped, 9 halved crosswise)**
2	**celery ribs, chopped**
1	**onion, peeled and quartered**
3	**bay leaves**
1	**tablespoon black peppercorns**
1	**tablespoon minced fresh thyme**
1	**teaspoon whole allspice**
3	**tablespoons unsalted butter**
1½	**pounds small red potatoes**
1	**head green cabbage (2 pounds), cut into 8 (2-inch) wedges**
	Pepper

1. Adjust oven rack to middle position and heat oven to 300 degrees. Combine beef, broth, water, chopped carrots, celery, onion, bay leaves, peppercorns, thyme, and allspice in Dutch oven. Cover and bake until fork slips easily in and out of meat, 4½ to 5 hours.

2. Transfer meat to 13 by 9-inch baking dish. Strain cooking liquid through fine-mesh strainer into large bowl, discard solids, and skim fat from liquid. Pour 1 cup cooking liquid over meat. Cover dish tightly with aluminum foil and let rest for 30 minutes.

3. Meanwhile, return remaining cooking liquid to Dutch oven, add butter, and bring to simmer over medium-high heat. Add potatoes and simmer until they begin to soften, about 10 minutes. Add carrot halves and cabbage, cover, and cook until tender, 10 to 15 minutes. Transfer vegetables to serving platter and season with pepper to taste.

4. Transfer beef to carving board and slice against grain into ¼-inch-thick slices. Serve with vegetables.

TO MAKE AHEAD: Prepare corned beef through step 2. Refrigerate moistened beef and cooking liquid separately for up to 24 hours.

To serve, adjust oven rack to middle position and heat oven to 350 degrees. Transfer meat to carving board; slice against grain into ¼-inch-thick slices and return to baking dish. Cover dish tightly with foil and bake until meat is heated through, about 25 minutes. While meat is heating, proceed with step 3.

CUTTING CABBAGE

To keep cabbage wedges together, quarter the cabbage, taking care to cut directly through the core. Cut each quarter in half for 8 (2-inch) wedges.

⌀ WHY THIS RECIPE WORKS

Homemade clam chowder is often one of two things: time-consuming and fantastic or quick and forgettable. We wanted to find a middle ground, eliminating laborious prep work without sacrificing flavor. We started by sautéing strips of bacon, saving the slices for garnishing and leaving the fat in the pan for our flavor base. To put the spotlight on the clams, we created a makeshift stock of clam juice and water. We skipped steaming and shucking by turning to preshucked chopped clams—these imparted fresh clam flavor that relegated the canned alternative to our no-fly list. We then turned our focus to thickening the broth. Instead of muting the rich and briny flavor with flour, we opted for crushed saltines and mashed potatoes for added body. Our chowder was thick, rich, and bursting with clam flavor in under an hour. Crispy, flaky Common Crackers pair perfectly with this chowder and can even be used in place of the store-bought saltines used to thicken it.

EASY NEW ENGLAND CLAM CHOWDER SERVES 6

If you buy frozen clams, thaw them before using. You can sub-stitute nine Common Crackers for the saltines.

4	slices bacon, chopped fine
1	onion, chopped fine
3	(8-ounce) bottles clam juice
2	cups water
1½	pounds russet potatoes, peeled and cut into ½-inch pieces
20	saltines, crushed
1	teaspoon minced fresh thyme
1	bay leaf
2	pounds chopped clams, rinsed, drained, and chopped fine
1	cup heavy cream
	Salt and pepper

1. Cook bacon in large saucepan over medium heat until crisp, 6 to 8 minutes. Using slotted spoon, transfer bacon to paper towel–lined plate. Pour off all but 1 tablespoon fat from saucepan. Add onion and cook over medium heat until softened, about 5 minutes. Stir in clam juice, water, potatoes, saltines, thyme, and bay leaf and bring to boil. Reduce heat to medium and simmer, stirring occasionally, until potatoes are tender, about 20 minutes.

2. Using slotted spoon, transfer ½ cup potatoes to bowl and mash with potato masher until smooth. Return mashed potatoes to pot. Reduce heat to low. Stir clams into pot and simmer until cooked through, 3 to 5 minutes. Off heat, stir in cream. Discard bay leaf, and season with salt and pepper to taste. Sprinkle with reserved bacon. Serve.

COMMON CRACKERS MAKES ABOUT 36

Use mild lager, such as Budweiser, to make this recipe.

2½	cups (12½ ounces) all-purpose flour
2	teaspoons baking powder
1¼	teaspoons salt
3	tablespoons vegetable shortening, cut into ½-inch pieces and chilled, plus 2 tablespoons melted and cooled
1	cup beer, chilled

1. Adjust oven rack to lower-middle position and heat oven to 350 degrees. Set wire rack in rimmed baking sheet. Pulse flour, baking powder, and salt in food processor until combined, about 5 pulses. Add chilled shortening and pulse until just combined, about 5 pulses.

2. Transfer flour mixture to large bowl. Stir in beer until combined. Turn dough onto lightly floured counter and knead briefly until dough comes together. Roll dough into 10 by 7-inch rectangle. Brush dough with melted shortening, then fold as you would a letter: Working from short edge, fold dough over itself, leaving ⅓ of dough uncovered. Fold opposite uncovered short edge over dough. Roll folded dough into 18 by 7-inch rectangle, about ¼ inch thick.

3. Using 2-inch biscuit cutter dipped in flour, cut out rounds and arrange on prepared rack. Gather remaining dough and roll into ¼-inch-thick circle. Cut rounds from dough and transfer to rack. Prick dough rounds twice using fork.

4. Bake until light golden brown and firm, 50 to 55 minutes. Let crackers cool completely, about 1 hour. Serve. (Crackers can be stored in closed paper bag for up to 3 days.)

⚲ WHY THIS RECIPE WORKS

This lesser-known take on New England's favorite soup gets its bold hue from tomatoes, and we wanted to make sure our red chowder boasted plenty of tomato flavor to balance out the briny clams. We started by steaming fresh cherrystones, removing the clams as they opened to ensure even cooking. We reserved some of the clam steaming liquid for our broth, diluting the salty liquid with bottled clam juice for great balanced flavor. Canned whole tomatoes and tomato paste added bright tomato taste and creamy texture to the broth. Cubed Yukon Gold potatoes took on the chowder's flavor and maintained their structure, ensuring that our chowder had a chunky element to contrast with the creamy base. To add a final boost of flavor, we simmered the chowder with slices of bacon and a bay leaf, removing both right before serving.

RHODE ISLAND RED CLAM CHOWDER

Be sure to use fresh clams for this soup. Red clam chowder is classically served with oyster crackers; however, it also tastes great with Garlic Toasts (recipe follows).

- 3 **cups water**
- 6 **pounds medium hard-shell clams, such as cherrystones, scrubbed**
- 2 **tablespoons unsalted butter**
- 1 **(28-ounce) can whole tomatoes, drained with juice reserved**
- 1 **medium onion, minced**
- 1 **tablespoon tomato paste**
- 2 **garlic cloves, minced**
- 3 **(8-ounce) bottles clam juice**
- 1½ **pounds Yukon Gold potatoes, peeled and cut into ½-inch pieces**
- 2 **slices bacon**
- 1 **bay leaf**
- 2 **tablespoons minced fresh parsley**
- 2 **teaspoons dry sherry**
  Salt and pepper

1. Bring water to boil in large Dutch oven. Add clams, cover, and cook for 5 minutes. Stir clams thoroughly, cover, and continue to cook until they just begin to open, 2 to 5 minutes. As clams open, transfer to large bowl and let cool slightly. Discard any unopened clams.

2. Measure out and reserve 2 cups clam steaming liquid, avoiding any gritty sediment that settled on bottom of pot. Remove clam meat from shells and chop coarse.

3. In clean Dutch oven, melt butter over medium heat. Add tomatoes, onion, and tomato paste and cook until dry and beginning to brown, 11 to 13 minutes. Stir in garlic and cook until fragrant, about 30 seconds. Stir in bottled clam juice and reserved clam steaming liquid, scraping up any browned bits.

4. Working in batches, puree soup until smooth, 1 to 2 minutes. Return soup to clean pot. Stir in potatoes, bacon, and bay leaf and bring to boil. Reduce heat to gentle simmer and cook until potatoes are tender, 20 to 25 minutes.

5. Off heat, remove bacon and discard bay leaf. Stir in parsley and sherry and season with salt and pepper to taste. Stir in chopped clams, cover, and let stand until warmed through, about 1 minute. Serve.

GARLIC TOASTS MAKES 8 SLICES

Be sure to use a high-quality crusty bread, such as a baguette; do not use sliced sandwich bread.

- 8 **(1-inch-thick) slices rustic bread**
- 1 **large garlic clove, peeled**
- 3 **tablespoons extra-virgin olive oil**
  Salt and pepper

Position oven rack 6 inches from broiler element and heat broiler. Spread bread in rimmed baking sheet and broil until golden brown on both sides, about 2 minutes per side. Briefly rub 1 side of each toast with garlic. Drizzle toasts with oil, season with salt and pepper to taste, and serve.

BRINGING BACK CHOWDER

While clam chowder aficionados debate the relative merits of New England versus Manhattan-style, there's a little-known third chowder in the region, one that we find especially intriguing: Rhode Island red clam chowder. Consisting of chopped fresh clams, tender chunks of potato, and a creamy-tasting, rich-flavored tomato and clam broth, this clam chowder is a minimalist expression of where the sea meets the land. Our research into the origins of this chowder brought us to the small coastal Rhode Island town of Warwick. It was there, in the Rocky Point Shore Dinner Hall (publicized as the "world's largest shore dinner hall"), that generations of sun-baked seaside visitors were first introduced to this unique bowl of soup. The dinner hall and adjacent amusement park closed a few years ago, but with our recipe you can enjoy this classic at home.

✓ WHY THIS RECIPE WORKS

When New England fishermen first started making fish chowders in the 18th century, they kept it simple: The catch of the day (usually cod or haddock) was tossed into a pot with water and salt pork, and the chowder was thickened with hardtack. Back on dry land, we hoped to stir together a chowder that honored the soup's simple roots, showcasing moist, tender morsels of fish in a delicate, clean-tasting broth. To capture salt pork's smoky flavor, we cooked two large chunks in butter with onions, thyme, salt, and a bay leaf. Forgoing fussy, from-scratch fish stock, we built an ultraquick base with just the fish and water. We removed the fillets once they turned opaque to prevent overcooking and then added the potatoes. Whole milk gave the broth just enough richness, and a tablespoon of cornstarch prevented curdling. We discarded the salt pork and bay leaf after stirring in the waiting fillets. Our light, delicate broth was studded with flavorful potatoes and perfectly highlighted the tender cod. Though not stirred up on the deck of a fishing vessel, our chowder more than paid homage to its New England pedigree.

NEW ENGLAND FISH CHOWDER

SERVES 6 TO 8

Haddock or other flaky white fish may be substituted for the cod. Garnish the chowder with minced fresh chives, crisp bacon bits, or oyster crackers.

2	tablespoons unsalted butter
2	onions, cut into ½-inch dice
4	ounces salt pork, rind removed, rinsed and cut into 2 pieces
1½	teaspoons minced fresh thyme
	Salt and pepper
1	bay leaf
5	cups water
2	pounds skinless cod fillets, sliced crosswise into 6 equal pieces
1½	pounds Yukon Gold potatoes, peeled and cut into ½-inch dice
2	cups whole milk
1	tablespoon cornstarch

1. Melt butter in Dutch oven over medium heat. Add onions, salt pork, thyme, ¾ teaspoon salt, and bay leaf; cook, stirring occasionally, until onions are softened but not browned, 3 to 5 minutes. Add water and bring to simmer. Remove pot from heat, gently place cod fillets in water, cover, and let fish stand until opaque and nearly cooked through, about 5 minutes. Using metal spatula, transfer cod to bowl.

2. Return pot to medium-high heat, add potatoes, and bring to simmer. Cook until potatoes are tender and beginning to break apart, about 20 minutes.

3. Meanwhile, whisk milk, cornstarch, and ½ teaspoon pepper together in bowl. Stir milk mixture into chowder and return to simmer. Return fish and any accumulated juices to pot. Remove pot from heat, cover, and let stand for 5 minutes. Remove and discard salt pork and bay leaf. Stir gently with wooden spoon to break fish into large pieces. Season with salt and pepper to taste. Serve immediately.

WHAT, EXACTLY, IS SALT PORK?

Many chowder, stew, soup, and baked bean recipes call for salt pork, which is made from the same cuts as bacon: the sides and belly of the pig. Salt pork is salt cured (in either dry salt or a salt brine), but it's not smoked, while bacon is. Another difference? It's fattier than bacon. We like salt pork in several of our stews and frequently use its plentiful rendered fat to brown and flavor the meat and vegetables. If you can't find salt pork, use bacon, but remember that it will add a smoky undertone. Don't confuse salt pork with fatback, which is unsalted and uncured and comes from the layer of fat running along the pig's back. Looking for a project? Use fatback to make your own lard and cracklings (and please invite us over to snack on the latter). You can find both salt pork and fatback in the meat section of the supermarket, usually next to packaged hot dogs.

✓ WHY THIS RECIPE WORKS

There is no shortage of good corn chowders being stirred together in New England kitchens, but we wanted to deliver all of their best qualities—velvety texture, strong corn flavor, and plump kernels—in one silver-bullet recipe. Aiming for ultimate corn flavor, we set out to include our key ingredient in every step, from kernel to cob. For a sweet and smoky starting place, we sautéed chopped bacon to render its fat and kept the crispy pieces to stir in at the end. Cooking the fresh kernels and onion in the fat created a toasty, caramelized base of flavor. Canned corn pureed with chicken broth served as a lush thickener that boosted the chowder's corn flavors. Last, we dropped our shucked cobs into the simmering pot for a subtle but significant final dose of corn taste, perfectly finishing off our top-to-bottom corn chowder. As irresistible as it was on its own, it also lent itself perfectly to the addition of some bold ingredients like andouille sausage and bell pepper for a spicy, savory, and salty kick.

CLASSIC CORN CHOWDER SERVES 6 TO 8

Be sure to save the cobs for the chowder.

- 6 **ears corn**
- 2 **(15-ounce) cans whole kernel corn, drained**
- 5 **cups chicken broth**
- 3 **slices bacon, chopped fine**
- 1 **onion, chopped**
  Salt and pepper
- 1 **pound red potatoes, scrubbed and cut into ½-inch dice**
- 1 **cup heavy cream**
- 4 **scallions, sliced thin**

1. Cut kernels from ears of corn by cutting cob in half crosswise, then standing each half on its flat, cut end. Using chef's knife, cut kernels off ear, 1 side at a time. Reserve kernels and cobs separately. Puree canned corn and 2 cups broth in blender until smooth.

2. Cook bacon in Dutch oven over medium heat until crisp, about 8 minutes. Using slotted spoon, transfer bacon to paper towel–lined plate and reserve. Cook onion, corn kernels, ½ teaspoon salt, and ¼ teaspoon pepper in bacon fat until vegetables are softened and golden brown, 6 to 8 minutes.

3. Add potatoes, corn puree, remaining 3 cups broth, and reserved corn cobs to Dutch oven and bring to boil. Reduce heat to medium-low and simmer until potatoes are tender, about 15 minutes. Discard cobs and stir in cream, scallions, and reserved bacon. Season with salt and pepper to taste. Serve. (Soup can be refrigerated in airtight container for up to 3 days.)

CORN CHOWDER WITH ANDOUILLE AND BELL PEPPER

Substitute 4 ounces finely chopped andouille sausage and 1 teaspoon vegetable oil for bacon and add 1 celery rib, chopped fine, and 1 red bell pepper, seeded and chopped fine, along with onion in step 2.

CORN CHOWDER WITH CHORIZO AND CHILES

Substitute 4 ounces finely chopped chorizo sausage and 1 teaspoon vegetable oil for bacon and ¼ cup chopped fresh cilantro for scallions. In step 2, add 1 to 2 jalapeño chiles, seeded and minced, and ½ teaspoon ground cumin along with onion.

CORN CHOWDER WITH SWEET POTATOES AND CAYENNE

Substitute 1 pound sweet potatoes, peeled and cut into ½-inch dice, for red potatoes. In step 3, stir in 1 tablespoon maple syrup and ¼ teaspoon cayenne pepper along with cream.

CORN CHOWDER WITH PROSCIUTTO AND SAGE

Substitute 4 ounces finely chopped deli prosciutto and 1 teaspoon vegetable oil for bacon and 2 tablespoons minced fresh sage for scallions.

CLEAN SHAVE

Cutting kernels from an ear of corn can be an awkward task. Here's how to steady the cob and keep the kernels from flying around the kitchen, all while maneuvering a sharp knife.

Cut cob in half crosswise, then stand each half on its flat, cut end. Using chef's knife, cut kernels off ear, 1 side at a time.

✔ WHY THIS RECIPE WORKS

Joe Booker the man may forever remain a mystery, but we were determined to perfect the stew that bears his name and was a favorite among Maine's ice fishermen and loggers. Unlike many beef stews, this one is meant to possess a lighter broth, be packed with vegetables, and boast tender dumplings. To keep our base both delicate and flavorful, we started by microwaving the salt pork and then rinsing it of excess salt. Observing the tenets of Yankee thrift, we used the rendered fat to brown the beef and to cook the chopped onions. We wanted our broth to be light but still robust, so we simmered equal parts water and beef broth together. We kept the dumplings simple, adding chopped parsley for flavor and baking powder for more leavening power. Combining the dry ingredients with milk and melted butter produced rich, tender dumplings, no kneading required. With a one-pot dinner this tasty on the table, we were sure Joe Booker—whoever he was—would be proud.

JOE BOOKER STEW
SERVES 6 TO 8

You can substitute peeled, chopped turnip or parsnip for the rutabaga. Use a Dutch oven with at least a 6-quart capacity.

STEW

- 8 ounces salt pork, quartered
- 3 pounds boneless beef chuck, cut into 1-inch chunks
  Pepper
- 2 onions, chopped
- 2 tablespoons all-purpose flour
- 4 cups beef broth
- 4 cups water
- 2 teaspoons minced fresh thyme
- 1½ pounds red potatoes, scrubbed and cut into ¾-inch chunks
- 1½ pounds rutabaga, peeled and cut into ¾-inch chunks
- 1 pound carrots, peeled and cut into ¾-inch chunks

DUMPLINGS

- 2 cups (10 ounces) all-purpose flour
- 5 teaspoons baking powder
- ½ cup minced fresh parsley
  Salt and pepper
- 1 cup milk
- 3 tablespoons unsalted butter, cut into ½-inch pieces

1. FOR THE STEW: Place salt pork in bowl and microwave until fat renders and pork is golden, 5 to 8 minutes. Pour off fat, reserving 2 tablespoons (if you have less, supplement with vegetable oil). When pork is cool enough to handle, rinse under running water to remove excess salt. Set aside.

2. Pat beef dry with paper towels and season with pepper. Heat 2 teaspoons reserved pork fat in large Dutch oven over medium-high heat until just smoking. Cook half of beef until well browned all over, about 8 minutes. Transfer to bowl and repeat with 2 teaspoons pork fat and remaining beef. Add remaining 2 teaspoons pork fat and onions to now-empty pot and cook until golden brown, about 5 minutes. Stir in flour and cook until lightly browned, about 1 minute.

3. Return beef and any accumulated juices to pot. Stir in broth, water, thyme, and rinsed salt pork and bring to boil. Reduce heat to low and simmer, covered, until meat is nearly tender, about 1 hour. Remove and discard salt pork. Add potatoes, rutabaga, and carrots to pot and continue to simmer, covered, until vegetables are just tender, 20 to 30 minutes.

4. FOR THE DUMPLINGS: When vegetables are nearly tender, combine flour, baking powder, parsley, 1 teaspoon salt, and 1 teaspoon pepper in large bowl. Combine milk and butter in liquid measuring cup and microwave, stirring once or twice, until butter melts, about 1 minute. Stir warm milk mixture into flour mixture until incorporated.

5. Once vegetables are tender, use small ice cream scoop or 2 large spoons to drop golf ball–size dumplings (about 2 tablespoons) onto stew about ¼ inch apart (you should have about 15 dumplings). Simmer gently, covered, until dumplings have doubled in size and toothpick inserted in center comes out clean, 18 to 22 minutes. Serve.

TO MAKE AHEAD: Stew can be made through step 3, covered, and refrigerated for up to 3 days. To serve, bring stew to simmer and proceed with step 4.

SCOOP-AND-DROP DUMPLINGS

No need to roll, cut, or knead. Our dumplings come together in minutes.

1. After combining flour, baking powder, and seasonings, stir in mixture of milk and melted butter.

2. Use small ice cream scoop (or 2 large spoons) to gently drop dumplings onto simmering stew about ¼ inch apart.

✓ WHY THIS RECIPE WORKS

Before bringing this western Pennsylvania favorite (also called Italian wedding soup) home to meet the in-laws, it needed some streamlining. To start, we kicked up the broth by mixing garlic and red pepper flakes cooked in olive oil into store-bought chicken broth. We turned to meatloaf mix (a tasty combination of beef, pork, and veal) for our meatballs. Poaching them in the broth saved time and added extra flavor to the base. Chopped kale held its own in the hot liquid, adding great texture and flavor without losing its hearty crunch, and orzo proved the right size for spooning up with the meatballs and greens. Having added some extra Parmesan and a drizzle of extra-virgin olive oil right before serving, we were in wedded bliss.

PITTSBURGH WEDDING SOUP

SERVES 6 TO 8

If meatloaf mix isn't available, substitute 1 pound of 85 percent lean ground beef. Using the large end of a melon baller guarantees uniform meatballs that cook evenly. Serve with extra Parmesan cheese and a drizzle of extra-virgin olive oil.

MEATBALLS

2	slices hearty white sandwich bread, torn into pieces
½	cup milk
1	large egg yolk
1	ounce Parmesan cheese, grated (½ cup)
3	tablespoons chopped fresh parsley
3	garlic cloves, minced
¾	teaspoon salt
½	teaspoon pepper
½	teaspoon dried oregano
1	pound meatloaf mix

SOUP

1	tablespoon extra-virgin olive oil
2	garlic cloves, minced
¼	teaspoon red pepper flakes
3	quarts chicken broth
1	large head kale or Swiss chard, stemmed, leaves chopped
1	cup orzo
3	tablespoons chopped fresh parsley
	Salt and pepper

1. FOR THE MEATBALLS: Using potato masher, mash bread and milk together in large bowl until smooth. Add remaining ingredients, except meatloaf mix, and mash to combine. Add meatloaf mix and knead by hand until well combined. Form mixture into 1-inch meatballs (you should have about 55 meatballs) and arrange in rimmed baking sheet. Cover with plastic wrap and refrigerate until firm, at least 30 minutes. (Meatballs can be made up to 24 hours in advance.)

2. FOR THE SOUP: Heat oil in Dutch oven over medium-high heat until shimmering. Cook garlic and pepper flakes until fragrant, about 30 seconds. Add broth and bring to boil. Stir in kale and simmer until softened, 10 to 15 minutes. Stir in meatballs and pasta, reduce heat to medium, and simmer until meatballs are cooked through and pasta is tender, about 10 minutes. Stir in parsley and salt and pepper to taste. Serve. (Leftover soup can be refrigerated for up to 3 days.)

PREPPING KALE

1A. Hold leaf at base of stem and use knife to slash leafy portion from either side of tough stem

1B. Alternatively, fold each leaf in half and cut along edge of rib to remove thickest part of rib and stem.

2. After separating leaves, stack several and either cut into strips or roll pile into cigar shape and coarsely chop.

3. Fill salad spinner bowl with cool water, add cut greens, and gently swish them around. Let grit settle to bottom of bowl, then lift greens out and drain water. Repeat until greens no longer release dirt.

✔ WHY THIS RECIPE WORKS

To liven up this classic salad while still paying homage to the original, we started with the standard ingredients first tossed together at New York's posh Waldorf Hotel: apples, celery, and mayonnaise. First, we balanced contrasting flavors, chopping three sweet apples (Gala or Braeburn) alongside three tart Granny Smiths, keeping the skin on for color. Toasting the walnuts enhanced their flavor, and golden raisins, plumped in a little water, added bursts of sweetness to the mix. We whisked cider vinegar into mayonnaise for our dressing, lightening an otherwise gloppy mayo coating and reinforcing the crisp apple taste. A spoonful of honey helped unite the flavors once the ingredients were tossed together. With this winning combination in place, we played with some other bright flavor combinations—and if you ask us, all proved worthy of a place on the Waldorf menu.

WALDORF SALAD

SERVES 4 TO 6

Toast the walnuts in a dry skillet over medium heat, stirring frequently, until lightly browned and fragrant, about 5 minutes. You can use reduced-fat mayonnaise here, and regular raisins will work in place of the golden raisins.

¾	cup golden raisins
¼	cup water
⅓	cup mayonnaise
3	tablespoons cider vinegar
1	tablespoon honey
3	Granny Smith apples, cored and cut into ½-inch pieces
3	Gala or Braeburn apples, cored and cut into ½-inch pieces
3	celery ribs, chopped fine
¾	cup toasted walnuts, chopped
	Salt and pepper

1. Combine raisins and water in bowl. Wrap tightly with plastic wrap and microwave until water begins to boil, about 1 minute. Let stand until raisins are soft and liquid has been absorbed, about 5 minutes.

2. Whisk mayonnaise, vinegar, and honey together in large bowl. Add apples, celery, walnuts, and plumped raisins to bowl and toss until well coated. Refrigerate, covered, for 30 minutes. Season with salt and pepper to taste. Serve. (Salad can be stored in airtight container for up to 2 days.)

WALDORF SALAD WITH DRIED CHERRIES AND PECANS

Substitute ¾ cup dried cherries for raisins and ¾ cup chopped pecans for walnuts.

WALDORF SALAD WITH RED GRAPES AND ALMONDS

Omit step 1. Substitute 1 cup seedless red grapes, halved, for plumped raisins and ¾ cup sliced almonds for walnuts.

CURRIED WALDORF SALAD WITH GREEN GRAPES AND PEANUTS

Omit step 1. In step 2, whisk 2 tablespoons peanut butter and 1 teaspoon curry powder into mayonnaise mixture and substitute 1 cup seedless green grapes, halved, for plumped raisins and ¾ cup dry-roasted peanuts for walnuts.

TOASTING NUTS

To toast a small amount (less than 1 cup) of nuts, put them in dry skillet over medium heat. Shake skillet occasionally to prevent scorching and toast until lightly browned and fragrant, 3 to 8 minutes. To toast a larger quantity, spread nuts in single layer on rimmed baking sheet and toast in 350-degree oven. To promote even toasting, shake baking sheet every few minutes, and toast until lightly browned and fragrant, 5 to 10 minutes.

✔ WHY THIS RECIPE WORKS

Like football and foliage, apple cider and hearty root vegetables are among the harbingers of autumn in New England. To capture those distinct fall flavors in this side dish, we focused on the vegetables. Chopping carrots into smaller pieces than the parsnips and turnips ensured that all three cooked evenly in the same amount of time. To coax more flavor out of them, we sautéed the vegetables in butter until browned and nicely caramelized. Though cider alone offered nice apple flavor, hard cider created a crisp, cleaner-tasting glaze; a few tablespoons of sugar tamped down any off-putting tartness. For a bright dose of enhanced apple flavor, we stirred in a diced Granny Smith and some cider vinegar. As a finishing touch, chopped fresh tarragon contributed a fresh herbal note.

CIDER-GLAZED ROOT VEGETABLES SERVES 8

If you prefer to use an equal amount of nonalcoholic sparkling or regular cider, reduce the sugar to 1 tablespoon.

4	tablespoons unsalted butter
1	pound carrots, peeled and cut into ½-inch pieces
12	ounces parsnips, peeled and cut into ¾-inch pieces
12	ounces turnips, peeled and cut into ¾-inch pieces
3	shallots, peeled and halved
2½	cups hard cider
3	tablespoons sugar
	Salt and pepper
1	Granny Smith apple, cored and cut into ½-inch pieces
2	tablespoons chopped fresh tarragon
2	teaspoons cider vinegar

1. Melt 1 tablespoon butter in 12-inch skillet over medium-high heat. Add carrots, parsnips, turnips, and shallots and cook until lightly browned, about 5 minutes. Add cider, sugar, 1½ teaspoons salt, and remaining 3 tablespoons butter and bring to boil. Reduce heat to medium-low, cover, and cook until vegetables are just tender, 7 to 10 minutes, stirring occasionally.

2. Uncover, increase heat to medium, and cook until vegetables are fully tender, about 13 minutes, stirring occasionally. Stir in apple and continue to cook until cider is syrupy and apple is just tender, about 2 minutes longer. Off heat, stir in tarragon and vinegar. Season with salt and pepper to taste. Transfer to serving dish and pour any remaining glaze over vegetables. Serve.

CIDER-GLAZED ROOT VEGETABLES WITH POMEGRANATE AND CILANTRO

Substitute chopped fresh cilantro for tarragon and add ¼ cup pomegranate seeds along with cilantro and vinegar.

THE HARD STUFF

Most of us associate cider with the unfiltered apple juice that appears in supermarkets every fall, but before Prohibition the word "cider" meant what we know today as "hard cider," an alcoholic drink made from fermented apple juice. Hard cider was once the most popular beverage in America—in fact, colonial settlers (even children) drank cider in place of water because public wells were considered unsanitary. But cider's popularity sharply declined as immigrants brought over beer from Europe, and by the early 1900s, hard cider had all but disappeared. But after this century-long dry spell, cider is having a revival—sales have been growing by more than 50 percent a year.

PREPPING TURNIPS

The long, slender shape of carrots and parsnips makes for simple prepping. Turnips require a few extra steps:

1. Trim top and bottom of turnip and peel off outer skin. Slice turnip into ¾-inch-thick planks.

2. Slice planks into ¾-inch-wide pieces.

3. Cut pieces into ¾-inch cubes.

✓ WHY THIS RECIPE WORKS

The sweet, smoky flavor of Boston baked beans is hard to top, but few home cooks are willing to devote a full day in the kitchen to making a humble side dish that will be scarfed down in mere minutes. Shooting for authentic beans in under 3 hours, we turned to baking soda to speed up the beans' cooking time. This addition triggered rapid softening, and after only 20 minutes on the stove, our beans were ready to bake. To create a slow-cooked, salty-sweet taste, we bolstered molasses with dark brown sugar and then upped the flavor with cider vinegar, Worcestershire, and Dijon mustard. Chopping and browning the salt pork rendered some of its fat and made it an edible addition to the beans (rather than a flavor booster fished out before serving). We moved our covered pot to the oven to bake for 1½ hours followed by 30 minutes uncovered, concentrating the liquid. Our beans emerged perfectly tender, and a final stir of extra molasses and mustard served to thicken and enrich the sauce.

QUICKER BOSTON BAKED BEANS SERVES 6 TO 8

Liquids evaporate faster in the oven in heavy cast-iron Dutch ovens than in lighter pots. If you're using a cast-iron pot, increase the water in step 2 to 4½ cups.

- 1 **pound (2½ cups) dried navy beans, picked over and rinsed**
- 1 **tablespoon baking soda**
- 6 **ounces salt pork, rind removed, cut into ¼-inch pieces**
- 1 **onion, chopped fine**
- 5 **tablespoons packed dark brown sugar**
- 5 **tablespoons molasses**
- 2 **tablespoons Worcestershire sauce**
- 4 **teaspoons Dijon mustard**
- 2 **teaspoons cider vinegar**
  Salt and pepper

1. Adjust oven rack to middle position and heat oven to 350 degrees. Bring 3 quarts water, beans, and baking soda to boil in Dutch oven over high heat. Reduce heat to medium-high and simmer briskly for 20 minutes. Drain beans in colander. Rinse beans and pot.

2. Cook salt pork in now-empty pot over medium heat, stirring occasionally, until browned, about 10 minutes. Add onion and cook until softened, about 5 minutes. Stir in 3 cups water, sugar, ¼ cup molasses, Worcestershire, 1 tablespoon mustard, vinegar, ¼ teaspoon pepper, and beans and bring to boil. Cover, transfer pot to oven, and cook until beans are nearly tender, about 1½ hours.

3. Remove lid and continue to bake until beans are completely tender, about 30 minutes. Stir in remaining 1 tablespoon molasses and remaining 1 teaspoon mustard. Season with salt and pepper to taste. Serve.

TO MAKE AHEAD: Beans can be made through step 3 and refrigerated for up to 4 days. Cover and heat over low heat, stirring occasionally, until heated through, 8 to 10 minutes, adjusting consistency with water as needed.

HOW SWEET IT WAS

Given the relative obscurity of molasses in today's economy, it's hard to understand that it was once an important commodity. From colonial times onward, it was distilled into rum, enjoyed by the colonists, and exported to Europe. But molasses, a byproduct of the cane-sugar refining process imported from the Caribbean and West Indies, could also be used to make industrial-grade alcohol. This was in turn used to manufacture gunpowder and other munitions, both in great demand during World War I. But with the end of the war in late 1918, the demand for industrial alcohol fell, and the coming of Prohibition signaled the end of the legal manufacture of drinking alcohol. In fact, the day after Boston's Great Molasses Flood, the state of Nebraska ratified the 18th Amendment to the Constitution, and Prohibition became the law of the land. Molasses never regained its importance in the New England economy.

✓ WHY THIS RECIPE WORKS

The knish is a hearty, savory pastry made famous by Eastern European Jews who immigrated to New York in the early 20th century. To master the knish at home, we started with a simple dough of flour, olive oil, salt, and water. Adding an egg allowed the oil and water to combine, making the dough more supple, and baking powder promoted lift and tenderness. For the filling, we mashed high-starch russet potatoes and deeply browned onions for intense flavor. To assemble, we rolled the dough into a very thin square and formed the filling into a rope along one of its edges. A thin coating of oil on the dough prevented the layers from fusing, creating a lighter pastry. We rolled the dough around the filling, sliced each cylinder into eight knishes, and stood each on end before pressing lightly to flatten the rolls. To ensure crisp bottoms, we brushed the parchment paper–lined baking sheet with oil before arranging the knishes on it.

POTATO KNISHES MAKES 16

A well-floured counter is essential here. To reheat baked knishes, place them in a 350-degree oven for 10 to 15 minutes.

FILLING

- 2¼ **pounds russet potatoes, peeled and cut into 1-inch pieces**
- **Salt and pepper**
- 1 **tablespoon olive oil**
- 3 **onions, chopped fine**

DOUGH

- 2 **cups (10 ounces) all-purpose flour**
- 1½ **teaspoons baking powder**
- ¾ **cup olive oil**
- ½ **cup water**
- 1 **large egg, plus 1 large egg beaten with 1 tablespoon water**
- 1 **teaspoon salt**

1. FOR THE FILLING: Combine potatoes and 1 tablespoon salt in Dutch oven and add water to cover by 1 inch. Bring to boil over high heat. Reduce heat to medium and cook until potatoes are tender, 20 to 25 minutes. Drain potatoes and return to pot. Cook over low heat until potatoes are thoroughly dry, about 1 minute. Mash potatoes with potato masher until very few lumps remain. Transfer to large bowl and stir in ½ teaspoon salt and ½ teaspoon pepper.

2. Heat oil in 12-inch nonstick skillet over medium-high heat until shimmering. Add onions and ½ teaspoon salt and cook, stirring occasionally, until well browned, about 10 minutes. Transfer to bowl with mashed potatoes and stir to combine. Let filling cool completely. (Filling can be made up to 24 hours in advance, covered, and refrigerated.)

3. FOR THE DOUGH: Whisk flour and baking powder together in large bowl. Whisk 6 tablespoons oil, water, 1 egg, and salt together in separate bowl. Add wet ingredients to dry ingredients and stir with rubber spatula until dough forms. Transfer dough to floured counter and knead until smooth, about 1 minute. Wrap in plastic wrap and let rest on counter for 1 hour or refrigerate for up to 4 hours (let dough come to room temperature before rolling).

4. Adjust oven rack to middle position and heat oven to 350 degrees. Line rimmed baking sheet with parchment paper and brush parchment with 2 tablespoons oil. Divide dough in half and form each half into 4-inch square on well-floured counter. Working with 1 square at a time (keep remaining dough covered with plastic), roll dough into 16-inch square. Lightly brush dough with 2 tablespoons oil, leaving 1-inch border at farthest edge.

5. Form half of filling into 1-inch log along near edge of dough, leaving 1-inch border on sides. Brush far edge of dough with water. Roll dough around filling and seal edge. Trim knish log on each end so log measures 16 inches long. Cut log into eight 2-inch pieces. Stand each knish on end and press to 1-inch thickness. Space evenly apart in prepared sheet. Repeat with remaining dough, remaining 2 tablespoons oil, and remaining filling.

6. Brush tops and sides of knishes with egg-water mixture. Bake until golden brown, 35 to 40 minutes, rotating sheet halfway through baking. Transfer knishes to wire rack and let cool for 15 minutes. Serve.

TO MAKE AHEAD: Knishes can be made through step 5 and frozen for up to 1 month. If baking from frozen, increase baking time to 50 to 55 minutes.

EASIER KNISH CONSTRUCTION

1. Roll half of dough into 16-inch square so thin you can see counter through it. Brush dough with oil, mound half of filling evenly in long rope, leaving about 1 inch clear at nearest edge and at ends.

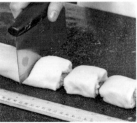

2. Roll dough around filling and seal seam. Trim edges, place seam side down, and cut tube into pieces. Stand each knish on cut end and lightly press. Place on oiled, parchment paper–lined baking sheet.

✔ WHY THIS RECIPE WORKS

After tasting the bialys at Kossar's in Manhattan's Lower East Side, we knew what we wanted from our own recipe: golden, chewy rolls with great salty flavor and a generous onion-filled dimple in the center. We started with the filling, sautéing chopped onions in olive oil and kosher salt until they turned golden brown. A tablespoon of poppy seeds stirred in off the heat finished off the filling. Turning to the rolls, the key was patience. After mixing a simple dough and kneading it, we let it rise for an hour. We divided the dough into 12 pieces, allowed them to rise, formed them into balls, and let them rise yet again. The three resting periods allowed the gluten to relax and the yeast to form large air pockets, resulting in very tender bialys. Sugar gave the exterior a crusty, golden appearance. We formed and filled the dimples right before baking, and our end result took us right back to New York City—but without the train fare.

BIALYS MAKES 12

If you substitute table salt for kosher, cut the salt amounts in half.

DOUGH
- 2 **cups warm water (110 degrees)**
- 1 **tablespoon sugar**
- 2 **teaspoons instant or rapid-rise yeast**
- 4¾ **cups (23¾ ounces) all-purpose flour**
- 2 **tablespoons kosher salt**

FILLING
- 3 **tablespoons olive oil**
- 3 **cups finely chopped onion**
- 1 **teaspoon kosher salt**
- 1 **tablespoon poppy seeds**

1. FOR THE DOUGH: In bowl of stand mixer, combine warm water, sugar, and yeast and let sit until foamy, about 3 minutes. Add flour and salt to yeast mixture. Fit stand mixer with dough hook and knead on low speed until dough comes together, about 3 minutes.

2. Turn out dough onto lightly floured counter and knead by hand until smooth, about 1 minute. Transfer dough to greased bowl and cover tightly with plastic wrap. Let dough rise at room temperature until almost doubled in size, about 1 hour.

3. Line 2 rimmed baking sheets with parchment paper and lightly flour parchment. Gently press center of dough to deflate. Transfer dough to lightly floured counter and divide into 12 equal pieces. Form each piece into rough ball by pulling dough edges underneath so top is smooth. Arrange 6 balls on each prepared sheet and cover loosely with plastic. Let dough rise at room temperature for 30 minutes.

4. FOR THE FILLING: Heat oil in 12-inch nonstick skillet over medium heat until shimmering. Add onions and salt and cook until golden brown, about 10 minutes. Off heat, stir in poppy seeds.

5. Adjust oven racks to upper-middle and lower-middle positions and heat oven to 475 degrees. On lightly floured counter, use your hands to gently press each dough ball into 5-inch round. Return to sheets and cover loosely with plastic. Let dough rise at room temperature until puffy, 15 to 20 minutes.

6. Grease and flour bottom of round 1-cup dry measuring cup (or 3-inch-diameter drinking glass). Press cup firmly into center of each dough round until cup touches sheet to make indentation for filling. (Reflour cup as needed to prevent sticking.)

7. Divide filling evenly among bialys (about 1 heaping tablespoon each) and smooth with back of spoon. Bake until spotty golden brown, 15 to 20 minutes, rotating and switching sheets halfway through baking. Transfer bialys to wire rack and let cool for 10 minutes. Serve.

BIALY'S BIRTHPLACE

When food writer Mimi Sheraton set out in 1992 to discover the origins of the bialy, common wisdom sent her straight to the widely acknowledged source: Bialystok, Poland. But despite vigorous sleuthing, she couldn't find a Bialystok bakery that produced bialys. Was she on the wrong track? Had Nazi occupation (German forces decimated Bialystok's once-thriving Jewish population) wiped out any evidence? Were bialys invented in the New World by expatriates who'd escaped turn-of-the-century pogroms? The mystery inspired her book *The Bialy Eaters*, in which Sheraton spoke with far-flung former Bialystokers around the world, from New York to Israel to Argentina.

Through her interviews and research, Sheraton determined that the bialy (*bialystoker kuchen*) and its precursor, the *pletzl*, were both known in Bialystok before World War II. Whether it was invented there, however, and who baked the first one, is a mystery.

✓ WHY THIS RECIPE WORKS

We wanted mahogany-brown soft pretzels that made it worth staying home to watch the big game. To start, we created a soft, sweet interior by using bread flour—its higher gluten content produces great chew— and brown sugar, which contributed a subtle malty flavor to the dough. Pretzels get their dark crust from exposure to an alkali solution, so we created our own with water and baking soda. Boiling our pretzels in this solution ensured proper browning and set the crust to protect the dense, chewy dough inside. After 30 seconds in the solution, we let the uncooked pretzels dry briefly on a wire rack to prevent them from adhering to the baking sheet. Baked after a generous sprinkling of kosher salt, these pretzels were ready for the big leagues.

BALLPARK PRETZELS MAKES 12

We use kosher salt on the exterior of our pretzels, but coarse pretzel salt may be substituted. However, be sure to use kosher salt in the dough. Keep in mind that the dough needs to rise for 1 hour, and then the shaped pretzels require a 20-minute rise before boiling and baking. These pretzels are best served warm, with mustard.

1½	cups warm water (110 degrees)
3	tablespoons vegetable oil
2	tablespoons packed dark brown sugar
2	teaspoons instant or rapid-rise yeast
3¾	cups (20⅔ ounces) bread flour
	Kosher salt
¼	cup baking soda

1. Lightly grease large bowl. In bowl of stand mixer, combine warm water, 2 tablespoons oil, sugar, and yeast and let sit until foamy, about 3 minutes. Combine flour and 4 teaspoons salt in separate bowl. Add flour mixture to yeast mixture. Fit stand mixer with dough hook and knead on low speed until dough comes together and clears sides of bowl, 4 to 6 minutes.

2. Turn out dough onto lightly floured counter and knead by hand until smooth, about 1 minute. Transfer dough to greased bowl and cover with plastic wrap. Let dough rise at room temperature until almost doubled in size, about 1 hour.

3. Gently press center of dough to deflate. Transfer dough to lightly greased counter, divide into 12 equal pieces, and cover with plastic.

4. Lightly flour 2 rimmed baking sheets. Working with 1 piece of dough at a time, roll into 22-inch-long rope. Shape rope into U with 2-inch-wide bottom curve and ends facing away from you. Crisscross ropes in middle of U, then fold ends toward bottom of U. Firmly press ends into bottom curve of U 1 inch apart to form pretzel shape. Transfer pretzels to prepared sheets, knot side up, 6 pretzels per sheet. Cover pretzels loosely with plastic and let rise at room temperature until slightly puffy, about 20 minutes.

5. Adjust oven racks to upper-middle and lower-middle positions and heat oven to 425 degrees. Dissolve baking soda in 4 cups water in Dutch oven and bring to boil over medium-high heat. Using slotted spatula, transfer 4 pretzels, knot side down, to boiling water and cook for 30 seconds, flipping halfway through cooking. Transfer pretzels to wire rack, knot side up, and repeat with remaining 8 pretzels in 2 additional batches. Let pretzels rest for 5 minutes.

6. Wipe flour from sheets and grease with remaining 1 tablespoon oil. Sprinkle each sheet with ½ teaspoon salt. Transfer pretzels to prepared sheets, knot side up, 6 pretzels per sheet. Sprinkle 1 teaspoon salt evenly over pretzels.

7. Bake pretzels until mahogany brown and any yellowish color around seams has faded, 15 to 20 minutes, switching and rotating sheets halfway through baking. Transfer pretzels to wire rack and let cool for 10 minutes. Serve.

TO MAKE AHEAD: Pretzels are best eaten day they are baked but will keep at room temperature in airtight container for up to 2 days. Freeze pretzels, wrapped well in plastic wrap, for up to 1 month. To reheat room-temperature pretzels, brush tops lightly with water, sprinkle with salt, and toast on baking sheet at 300 degrees for 5 minutes. Let frozen pretzels thaw before reheating.

SHAPE SHIFTER

1. After rolling each ball into 22-inch rope, bend into U shape with ends facing away.

2. Cross rope ends in middle of U, then cross again. Fold ends over top toward bottom of U and press ends firmly into bottom of curve, about 1 inch apart.

✓ WHY THIS RECIPE WORKS

Johnnycakes are rich, crisp corn cakes that aren't just for breakfast. Rhode Islanders regularly serve up this colonial-era dish, and the local love for johnnycakes is put on proud display at the annual Johnny Cake Festival in Richmond, Rhode Island. For johnnycakes that would stack up in our own kitchen, we took a tip from polenta recipes, combining the dry ingredients before whisking them into a pot of boiling water. This step allowed the cornmeal to cook more thoroughly, softening its naturally gritty texture. Resting the batter for 15 minutes thickened it to the consistency of mashed potatoes. After plopping mounds of batter into the pan, we let the cakes cook for at least 6 minutes to form a crust on the bottom, preventing them from breaking apart when flipped. Gently flattening the cakes to about ¼ inch allowed them to cook through. As is, these were a perfect side dish; served with a simple maple butter, they proved a standout alternative to pancakes.

RHODE ISLAND JOHNNYCAKES MAKES 12

Johnnycakes are best served warm with Maple Butter (recipe follows) or maple syrup for breakfast, or as a side dish for soups and stews. Do not try to turn the johnnycakes too soon or they will fall apart. If you prefer crispier johnnycakes, press the pancakes thinner in step 5.

- 1 cup johnnycake meal or stone-ground cornmeal
- 2 teaspoons sugar
- ¾ teaspoon salt
- 2¾ cups water, plus extra hot water for thinning batter
- 2 tablespoons unsalted butter
- 2 tablespoons vegetable oil

1. Adjust oven rack to middle position and heat oven to 200 degrees. Set wire rack in rimmed baking sheet.

2. Whisk johnnycake meal, sugar, and salt together in bowl. Bring water to boil in large saucepan. Slowly whisk johnnycake meal mixture into boiling water until no lumps remain; continue to cook until thickened, about 30 seconds. Off heat, whisk in butter. Pour batter into bowl, cover with plastic wrap, and let sit until slightly firm, about 15 minutes.

3. Rewhisk batter until smooth. Batter should be consistency of ploppable mashed potatoes; if not, thin with 1 to 2 tablespoons extra hot water until mixture will drop easily from spoon.

4. Heat 1 tablespoon oil in 12-inch nonstick skillet over medium heat until shimmering (or heat nonstick griddle to 400 degrees). Using greased ¼-cup dry measuring cup, drop 6 evenly spaced scoops of batter into skillet, using spoon to help release batter from cup as needed. Cook johnnycakes, without moving them, until edges appear crispy and golden brown, 6 to 8 minutes.

5. Carefully flip johnnycakes and press with spatula to flatten into 2½- to 3-inch-diameter pancakes. Continue to cook until well browned on second side, 5 to 7 minutes. Transfer johnnycakes to prepared wire rack and place in oven to keep warm. Whisk 2 to 4 tablespoons extra hot water into remaining batter to return to correct consistency. Repeat cooking with remaining 1 tablespoon oil and remaining batter. Serve.

MAPLE BUTTER MAKES ¼ CUP

Maple butter will keep, covered and refrigerated, for one week. Try it on roasted vegetables, cornbread, or pork chops, as well as johnnycakes.

- 4 tablespoons unsalted butter, softened
- 1 tablespoon pure maple syrup
- ¼ teaspoon salt

Whisk butter, maple syrup, and salt together in bowl until combined.

WHAT'S IN A NAME?

Recipes unique to a particular area inspire fierce loyalty among their fans, not to mention raging arguments about the "real" version and who first made it. Even the proper spelling can be a subject of disputes. Rhode Island johnnycakes are a perfect example. Americans have been eating cornmeal-based hotcakes ever since the first settlers adopted them from the Native Americans. The earliest English name for them was "journeycakes," thought to derive from the fact that Native Americans took the cakes with them on their travels. Over the years, regional variations multiplied, and ownership of the best or most authentic version was hotly debated. Nowhere did the argument rage more fiercely than in Rhode Island, where, as it turns out, the spelling was as important as the recipe. At some point not long after the Revolutionary War, "journeycake" was replaced by "Johnnycake" throughout the colonies. But some Rhode Islanders objected that this new spelling could be construed as honoring John Bull, the colonial name for an Englishman. How much more patriotic, they said, to call them "Jonnycakes," since "Jonathan" (no *h*) was the nickname for the new Americans. In the 1890s, the Rhode Island legislature proclaimed "Jonnycake" the state's official spelling (although "johnnycake" or "johnny cake" is most common now).

✓ WHY THIS RECIPE WORKS

As a rule, biscuits should be light and flaky, requiring minimal prep and delivering maximum richness in every bite. How could we incorporate potatoes, said to make baked goods extra-tender, into that delicate balance? We discovered that instant mashed potatoes provided the benefit of potato starch without any added weight. After testing different proportions, we found that ¾ cup dehydrated potato to 2½ cups all-purpose flour produced incredibly flaky biscuits that resisted crumbling. For a biscuit that rose as high as its buttermilk cousins, we turned to extra baking powder for leavening power. Chopped fresh chives reinforced the earthy potato taste, rounding out the flavor of these tender, savory biscuits.

POTATO BISCUITS WITH CHIVES MAKES 12

We like the texture of biscuits made with both butter and shortening, but if you prefer to use all butter, omit the shortening and use 12 tablespoons of chilled butter in step 1.

2½	cups (12½ ounces) all-purpose flour
¾	cup instant potato flakes
⅓	cup chopped fresh chives
4	teaspoons baking powder
½	teaspoon baking soda
1	tablespoon sugar
1	teaspoon salt
8	tablespoons unsalted butter, cut into ½-inch pieces and chilled, plus 2 tablespoons unsalted butter, melted
4	tablespoons vegetable shortening, cut into ½-inch pieces and chilled
1¼	cups buttermilk, chilled

1. Adjust oven rack to middle position and heat oven to 450 degrees. Line rimmed baking sheet with parchment paper. Process flour, potato flakes, chives, baking powder, baking soda, sugar, and salt in food processor until combined, about 15 seconds. Add chilled butter and shortening and pulse until mixture resembles coarse crumbs, 7 to 9 pulses.

2. Transfer flour mixture to large bowl. Stir in buttermilk with rubber spatula until combined, turning and pressing until no dry flour remains. Turn out dough onto lightly floured counter and knead briefly, 8 to 10 times, to form smooth, cohesive ball. Roll out dough into 9-inch circle, about ¾ inch thick.

3. Using floured 2½-inch round cutter, stamp out 8 to 9 biscuits and arrange upside down on prepared sheet. Gather dough scraps and gently pat into ¾-inch-thick circle. Stamp out remaining 3 to 4 biscuits and transfer to sheet.

4. Bake until biscuits begin to rise, about 5 minutes, then rotate sheet and reduce oven temperature to 400 degrees. Continue to bake until golden brown, 10 to 12 minutes longer. Brush biscuit tops with melted butter. Transfer to wire rack and let cool for 5 minutes before serving.

POTATO BISCUITS WITH CHEDDAR AND SCALLIONS

Omit chives and process ¾ cup shredded extra-sharp cheddar cheese and 4 thinly sliced scallions with flour in step 1.

POTATO BISCUITS WITH BACON

Cook 6 slices of bacon in 12-inch skillet over medium heat until crispy, 7 to 9 minutes; transfer to paper towel–lined plate. Crumble bacon when cool enough to handle. Omit chives and process crumbled bacon with flour in step 1.

FLAKING OUT

It was 1953, and chemical engineers James Cording and Miles J. Willard had a challenge: a potato glut. Cording and Willard, working for the Department of Agriculture in Wyndmoor, Pennsylvania, set out to find a way to preserve the bounty by creating a potato product that was shelf-stable, lightweight, and pleasant to eat—something the military, for example, could use for rations. After many gluey failures, they developed the three-step "Philadelphia Cook": The potatoes are cooked at 150 to 165 degrees for 20 minutes to gelatinize the starch, then cooled and cooked again in a steam cooker to separate the potato cells without rupturing them (ruptured cells make paste, not mash). Finally, the potatoes are dried and broken into flakes. The result: easy-to-rehydrate, shelf-stable, light potatoes. Cording and Willard were granted a patent for the process in 1956. Today, about 10 percent of the U.S. potato crop is dehydrated, mostly for use in military, school, and food aid programs here and abroad.

🥄 WHY THIS RECIPE WORKS

Could we bring soft, chewy, and supremely garlicky garlic knots home without the help of a pizza delivery guy? Since potent garlic flavor is their defining characteristic, we set out to infuse our garlic knots with it. We started by cooking 10 minced garlic cloves in butter, adding water to draw out the cooking time for better browning. Letting the pan sit off the heat allowed the butter to steep before the garlic solids were strained and set aside. After discovering that simply brushing the surface with our garlic butter wasn't quite enough, we stirred some of the butter and the reserved toasty garlic solids into the dough to ramp up the flavor. Brushing the surface with our browned butter twice during baking produced the potent garlicky knots we were craving.

GARLIC KNOTS   MAKES 12

You'll need 2 tablespoons of minced garlic. Adding 1 teaspoon of water in step 2 allows the garlic to brown before the butter burns.

10	garlic cloves, minced
6	tablespoons unsalted butter
1	teaspoon water, plus ¾ cup warm water (110 degrees)
1½	teaspoons instant or rapid-rise yeast
2	cups (10 ounces) all-purpose flour
1	teaspoon salt

1. Adjust oven rack to middle position and heat oven to 200 degrees. When oven reaches 200 degrees, turn it off. Grease large bowl.

2. Cook garlic, 1 tablespoon butter, and 1 teaspoon water in small nonstick skillet over low heat, stirring occasionally, until garlic is straw colored, 8 to 10 minutes. Add remaining 5 tablespoons butter, stirring until melted. Let stand for 10 minutes off heat. Strain garlic butter through fine-mesh strainer into small bowl; reserve garlic solids.

3. Whisk remaining ¾ cup warm water, 1 tablespoon garlic butter, reserved garlic solids, and yeast together in liquid measuring cup until yeast dissolves. In bowl of stand mixer fitted with dough hook, mix flour and salt until combined. With mixer on low, add water mixture in steady stream and mix until dough comes together, about 1 minute. Increase speed to medium and knead until dough is smooth and comes away from sides of bowl, about 6 minutes. Turn out dough onto clean counter and knead briefly to form smooth, cohesive ball. Transfer dough to prepared bowl and turn to coat. Cover with plastic wrap and place in turned-off oven until dough has doubled in size, 40 to 50 minutes.

4. Line baking sheet with parchment paper. Punch down dough on floured counter. Roll dough into 12 by 6-inch rectangle and cut into twelve 6-inch strips. With flat hands, roll strips into 12-inch ropes. Gather ends of each rope and make 1½-inch loop by threading ends of rope underneath each other and pulling as if tying shoelaces. Tuck one tail into center of loop and pull other tail up through center of loop.

5. Place knots on prepared baking sheet, cover loosely with plastic, and return to turned-off oven until doubled in size, about 20 minutes.

6. Remove knots from oven and discard plastic. Heat oven to 500 degrees. Return knots to oven and bake until set, about 5 minutes. Remove knots from oven and brush with 2 tablespoons garlic butter. Rotate sheet, return it to oven, and bake until knots are golden, about 5 minutes. Brush knots with remaining garlic butter and let cool for 5 minutes. Transfer to wire rack. Serve warm.

TO MAKE AHEAD: Shaped knots can be refrigerated, covered, for 24 hours. Let sit at room temperature for 30 minutes. Meanwhile, heat oven to 200 degrees and turn off. Put knots in turned-off oven until doubled in size, about 20 minutes. Proceed with step 6.

TYING THE KNOT

1. Making 1½-inch loop, tie rope as in first step of tying shoelaces.

2. Tuck 1 tail into center of loop from top.

3. Pull other tail up through bottom so end pokes up through center.

✔ WHY THIS RECIPE WORKS

What's the secret to perfecting this classic New England cornmeal and molasses loaf? More cornmeal and molasses. Hoping to achieve a strong cornmeal flavor without sacrificing the bread's structure, we upped the amount of cornmeal and then added yeast to make up for the loss of gluten and help our loaves rise high. To perfect the texture, we turned to all-purpose flour instead of whole wheat (which produced heavy bread), and we chose water over milk for a nicer chew. For more noticeable molasses flavor, we added a whopping ½ cup, which also gave the bread a beautiful caramel-brown color.

ANADAMA BREAD

MAKES 2 LOAVES

This recipe is easily halved.

1	cup (5 ounces) cornmeal, plus extra for dusting
2	cups warm water (110 degrees)
½	cup molasses
5	tablespoons unsalted butter, melted
5½	cups (27½ ounces) all-purpose flour
1	tablespoon instant or rapid-rise yeast
2½	teaspoons salt

1. Grease large bowl. Grease two 8½ by 4½-inch loaf pans and dust with extra cornmeal. Whisk water, molasses, and melted butter together in bowl or large measuring cup until combined.

2. Using stand mixer fitted with dough hook, mix flour, yeast, salt, and cornmeal together on low speed until combined, about 5 seconds. Slowly add molasses mixture and knead until cohesive mass starts to form, about 2 minutes. Increase speed to medium-low and knead until dough is smooth and elastic, 6 to 8 minutes. (Dough should clear sides of bowl but will stick to bottom.) Turn out dough onto lightly floured counter and knead for 1 minute.

3. Transfer dough to prepared bowl and cover with plastic wrap. Let rise at room temperature until almost doubled in size and fingertip depression in dough springs back slowly, 1 to 1½ hours.

4. Gently press down on center of dough to deflate. Place dough on lightly floured counter and divide in half. Working with 1 half at a time, pat dough into 17 by 8-inch rectangle. With short side facing you, roll dough away from you into tight cylinder. Pinch seam closed. Place loaf seam side down in prepared pan, pressing gently into corners. Repeat with remaining dough.

5. Cover loaves loosely with plastic and let rise at room temperature until almost doubled in size, 1 to 1½ hours (tops of loaves should rise about 1 inch above lips of pans). About 20 minutes before dough is fully risen, adjust oven rack to lower-middle position and heat oven to 425 degrees.

6. Place pans in oven and reduce oven temperature to 375 degrees. Bake until crust is brown and bread registers 200 degrees, 35 to 45 minutes, switching and rotating pans halfway through baking. Turn out loaves onto wire rack and let cool completely before serving, about 2 hours.

SHAPING SANDWICH BREAD

Our anadama dough is easy to work with and requires no special tricks—it's shaped just like regular sandwich bread.

1. After first rise, divide dough in half and pat dough into rectangle.

2. Roll dough into tight cylinder.

3. Pinch seam closed.

4. Transfer loaf, seam side down, to prepared loaf pan.

✔ WHY THIS RECIPE WORKS

Much better than run-of-the-mill cinnamon bread, babka has been perfected in bakeries across the Big Apple. For our take on this multilayered classic, we wanted a rich, moist loaf of bread swirled with gooey cinnamon sugar. Starting with brioche-style dough (a yeasted dough made with butter, eggs, sugar, and milk), we reduced the amount of butter and replaced one whole egg with two yolks and some milk for a luxuriously tender yet sturdy dough. Adding flour and an egg white to the filling kept the cinnamon sugar from sinking through the dough, maintaining the desired swirl from top to bottom. To create this bread's signature layers, we rolled out the chilled dough, spread it with the filling, and rolled it into a cylinder, then spread more filling on top of the cylinder before folding it over on itself. Last, we gently twisted the folded dough twice into a double figure eight. We allowed the loaf to rise, brushed it with an egg wash, then baked it until it was a beautiful deep golden color.

BABKA   MAKES 1 LOAF

Once you've added the butter in step 3, if the dough is still sticking to the sides of the bowl after 5 minutes of mixing, add 2 to 4 tablespoons of extra flour. The test kitchen's favorite loaf pan measures 8½ by 4½ inches; if you use a standard 9 by 5-inch loaf pan, start checking the babka for doneness after 40 minutes.

FILLING
- 1 cup packed (7 ounces) light brown sugar
- ¼ cup (1¼ ounces) all-purpose flour
- 2 tablespoons unsalted butter, melted and cooled
- 1 large egg white
- 2 teaspoons ground cinnamon
- ⅛ teaspoon salt

DOUGH
- ½ cup warm whole milk (110 degrees)
- 2 large egg yolks plus 1 large egg
- 1 teaspoon vanilla extract
- 2 cups (10 ounces) all-purpose flour
- ¼ cup (1¾ ounces) granulated sugar
- 1½ teaspoons instant or rapid-rise yeast
- ½ teaspoon salt
- 8 tablespoons unsalted butter, cut into 8 pieces and softened

1. FOR THE FILLING: Combine all ingredients in medium bowl. Set aside 1 tablespoon filling.

2. FOR THE DOUGH: Adjust oven rack to middle position and heat oven to 200 degrees. When oven reaches 200 degrees, turn it off. Grease large bowl. Whisk milk, egg yolks, and vanilla together in 1-cup liquid measuring cup.

3. Using stand mixer fitted with dough hook, mix together flour, sugar, yeast, and salt on low speed until combined. Slowly add milk mixture and mix until dough comes together, about 3 minutes. Increase speed to medium-low and add butter, 1 piece at a time, until incorporated, about 1 minute. Continue to mix until dough is smooth and comes away from sides of bowl, 10 to 12 minutes. Transfer dough to prepared bowl, cover with plastic wrap, and place in turned-off oven until dough has risen slightly, about 1 hour. Place in refrigerator until dough is firm and has doubled in size, at least 1 hour.

4. Line 8½ by 4½-inch loaf pan with parchment paper, allowing excess to hang over edges. Punch down dough on lightly floured counter. Roll out dough to 20 by 14-inch rectangle. Spread all but reserved 1 tablespoon filling over dough, leaving ½-inch border around edges. Working from short side, roll dough into cylinder and pinch along seam to seal. Position cylinder seam side up and roll back and forth until stretched to 18-inch length. Spread reserved filling on top of cylinder. Fold cylinder on top of itself and pinch ends to seal. Gently twist double cylinder twice to form double figure eight. Place shaped dough seam side down in prepared pan, cover loosely with plastic, and let rise in turned-off oven until doubled in size, about 1 hour.

5. Lightly beat whole egg in bowl. Remove loaf from oven and discard plastic. Heat oven to 350 degrees. Brush loaf with beaten egg. Bake until deep golden brown and loaf registers 190 degrees, about 45 minutes. Let cool in pan on wire rack for 20 minutes. Remove loaf from pan and cool completely, about 2 hours. Serve.

TO MAKE AHEAD: Instead of letting dough rise in step 4, cover shaped loaf with plastic wrap and refrigerate for up to 24 hours. Let dough sit at room temperature for 1 hour before baking.

CREATING BABKA'S SIGNATURE SWIRL

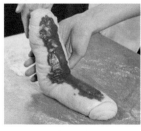

1. After stretching log of dough to 18 inches and rolling it back and forth, spread remaining filling over top of log. Fold log onto itself and pinch ends to seal.

2. Twist log twice to form double figure eight and place seam side down in loaf pan.

✔ WHY THIS RECIPE WORKS

Hermits, a New England specialty, should be soft, chewy raisin cookies with balanced, spicy sweetness. For cookies with the perfect texture, we melted the butter in a saucepan and cooked it until slightly brown. The browned butter added moisture and a nutty flavor to the cookies. We wanted warm, delicate spices in these hermits, so we bloomed the aromatic flavors of cinnamon and allspice in the browned butter. Pureeing raisins and crystallized ginger into a paste helped distribute their potent, sweet flavors into every bite. Baking the dough as a log before slicing it into bars made for chewier, moister cookies. Drizzled with a simple glaze of confectioners' sugar and orange juice, these old-fashioned cookies earned their place in our cookie jar.

HERMIT COOKIES MAKES ABOUT 20

For this recipe, we prefer using mild (or light) molasses instead of the robust or blackstrap varieties.

1	cup raisins
2	tablespoons finely chopped crystallized ginger
8	tablespoons unsalted butter
1	teaspoon ground cinnamon
¼	teaspoon ground allspice
2	cups (10 ounces) all-purpose flour
½	teaspoon baking soda
½	teaspoon salt
¾	cup packed (5¼ ounces) dark brown sugar
½	cup molasses
2	large eggs
1½	tablespoons orange juice
¾	cup (3 ounces) confectioners' sugar

1. Adjust oven racks to upper-middle and lower-middle positions and heat oven to 350 degrees. Line 2 baking sheets with parchment paper. Process raisins and ginger in food processor until mixture sticks together and only small pieces remain, about 10 seconds. Transfer mixture to large bowl.

2. Heat butter in small saucepan over medium-low heat, swirling pan occasionally, until nutty brown in color, about 10 minutes. Stir in cinnamon and allspice and cook until fragrant, about 15 seconds. Stir butter mixture into raisin mixture until well combined; let cool to room temperature.

3. Combine flour, baking soda, and salt in bowl. Stir brown sugar, molasses, and eggs into cooled butter-raisin mixture until incorporated. Fold in flour mixture (dough will be very sticky) and refrigerate, covered, until firm, at least 1½ hours or up to 24 hours.

4. Divide dough into quarters. Transfer 1 piece of dough to lightly floured counter and roll into 10-inch log. Transfer to prepared baking sheet and use ruler to neatly square off sides. (Each sheet will contain 2 logs.) Repeat with remaining dough. Bake until only shallow indentation remains on edges when touched (center will appear slightly soft), 15 to 20 minutes, switching and rotating sheets halfway through baking. Let cool on sheets for 5 minutes, then transfer parchment to wire racks and let cool completely.

5. Whisk orange juice and confectioners' sugar together in small bowl until smooth. Drizzle glaze onto cooled logs and let sit until glaze hardens, about 15 minutes. Cut logs into 2-inch bars. Serve. (Cookies can be stored in airtight container at room temperature for up to 5 days.)

PERFECTING HERMITS

1. Roll each quarter of dough into 10-inch log, transfer to baking sheet, then use ruler to neatly square off sides before baking.

2. Once completely cooled, drizzle baked hermits with glaze before slicing into individual bars.

✔ WHY THIS RECIPE WORKS

To make this odd but intriguing-sounding cookie recipe work, we wanted to harness the salty flavor and crunch of potato chips while skipping any excess grease. To incorporate potato chip crumbs with ample crunch into our dough, we crushed them in a zipper-lock bag with a rolling pin. Reduced-fat chips meant less browning and no oily taste. Using both granulated and confectioners' sugars produced cookies that were both chewy and crumbly, and adding a single egg yolk made for the most tender texture. Toasted and chopped pecans were all that were needed to solidify this lip-smacking salty-sweet matchup. How could we possibly improve on this one-of-a-kind cookie? With a dip in melted chocolate and a sprinkling of coarse salt.

POTATO CHIP COOKIES

MAKES 24

Cape Cod 40% Reduced Fat Potato Chips are the test kitchen favorite among reduced-fat chips. In this recipe, they make for extremely crunchy cookies. To prevent sticking, dip the drinking glass in flour before flattening each cookie. Toast the pecans in a small, dry skillet over medium heat, shaking the skillet often, until they begin to darken, 3 to 5 minutes.

¾   cup (3¾ ounces) all-purpose flour
1½   ounces reduced-fat potato chips,
      crushed fine (½ cup)
¼   cup pecans, toasted and chopped fine
¼   teaspoon salt
8   tablespoons unsalted butter, cut into
      8 pieces and softened
¼   cup (1¾ ounces) granulated sugar
¼   cup (1 ounce) confectioners' sugar
1   large egg yolk
½   teaspoon vanilla extract

1. Adjust oven rack to middle position and heat oven to 350 degrees. Line 2 rimmed baking sheets with parchment paper. Combine flour, potato chips, pecans, and salt in bowl.

2. Using stand mixer fitted with paddle, beat butter, granulated sugar, and confectioners' sugar together on medium-high speed until pale and fluffy, about 3 minutes. Add egg yolk and vanilla and beat until combined. Reduce speed to low and slowly add flour mixture in 3 additions. Roll dough into 1-inch balls and space 3 inches apart on baking sheets. Flatten dough balls to ¼-inch thickness with bottom of floured drinking glass.

3. Bake, 1 sheet at a time, until cookies are just set and lightly browned on bottom, 10 to 13 minutes, rotating sheet halfway through baking. Let cookies cool completely on sheets, about 15 minutes. Serve. (Cookies can be stored in airtight container at room temperature for up to 2 days.)

CHOCOLATE-DIPPED POTATO CHIP COOKIES

Microwave 10 ounces finely chopped bittersweet chocolate in bowl at 50 percent power, stirring occasionally, until melted, 2 to 4 minutes. Carefully dip half of each cooled cookie in chocolate, scraping off excess with finger, and place on parchment paper–lined baking sheet. Sprinkle coarse salt over warm chocolate and refrigerate until chocolate sets, about 15 minutes. Serve.

THE CHIP CAME FIRST

America's love affair with potato chips began more than 150 years ago when an enterprising chef at Moon's Lake House in Saratoga Springs, New York, sent thick slices of potato on a historic salty plunge into the deep fryer and unwittingly changed the snack food business forever.

Saratoga Springs was (and is) a small, upstate town, but plenty of well-heeled New Yorkers relaxed there during the summer in the 1850s, which may account for the spotlight shone on the early chip. "You begin to eat fried potatoes as soon as you arrive at the lake; you continually eat them til you depart; and I have heard of ladies who have taken French cambric pocket-handkerchiefs full of fried potatoes home with them, and kept them under their pillows," British journalist George Augustus Sala wrote in the *Daily Telegraph*. (He was reporting on American manners and customs during the Civil War.)

"I have seen them eaten by ladies with lavender kid gloves on," he continued, "and they are so crisp and croquant and so clean-looking, that you generally dispense with a plate while eating them at dinner, and keep a pile of fried potatoes on the table-cloth by your side. They are eaten with fish, they are eaten with game, they are eaten with sherry-coblers, and they are eaten with ice-creams." In addition to eating them in our cookies, we like our chips straight out of the bag.

✔ WHY THIS RECIPE WORKS

Translating Boston cream pie into handheld form required a sturdy but tender cake, rich, creamy custard that held its shape, and a rich chocolate glaze to top it off. For the cake, reverse creaming (cutting butter into the dry ingredients before beating in the liquid ingredients) created a moist, fine crumb, easily handled and ready for filling. Heavy cream, egg yolks, and cornstarch created the perfect consistency for the custard. Bittersweet chocolate blended with corn syrup gave the glaze a full, strong flavor and an appealing sheen. To assemble the components, we carved out a cone of cake from the top of each dome and cut off all but the top disk of cake to contain the filling. After we spooned the custard into the middle of the cupcake and replaced the top, the glaze concealed the incision for a flawless bakery-fresh look.

BOSTON CREAM CUPCAKES MAKES 12

Bake the cupcakes in a greased and floured muffin tin rather than paper cupcake liners so the chocolate glaze can run down the sides of the cooled cakes.

PASTRY CREAM
- 1⅓ **cups heavy cream**
- 3 **large egg yolks**
- ⅓ **cup (2⅓ ounces) sugar**
- **Pinch salt**
- 1 **tablespoon plus 1 teaspoon cornstarch**
- 2 **tablespoons unsalted butter, chilled and cut into 2 pieces**
- 1½ **teaspoons vanilla extract**

CUPCAKES
- 1¾ **cups (8¾ ounces) all-purpose flour**
- 1½ **teaspoons baking powder**
- ¾ **teaspoon salt**
- 1 **cup (7 ounces) sugar**
- 12 **tablespoons unsalted butter, cut into 12 pieces and softened**
- 3 **large eggs**
- ¾ **cup milk**
- 1½ **teaspoons vanilla extract**

GLAZE
- ¾ **cup heavy cream**
- ¼ **cup light corn syrup**
- 8 **ounces bittersweet chocolate, chopped**
- ½ **teaspoon vanilla extract**

1. FOR THE PASTRY CREAM: Heat cream in medium saucepan over medium heat until simmering, stirring occasionally. Meanwhile, whisk egg yolks, sugar, and salt together in medium bowl. Add cornstarch and whisk until mixture is pale yellow and thick, about 15 seconds.

2. When cream reaches full simmer, slowly whisk into yolk mixture. Return mixture to saucepan and cook over medium heat, whisking constantly, until thick and glossy, 1 to 2 minutes. Off heat, whisk in butter and vanilla. Transfer pastry cream to small bowl, press plastic wrap directly onto surface, and refrigerate until set, at least 2 hours or up to 2 days.

3. FOR THE CUPCAKES: Adjust oven rack to middle position and heat oven to 350 degrees. Spray 12-cup muffin tin with vegetable oil spray, flour generously, and tap pan to remove excess flour.

4. Using stand mixer fitted with paddle, combine flour, baking powder, salt, and sugar on low speed. Add butter, 1 piece at a time, and combine until mixture resembles coarse sand. Add eggs, 1 at a time, and mix until combined. Add milk and vanilla, increase speed to medium, and mix until light and fluffy and no lumps remain, about 3 minutes.

5. Fill muffin cups three-quarters full of batter (do not overfill). Bake until toothpick inserted in center of cupcake comes out clean, 18 to 20 minutes. Let cupcakes cool in pan for 5 minutes, then transfer them to wire rack to cool completely.

6. FOR THE GLAZE: Cook cream, corn syrup, chocolate, and vanilla in small saucepan over medium heat, stirring constantly, until smooth. Set glaze aside to cool and thicken for 30 minutes.

7. Insert tip of small knife at 45-degree angle about ¼ inch from edge of cupcake and cut all the way around. Remove cone and cut away all but top ¼ inch, leaving small disk of cake. Fill cupcake with 2 tablespoons pastry cream and top with disk of cake. With cupcakes on wire rack set over parchment paper, spoon glaze over each cupcake, allowing it to drip down sides. Refrigerate cupcakes until glaze is just set, about 10 minutes. (Cupcakes can be refrigerated in airtight container for up to 2 days; bring to room temperature before serving.)

FILLING BOSTON CREAM CUPCAKES

1. Insert knife tip at 45-degree angle ¼ inch from cupcake edge, cut all the way around, and remove cone of cake.

2. Cut off all but top ¼ inch of cone, leaving only small disk of cake. Fill cupcake and cover filling with cake disk.

✓ WHY THIS RECIPE WORKS

For century-old Wellesley fudge cake to make an impact on modern palates accustomed to ramped-up chocolate flavor and silken ganaches (not to mention high-quality chocolate), we needed a thick, extra-fudgy frosting and a rich but sturdy cake to support its weight. Starting with the cake, we turned to all-purpose flour for more structure and cocoa powder for deep chocolate flavor, which deepened further when whisked with hot water. For the signature frosting, we created a caramel-like base of evaporated milk, butter, and sugar. We opted for light brown sugar over granulated for its resistance to crystallizing during cooking. Stirring in more butter and evaporated milk off the heat cooled the base and prevented the bittersweet chocolate's fat from separating and turning grainy. Adding sifted confectioners' sugar and cooling the mixture thickened the frosting to a spreadable consistency. Refrigerating the iced cake for an hour made for easy slicing.

WELLESLEY FUDGE CAKE SERVES 12

We prefer Dutch-processed cocoa powder here, but natural cocoa powder can also be used.

CAKE

- 2½ cups (12½ ounces) all-purpose flour
- 2 teaspoons baking soda
- 1 teaspoon baking powder
- ½ teaspoon salt
- ¾ cup hot water
- ½ cup (1½ ounces) unsweetened cocoa powder
- 16 tablespoons unsalted butter, cut into 16 pieces and softened
- 2 cups (14 ounces) granulated sugar
- 2 large eggs
- 1 cup buttermilk, room temperature
- 2 teaspoons vanilla extract

FROSTING

- 1½ cups packed (10½ ounces) light brown sugar
- 1 cup evaporated milk
- 8 tablespoons unsalted butter, cut into 8 pieces and softened
- ½ teaspoon salt
- 8 ounces bittersweet chocolate, chopped
- 1 teaspoon vanilla extract
- 3 cups (12 ounces) confectioners' sugar, sifted

1. FOR THE CAKE: Adjust oven rack to middle position and heat oven to 350 degrees. Grease and flour two 8-inch square cake pans. Combine flour, baking soda, baking powder, and salt in bowl; set aside. In small bowl, whisk hot water and cocoa together until smooth; set aside. Using stand mixer fitted with paddle, beat butter and sugar together on medium-high speed until pale and fluffy, about 3 minutes. Add eggs, 1 at a time, and beat until combined. Reduce speed to low and add flour mixture in 3 additions, alternating with buttermilk in 2 additions, scraping down bowl as needed. Slowly add cocoa mixture and vanilla and mix until incorporated. Give batter final stir by hand.

2. Divide batter evenly between prepared pans and smooth tops with rubber spatula. Bake until toothpick inserted in center comes out with few crumbs attached, 25 to 30 minutes, rotating pans halfway through baking. Let cakes cool in pans on wire rack for 15 minutes. Remove cakes from pans and let cool completely on rack, about 2 hours.

3. FOR THE FROSTING: Heat brown sugar, ½ cup evaporated milk, 4 tablespoons butter, and salt in large saucepan over medium heat until small bubbles appear around perimeter of pan, 4 to 8 minutes. Reduce heat to low and simmer, stirring occasionally, until large bubbles form and mixture has thickened and turned deep golden brown, about 6 minutes. Transfer to large bowl. Stir in remaining ½ cup evaporated milk and remaining 4 tablespoons butter until mixture is slightly cooled. Add chocolate and vanilla and stir until smooth. Whisk in confectioners' sugar until incorporated. Let cool completely, stirring occasionally, about 1 hour.

4. Line edges of cake platter with 4 strips of parchment paper to keep platter clean. Place 1 cake layer on platter. Spread 1 cup frosting evenly over top, right to edge of cake. Top with second cake layer and press lightly to adhere. Spread remaining frosting evenly over top and sides of cake. Refrigerate cake until frosting is set, about 1 hour. Carefully remove parchment strips before serving.

COLLEGE CONTRABAND

Unbelievable as it may sound, roughly 100 years ago, fudge (yes, fudge) was a contraband treat coveted by Wellesley College students in Massachusetts. The girls were expected to stick to "plain" food and avoid sweets, as college founder Henry Fowle Durant held that "pies, lies, and doughnuts should never have a place in Wellesley College." But the students held secret fudge-making parties in their dorm rooms and, according to an undated newspaper article, "put on great airs over their skill in making fudge." Within 10 years, several tearooms in the town of Wellesley were known for their Wellesley fudge cake, with its luscious fudge frosting, and recipes for the cake proliferated.

✅ WHY THIS RECIPE WORKS

Once a German bakery favorite in Queens, New York, *bienenstich*, or bee sting cake, boasts lightly sweet, yeasted cake, creamy filling, and a crunchy honey-almond crown. We found its sticky dough best suited to a brioche-making method: combining wet and dry ingredients before kneading in butter (a whole stick for extra richness) a tablespoon at a time. As with all yeasted doughs, this cake requires two rises before baking. After letting the dough rise, we pressed it into a cake pan, pierced it with a fork to eliminate air bubbles, and let it rise again. To create the signature honey-almond topping, we boiled butter, honey, sugar, and salt before stirring in sliced almonds. The cake baked to a gorgeous golden brown, and once it had cooled, we used a trick borrowed from baker Nick Malgieri to assemble it: After splitting the cake in half and covering the bottom with pastry cream—a lush vanilla custard stabilized with a little gelatin—we sliced the top into 12 wedges and reassembled it over the filling. This step ensured a clean slice through the cream and bottom layer. Our buzz-worthy cake was a beauty to behold and it had the sweetness to match.

BEE STING CAKE SERVES 12

If your cake pan is dark, start checking the cake after 25 minutes in step 7. If the sides of your pan are less than 2½ inches high, bake the cake on a foil-lined rimmed baking sheet to catch drips. The pastry cream and dough require 3 hours of prep time.

PASTRY CREAM
- 1 teaspoon unflavored gelatin
- 1 tablespoon water
- 6 large egg yolks
- ½ cup (3½ ounces) sugar
- ¼ teaspoon salt
- 1¾ cups milk
- ¼ cup (1 ounce) cornstarch
- 2 tablespoons unsalted butter
- 1 tablespoon vanilla extract

CAKE
- ¾ cup milk
- 1 large egg plus 2 large yolks
- 2¾ cups (13¾ ounces) all-purpose flour
- ¼ cup (1¾ ounces) sugar
- 2¼ teaspoons instant or rapid-rise yeast
- ½ teaspoon salt
- 8 tablespoons unsalted butter, cut into 8 pieces and softened

TOPPING
- 4 tablespoons unsalted butter
- ¼ cup honey
- 2 tablespoons sugar
- ⅛ teaspoon salt
- ⅔ cup blanched sliced almonds

1. FOR THE PASTRY CREAM: Sprinkle gelatin over water in small bowl and let sit until gelatin softens, about 5 minutes. Whisk egg yolks, sugar, and salt in medium bowl until pale yellow. Whisk ¼ cup milk and cornstarch into egg mixture until smooth. Heat remaining 1½ cups milk in medium saucepan over medium heat until hot but not simmering. Slowly whisk hot milk into egg mixture.

2. Transfer egg mixture back to saucepan and cook over medium-low heat, whisking constantly, until mixture thickens to pudding consistency, about 5 minutes. Off heat, vigorously whisk in gelatin mixture until dissolved. (If pastry cream is lumpy, strain through fine-mesh strainer.) Transfer pastry cream to clean bowl and whisk in butter and vanilla. Cover and refrigerate until firm, at least 3 hours or up to 24 hours.

3. FOR THE CAKE: Grease large bowl. Whisk milk and egg and yolks together in 2-cup liquid measuring cup until combined. Using stand mixer fitted with dough hook, mix flour, sugar, yeast, and salt together on medium-low speed until combined, about 5 seconds. With mixer running, slowly add milk mixture and knead until cohesive dough forms and no dry flour remains, 3 to 5 minutes, scraping down bowl and dough hook as needed.

4. With mixer still running, add butter 1 piece at a time until incorporated. Continue kneading until dough is uniformly combined, 8 to 10 minutes (dough will be sticky and will not completely clear sides of bowl). Turn out dough onto lightly floured counter and knead until smooth, about 1 minute. Form dough into tight ball and transfer to greased bowl, turning to coat. Cover with plastic wrap and let rise at room temperature until nearly doubled in size, 1 to 1½ hours.

5. Grease light-colored 9-inch round cake pan, line with parchment paper, and grease parchment. Transfer dough to lightly floured counter and press into 9-inch round. Transfer dough to prepared pan and press in even layer to edges of pan. Using fork, poke dough all over. Cover pan loosely with plastic and let rise at room temperature until puffy, 35 to 50 minutes. (After rising, dough and pan can be wrapped tightly in plastic and refrigerated for up to 24 hours. Let dough come to room temperature before baking.)

6. FOR THE TOPPING: Meanwhile, bring butter, honey, sugar, and salt to boil in small saucepan over medium heat, stirring often. Once boiling, stir in almonds and remove from heat.

7. Adjust oven rack to middle position and heat oven to 350 degrees. Spread almond mixture evenly over top of dough. Bake until topping is deep golden brown, 30 to 40 minutes, rotating pan halfway through baking. Let cake cool in pan on wire rack for 20 minutes. Remove cake from pan and let cool completely on rack, about 2 hours.

8. Stir chilled pastry cream with fork to loosen. Transfer cake to cutting board topping side up. Using long serrated knife, split cake in half horizontally. Transfer cake bottom to serving platter and spread pastry cream evenly over cut side. Cut cake top into 12 wedges and reassemble on top of pastry cream. To serve, use cuts in top layer as guide to slice cake into 12 pieces.

✔ WHY THIS RECIPE WORKS

For cranberry upside-down cake that looks as good as it tastes, we needed a cohesive sweet-tart topping and a sturdy but tender cake to support it. Ground almonds created a cake with a hearty, coarse crumb, stable enough to bear the berries' weight, and whipped egg whites folded into the batter kept the texture light. For the topping, we briefly cooked the cranberries with fruit flavor–boosting raspberry jam and sugar on the stovetop to evaporate some of the moisture and then strained and reduced the juices into a concentrated syrup. Turning the cake out of its pan before it was fully cooled prevented the topping from sticking to the bottom, ensuring an attractive ruby-red dessert.

CRANBERRY UPSIDE-DOWN CAKE SERVES 8

To prevent this cake from sticking, do not let it cool in the pan for more than 10 minutes before turning it out.

TOPPING

6	tablespoons unsalted butter
3	cups fresh or defrosted frozen cranberries
¾	cup (5¼ ounces) sugar
2	tablespoons seedless raspberry jam
½	teaspoon vanilla extract

CAKE

¼	cup blanched slivered almonds
1	cup (5 ounces) all-purpose flour
1	teaspoon baking powder
¼	teaspoon salt
½	cup milk
½	teaspoon vanilla extract
½	teaspoon almond extract
6	tablespoons unsalted butter, softened
¾	cup (5¼ ounces) sugar
3	large eggs, separated

1. FOR THE TOPPING: Adjust oven rack to middle position and heat oven to 350 degrees. Grease and flour 9-inch round cake pan, line with parchment paper, and spray with vegetable oil spray. Melt butter in large non-stick skillet over medium heat. Add cranberries, sugar, and jam and cook until cranberries are just softened, about 4 minutes. Strain cranberry mixture over bowl, reserving juices.

2. Add strained juices to now-empty skillet and simmer over medium heat until syrupy and reduced to 1 cup, about 4 minutes. Off heat, stir in vanilla. Arrange strained berries in single layer in prepared pan. Pour juice mixture over berries and refrigerate for 30 minutes.

3. FOR THE CAKE: Process almonds and ¼ cup flour in food processor until finely ground, about 10 seconds. Add remaining ¾ cup flour, baking powder, and salt and pulse to combine. Whisk milk and extracts together in measuring cup. In stand mixer fitted with paddle, beat butter and sugar together until fluffy, about 2 minutes. Beat in egg yolks, 1 at a time, until combined. Reduce speed to low and add flour mixture in 3 additions, alternating with 2 additions of milk mixture.

4. Using clean bowl and beaters, beat egg whites on medium-high speed until they hold soft peaks, about 2 minutes. Whisk one-third of whites into batter, then fold in remaining whites. Pour batter over chilled cranberry mixture and bake until toothpick inserted in center comes out clean, 35 to 40 minutes. Cool on wire rack for 10 minutes, then run paring knife around cake and invert onto serving platter. Serve.

A CLEAN TURNOUT

Our cranberry upside-down cake is a real showstopper—if it comes out of the pan cleanly. To ensure that this happens, allow the cake to cool for 10 minutes, then gently run the tip of a paring knife around the outside of the cooled cake.

1. Cover cake with clean serving plate and invert.

2. Using straight upward motion, carefully remove cake pan, shaking gently as needed to get clean release of cake and topping.

✔ WHY THIS RECIPE WORKS

For this classic New England favorite, we wanted a pie with major maple flavor and a lush, smooth texture. Cooking the syrup, cream, butter, and cornstarch on the stovetop proved the best way to create a rich, balanced filling. Using cornstarch instead of flour created a creamier consistency and made the pie easy to slice. To keep the pie's sweetness in check without sacrificing any maple flavor, we turned to a test kitchen trick: adding an acidic ingredient. Stirring 2 teaspoons of tangy cider vinegar into our filling produced remarkable results: That touch of acidity brightened the maple, bringing it to the forefront where it belonged. A dollop of homemade crème fraîche offered a smooth, mildly tart finish.

MAPLE SYRUP PIE SERVES 8

Homemade crust tastes the best, but you can use store-bought pie dough in this recipe. Serve with Crème Fraîche (recipe follows).

CRUST

1¼	cups (6¼ ounces) all-purpose flour
1	tablespoon sugar
½	teaspoon salt
4	tablespoons vegetable shortening, cut into ½-inch pieces and chilled
6	tablespoons unsalted butter, cut into ¼-inch pieces and chilled
3–4	tablespoons ice water

FILLING

1¾	cups pure maple syrup
⅔	cup heavy cream
¼	teaspoon salt
5	tablespoons unsalted butter
2	tablespoons cornstarch
3	large eggs plus 2 large yolks
2	teaspoons cider vinegar

1. FOR THE CRUST: Process flour, sugar, and salt in food processor until combined, about 5 seconds. Scatter shortening over top and process until mixture resembles coarse cornmeal, about 10 seconds. Scatter butter over top and pulse until mixture resembles coarse crumbs, about 10 pulses. Transfer to bowl.

2. Sprinkle 3 tablespoons ice water over flour mixture. Using rubber spatula, stir and press dough until it sticks together. If dough does not come together, stir in remaining 1 tablespoon ice water. Flatten dough into 4-inch disk, wrap tightly in plastic wrap, and refrigerate for 1 hour. (Wrapped dough can be refrigerated for up to 2 days or frozen for up to 1 month. If frozen, let dough thaw completely on counter before rolling.) Let chilled dough sit on counter to soften slightly, about 10 minutes, before rolling.

3. Adjust oven rack to middle position and heat oven to 375 degrees. Grease 9-inch pie plate. Roll dough into 12-inch circle on lightly floured counter. Loosely roll dough around rolling pin and gently unroll it onto prepared pie plate, letting excess dough hang over edge. Ease dough into plate by gently lifting edge of dough with 1 hand while pressing into plate bottom with your other hand.

4. Trim overhang to ½ inch beyond lip of pie plate. Tuck overhang under itself; folded edge should be flush with edge of pie plate. Crimp dough evenly around edge of pie plate using your fingers. Wrap dough-lined pie plate loosely in plastic and freeze until dough is firm, about 30 minutes.

5. Line chilled pie shell with parchment paper or double layer of aluminum foil, covering edges to prevent burning, and fill with pie weights. Bake until edges are light golden brown, 18 to 25 minutes, rotating pie plate halfway through baking. Remove weights and parchment and continue to bake until center begins to look opaque and slightly drier, 3 to 6 minutes. Remove from oven and let cool for at least 30 minutes. (Baked, cooled crust can be wrapped in plastic and stored at room temperature for up to 24 hours.)

6. FOR THE FILLING: Reduce oven temperature to 350 degrees. Bring maple syrup, cream, and salt to boil in medium saucepan. Add butter and whisk until melted. Reduce heat to medium-low and whisk in cornstarch. Bring to simmer and cook for 1 minute, whisking frequently. Transfer to large bowl and let cool for at least 30 minutes. Whisk in eggs and yolks and vinegar until smooth. (Cooled filling can be refrigerated for up to 24 hours. Whisk to recombine and proceed with step 7, increasing baking time to 55 to 65 minutes.)

7. Place cooled crust on rimmed baking sheet and pour filling into crust. Bake until just set, 35 to 45 minutes. Let pie cool completely on wire rack, about 2 hours. Transfer to refrigerator and chill until fully set, at least 2 hours or up to 24 hours. Serve cold or at room temperature.

CRÈME FRAÎCHE MAKES 1 CUP

The ideal temperature for the crème fraîche to culture is 75 degrees. It will work at lower temperatures but may take up to 36 hours.

1	cup pasteurized heavy cream, room temperature
2	tablespoons buttermilk, room temperature

Combine cream and buttermilk in 1-pint jar. Cover jar with triple layer of cheesecloth and secure with rubber band. Let sit in warm place (about 75 degrees) until thickened but still pourable, 12 to 24 hours. Stir to recombine. Serve. (Crème fraîche can be refrigerated for up to 1 month.)

✔ WHY THIS RECIPE WORKS

Marlborough pie, the lesser-known open-faced New England pie, combines the comforting apple-and-spice flavors of traditional apple pie with sweet custard. Pre–Civil War bakers turned out these pies as a tasty way to use up the bruised, aging apples from their root cellars. Looking to mimic the same bracing tang straight from the supermarket, we worked with a mix of Granny Smiths (for tart flavor that doesn't quit) and Fuji, Gala, or Golden Delicious (for contrasting sweetness). We grated our apples, then sautéed them in butter to draw out moisture and concentrate the apple flavor. Prebaking the pie crust further guaranteed a flaky, crisp shell. Lemon zest contributed enough tang to the filling without becoming bitter, and sherry, cinnamon, and mace rounded out the pie's rich spiced flavor. Baking the pie at a gentle 325 degrees kept the filling from curdling, resulting in a creamy, sweetly boozy apple pie.

MARLBOROUGH APPLE PIE SERVES 8

Homemade crust tastes the best, but you can use store-bought pie dough in this recipe; prebake it according to the package instructions. Shred the apples on the large holes of a box grater. Store the pie in the refrigerator for up to 24 hours.

CRUST

- 1¼ cups (6¼ ounces) all-purpose flour
- 1 tablespoon sugar
- ½ teaspoon salt
- 4 tablespoons vegetable shortening, cut into ½-inch pieces and chilled
- 6 tablespoons unsalted butter, cut into ¼-inch pieces and chilled
- 3–4 tablespoons ice water

FILLING

- 4 tablespoons unsalted butter
- 2 Granny Smith apples, peeled and shredded (2 cups)
- 2 Fuji, Gala, or Golden Delicious apples, peeled and shredded (2 cups)
- ½ cup (3½ ounces) sugar
- ¼ teaspoon ground cinnamon
- ¼ teaspoon ground mace
- ¼ teaspoon salt
- 3 large eggs, lightly beaten
- ½ cup heavy cream
- 5 tablespoons dry sherry
- 1 teaspoon grated lemon zest
- 1 teaspoon vanilla extract

1. FOR THE CRUST: Process flour, sugar, and salt in food processor until combined, about 5 seconds. Scatter shortening over top and process until mixture resembles coarse cornmeal, about 10 seconds. Scatter butter over top and pulse until mixture resembles coarse crumbs, about 10 pulses. Transfer to bowl.

2. Sprinkle 3 tablespoons ice water over flour mixture. Using rubber spatula, stir and press dough until it sticks together. If dough does not come together, stir in remaining 1 tablespoon ice water. Flatten dough into 4-inch disk, wrap tightly in plastic wrap, and refrigerate for 1 hour. (Wrapped dough can be refrigerated for up to 2 days or frozen for up to 1 month. If frozen, let dough thaw completely on counter before rolling.) Let chilled dough sit on counter to soften slightly, about 10 minutes, before rolling.

3. Adjust oven rack to middle position and heat oven to 375 degrees. Grease 9-inch pie plate. Roll dough into 12-inch circle on lightly floured counter. Loosely roll dough around rolling pin and gently unroll it onto prepared pie plate, letting excess dough hang over edge. Ease dough into plate by gently lifting edge of dough with 1 hand while pressing into plate bottom with your other hand.

4. Trim overhang to ½ inch beyond lip of pie plate. Tuck overhang under itself; folded edge should be flush with edge of pie plate. Crimp dough evenly around edge of pie plate using your fingers. Wrap dough-lined pie plate loosely in plastic and freeze until dough is firm, about 30 minutes.

5. Line chilled pie shell with parchment paper or double layer of aluminum foil, covering edges to prevent burning, and fill with pie weights.

6. Bake until pie dough looks dry and is light in color, 25 to 30 minutes. Transfer pie plate to wire rack and remove weights and parchment. (Crust must still be warm when filling is added.)

7. FOR THE FILLING: Adjust oven rack to lower-middle position and reduce oven temperature to 325 degrees. Melt butter in 12-inch skillet over medium heat. Add apples and cook, stirring frequently, until pan is dry and apples have softened, 12 to 14 minutes. Transfer apples to bowl and let cool to room temperature, about 20 minutes.

8. Whisk sugar, cinnamon, mace, and salt together in large bowl. Add eggs, cream, sherry, lemon zest, and vanilla and whisk until smooth. Add cooled apples and stir to combine.

9. Pour mixture into pie shell and bake until center is just set, about 40 minutes. Cool completely on wire rack, about 4 hours. Serve.

☙ WHY THIS RECIPE WORKS

Many blueberry crumbles are plagued by soupy fillings that turn their crunchy toppings into mush—a major misuse of summer's fresh blueberry crop. Looking for a streamlined recipe that allowed juicy, ripe blueberries to shine without drowning the streusel topping, we kept our filling simple. Sugar and a pinch of salt proved to be all the seasoning we needed, and cornstarch thickened the filling without muting the flavor of the berries. For our topping, we wanted an extra-chunky streusel that would stay crunchy on top of the berries, so we pulsed flour, butter, brown sugar, oats, and a touch of cinnamon in the food processor until large dime-size crumbles formed. We pinched any powdery bits together with our fingers before sprinkling the topping over the berry filling. After 30 minutes in the oven, our crumble emerged browned and bubbling, the streusel still crisp atop the juicy, deep purple filling.

SUMMER BLUEBERRY CRUMBLE SERVES 6

Avoid instant or quick oats here—they are too soft and will make the crumble mushy. In step 2, do not press the topping into the berry mixture or it may sink and become soggy. Frozen berries do not work in this recipe because they shed too much liquid. Serve with vanilla ice cream or lightly sweetened whipped cream.

½	cup (3½ ounces) granulated sugar
4	teaspoons cornstarch
	Salt
25	ounces (5 cups) blueberries
⅔	cup (3⅓ ounces) all-purpose flour
½	cup (1½ ounces) old-fashioned rolled oats
⅓	cup packed (2⅓ ounces) light brown sugar
½	teaspoon ground cinnamon
6	tablespoons unsalted butter, cut into 6 pieces and chilled

1. Adjust oven rack to lower-middle position and heat oven to 375 degrees. Whisk granulated sugar, cornstarch, and ⅛ teaspoon salt together in large bowl. Add blueberries to bowl and toss to coat. Transfer to 8-inch square baking dish.

2. Pulse flour, oats, brown sugar, cinnamon, and ⅛ teaspoon salt in food processor until combined, about 5 pulses. Scatter butter over top and pulse until dime-size clumps form, about 15 pulses. Transfer topping to bowl and pinch together any powdery parts. Sprinkle topping evenly over blueberries.

3. Bake until filling is bubbling around edges and topping is golden brown, about 30 minutes, rotating dish halfway through baking. Transfer dish to wire rack and let cool for at least 30 minutes before serving. (When completely cool, crumble can be wrapped in plastic wrap and refrigerated for up to 24 hours. Let crumble sit at room temperature for 30 minutes before serving.)

CRUMBLE WITHOUT A FOOD PROCESSOR

In step 2, mix flour, oats, brown sugar, cinnamon, and ⅛ teaspoon salt together in large bowl. Add chilled butter to bowl and, using pastry blender or 2 knives, cut butter into dry ingredients until dime-size clumps form. Pinch together any powdery parts, then sprinkle crumbs evenly over berries. Proceed with recipe as directed.

FRUIT FOR DESSERT

There is an astonishing array of old-fashioned American desserts that consist of fruit baked with oats, bread, cake crumbs, flour and butter, and the like. These desserts were an easy way for frugal cooks to use up stale leftovers while providing a bit of variety in terms of texture and flavor. Most of these simple desserts have funny names that are hard to keep straight. While regional differences exist, most American cookbooks agree on the following formulations:

BETTY: Fruit combined with buttered bread or cake crumbs and baked. Similar to a crisp, except that the crumbs are usually layered with the fruit instead of placed on top.

BUCKLE: Fruit mixed with simple yellow cake batter and baked. Cake batter can be topped with streusel crumbs.

COBBLER: Fruit topped with a crust, which can be made from cookie dough, pie pastry, or biscuit topping, and baked.

CRUMBLE: Fruit topped with a "rubbed" mixture of oats, butter, sugar, and flour, then baked.

GRUNT: Fruit topped with biscuit dough, covered, and baked so that the biscuits steam rather than bake. The texture is akin to that of dumplings and is often gummy. Also called a slump.

PANDOWDY: Fruit covered with pastry dough and baked. The dough is cut, scored, and pressed into the fruit. Sometimes the crust is pressed into the fruit during baking; other recipes "dowdy" the crust after baking.

✔ WHY THIS RECIPE WORKS

We thought this retro lemon foam "snow" dessert deserved some reviving. We started with fresh lemons—a combination of lemon zest and fresh juice gave the snow a bright, pleasantly tart bite. We whisked the zest and juice into dissolved gelatin and, once it was set, whipped the lemon gelatin with egg whites, creating a light, creamy foam that resembled fresh snowdrifts. For the custard topping, we used the egg yolks left from the foam, whisking them with sugar and salt before tempering them with boiling milk. A tablespoon of butter added richness to the custard and thickened it into a creamy sauce to spoon over our airy dessert.

LEMON SNOW

SERVES 8 TO 10

If you're concerned about eating raw egg whites, use pasteurized shell eggs. Plan ahead, as both the gelatin mixture and the "snow" need to chill. To reduce the chilling time, place the bowl with the gelatin mixture over a second, larger bowl of ice water and stir occasionally. To make orange snow, use orange juice and zest in place of the lemon.

LEMON SNOW

- ¼ cup cold water
- 2 teaspoons unflavored gelatin
- 1 cup boiling water
- 1 cup (7 ounces) sugar
- 1 teaspoon grated lemon zest plus ⅓ cup juice (2 lemons)
  Pinch salt
- 3 large egg whites

CUSTARD SAUCE

- 3 large egg yolks
- ¼ cup (1¾ ounces) sugar
  Pinch salt
- 1¼ cups whole milk
- 1 tablespoon unsalted butter
- 1¼ teaspoons vanilla extract

1. FOR THE LEMON SNOW: Place cold water in medium bowl. Sprinkle gelatin over water and let sit until gelatin softens, about 5 minutes. Whisk boiling water into mixture until gelatin dissolves. Whisk sugar, lemon zest and juice, and salt into gelatin mixture until dissolved. Cover with plastic wrap and refrigerate until cool and slightly gelatinous, about 2 hours.

2. Combine egg whites and gelatin mixture in bowl of stand mixer fitted with whisk. Whip on medium-low speed until foamy, about 1 minute. Increase speed to medium-high and whip until soft peaks form, 11 to 14 minutes. Scrape lemon snow into bowl, or divide among dessert glasses, and refrigerate until set, about 2 hours.

3. FOR THE CUSTARD: Whisk egg yolks, sugar, and salt together in bowl until combined. Bring milk to boil in small saucepan. Slowly stir milk into yolk mixture with wooden spoon. Return milk-yolk mixture to pot, reduce heat to low, and cook, stirring constantly, until sauce is slightly thickened and registers 175 to 180 degrees, 2 to 4 minutes. Pour through fine-mesh strainer into 2-cup liquid measuring cup. Stir in butter and vanilla until incorporated. Refrigerate until cool and serve with lemon snow.

THE ORIGINAL "EGG BEATERS"

When we say lemon snow, we mean a chilled, gelatin-set lemon foam topped with a sweet, egg-thickened cream sauce. But as it turns out, "snow" wasn't always just a metaphor. Before the use of stiffly beaten egg whites became common—beating eggs was slow going in the days when a bundle of twigs was used for a whisk—freshly fallen snow was often beaten with cream and flavorings to create a cool, light dessert pudding. And that wasn't the only way inventive cooks handled snow in the kitchen. According to several early 19th-century cookbook authors, notably Maria Rundell, snow was quite useful. "Snow is an excellent substitute for eggs, either in puddings or pancakes," she wrote in *A New System of Domestic Cookery* (1808). "Two large spoonfuls will supply the place of one egg, and the article it is used in will be equally good." This may have been true in the 19th century, when eggs were few and far between in the winter, but since we can buy eggs at the supermarket whenever we please, we think we'll leave the snow where it belongs: outside.

APPALACHIA AND THE SOUTH

WEST VIRGINIA
PEPPERONI ROLLS
FAIRMONT, WV

MARYLAND CRAB FLUFF
BALTIMORE, MD

THOROUGHBRED PIE
LOUISVILLE, KY

MEMPHIS SPARERIBS
MEMPHIS, TN

CANADA

MD

DE

WEST
VIRGINIA

VIRGINIA

KENTUCKY

ARKANSAS

TENNESSEE

NORTH
CAROLINA

SOUTH
CAROLINA

SOUTH CAROLINA
SHRIMP BOIL
SOUTH CAROLINA COAST

MISSISSIPPI

ALABAMA

GEORGIA

LOUISIANA

FLORIDA

ATLANTIC OCEAN

MAQUE CHOUX
SOUTHERN LOUISIANA

BLACKBERRY JAM CAKE
APPALACHIAN MOUNTAINS

CREAM CHEESE
BISCUITS
CHARLESTON, SC

GULF OF MEXICO

79   **Pimento Cheeseburgers**

81   **New Orleans Muffulettas** ★

83   **Football Sandwiches**

      Pastrami and Swiss Football

         Sandwiches

85   **West Virginia Pepperoni Rolls**

87   **Maryland Crab Fluff**

      Cocktail Sauce

89   **Oyster Po' Boys**

91   **Maque Choux**

      with Shrimp

93   **Senate Navy Bean Soup**

95   **Kentucky Burgoo** ★

97   **Authentic Maryland Fried Chicken**

      and Gravy

99   **Carolina Chicken Bog** ★

101   **Country Captain Chicken**

103   **Chicken Bonne Femme**

105   **Memphis Spareribs**

107   **Pork Chops with Tomato Gravy**

109   **Country Ham**

      Jezebel Sauce

111   **Biscuit Dressing**

113   **Fried Catfish** ★

      Comeback Sauce

115   **South Carolina Shrimp Burgers**

117   **Perfect Shrimp Jambalaya**

119   **South Carolina Shrimp Boil**

121   **Shrimp Étouffée**

      White Rice

123   **Southern-Style Green Beans**

125   **Baked Cheese Grits**

127   **Fried Green Tomatoes**

129   **Caramel Tomatoes**

131   **Carolina Red Slaw** ★

133   **Lowcountry Red Rice**

135   **Dirty Rice**

137   **Red Beans and Rice**

139   **Hoppin' John**

141   **Ham Steak with Red-Eye Gravy**

      Short-Order Home Fries

143   **Hushpuppies**

      Corn and Red Pepper Hushpuppies

      Crab and Chive Hushpuppies

      Ham and Cheddar Hushpuppies

145   **Biscuits and Sausage Gravy**

147   **Sweet Potato Biscuits**

149   **Cream Cheese Biscuits**

      Chocolate Gravy

151   **Cracklin' Cornbread**

153   **Blackberry Jam Cake**

155   **Moravian Sugar Cake** ★

157   **Jefferson Davis Pie**

      Bourbon Whipped Cream

159   **Fudgy Tar Heel Pie**

161   **Peanut Butter Pie**

      with Chocolate Graham Crust

      Homemade Candied Peanuts

163   **Thoroughbred Pie**

165   **Grasshopper Pie**

167   **Buttermilk Pie**

169   **Carolina Sweet Potato Sonker**

★   FIND A LOCAL HOT SPOT

✓ WHY THIS RECIPE WORKS

The original recipes for South Carolina's famous pimento cheeseburgers are under lock and key, so we let our memories of the burgers we ate in Columbia, South Carolina, lead the way. To start, we bypassed store-bought pimento cheese for our own blend of grated extra-sharp cheddar, chopped pimentos, cayenne pepper, mayo, and dry mustard. Though seasoning ground beef with salt, pepper, and Worcestershire turned out tasty patties, we wanted our creamy pimento cheese to be front and center, so we mixed half of our cheese into balls and froze them for easier patty shaping. Cutting the usual mayo from our cheese center ensured that we didn't burn our chins with a spurt of hot cheese—using slow-melting cream cheese instead kept the scorching ooze at bay. We split each patty in half and sealed the pimento cheese in the middle, then flattened the patty. With this double dose of sweet-and-spicy homemade pimento cheese both topping and filling our perfectly seasoned burgers, we could hardly keep this recipe a secret.

PIMENTO CHEESEBURGERS SERVES 4

Stick with 85 percent lean ground beef here, since leaner meat is likely to dry out. Allow the cooked cheeseburgers to rest for a full 5 minutes (tented with aluminum foil) before eating them, or the hot, cheesy center will spurt out. If you like your burger more or less done, adjust the cooking times accordingly.

PIMENTO CHEESE

- 6 ounces extra-sharp cheddar cheese, shredded (1½ cups)
- ⅓ cup jarred pimentos, chopped fine
- 2 ounces cream cheese, softened
- ½ teaspoon dry mustard
- ⅛ teaspoon cayenne pepper
- 1 tablespoon mayonnaise

HAMBURGERS

- 1½ pounds 85 percent lean ground beef
- 1 tablespoon Worcestershire sauce
- ½ teaspoon salt
- ½ teaspoon pepper
- 4 hamburger buns

1. FOR THE PIMENTO CHEESE: Mix cheddar, pimentos, cream cheese, mustard, and cayenne together in bowl until well combined. Drop four 2-tablespoon portions of cheddar mixture on plate and lightly flatten with your palm. Cover plate tightly with plastic wrap and freeze until cheese is firm, at least 2 hours. Combine remaining cheddar mixture with mayonnaise, cover bowl with plastic, and refrigerate.

2. FOR THE HAMBURGERS: Combine beef, Worcestershire, salt, and pepper in large bowl and gently knead until well combined. Divide meat into 4 equal portions. Divide each portion of meat in half and wrap 1 half portion around each disk of frozen cheese, taking care to completely and snugly enclose cheese. Mold remaining half portions of meat around mini patties and tightly seal edges. Gently and uniformly flatten each patty to 1-inch thickness.

3A. FOR A CHARCOAL GRILL: Open bottom vent completely. Light large chimney starter filled with charcoal briquettes (6 quarts). When top coals are partially covered with ash, pour evenly over grill. Set cooking grate in place, cover, and open lid vent completely. Heat grill until hot, about 5 minutes.

3B. FOR A GAS GRILL: Turn all burners to high, cover, and heat grill until hot, about 15 minutes. Leave all burners on high.

4. Clean and oil cooking grate. Place patties on grill and cook without pressing on them until well browned on first side, 3 to 4 minutes. Flip burgers and cook on second side until cooked through, 3 to 4 minutes.

5. Distribute cheddar-mayonnaise mixture evenly on top of burgers, cover, and cook until mixture is slightly melted, about 1 minute. Transfer burgers to plate, tent with aluminum foil, and let rest for 5 minutes. Serve on hamburger buns.

BUILD A BETTER PIMENTO CHEESEBURGER

The homemade pimento cheese on top of our burgers was so tasty, we wanted even more—so we stuffed the burgers with extra cheese. But there's no point to stuffing the burgers if the cheese dribbles (or gushes) away with your first bite. Our construction technique forms burgers with a tight seal.

1. Divide each portion of meat in 2 and wrap half around 1 disk of frozen cheese, taking care to completely and snugly enclose cheese.

2. Mold remaining half portion of meat around mini patty and tightly seal edges. Flatten to form 1-inch-thick patty.

✅ WHY THIS RECIPE WORKS

Since biting into our first muffuletta, we'll never again look at a cold-cut sandwich the same way. Muffulettas are French Quarter favorites because of their briny olive salad paired with rich deli meats, provolone cheese, and sesame seed–covered bread. For our cold cuts, we layered the provolone with three standards: salami, mortadella, and capicola (alternating them for greater sandwich stability). Our olive salad combined green and black olives, giardiniera, garlic, and capers; rinsing the capers and using more green olives than black controlled the salad's salty taste. To infuse our salad with more zest, we added red wine vinegar, oregano, and thyme. After processing these ingredients until coarsely chopped, adding olive oil made the salad spreadable. For easy muffuletta bread, we used store-bought pizza dough, sprinkling it with seeds and baking it into round rolls. After slicing them in half, we spread the salad on the cut sides and layered the meats and cheese. We wrapped the sandwiches in plastic wrap and pressed them under a weighted baking sheet for compact, sliceable muffulettas. This also let the salad's juices seep into the bread, making every bite as zesty as the last.

NEW ORLEANS MUFFULETTAS SERVES 8

Using store-bought pizza dough makes for easy homemade muffuletta bread. You will need one 16-ounce jar of giardiniera to yield 2 cups drained. If you like a spicier sandwich, increase the amount of pepper flakes to ½ teaspoon.

2	(1-pound) balls pizza dough
2	cups drained jarred giardiniera
1	cup pimento-stuffed green olives
½	cup pitted kalamata olives
2	tablespoons capers, rinsed
1	tablespoon red wine vinegar
1	garlic clove, minced
½	teaspoon dried oregano
¼	teaspoon red pepper flakes
¼	teaspoon dried thyme
½	cup extra-virgin olive oil
¼	cup chopped fresh parsley
1	large egg, lightly beaten
5	teaspoons sesame seeds
4	ounces thinly sliced Genoa salami
6	ounces thinly sliced aged provolone cheese
6	ounces thinly sliced mortadella
4	ounces thinly sliced hot capicola

1. Form dough balls into 2 tight round balls on oiled baking sheet, cover loosely with greased plastic wrap, and let sit at room temperature for 1 hour.

2. Meanwhile, pulse giardiniera, green olives, kalamata olives, capers, vinegar, garlic, oregano, pepper flakes, and thyme in food processor until coarsely chopped, about 6 pulses, scraping down sides of bowl as needed. Transfer to bowl and stir in oil and parsley. Let sit at room temperature for 30 minutes. (Olive salad can be refrigerated for up to 1 week.)

3. Adjust oven rack to middle position and heat oven to 425 degrees. Keeping dough balls on sheet, flatten each into 7-inch disk. Brush tops of disks with egg and sprinkle with sesame seeds. Bake until golden brown and loaves sound hollow when tapped, 18 to 20 minutes, rotating sheet halfway through baking. Transfer loaves to wire rack and let cool completely, about 1 hour. (Loaves can be wrapped in plastic and stored at room temperature for up to 24 hours.)

4. Slice loaves in half horizontally. Spread one-fourth of olive salad on cut side of each loaf top and bottom, pressing firmly with rubber spatula to compact. Layer 2 ounces salami, 1½ ounces provolone, 3 ounces mortadella, 1½ ounces provolone, and 2 ounces capicola in order on each loaf bottom. Cap with loaf tops and individually wrap sandwiches tightly in plastic.

5. Place baking sheet on top of sandwiches and weigh down with heavy Dutch oven or two 5-pound bags of flour or sugar for 1 hour, flipping sandwiches halfway through pressing. Unwrap and slice each sandwich into quarters and serve. (Pressed, wrapped sandwiches can be refrigerated for up to 24 hours. Bring to room temperature before serving.)

EATING LOCAL ★ NEW ORLEANS, LA

Looking for a quick lunch in the French Quarter of New Orleans? Check out **CENTRAL GROCERY** on Decatur Street. The signature—and only—sandwich served there is the muffuletta, a hefty round of seeded bread stuffed with Italian meats, cheeses, and olive spread. And just like every signature sandwich, it's got an origin story to match. In 1906, Salvatore Lupo, the owner of Central Grocery, noticed Sicilian immigrants on their lunch breaks eating meals of meats, cheeses, olives, and bread. The enterprising grocer decided to save the workers some trouble by putting all the components together in a convenient, handheld sandwich. Thus was born the muffuletta, named after the round Sicilian bread it's made on and served at Central Grocery—and elsewhere all over the city—ever since.

**CENTRAL GROCERY
AND DELI**
923 Decatur St.
New Orleans, LA

✔ WHY THIS RECIPE WORKS

At first glance, football sandwiches look like simple ham sliders, but the secret to their popularity among Southern sports fans lies in the savory, buttery poppy seed sauce that flavors the rolls. To make our sauce, we chopped and microwaved onion with butter and poppy seeds. Worcestershire and garlic whisked into the melted butter mixture enhanced the savory-sweet flavors of the sauce. Turning to the rolls, we arranged the bottoms in a baking dish and layered mustard, ham, and Swiss on each, then placed the tops on the sandwiches before brushing each with poppy seed sauce. We spooned the remaining sauce over all of the sandwiches and let them sit for 10 minutes to soak up the flavors. Covering and baking the sandwiches for 20 minutes melted the cheese; a few minutes uncovered in the oven crisped the tops nicely. In almost no time at all, our sandwiches emerged melty, warm, and ready for game day.

FOOTBALL SANDWICHES SERVES 6

We prefer the soft white dinner rolls found in the bakery section of the supermarket, but dinner-size potato rolls will also work.

12	square soft white dinner rolls
6	tablespoons yellow mustard
12	thin slices deli Black Forest ham (8 ounces)
12	thin slices deli Swiss cheese (8 ounces)
	Pepper
4	tablespoons unsalted butter
2	tablespoons finely chopped onion
1	tablespoon poppy seeds
2	tablespoons Worcestershire sauce
1	teaspoon garlic powder

1. Adjust oven rack to middle position and heat oven to 350 degrees. Slice rolls in half horizontally. Spread 4 tablespoons mustard evenly on cut sides of roll tops and bottoms. Arrange roll bottoms, cut side up and side by side, in 13 by 9-inch baking dish. Fold ham slices in thirds, then once in half; place 1 slice on each roll bottom. Fold Swiss like ham, then place over ham. Season with pepper and cap with roll tops.

2. Combine butter, onion, and poppy seeds in bowl. Microwave until butter is melted and onion is softened, about 1 minute. Whisk Worcestershire, garlic powder, and remaining 2 tablespoons mustard into butter mixture until combined. Generously brush tops and edges of sandwiches with all of butter mixture. Spoon any remaining solids over sandwiches.

3. Cover dish with aluminum foil and let sit for 10 minutes to allow sandwiches to absorb sauce. Bake for 20 minutes. Uncover and continue to bake until cheese is melted around edges and tops are slightly firm, 7 to 9 minutes. Let cool for 10 minutes. Serve.

TO MAKE AHEAD: Sandwiches can be brushed with sauce, covered, and refrigerated up to 1 day in advance. Bring to room temperature before cooking.

PASTRAMI AND SWISS FOOTBALL SANDWICHES

Substitute 36 thin slices (8 ounces) deli peppered pastrami brisket for ham. Fold pastrami in thirds and use 3 slices per sandwich. Top pastrami with 1 pound sauerkraut, drained and squeezed dry, before adding cheese.

ALL ABOUT YELLOW MUSTARD

Smooth and mild, yellow mustard is a North American thing. In other parts of the world, mustards are hotter, darker, and grainier. But what yellow mustard may lack in worldliness and guts, it makes up for in versatility. Yellow mustard is as much at home on a ballpark hot dog as it is on cold cuts or in potato salad, barbecue sauce, salad dressing, or marinades for chicken or pork.

Yellow mustard is made from white (also called yellow) mustard seed, which is flavorful but doesn't cause any of the nasal burn of brown or black mustard seed; these last two are used in Dijon, Chinese, and other spicy mustards. Our tasters wanted to actually taste the mustard seed, and the brands they judged to have the most mustard flavor listed mustard seed second in their ingredients. The amount of salt also proved key. We often prefer saltier foods in our tastings, but this time the mustards with the least sodium tended to score higher. Why the break in preference? Vinegar adds so much pungency, these yellow mustards didn't need extra seasoning; indeed, too much salt threw the flavors out of balance.

And here's something else to keep in mind when you're shopping: The molecule that gives yellow mustard its assertive taste (4-hydroxybenzyl isothiocyanate, or PHBIT) dissipates over time, so note the freshness date on the jar.

✔ WHY THIS RECIPE WORKS

Pepperoni rolls are a spicy, on-the-go snack beloved across West Virginia; we wanted to extend that popularity to our kitchen and beyond. For rolls packed with flavor, we sliced pepperoni sticks into wedges and microwaved them, reserving the rendered oil. We made a dough of all-purpose flour, yeast, milk, and a little sugar to offset the pepperoni's spice. Instead of butter, we added the reserved oil to flavor the dough; letting the dough rise in the bowl used to microwave the pepperoni helped the meat's spicy heat permeate even further. To assemble, we tossed the pepperoni wedges with flour so the dough could adhere to their surfaces (avoiding gaping holes in the rolls' centers) and rolled the dough into 16 balls before flattening. We laid four evenly spaced wedges on the dough and rolled them into a tight cylinder. Brushing the surface with an egg wash and sprinkling with sesame seeds gave the rolls their signature look. Arranging them closely on a baking sheet resulted in soft, tender edges as they baked against one another. Our sesame-topped rolls emerged a beautiful golden brown with bold pepperoni flavor through and through.

WEST VIRGINIA PEPPERONI ROLLS MAKES 16

Be sure to reserve the pepperoni oil after microwaving the pepperoni, as it gives the dough flavor.

4	(7- to 8-ounce) sticks pepperoni, 8 inches long
1½	cups water
1	cup whole milk
2	tablespoons plus 2 teaspoons sugar
6⅔	cups (33⅓ ounces) plus 1 tablespoon all-purpose flour, plus extra as needed
1	tablespoon instant or rapid-rise yeast
2	teaspoons salt
1	large egg, lightly beaten with 1 tablespoon water
4	teaspoons sesame seeds

1. Line rimmed baking sheet with parchment paper. Cut pepperoni sticks in half crosswise, then cut each half in half lengthwise. Slice each quarter lengthwise into four 4-inch-long wedges. (You should have 64 wedges.) Microwave pepperoni in large bowl until fat is rendered, about 3 minutes. Using tongs, transfer pepperoni to paper towel–lined plate; reserve 3 tablespoons pepperoni oil. Do not wash bowl.

2. Combine water, milk, and sugar in 4-cup liquid measuring cup. Microwave until liquid registers 110 degrees, 1 to 2 minutes. Stir in reserved pepperoni oil

3. Using stand mixer fitted with dough hook, mix together 6⅔ cups flour, yeast, and salt on low speed until combined, about 30 seconds. With mixer running, slowly add water mixture until incorporated. Increase speed to medium and knead until dough is shiny and smooth and pulls away from sides of bowl, about 8 minutes. (If dough appears wet, add extra flour, 1 tablespoon at a time, as needed.) Turn out dough onto lightly floured counter and knead briefly to form cohesive ball. Transfer dough to reserved bowl and turn to coat with residual pepperoni oil in bowl. Cover with plastic wrap and let rise in warm place until doubled in size, 50 minutes to 1 hour.

4. Transfer dough to lightly floured counter and divide into 16 equal (3½-ounce) pieces. Working with 1 piece at a time (keep remaining pieces covered with plastic), form dough into balls, cover with plastic, and let rest for 5 minutes.

5. Toss pepperoni wedges with remaining 1 tablespoon flour to coat. Working with 1 dough ball at a time, use your hands to press ball into 6 by 4-inch rectangle. Starting along short side of rectangle, lay 4 pepperoni wedges side by side, ½ inch apart, and roll into tight cylinder, pinching seam to seal. Leave ends of rolls open. Arrange rolls seam side down on prepared sheet, end to end, ½ inch apart, and 4 per row. Cover with plastic and let rise until doubled in size, 50 minutes to 1 hour. Adjust oven rack to middle position and heat oven to 375 degrees.

6. Brush rolls with egg mixture and sprinkle with sesame seeds. Bake until golden brown, 24 to 28 minutes, rotating sheet halfway through baking. Transfer sheet to wire rack and let rolls cool for at least 15 minutes before serving.

TO MAKE AHEAD: Baked and cooled rolls can be wrapped in plastic, placed in zipper-lock bag, and frozen for up to 1 month. To reheat, adjust oven rack to middle position and heat oven to 350 degrees. Remove plastic and wrap each roll in aluminum foil. Bake directly on oven rack until heated through, 35 to 45 minutes.

"HOT POCKETS" OF THE COAL MINES

When deep-shaft mining became a big industry in late 19th-century America, many workers were recruited from Old World communities, where they had either been doing the same type of work or were so poor that they figured anything in America had to be better. Naturally, where a miner came from largely determined what he brought down the shaft in his lunch bucket. Food that formed its own package, with a filling inside a sturdy dough crust, was the most practical meal for a miner. So Cornish miners in the Upper Peninsula of Michigan ate pasties; Slavic miners in eastern Pennsylvania often carried baked pierogi in their lunch pails; and for the Italian immigrants who came to work in the West Virginia mines, the lunch of choice was pepperoni rolls, invented by a baker in Fairmont in the early 20th century.

✔ WHY THIS RECIPE WORKS

For finger-licking mini crab fritters, called "fluff," a diminutive cousin of Maryland crab cakes, we first focused on the frying. With the lightness of tempura in mind, we stirred together a batter of flour, baking powder, and seltzer. Instead of just coating our crab cakes with the tempura mixture, we combined it with the crabmeat mixture itself, which in addition to crabmeat included saltines, egg, mayonnaise, and seasonings. The batter stiffened the fluff just enough to promise a crisp shell. Sliced scallions, Dijon mustard, and hot sauce added an extra flavor boost. Reducing the size of each ball from ½ cup to ¼ cup made for faster frying with less grease absorption, and refrigerating the mix for 30 minutes before frying ensured that each ball held together in the oil. Our fritterlike crab fluff fried up golden and crisp, ready for any occasion.

MARYLAND CRAB FLUFF MAKES 12

You can buy jumbo lump crabmeat fresh or pasteurized; the latter is slightly cheaper. Serve fluff with Cocktail Sauce (recipe follows) or tartar sauce (to make your own, see page 115).

10	square or 11 round saltines, crushed fine
½	cup all-purpose flour
1½	teaspoons Old Bay seasoning
½	teaspoon baking powder
⅛	teaspoon cayenne pepper
½	cup seltzer
2	scallions, sliced thin
1	large egg plus 1 large yolk
2	tablespoons mayonnaise
1	tablespoon Dijon mustard
1	tablespoon hot sauce
1	pound jumbo lump crabmeat, picked over for shells and pressed dry between paper towels
2	quarts peanut or vegetable oil

1. Whisk crushed saltines, flour, Old Bay, baking powder, and cayenne together in large bowl. Whisk seltzer, scallions, egg and yolk, mayonnaise, mustard, and hot sauce into saltine mixture until combined. Gently fold crabmeat into batter until well combined. Cover and refrigerate for at least 30 minutes or up to 2 hours.

2. Set wire rack in rimmed baking sheet and line half of rack with triple layer of paper towels. Add oil to large Dutch oven until it measures about 1½ inches deep and heat over medium-high heat to 350 degrees.

3. Spray ¼-cup dry measuring cup with vegetable oil spray. Place 6 packed scoops of crab mixture in hot oil, using spoon to help dislodge batter from cup. Adjust burner, if necessary, to maintain oil temperature between 325 and 350 degrees. Fry until deep golden brown and hot throughout, about 5 minutes. Transfer crab fluff to paper towel–lined side of prepared rack and let drain for 1 minute, then move to unlined side of rack. Return oil to 350 degrees and repeat with remaining crab mixture. Serve.

COCKTAIL SAUCE MAKES 1 CUP

1	cup ketchup
2	tablespoons lemon juice
2	tablespoons prepared horseradish, plus extra for seasoning
2	teaspoons hot sauce, plus extra for seasoning
⅛	teaspoon salt
⅛	teaspoon pepper

Stir all ingredients together in small bowl and season with additional horseradish and hot sauce as desired. (Sauce can be refrigerated for up to 1 day.)

SAFE PORTIONING INTO HOT OIL

First chill batter so it's not too loose. Next, coat ¼-cup dry measuring cup with vegetable oil spray, scoop batter, and gently nudge each fluff into oil with spoon.

✓ WHY THIS RECIPE WORKS

The combination of spicy fried oysters and creamy mayo in a crusty baguette make the po' boy sandwich a proven winner, so we decided to find a way to re-create this New Orleans classic at home. Starting with fresh shucked oysters bought at our supermarket's fish counter, we created a delicate crust by rolling the oysters in a cornmeal and flour mixture. The oysters' natural juices (known as liquor) allowed the breading to cling without the extra weight of an egg wash. Salt, pepper, and cayenne blended into our crunchy cornmeal breading infused each bite with great flavor. Frying the oysters at a high temperature browned the crust while keeping the oysters tender and moist inside. With our oysters at the ready, we removed a 1-inch channel down the top and bottom of halved baguettes. We spread mayonnaise over the hollows and sprinkled lemon juice, salt, and pepper over both halves before adding diced pickles to the bottom halves. Once the oysters, sliced tomato, and lettuce were nestled under the top baguette halves, our po' boys tasted as good as sandwiches in the Big Easy . . . maybe better.

OYSTER PO' BOYS SERVES 4

Use a Dutch oven that holds 6 quarts or more for this recipe. Don't use stone-ground or coarse-ground cornmeal as it is too hearty for the delicate oysters. A spider skimmer makes quick work of removing the fried oysters from the oil.

- 6 **tablespoons fine-ground cornmeal**
- 6 **tablespoons all-purpose flour**
  Salt and pepper
- ⅛ **teaspoon cayenne pepper**
- 8 **ounces shucked oysters in their liquor (20–24 oysters), picked over for shells**
- 3 **cups peanut or vegetable oil**
- 1 **(24-inch) baguette, cut into 4 (6-inch) lengths**
- ½ **cup mayonnaise**
- 2 **teaspoons lemon juice**
- ½ **cup dill pickles, cut into ¼-inch pieces**
- 1 **tomato, cored and cut into ⅛-inch-thick slices**
- 4 **lettuce leaves**

1. Adjust oven rack to middle position, place wire rack set in rimmed baking sheet on oven rack, and heat oven to 200 degrees. Combine cornmeal, flour, ¾ teaspoon salt, ½ teaspoon pepper, and cayenne in shallow dish. Place oysters and their liquor in medium bowl. Using slotted spoon, scoop up about 8 oysters, briefly allowing excess liquor to drip off, and scatter across cornmeal mixture. Shake dish to coat oysters evenly with cornmeal mixture. Transfer oysters to second wire rack set in second rimmed baking sheet. Repeat with remaining oysters.

2. Line plate with triple layer of paper towels. Add oil to large Dutch oven and heat over medium-high heat to 400 degrees. (Adjust burner, if necessary, to maintain oil temperature of 400 degrees.) Working with one-third of oysters at a time, fry oysters, stirring with spider skimmer to prevent oysters from fusing together, until golden brown and frying has slowed, about 2 minutes. Transfer oysters to prepared plate, then transfer batch to prepared rack in oven. Return oil to 400 degrees and repeat with remaining oysters.

3. Cut each baguette length in half lengthwise. Using your fingers, pull out 1-inch-wide channel of bread from interior of top and bottom pieces of each length. Spread 1 tablespoon mayonnaise over each channel, sprinkle each piece with ¼ teaspoon lemon juice, and season with salt and pepper to taste. Sprinkle 2 tablespoons pickles over each bottom piece, then place 4 to 5 fried oysters, 2 to 3 slices of tomato, 1 leaf of lettuce, and top baguette pieces over pickles. Serve.

SHUCKING AN OYSTER

1. Hold oyster flat shell down in dish towel. Push blade into hinge, wiggling it back and forth to pry open shell; you will hear and feel pop. Move blade between shells to loosen, then twist to pry open.

2. Without spilling liquor that surrounds oyster, slide knife under oyster to sever muscle that holds meat to bottom shell.

✓ WHY THIS RECIPE WORKS

Every Louisiana family turns out its own version of *maque choux*, a spicy stewed corn dish studded with vegetables and plenty of Cajun seasoning. We wanted ours to be thick and creamy and loaded with smoky flavor, so we started by cooking bacon and using its rendered fat to brown andouille sausage, bell pepper, onion, and celery. For bright, fresh corn flavor and a thick, creamy texture, we stripped the kernels from six ears of corn and grated the kernels of two more ears, combining the kernels, starchy grated corn, and accumulated corn milk into a single bowl before adding the reserved bacon. We added the bacon-corn mixture and canned diced tomatoes to the cooked vegetables and sausage, reducing the liquid before adding the reserved tomato juice. The starch released by the grated corn quickly thickened the liquid, turning our simmering pot of vegetables and sausage into a creamy Cajun stew to ladle over rice.

MAQUE CHOUX SERVES 4 TO 6

Fresh corn is best. For frozen corn, use 6 cups of thawed kernels; process 1½ cups of kernels with ½ cup of water in a blender until coarsely ground to replace the grated corn in step 1.

- 8 ears corn, husks and silk removed
- 4 slices bacon, chopped fine
- 2 tablespoons vegetable oil
- 5 ounces andouille sausage, halved lengthwise and sliced thin
- 1 green bell pepper, stemmed, seeded, and chopped
- 1 onion, chopped
- 1 celery rib, minced
  Salt and pepper
- 4 garlic cloves, minced
- 1 tablespoon tomato paste
- ¼ teaspoon cayenne pepper
- 2 cups water
- 1 (14.5-ounce) can diced tomatoes, drained with juice reserved
- 6 scallions, sliced thin

1. Cut kernels from 6 ears of corn. Break remaining 2 ears in half and grate over plate on large holes of box grater. Combine cut kernels, grated corn, and any accumulated corn milk in bowl; set aside. Cook bacon in Dutch oven over medium heat until crisp, 6 to 8 minutes. Using slotted spoon, transfer bacon to bowl with corn.

2. Add oil to rendered bacon fat in pot and return to medium heat. Add sausage and cook until lightly browned, about 2 minutes. Add bell pepper, onion, celery, and ½ teaspoon salt and cook, stirring occasionally, until vegetables begin to soften and brown, 8 to 10 minutes. Stir in garlic, tomato paste, and cayenne and cook until fragrant, about 30 seconds.

3. Stir in corn-bacon mixture, water, and tomatoes and bring to boil, scraping up any browned bits. Reduce heat to low and simmer, stirring often, until liquid has reduced by three-fourths, 25 to 30 minutes. Stir in reserved tomato juice and cook until liquid is reduced by two-thirds and mixture is slightly thickened and creamy, about 10 minutes longer. Off heat, stir in scallions and season with salt and pepper to taste. Serve.

MAQUE CHOUX WITH SHRIMP

Stir in 1½ pounds extra-large shrimp (21 to 25 per pound), peeled and deveined, after tomato juice has reduced in step 3. Cook until shrimp are cooked through, about 5 minutes. Add scallions and serve.

SHOPPING FOR AND STORING CORN

Corn loses its sweetness soon after it is harvested, so buy the freshest corn you can find. Look for plump ears with green husks and golden silk extending from the tops (the more silk the better, since it is an indicator of the number of kernels). Peel back the husk to check for brown spots and to make sure the kernels are firm.

If you must store corn, wrap it, husk and all, in a wet paper bag and then in a plastic bag and place it in the refrigerator for up to 24 hours.

✓ WHY THIS RECIPE WORKS

It has been a fixture on the menu in the U.S. Senate cafeteria for more than a century, but we thought this simple navy bean and potato soup was in need of flavor reform. Brining the beans ensured that they would be creamy and soft, and cooking the onion, celery, and garlic separately from the long-simmering pot kept their crunch intact. For a gentle infusion of spice, we studded one of the ham hocks with whole cloves and slowly cooked the hocks and beans in water at a gentle medium-low heat for 45 minutes. This soup is typically thickened with mashed potatoes, but we found that cooking cubed russets and mashing them together with the softened beans right in the pot made perfecting the texture a breeze. We shredded the cooked hocks and returned the meat to the pot before finishing with a touch of cider vinegar for tang and sweetness. With meaty, salty, creamy flavors brimming in every piping-hot bowl, our soup made a lame duck of its predecessor.

SENATE NAVY BEAN SOUP

SERVES 6 TO 8

The finished texture of the soup should be creamy but not too thick. We use whole cloves because ground cloves turn the soup an unsightly gray color.

Salt and pepper
1   pound (2½ cups) navy beans, picked over and rinsed
1   tablespoon vegetable oil
1   onion, chopped fine
2   celery ribs, chopped fine
2   garlic cloves, minced
3   whole cloves
2   (12-ounce) smoked ham hocks
8   ounces russet potatoes, peeled and cut into ¼-inch pieces
1   tablespoon cider vinegar

1. Dissolve 3 tablespoons salt in 4 quarts cold water in large container. Add beans and soak at room temperature for at least 8 hours or up to 24 hours. Drain and rinse well.

2. Heat oil in Dutch oven over medium heat until shimmering. Add onion, celery, and 1 teaspoon salt and cook until softened, 8 to 10 minutes. Stir in garlic and cook until fragrant, about 30 seconds. Transfer onion mixture to bowl.

3. Insert cloves into skin of 1 ham hock. Add 8 cups water, ham hocks, and beans to now-empty pot and bring to boil over high heat. Reduce heat to medium-low and simmer, covered with lid slightly ajar, until beans are tender, 45 to 60 minutes, stirring occasionally.

4. Stir potatoes and onion mixture into soup and simmer, uncovered, until potatoes are tender, 10 to 15 minutes; remove pot from heat. Transfer ham hocks to cutting board and let cool slightly. Discard cloves, then shred meat, discarding bones and skin.

5. Using potato masher, gently mash beans and potatoes until soup is creamy and slightly thickened, 8 to 10 strokes. Add ½ teaspoon pepper and shredded meat and return to simmer over medium heat. Stir in vinegar. Season with salt and pepper to taste. Serve.

A GRIDLOCKED DEBATE

Senate navy bean soup is a mainstay at the U.S. Capitol cafeteria. In fact, it's been on the menu for over 100 years. But how did it get there? Even the Senate historian, Don Ritchie, isn't sure: "Some accounts attribute it to Idaho Senator Fred Dubois (b. 1851), who . . . pushed a resolution to require the bean soup on the menu every day. The other story attributes it to Minnesota Senator Knute Nelson (b. 1843), who got the Rules Committee to adopt a resolution in 1907. It's possible that both stories are true." We may never uncover the real story of Senate navy bean soup, but we know one thing for sure: This hearty soup is here to stay.

⚓ WHY THIS RECIPE WORKS

Pots of burgoo, a chunky stew of tomatoes, corn, potatoes, chicken, and mutton, are often made and served up at gatherings all over Kentucky, and the ingredients are often determined by what the cook happens to have on hand at the time. To stir up a heady, flavorful burgoo on a much smaller scale, we had to refine the ingredient list. We opted for readily available lamb shoulder chops over mutton and found that their bones added great flavor and body to the broth. Using a combination of fresh, frozen, and canned vegetables, we minimized prep time without putting a damper on the stew's flavors. After browning the lamb and chicken thighs, we used the rendered fat to cook the onions and garlic. Worcestershire sauce along with chicken broth and tomatoes gave the stew depth and richness. We let the chicken and lamb cook in the broth, removing the chicken after 30 minutes and cooking the lamb until tender. We cooked the vegetables last, simmering the potatoes first before adding the corn and lima beans. Pepper stirred in at the end restored the stew's pleasant, spicy heat, and lemon juice contributed a bright finishing touch.

KENTUCKY BURGOO SERVES 6 TO 8

If you can't find lamb shoulder blade chops at your market, you can substitute 1½ pounds of lamb stew meat or beef chuck stew meat. We like to use the rendered chicken fat (left over after browning the chicken in step 1) to brown the meat and sauté the vegetables.

4	(5- to 7-ounce) bone-in, skin-on chicken thighs
6	(6- to 8-ounce) lamb shoulder blade chops, each about ½ inch thick
	Salt and pepper
1	tablespoon vegetable oil, plus extra as needed
2	onions, chopped
2	tablespoons all-purpose flour
2	garlic cloves, minced
6	cups chicken broth
1	(14.5-ounce) can diced tomatoes
¼	cup Worcestershire sauce
1½	pounds Yukon Gold potatoes, peeled and cut into ½-inch chunks
1½	cups frozen corn
1½	cups frozen baby lima beans
¼	cup lemon juice (2 lemons)

1. Pat chicken and lamb dry with paper towels and season with salt and pepper. Heat oil in Dutch oven over medium-high heat until just smoking. Brown chicken, about 5 minutes per side; transfer to plate. Pour off fat from pan and reserve. (You should have about 3 tablespoons fat; if you have less, supplement with vegetable oil.) Add 1 tablespoon reserved fat to now-empty Dutch oven and heat until just smoking. Brown half of chops, about 5 minutes per side; transfer to plate. Repeat with additional 1 tablespoon fat and remaining chops.

2. Add remaining 1 tablespoon fat and onions to now-empty pot and cook until softened, about 5 minutes. Add flour and garlic and cook until fragrant, about 1 minute. Stir in broth, tomatoes, and Worcestershire, scraping up any browned bits. Return chicken and lamb to pot and bring to boil.

3. Reduce heat to medium-low and simmer, covered, until chicken is tender, about 30 minutes. Transfer chicken to plate. When cool enough to handle, pull chicken into bite-size pieces and reserve in refrigerator; discard bones and skin. Continue to simmer stew until lamb is tender, about 40 minutes longer. Transfer lamb to plate. When cool enough to handle, pull lamb into bite-size pieces and reserve in refrigerator; discard bones.

4. Add potatoes to pot and simmer until tender, about 15 minutes. Add corn, lima beans, reserved chicken, and reserved lamb and simmer until heated through, about 5 minutes. Stir in lemon juice and ¾ teaspoon pepper. Season with salt to taste. Skim fat if necessary. Serve.

EATING LOCAL ★ OWENSBORO, KY

Although Kentucky burgoo began as a way to make use of whatever was hunted or ready to harvest (including cabbage, lima beans, squirrel, opossum, or deer), today, burgoo is a bit more formulaic. The chunky stew is made with tomatoes, corn, potatoes, chicken, and mutton (mature lamb). Locals developed their taste for mutton in the 19th century, when sheep farming was big business, both in the region and elsewhere in America. This unusual local specialty garners lots of attention at the **INTERNATIONAL BAR-B-Q FESTIVAL** in Owensboro, Kentucky, where mutton is both barbecued and served in burgoo. Outside of Owensboro, mutton isn't very common (our local market doesn't even carry it), but the residents of Owensboro still devour more than 20,000 pounds of mutton at the festival each year.

**INTERNATIONAL
BAR-B-Q FESTIVAL**
Courthouse Square, 2nd St.
Owensboro, KY

✓ WHY THIS RECIPE WORKS

In Maryland, fried chicken is marked by a thin, crisp crust, standout seasoning, and a dribble of peppery cream gravy. To get our version of this chicken on the right track, we injected a kick of spicy flavor with a generous dose of dry mustard, salt, and garlic powder. Dredging in flour and baking powder, then refrigerating the seasoned chicken before frying in peanut oil, made for an extra-crisp coating. A sprinkling of Old Bay on the just-fried pieces reinforced the chicken's bold seasoning. With chicken this crisp and flavorful, we wanted a traditional cream gravy. Using some of the remaining frying oil in our pot, we browned flour and whisked in chicken broth, heavy cream, and pepper. After the mixture thickened for about 5 minutes, our Maryland fried chicken had an equally authentic gravy to match.

AUTHENTIC MARYLAND FRIED CHICKEN AND GRAVY

SERVES 4 TO 6

Be sure to use peanut oil or vegetable shortening in this recipe, as vegetable oil can break down and impart off-flavors to the chicken.

FRIED CHICKEN

- 4 pounds bone-in chicken pieces, breasts halved crosswise and leg quarters separated into drumsticks and thighs, trimmed
- 1 tablespoon dry mustard
- 1 tablespoon garlic powder
- 1 teaspoon salt
- 2 cups all-purpose flour
- 1 teaspoon baking powder
- 3 cups peanut oil or vegetable shortening
  Old Bay seasoning

CREAM GRAVY

- ¼ cup all-purpose flour
- 2 cups chicken broth
- 1 cup heavy cream
- 1 teaspoon pepper
  Salt

1. FOR THE FRIED CHICKEN: Pat chicken dry with paper towels. Combine mustard, garlic powder, and salt in small bowl and sprinkle mixture evenly over chicken. Combine flour and baking powder in shallow dish. Working with 1 piece at a time, dredge chicken in flour mixture until well coated, shaking off excess. Transfer to plate and refrigerate for at least 30 minutes or up to 2 hours.

2. Adjust oven rack to middle position and heat oven to 200 degrees. Set wire rack in rimmed baking sheet. Heat oil in Dutch oven over medium-high heat to 375 degrees. Place half of chicken skin side down in pot, cover, and fry until well browned, about 5 minutes per side. Reduce heat to medium, adjusting burner, if necessary, to maintain oil temperature between 300 and 325 degrees. Cook, uncovered and turning chicken as needed, until breasts register 160 degrees and drumsticks/thighs register 175 degrees, about 5 minutes. Transfer chicken to prepared wire rack, season with Old Bay, and keep warm in oven. Return oil to 375 degrees and repeat with remaining chicken.

3. FOR THE CREAM GRAVY: Pour off all but ¼ cup oil from pot. Stir in flour and cook until golden, about 2 minutes. Slowly whisk in broth, cream, and pepper and simmer gravy until thickened, about 5 minutes. Season with salt to taste. Serve chicken with gravy.

OIL MATTERS

While we were developing this fried chicken recipe, batch after batch of the chicken was marred by an odd "fishy" flavor. To find the culprit, we tried adjusting every variable in the recipe, but nothing worked. As a last resort, we switched from vegetable oil (our usual frying medium) to peanut oil (another commonly used frying oil), and the problem was solved. As it turns out, after a total frying time of roughly 30 minutes, the vegetable oil was beginning to break down and impart a spoiled, fishy flavor to the chicken. Peanut oil (which has a higher smoke point) fared better and didn't break down, resulting in no off-flavors in the chicken. We also tried safflower oil, canola oil, and vegetable shortening. The peanut oil was still best, but the vegetable shortening was the runner-up, winning praise for its "clean" flavor.

✅ WHY THIS RECIPE WORKS

By name it may not sound like much, but chicken bog—a one-pot dish of chicken, smoky sausage, and white rice—is a delicious dish from South Carolina kitchens, packing hearty taste into every last bite. To get in on that flavor, we set our sights on pilaf-like rice cooked in a deeply flavorful broth with generous chunks of chicken and sausage. Rather than risk overcooking white meat, we turned to chicken thighs for juicy meat and maximum flavor. We browned the thighs and set them aside, using the skin's rendered fat to infuse chicken flavor into the onion and kielbasa. Next, we created an aromatic broth, blooming minced garlic before stirring in chicken broth. The thighs cooked in this superflavorful liquid at a low simmer before we added the rice. As the rice cooked to a tender, slightly sticky consistency, we shredded the chicken and folded it into the sausage-studded rice. We now had all of the meaty, seasoned flavors of a Loris Bog-Off Festival contender, but in the comfort of our own kitchen.

CAROLINA CHICKEN BOG

SERVES 6 TO 8

6 (5- to 7-ounce) bone-in chicken thighs, trimmed
Salt and pepper
1 tablespoon vegetable oil
8 ounces smoked kielbasa sausage,
cut into ½-inch-thick rounds
1 onion, chopped fine
3 garlic cloves, minced
4 cups chicken broth
2 cups long-grain white rice

1. Pat chicken dry with paper towels and season with salt and pepper. Heat oil in Dutch oven over medium heat until just smoking. Cook chicken, skin side down, until well browned, 6 to 8 minutes; transfer chicken to plate. Discard skin.

2. Pour off all but 1 tablespoon fat from pot and return to medium heat. Add sausage and onion and cook until onion is translucent and sausage begins to brown, 3 to 5 minutes. Add garlic and cook until fragrant, about 30 seconds. Add broth, chicken, 1 teaspoon salt, and 1 teaspoon pepper and bring to boil. Reduce heat to low, cover, and simmer until chicken is tender, about 30 minutes.

3. Remove chicken from pot and set aside. Stir rice into pot, cover, and continue to cook over low heat until rice is tender, about 20 minutes.

4. Shred chicken into bite-size pieces; discard bones. Gently fold shredded chicken into rice mixture. Remove from heat and let sit, covered, for 10 minutes. Serve.

RINSING CHICKEN?

Both the U.S. Department of Agriculture and the Food and Drug Administration advise against washing poultry. According to their research, while rinsing may remove some bacteria, the only way to ensure that all bacteria are killed is through proper cooking. Moreover, splashing bacteria around the sink can be dangerous, especially if water lands on food that is ready to be served. All the same, some people will argue that chicken should be rinsed for flavor—not safety—reasons. After sitting in its own blood and juices for days, they argue, chicken should be unwrapped and refreshed under running water. To find out if rinsing had any impact on flavor, we roasted four chickens—two rinsed, two unrinsed—and held a blind tasting. Tasters couldn't tell the difference. Our conclusion? Skip the rinsing.

EATING LOCAL ★ LORIS, SC

We traveled down to Loris, South Carolina, to watch local bog masters at work at the annual **LORIS BOG-OFF FESTIVAL**, a hotly contested affair. Entrants cook up bogs in large cast-iron Dutch ovens, carefully stirring with wooden "bogging spoons" worn down from years of pot stirring. Recipes are guarded jealously, but the basics—chicken, sausage, and white rice—are the three key ingredients shared by all.

LORIS BOG-OFF FESTIVAL
Main St., Loris, SC

⚫ WHY THIS RECIPE WORKS

With recipes for this mildly curried chicken dating back centuries, country captain represents one of America's earliest forays into multicultural cuisine. We wanted to freshen up this dish so it boasted the perfect balance of heat and sweet. After browning the chicken, we used the rendered fat to cook the onions and green bell pepper. We upped our spices' impact by cooking a generous amount of curry powder and garlic with tomato paste, flour, and brown sugar. Raisins and chopped sweet-tart apple were promoted from garnish to key ingredient—we found they contributed subtle sweetness and brightness when stirred in with canned diced tomatoes. We cooked the chicken in this flavorful sauce and added lime juice before serving for a final citrusy kick.

COUNTRY CAPTAIN CHICKEN SERVES 6

If you can't find petite diced tomatoes, pulse one 28-ounce can of diced tomatoes in a food processor until coarsely ground. This dish is traditionally served with rice and a host of garnishes that include bacon, scallions, toasted coconut, almonds, chopped banana, peanuts, and pineapple; use as many or as few of those as you like.

- 4 pounds bone-in chicken pieces, breasts halved crosswise and leg quarters separated into drumsticks and thighs, trimmed
  Salt and pepper
- 1 tablespoon vegetable oil
- 2 onions, chopped fine
- 1 green bell pepper, stemmed, seeded, and chopped fine
- 2 tablespoons tomato paste
- 2 tablespoons curry powder
- 2 tablespoons all-purpose flour
- 2 garlic cloves, minced
- 1 teaspoon packed brown sugar
- 1 (28-ounce) can petite diced tomatoes
- 1 Granny Smith apple, cored, halved, and chopped fine
- ½ cup raisins or dried currants
- 2 teaspoons lime juice

1. Pat chicken dry with paper towels and season with salt and pepper. Heat oil in Dutch oven over medium-high heat until just smoking. Brown half of chicken well, about 5 minutes per side; transfer to plate. Repeat with remaining chicken. When cool enough to handle, discard skin.

2. Pour off all but 2 tablespoons fat from pot. Add onions and bell pepper and cook, covered, until softened, about 8 minutes. Stir in tomato paste, curry powder, flour, garlic, and sugar and cook until fragrant and color deepens, about 2 minutes. Stir in tomatoes and their juice, apple, and raisins and bring to boil.

3. Return chicken and any accumulated juices to pot. Reduce heat to low and simmer, covered, until breasts register 160 degrees and drumsticks/thighs register 175 degrees, 20 to 25 minutes. Stir in lime juice, season with salt and pepper to taste, and serve.

A GEORGIA CLASSIC

Although some sources claim this recipe was invented in the American South, most food historians believe this vibrant stew was introduced to the residents of Savannah by British sea captains who had traveled along the spice route during the late 18th or early 19th century. In any case, the dish has its roots in India. The first printed recipe appeared in *Miss Leslie's New Cookery Book* (1857), and from the 20th century onward country captain became a staple in many Southern and all-purpose cookbooks, including the original *Joy of Cooking* (1931). President Franklin D. Roosevelt is said to have been a fan of this dish, having enjoyed it during his frequent visits to Warm Springs, Georgia, for rest and recuperation.

✓ WHY THIS RECIPE WORKS

To bring this slow-cooked Creole chicken dish into the 21st century, we lightened up the ingredients and sped up the prep time of chicken *bonne femme*. Swapping the traditional fried chicken for braised handily turned our bonne femme into a one-pot meal. We opted for chicken thighs for their rich flavor and ability to stay moist during long, slow cooking. Bacon is a key flavor in bonne femme. After browning it, we kept a tablespoon of the rendered fat in the pot and used it to brown the thighs. Once cooked, we removed the thighs, discarded their skin, and left some fat in the pot to brown the potato halves and aromatics. We built the sauce gradually, first adding onion, then garlic and thyme, and finishing with dry white wine, chicken broth, some of the bacon, and hot sauce. We returned the skinless thighs to the pot to braise in the zesty sauce. The chicken emerged loaded with Creole flavor, needing only a sprinkling of sliced scallions, fresh parsley, and the rest of the bacon.

CHICKEN BONNE FEMME

SERVES 4 TO 6

To ensure even cooking and browning, use small red potatoes measuring no more than 1½ inches in diameter for this recipe.

- 3 **pounds bone-in chicken thighs, trimmed**
  Salt and pepper
- 5 **slices bacon, chopped**
- 1½ **pounds small red potatoes, unpeeled, halved**
- 1 **onion, chopped fine**
- 4 **garlic cloves, minced**
- 2 **teaspoons minced fresh thyme**
- ¾ **cup dry white wine**
- ½ **cup chicken broth**
- 1 **teaspoon hot sauce**
- 3 **scallions, sliced thin**
- 2 **tablespoons chopped fresh parsley**

1. Pat chicken dry with paper towels and season with salt and pepper. Cook bacon in Dutch oven over medium heat until crisp, 5 to 7 minutes. Using slotted spoon, transfer bacon to paper towel–lined plate. Pour off all but 1 tablespoon fat from pot. Heat fat over medium-high heat until just smoking. Add chicken to pot and cook until thighs are well browned, 3 to 4 minutes per side; transfer to plate. When chicken is cool enough to handle, discard skin.

2. Pour off all but 1½ tablespoons fat from pot. Arrange potatoes cut side down in pot and cook over medium heat until golden brown, about 10 minutes. Stir in onion and cook until softened, about 5 minutes. Add garlic and thyme and cook until fragrant, about 30 seconds. Stir in wine, broth, hot sauce, and half of bacon and bring to boil.

3. Return chicken and any accumulated juices to pot. Reduce heat to medium-low and cook, covered, until potatoes are tender and meat registers 175 degrees, about 25 minutes. Sprinkle with scallions, parsley, and remaining bacon. Season with salt and pepper to taste and serve.

BROWN, BABY, BROWN

Most chicken braises call for browning the meat before adding liquid. For another layer of flavor in our bonne femme, we browned the potato halves in a combination of bacon and chicken fat.

TURNING TO CHICKEN THIGHS

Our Chicken Bonne Femme is a hearty one-pot meal, and meaty chicken thighs promised richness without drying out. Here's how we maximized the thighs' flavors:

1. Pat chicken dry with paper towels and season with salt and pepper.

2. With 1 tablespoon of bacon fat left in pot, cook chicken until well browned on both sides.

3. When chicken is cool enough to handle, discard skin and set chicken aside.

☑ WHY THIS RECIPE WORKS

Rather than smothering ribs in sauce, Memphis pit masters rely on a potent spice rub to infuse the meat with unmistakable flavor. To replicate that Memphis-style rub at home, we started at our spice rack and chose a handful of spices that wouldn't taste too harsh straight from the jar. Beginning with salt and brown sugar for its subtle molasses notes, we combined paprika, chili powder, pepper, garlic powder, onion powder, and cayenne to create a perfectly balanced rub. We worked it over our ribs and then let them sit while the wood chips soaked. After grilling for the first hour, we flipped the ribs and brushed them with a sweet and sour mop of apple cider and cider vinegar, repeating this step every half hour. With the smoky crust in place, wrapping the ribs in foil and moving them to the oven to finish ensured an irresistibly tender texture. We sprinkled them with more of the spice rub and gave them 2 minutes under the broiler for a final browning. While the ribs rested, we reduced the mop into a dipping sauce, adding in our remaining spice rub and hot sauce for extra heat. Our Memphis-style ribs were an unbeatable combination of smoke, spice, and pork.

MEMPHIS SPARERIBS   SERVES 4 TO 6

These ribs are moderately spicy; adjust the cayenne and hot sauce as you wish. To reheat leftovers, place the ribs in an ovenproof dish, add a few tablespoons of water, cover with aluminum foil, and place in a 250-degree oven for 20 to 30 minutes.

¼   **cup paprika**
3   **tablespoons packed brown sugar**
2   **tablespoons chili powder**
2   **teaspoons garlic powder**
2   **teaspoons onion powder**
1   **teaspoon cayenne pepper**
    Salt and pepper
2   **(2½- to 3-pound) racks St. Louis–style spareribs, trimmed, membrane removed**
3   **cups apple cider**
1   **cup cider vinegar**
2   **cups wood chips, soaked in water for 15 minutes and drained**
2   **teaspoons hot sauce**

1. Combine paprika, sugar, chili powder, garlic powder, onion powder, cayenne, 2 tablespoons pepper, and 1 tablespoon salt in bowl. Reserve 7 teaspoons of spice mixture separately for finishing ribs and sauce. Pat ribs dry with paper towels and rub evenly with remaining spice mixture. Wrap ribs in plastic wrap and let sit at room temperature for at least 1 hour, or refrigerate for up to 24 hours.

2. Bring cider and vinegar to simmer in small saucepan; remove from heat and cover to keep warm. Using large piece of heavy-duty aluminum foil, wrap soaked chips in foil packet and cut several vent holes in top.

3A. FOR A CHARCOAL GRILL: Open bottom vent halfway. Light large chimney starter three-quarters filled with charcoal briquettes (4½ quarts). When top coals are partially covered with ash, pour into steeply banked pile against side of grill. Place wood chip packet on coals. Set cooking grate in place, cover, and open lid vent halfway. Heat grill until hot and wood chips are smoking, about 5 minutes.

3B. FOR A GAS GRILL: Remove cooking grate and place wood chip packet directly on primary burner. Set cooking grate in place, turn all burners to high, cover, and heat grill until hot and wood chips are smoking, about 15 minutes. Turn primary burner to medium-high and turn off other burner(s). (Adjust primary burner as needed to maintain grill temperature around 325 degrees.)

4. Clean and oil cooking grate. Unwrap ribs and place, meat side down, on cooler side of grill; ribs may overlap slightly. Cover (position lid vent over meat if using charcoal) and cook until ribs are deep red and smoky, about 2 hours, flipping, rotating, and switching ribs and basting with warm cider mop every 30 minutes. During final 20 minutes of grilling, adjust oven rack to middle position and heat oven to 250 degrees.

5. Transfer ribs, meat side up, to rimmed baking sheet and cover tightly with foil. Continue to cook ribs in oven until tender and fork inserted into ribs meets no resistance, 1½ to 2½ hours, basting with warm mop every 30 minutes.

6. Remove ribs from oven and unwrap. Adjust oven rack 6 inches from broiler element and heat broiler. Sprinkle ribs with 2 tablespoons reserved spice mixture and broil until browned and dry on surface and spices are fragrant, about 2 minutes, flipping ribs halfway through broiling.

7. Remove ribs from oven, tent with foil, and let rest for 30 minutes. While ribs rest, add remaining 1 teaspoon spice mixture to remaining mop and simmer, uncovered, until thickened and saucy, 10 to 15 minutes. Stir in hot sauce and season with salt and pepper to taste. Slice ribs between bones and serve with sauce.

READYING RIBS FOR THE GRILL

Removing the membrane on the underside of the ribs will help the fat render more quickly.

1. At 1 end of rack, loosen edge of membrane with tip of paring knife or your fingernail.

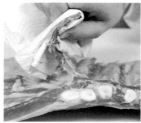

2. Grab membrane with paper towel to keep it from slipping. Pull slowly—it should come off in 1 piece.

🗹 WHY THIS RECIPE WORKS

Like many of our favorite Louisiana dishes, these pork chops traditionally have the bold flavor that results from long, slow cooking; could we capture the bold, meaty flavors we loved without the wait? We infused the chops with Cajun spice using a rub of paprika, sugar, and cayenne and then turned to finely chopped bacon for our salty, smoky flavor base. After cooking the bits in a skillet, we removed the bacon and used its rendered fat to brown the pork chops on one side to develop fond—those flavorful browned bits at the bottom of the pan. With the browned chops set aside, we cooked oil, onion, celery, and garlic in the same skillet. To establish our gravy's flavorful roux, we added flour and tomato paste, allowing them to brown and bloom before also whisking in broth, tomato sauce, thyme, bay leaf, and the reserved bacon. Our sauce was now thick, smoky, and rich. We arranged the chops in the skillet, browned side up, and let them braise in the simmering sauce until done. The finished chops boasted a crisp, tasty crust and a deep, full-flavored tomato gravy to match—and with time to spare.

PORK CHOPS WITH TOMATO GRAVY   SERVES 4

For the best presentation, make sure the seared side is facing up when plating these chops. Arrange the pork chops in a pinwheel pattern so they fit easily in the skillet. We like to serve these chops over rice or with grits.

	Salt and pepper
½	teaspoon paprika
½	teaspoon sugar
¼	teaspoon cayenne pepper
4	(8- to 10-ounce) bone-in pork rib chops, 1 inch thick, trimmed
4	slices bacon, chopped fine
2	tablespoons vegetable oil
1	onion, chopped fine
1	celery rib, minced
1	garlic clove, minced
3	tablespoons all-purpose flour
1	tablespoon tomato paste
1	cup chicken broth
1	(8-ounce) can tomato sauce
1	teaspoon minced fresh thyme
1	bay leaf

1. Combine 1 teaspoon salt, 1 teaspoon pepper, paprika, sugar, and cayenne in bowl. Pat chops dry with paper towels and sprinkle evenly with spice mixture.

2. Cook bacon in 12-inch nonstick skillet over medium heat until crisp, 5 to 7 minutes. Using slotted spoon, transfer bacon to paper towel–lined plate. Pour off all but 1 tablespoon fat from skillet. Increase heat to medium-high and brown chops well on 1 side, about 5 minutes. Transfer to plate, browned side up.

3. Reduce heat to medium, add oil, and heat until shimmering. Add onion, celery, and garlic and cook until softened, 5 to 7 minutes. Add flour and tomato paste and cook, stirring constantly, for 2 minutes. Whisk in broth, tomato sauce, thyme, bay leaf, and reserved bacon and bring to boil.

4. Transfer chops, browned side up, and any accumulated juices to pan. Reduce heat to low, cover, and simmer until chops register 145 degrees, 8 to 12 minutes. Transfer chops to serving platter, tent loosely with aluminum foil, and let rest for 5 to 10 minutes. Season gravy with salt and pepper to taste, discard bay leaf, cover, and keep warm. Stir any accumulated juices from platter into gravy and pour over chops. Serve.

PORKY PERFECTION

For years the standard internal temperature for pork was 180 degrees—an appropriate temperature for pre-WWII pork, but hardly right for today's young, lean, "other white meat." The National Pork Producers Council currently promotes 160 degrees as the new standard, but we found pork cooked to this temperature was still too dry. The test kitchen suggests a final temperature of 145 degrees, keeping in mind that larger cuts of pork can be removed from heat at roughly 135 degrees, covered, and allowed to rest, during which time the temperature will rise by at least 10 degrees. (Be sure to check the final temperature before serving to make certain that it reaches 145 degrees.)

Is it safe to cook pork to this temperature? In a word, yes. Given the controlled grain-based diet of pigs these days, trichinosis is virtually non-existent. According to David Meisinger, assistant vice president of pork quality for the National Pork Producers Council, the very few reported incidents are a result of privately raised pigs and rustic production conditions. Even so, trichinosis is killed at 140 degrees.

In an effort to keep customers happy and pork juicy even if it's been somewhat overcooked, pork producers have introduced a product called "enhanced pork" to the market. Enhanced pork is injected with a solution of water, salt, and sodium phosphate, all of which are among the ingredients used to cure pork when making bacon. The objective is to both season the pork from within and to make it more resistant to drying out when cooked. The process is similar to that used by some turkey producers in an effort to keep the breast meat from drying out during cooking.

Curious about enhanced pork, we purchased two packages of pork chops at local markets, one of which was labeled "enhanced." We sautéed the chops, cooking them to a temperature of 145 degrees, then let them sit, covered, for five minutes to let the juices redistribute themselves throughout the meat. The results? Most tasters found the enhanced pork juicier and more tender. But while the unenhanced pork was found to be drier and tougher to chew, it was also described by some tasters as having a more natural pork flavor, which they preferred to the somewhat salty taste of the enhanced pork.

✔ WHY THIS RECIPE WORKS

Tradition dictates that country ham—the South's salty, aged cousin to today's spiral-cut hams—requires lengthy soaking before scoring and baking. We were ready to follow suit until we discovered that soaking the ham neither drew out excess salt nor increased moisture—the long-accepted reasoning behind this time-consuming prep. Working with country hams aged between three and six months, we skipped the soaking and simmering altogether. We scrubbed off the mold (a normal result of the aging process), trimmed off the skin, and scored the surface, then moved the ham right to the oven. We placed the ham fat side up in a roasting pan and ensured plenty of moisture-boosting steam by pouring in water and covering the pan with aluminum foil. After baking the ham for 4 to 5 hours, we mixed together a glaze of brown sugar, dry mustard, and pepper and rubbed it over the ham's surface. We returned the ham to the oven for a few more minutes to set the glaze and then let it rest on a carving board before slicing. In record time, we had moist slices of country ham with a crusty sugar coating on our plates, perfectly paired with spicy-sweet Jezebel Sauce.

COUNTRY HAM

SERVES 12 TO 15

Use hams aged six months or less for this recipe. Mold on country ham is not a sign of spoilage; it is a natural effect of the curing and aging process. Serve ham on biscuits with Jezebel Sauce (recipe follows). Leftover ham is delicious in scrambled eggs, cheese grits, macaroni and cheese, and all manner of things.

1 (13- to 15-pound) 3- to 6-month-old bone-in country ham
½ cup packed light brown sugar
1 tablespoon dry mustard
2 teaspoons pepper

1. Adjust oven rack to middle position and heat oven to 325 degrees. Using clean, stiff-bristled brush, scrub ham under cold running water to remove any surface mold. Transfer ham to cutting board and trim off dry meat, skin, and all but ¼ inch of fat. Score fat cap in ½-inch crosshatch pattern, ¼ inch deep.

2. Transfer ham to roasting pan fat side up, add 1 quart water, and cover pan tightly with aluminum foil. Bake until thickest part of meat registers 140 degrees, 4 to 5 hours. Remove ham from oven, discard foil, and increase oven temperature to 450 degrees.

3. Combine sugar, mustard, and pepper in bowl and rub over top of ham. Return ham to oven and cook, uncovered, until glazed, 12 to 17 minutes. Transfer ham to carving board and let rest for 20 minutes. Carve thin slices and serve.

JEZEBEL SAUCE MAKES ABOUT 2 CUPS

Granted, it's an odd-sounding mix of ingredients, but it's actually a surprisingly great pairing with country ham. We like this sauce on a turkey sandwich, too.

⅓ cup pineapple preserves
⅓ cup apple jelly
⅓ cup yellow mustard
⅓ cup prepared horseradish
1½ teaspoons pepper
¼ teaspoon cayenne pepper

Combine all ingredients in blender and process until smooth, 20 to 30 seconds.

COUNTRY HAMS ON THE RISE

Europe has its fabled cured hams—prosciutto in Italy, *jamón ibérico* in Spain—but we've got one, too. Country ham is a strong, salty, dry-cured product produced primarily in Virginia, North Carolina, Tennessee, Kentucky, and Missouri. Just seven million country hams are sold annually in the United States, but with increased interest in artisanal and local foods, the current love affair with anything pig, and the explosion of Internet mail ordering, these small-town Southern hams seem poised to hit the big time. Being ham lovers ourselves, we wanted in.

By definition, a ham is the cut of meat taken from the upper part of a pig's back leg; for many, it's a holiday table centerpiece, spiral-cut and lacquered with a sugary glaze. But that is a city ham, made by injecting or soaking a fresh ham in brine and sold cooked, to be simply heated and served.

While city hams can be ready for market in 24 hours, country hams cure for anywhere from three months to years. Traditionally, it was a way to preserve the meat in prerefrigeration days: Hogs were slaughtered in the fall; the hams were rubbed with salt, sugar, and spices and then left to cure during the winter, with the salt drawing out moisture. Come spring, they were cleaned and hung, and some were smoked. Finally, in the warm summer months, the hams were aged. The heat accelerated enzymatic activity, which imparted the robust, pungent flavors that one producer has described as the ham's "country twang." This centuries-old seasonal style of making country ham is known as an "ambient" cure. Today, virtually all commercial cured-ham makers use special aging rooms to mimic the seasons, with temperature, airflow, and humidity under carefully monitored control.

Much as barbecue fanatics fight over Memphis versus Carolina versus Texas, country ham pros have partisan loyalties. Tasting hams from different states, they warned us, was like comparing apples with oranges. We tasted hams across the geographic range and loved their porky, complex flavors, developed from aging temperatures that run 10 to 30 degrees hotter than those used for European cured hams.

With all due respect, when it comes to these robust, salty hams from down South, it's not apples and oranges. McIntosh and Granny Smith might be more apt.

✔ WHY THIS RECIPE WORKS

While many of the century-old recipes we uncovered for this Appalachian stuffing were vague in their instructions, there was no question about their crowning feature: the buttery flavor of biscuits. In order to bake up our own dressing without the two-day wait, we started with a simple dump-and-stir buttermilk biscuit recipe. We portioned 1-inch pieces of biscuit dough onto a baking sheet and intentionally overbaked them, turning out crunchy miniature biscuits—as good as stale in just 25 minutes. As for the vegetables, we opted for a savory combination of onion and celery sautéed in butter and seasoned with thyme and sage. To assemble, we crumbled the biscuits into a bowl, added the vegetables, and stirred in a mixture of egg and chicken broth. Baked for 40 minutes, the dressing emerged with a beautiful brown crust, moist center, and that distinctly buttery biscuit goodness.

BISCUIT DRESSING

Flour your fingers to keep the biscuit dough from sticking in step 2. The biscuits can be baked and cooled a day ahead of time and stored at room temperature.

BISCUITS

3	cups (15 ounces) all-purpose flour
1	tablespoon baking powder
¾	teaspoon baking soda
1½	teaspoons sugar
1¼	teaspoons salt
1½	cups buttermilk, chilled
12	tablespoons unsalted butter, melted

DRESSING

2	tablespoons unsalted butter
2	onions, chopped fine
3	celery ribs, minced
2	tablespoons chopped fresh sage
2	tablespoons chopped fresh thyme
1½	teaspoons pepper
1	teaspoon salt
4	cups chicken broth
4	large eggs

1. FOR THE BISCUITS: Adjust oven racks to upper-middle and lower-middle positions and heat oven to 400 degrees. Line 2 rimmed baking sheets with parchment paper. Whisk flour, baking powder, baking soda, sugar, and salt together in large bowl. Combine buttermilk and melted butter in bowl and stir until butter forms clumps. Add buttermilk mixture to dry ingredients and stir with rubber spatula until just incorporated.

2. Using floured fingers, break off 1-inch pieces of dough and scatter evenly on baking sheets. Bake until tops are deep golden brown, about 25 minutes, switching and rotating sheets halfway through baking. Let biscuits cool on sheets. Do not turn oven off. (Completely cooled biscuits can be stored at room temperature for up to 24 hours.) When biscuits are cool enough to handle, crumble into ½-inch pieces into large bowl.

3. FOR THE DRESSING: Grease 13 by 9-inch baking dish. Melt butter in 12-inch skillet over medium-low heat. Add onions and celery and cook, covered, until softened and lightly browned, 10 to 12 minutes, stirring occasionally. Stir in sage, thyme, pepper, and salt and cook until fragrant, about 30 seconds. Add vegetable mixture to bowl with biscuits.

4. Whisk broth and eggs together in bowl. Add broth mixture to biscuits and vegetables and stir gently to combine. Let sit until biscuits have softened slightly, about 3 minutes. Transfer to prepared baking dish and press gently into even layer. Bake dressing on lower-middle rack until top is golden brown and crisp, 35 to 40 minutes, rotating dish halfway through baking. Let cool for 20 minutes before serving.

BISCUIT BITS

We needed biscuits that wouldn't fall apart even after we moistened them to build the dressing. So we made tiny biscuits, pinching the dough into 1-inch bits, to yield more firm edges and less fluffy middle. We also "prestaled" them by baking them nearly twice as long as a full-size biscuit would bake.

✓ WHY THIS RECIPE WORKS

Very few Mississippi restaurants don't have fried catfish on the menu, but this firm, mild fish rarely makes much of an impact north of the delta. We wanted to re-create the crunchy, seasoned coating we fell for down South using ingredients we could track down at any supermarket. To make sure our coating stayed put, we dunked the catfish in a flavorful mixture of buttermilk and hot sauce before rolling each fillet in cornmeal. Slicing our catfish fillets in half made for more manageable frying and increased each piece's surface area, upping our coating-to-fish ratio. Using a combination of coarse and finely ground cornmeal produced the best crunch and texture. On top of the spicy kick we got from the hot sauce–buttermilk dunk, we boosted flavor further by adding salt, pepper, garlic, and cayenne to the cornmeal blend. Our fried catfish "tenders" boasted appealing crunch and spice in every bite, only made better with the creamy, sweet-and-spicy flavors of our homemade Comeback Sauce.

FRIED CATFISH   SERVES 4 TO 6

Use a Dutch oven that holds 6 quarts or more for this recipe. If your spice grinder is small, grind the cornmeal in batches or process it in a blender for 60 to 90 seconds. Serve with Comeback Sauce (recipe follows).

- 2 **cups buttermilk**
- 1 **teaspoon hot sauce**
- 2 **cups cornmeal**
- 4 **teaspoons salt**
- 2 **teaspoons pepper**
- 2 **teaspoons granulated garlic**
- 1 **teaspoon cayenne pepper**
- 4 **(6- to 8-ounce) catfish fillets, halved lengthwise along natural seam**
- 2 **quarts peanut or vegetable oil**
   Lemon wedges

1. Set wire rack in rimmed baking sheet and line half of rack with triple layer of paper towels. Whisk buttermilk and hot sauce together in shallow dish. Process 1 cup cornmeal in spice grinder to fine powder, 30 to 45 seconds. Whisk salt, pepper, granulated garlic, cayenne, remaining 1 cup cornmeal, and ground cornmeal together in second shallow dish.

2. Pat fish dry with paper towels. Working with 1 piece of fish at a time, dip fish in buttermilk mixture, letting excess drip back into dish. Dredge fish in cornmeal mixture, shaking off excess, and transfer to large plate.

3. Add oil to large Dutch oven until it measures about 1½ inches deep and heat over medium-high heat to 350 degrees. Working with 4 pieces of fish at a time, add fish to hot oil. Adjust burner, if necessary, to maintain oil temperature between 325 and 350 degrees. Fry fish until golden brown and crisp, about 5 minutes. Transfer fish to paper towel–lined side of prepared rack and let drain for 1 minute, then move to unlined side of rack. Return oil to 350 degrees and repeat with remaining fish. Serve with lemon wedges.

COMEBACK SAUCE   MAKES ABOUT 1 CUP

Chili sauce, a condiment similar to ketchup, has a sweet flavor and subtle spicy kick; do not substitute Asian chili-garlic sauce.

- ½ **cup mayonnaise**
- ⅓ **cup chopped onion**
- 2 **tablespoons vegetable oil**
- 2 **tablespoons chili sauce**
- 1 **tablespoon ketchup**
- 2½ **teaspoons Worcestershire sauce**
- 2½ **teaspoons hot sauce**
- 1 **teaspoon yellow mustard**
- 1 **teaspoon lemon juice**
- 1 **garlic clove, minced**
- ¾ **teaspoon pepper**
- ⅛ **teaspoon paprika**

Process all ingredients in blender until smooth, about 30 seconds. Sauce can be refrigerated for up to 5 days.

EATING LOCAL ⭐ TAYLOR, MS

Lynn Hewlett bought **TAYLOR GROCERY** in 1998, although the storied business has been in operation since 1890. Like most boys in the area, Hewlett grew up fishing for catfish in local streams. Now, he makes a living selling his famous catfish in several versions: fried whole catfish, fried fillets, blackened, and grilled catfish. For his fried fish, he rinses and holds catfish in very cold water to remove off-flavors and keep the fish firm before coating each piece in a mixture of cornmeal, cream meal (finely ground cornmeal), and his own Taylor seasoning (a blend of salt, pepper, garlic, and other spices). He fries in oil heated to 325 degrees, a little lower than most recipes, to produce a coating that is crisp but not hard. He takes great pride in this process. "Food is a big deal down here," he explains. "Other places, people eat to live. Down here people live to eat. It's all about the food." We can get behind that.

TAYLOR GROCERY
4-A Depot St., Taylor, MS

✔ WHY THIS RECIPE WORKS

New England has the lobster roll and Maryland its famous crab cakes, but when it comes to shrimp, it's time to head south. The shrimp burgers served up in South Carolina put the region's sweet shrimp front and center. We wanted to re-create the clean shrimp taste and crisp crust at home, but without a deep fryer on hand we had to be resourceful. We created the patty's meaty texture by finely chopping a third of the shrimp in a food processor and coarsely chopping the remaining shrimp. This step also made our shrimp slightly sticky for easy binding, aided further by some cayenne-seasoned mayonnaise. Chopped scallions gave our burgers extra fresh flavor. For a crunchy coating ready to crisp up in our skillet, we processed panko bread crumbs, creating a fine crumb that evenly coated the patties. We fried these burgers in oil until they emerged crisp and brown. We put the finishing touches on our shrimp burgers by serving them on a soft bun with a smear of homemade tartar sauce.

SOUTH CAROLINA SHRIMP BURGERS SERVES 4

We prefer untreated shrimp—those without added sodium or preservatives like sodium tripolyphosphate (STPP). Most frozen shrimp have been treated (the ingredient list should tell you). If you're using untreated shrimp, increase the amount of salt to ½ teaspoon. If you're purchasing shell-on shrimp, you should buy about 1½ pounds.

TARTAR SAUCE
- ¾   **cup mayonnaise**
- 3   **tablespoons finely chopped dill pickles plus 1 teaspoon brine**
- 1   **small shallot, minced**
- 1   **tablespoon capers, rinsed and chopped fine**
- ¼   **teaspoon pepper**

BURGERS
- 1   **cup panko bread crumbs**
- 1¼   **pounds large shrimp (26 to 30 per pound), peeled, deveined, and tails removed**
- 2   **tablespoons mayonnaise**
- ¼   **teaspoon pepper**
- ⅛   **teaspoon salt**
- ⅛   **teaspoon cayenne pepper**
- 3   **scallions, chopped fine**
- 3   **tablespoons vegetable oil**
- 4   **hamburger buns**
- 4   **leaves Bibb lettuce**

1. FOR THE TARTAR SAUCE: Combine all ingredients in bowl and refrigerate until needed.

2. FOR THE BURGERS: Pulse panko in food processor until finely ground, about 15 pulses; transfer to shallow dish. Place one-third of shrimp (1 cup), mayonnaise, pepper, salt, and cayenne in now-empty processor and pulse until shrimp are finely chopped, about 8 pulses. Add remaining two-thirds of shrimp (2 cups) to shrimp mixture in processor and pulse until coarsely chopped, about 4 pulses, scraping down sides of bowl as needed. Transfer shrimp mixture to bowl and stir in scallions.

3. Divide shrimp mixture into four ¾-inch-thick patties (about ½ cup each). Working with 1 patty at a time, dredge both sides of patties in panko, pressing lightly to adhere, and transfer to plate.

4. Heat oil in 12-inch nonstick skillet over medium heat until shimmering. Place patties in skillet and cook until golden brown on first side, 3 to 5 minutes. Carefully flip and continue to cook until shrimp registers 140 to 145 degrees and second side is golden brown, 3 to 5 minutes longer. Transfer burgers to paper towel–lined plate and let drain, about 30 seconds per side. Spread tartar sauce on bun bottoms, then place burgers and lettuce on top. Cover with bun tops. Serve.

PEELING AND DEVEINING SHRIMP

1. Break shell under swimming legs, which will come off as shell is removed. Leave tail intact if desired, or tug tail to remove shell.

2. Use paring knife to make shallow cut along back of shrimp to expose vein. Use tip of knife to lift out vein. Discard vein by wiping blade against paper towel.

✔ WHY THIS RECIPE WORKS

When it comes to one-pot meals, you can't top shrimp jambalaya. For a satisfying Cajun medley of perfectly cooked shrimp, sausage, rice, and vegetables, we cooked the ingredients in stages, ensuring optimal flavor and texture in every bite. Browning half-moon slices of andouille released the sausage's smoky, spicy oil, which we used to brown our shell-on shrimp. The shells contributed extra shrimp flavor, and adding briny clam juice instead of chicken broth to cook the rice highlighted the seafood notes even further. Tomato paste, diced tomatoes, and reserved tomato juice gave the jambalaya its color and bright tomato flavors. For moist, tender rice, we transferred our jump-started jambalaya from the stovetop to the oven to finish cooking, adding a layer of aluminum foil on top of the rice to contain the steam. Peeling the shrimp and adding them for the last 5 minutes in the oven resulted in perfectly cooked crustaceans.

PERFECT SHRIMP JAMBALAYA   SERVES 4 TO 6

If you can't find andouille sausage, substitute an equal amount of Spanish-style chorizo.

2   teaspoons vegetable oil
8   ounces andouille sausage, halved lengthwise and sliced ¼ inch thick
1   pound shell-on large shrimp (26 to 30 per pound)
1   large onion, chopped fine
1   celery rib, minced
1   green bell pepper, stemmed, seeded, and chopped fine
5   garlic cloves, minced
1½   cups long-grain white rice
1   tablespoon tomato paste
1   teaspoon salt
½   teaspoon minced fresh thyme
2   (8-ounce) bottles clam juice
1   (14.5-ounce) can diced tomatoes, drained with ¼ cup juice reserved
1   bay leaf
2   scallions, sliced thin

1. Adjust oven rack to middle position and heat oven to 325 degrees.

2. Heat oil in Dutch oven over medium-high heat until shimmering. Add sausage and cook until browned, 3 to 5 minutes. Using slotted spoon, transfer sausage to paper towel–lined plate. Add shrimp to pot and cook until shells are lightly browned on both sides, about 1 minute per side. Transfer shrimp to large bowl, cover with plastic wrap, and refrigerate. (Shrimp and sausage can be refrigerated separately for up to 24 hours.)

3. Reduce heat to medium and add onion, celery, bell pepper, and garlic to pot. Cook, stirring occasionally, until vegetables have softened, 5 to 10 minutes. Add rice, tomato paste, salt, and thyme and cook until rice is coated with fat, about 1 minute. Stir in clam juice, tomatoes and reserved juice, bay leaf, and sausage. Place square of aluminum foil directly on surface of rice and press against sides of pot. Bring to boil, cover pot, transfer to oven, and bake until rice is almost tender and most of liquid is absorbed, about 20 minutes.

4. Meanwhile, peel and devein shrimp and discard shells. Remove pot from oven, lift off foil, and gently stir in peeled shrimp and any accumulated juices. Replace foil and lid, return pot to oven, and cook until rice is fully tender and shrimp are cooked through, about 5 minutes. Remove pot from oven, discard foil and bay leaf, fold in scallions, and serve.

FOILED AGAIN!

Baking the jambalaya in the oven ensures that the rice won't scorch, as often happens when this dish is prepared on top of the stove. A great form of insurance against any persistently crunchy grains of rice is a sheet of aluminum foil, placed directly on the surface of the rice (and pressed against the sides of the pot) before the jambalaya goes into the oven. The foil holds in steam and heat, ensuring that every grain of rice cooks perfectly. And, whatever you do, don't stir the rice as it cooks—this will only make it gluey.

✓ WHY THIS RECIPE WORKS

Inspired by Frogmore stew (which contains no frogs and isn't even a stew), shrimp boils make a regular appearance at backyard picnics and along South Carolina's coast in casual seaside restaurants. Though Old Bay is this stew's star seasoning, we wanted the summery notes of shrimp and corn to really shine, so we staggered their cooking times and injected bright, robust flavors along the way. We browned pieces of smoky, spicy andouille sausage and left its rendered fat in the pot to carry its flavor into the briny broth of clam juice and water. We simmered Old Bay, a bay leaf, tomatoes, potatoes, and cut-up ears of corn until the potatoes were just tender, then added the browned sausage back to the pot. To add flavor and keep them moist, we cooked seasoned, shell-on shrimp in a steamer basket set atop the vegetables. With our shrimp boil cooked to perfection, all we were missing was the picnic table.

SOUTH CAROLINA SHRIMP BOIL SERVES 8

This dish is always made with shell-on shrimp, and we think peeling them is half the fun. If you prefer peeled shrimp, use only 1 teaspoon of Old Bay in step 3. Can't find andouille? Substitute kielbasa sausage and add ¼ teaspoon of cayenne pepper to the broth in step 2. Use small red potatoes measuring 1 to 2 inches in diameter.

1½	**pounds andouille sausage, cut into 2-inch lengths**
2	**teaspoons vegetable oil**
4	**cups water**
1	**(8-ounce) bottle clam juice**
1	**(14.5-ounce) can diced tomatoes**
5	**teaspoons Old Bay seasoning**
1	**bay leaf**
1½	**pounds small red potatoes, scrubbed and halved**
4	**ears corn, husks and silk removed, cut into 2-inch rounds**
2	**pounds extra-large shrimp (21 to 25 per pound)**

1. Heat sausage and oil in Dutch oven over medium-high heat until fat renders and sausage is browned, about 5 minutes; using slotted spoon, transfer sausage to plate.

2. Add water, clam juice, tomatoes, 3 teaspoons Old Bay, bay leaf, potatoes, and corn to pot and bring to boil. Reduce heat to medium-low and simmer, covered, until potatoes are barely tender, about 10 minutes.

3. Return browned sausage to pot. Toss shrimp with remaining 2 teaspoons Old Bay and transfer to collapsible steamer basket. Nestle steamer basket into pot. Cook, covered, stirring shrimp occasionally, until cooked through, about 10 minutes. Strain stew and discard bay leaf. Serve.

OLD BAY'S ORIGINS

Old Bay seasoning, a key ingredient in our South Carolina Shrimp Boil, was created in 1941 by a German-Jewish spice merchant and refugee. Gustav Brunn had arrived in America just two years earlier, after spending 16 days in a concentration camp. The family managed to secure his release and fled to America with Brunn's spice grinder. Brunn, who spoke little English, had trouble getting a job, so he opened a business by the port of Baltimore. Observing seafood merchants steaming crabs in their own spice blends, he developed his own blend, naming it Old Bay after a defunct steamship line. The business remained in the family until the 1980s. McCormick & Company now owns Old Bay and still follows the original recipe.

LAYERED COOKING

Our staggered cooking method develops flavor and guarantees that each ingredient is perfectly cooked.

1. Browning sausage renders fat and builds flavor, giving stew a spicy base of flavor.

2. Potatoes and corn get a head start, giving them time to soak up flavors and become tender.

3. For tender sausage, return browned sausage to pot for last 10 minutes of cooking.

4. Steam seasoned shrimp over simmering stew to ensure they are just tender and well seasoned.

☑ WHY THIS RECIPE WORKS

Étouffée is a classic Creole seafood stew served over rice. To re-create its lush, velvety sauce, we started by making our own shrimp stock. We used the shells of 2 pounds of extra-large shrimp as the base, cooking them in butter with onions and celery before adding spices and water to the pot. While that simmered, we turned our attention to the roux. We discovered that toasting flour in a dry pot until it turned fragrant and light brown sped up this step considerably. *Voilà*—our roux was ready in about 5 minutes. We stirred in chopped vegetables and fragrant spices, saving diced tomatoes and their juice for last. Once the sauce had reduced, we slowly added our stock and let it thicken. The shrimp were added last, simmered for just 5 minutes. Finished with scallions and Worcestershire, our étouffée was ready to be spooned over a bed of white rice.

SHRIMP ÉTOUFFÉE SERVES 4 TO 6

You will need 3 cups of chopped onion and 1½ cups of chopped celery, which are divided between the shrimp stock and the étouffée. If you can't find shell-on shrimp, skip step 1 and substitute 3 cups of water, 1 (8-ounce) bottle of clam juice, and ¾ teaspoon of salt for the stock in step 3. Serve with White Rice (recipe follows).

9	tablespoons unsalted butter, cut into 9 pieces
2	pounds extra-large shrimp (21 to 25 per pound), peeled and deveined, shells reserved
3	onions, chopped
3	celery ribs, chopped
	Salt and pepper
5	cups water
8	garlic cloves (2 peeled and smashed, 6 minced)
1	tablespoon peppercorns
3	bay leaves
2	sprigs fresh thyme, plus 1 teaspoon minced
½	cup all-purpose flour
1	green bell pepper, stemmed, seeded, and chopped
1	teaspoon smoked paprika
¼	teaspoon cayenne pepper
1	(14.5-ounce) can diced tomatoes
3	scallions, sliced thin
2	teaspoons Worcestershire sauce
	Hot sauce
	Lemon wedges

1. Melt 1 tablespoon butter in Dutch oven over medium heat. Add shrimp shells, 2 cups onions, ½ cup celery, and 1 teaspoon salt and cook, stirring occasionally, until shells are spotty brown, about 10 minutes. Add water, smashed garlic, peppercorns, bay leaves, and thyme sprigs and bring to boil. Reduce heat to low, cover, and simmer for 30 minutes. Strain shrimp stock through fine-mesh strainer set over large bowl, pressing on solids to extract as much liquid as possible; discard solids. Wash and dry pot. (Stock can be refrigerated for up to 3 days or frozen for up to 1 month.)

2. Toast flour in now-empty pot over medium heat, stirring constantly, until just beginning to brown, about 5 minutes. Whisk in remaining 8 tablespoons butter until melted and combined with flour. Continue to cook, whisking constantly, until deep brown, 4 to 6 minutes.

3. Add bell pepper, remaining onions, remaining celery, 1 teaspoon salt, and ½ teaspoon pepper and cook, stirring often, until vegetables are softened, 10 to 12 minutes. Add paprika, cayenne, minced garlic, and minced thyme and cook until fragrant, about 1 minute. Stir in tomatoes and their juice and cook until dry, about 1 minute. Slowly whisk in 4 cups shrimp stock until incorporated (reserve any remaining stock for another use). Bring to boil, reduce heat to medium-low, and simmer until slightly thickened, about 25 minutes.

4. Season shrimp with salt and pepper, add to pot, and simmer until cooked through, about 5 minutes. Stir in scallions and Worcestershire. Season with salt and pepper to taste. Serve over rice with hot sauce and lemon wedges.

WHITE RICE SERVES 6 TO 8

Rinsing the rice, which removes much of the exterior starch, produces the lightest, fluffiest result.

2	cups long-grain white rice
1	tablespoon unsalted butter
3	cups water
1	teaspoon salt

1. Place rice in fine-mesh strainer set over large bowl. Rinse under running water until water runs clear, about 1 minute. Drain rice well.

2. Melt butter in large saucepan over medium heat. Add rice and cook, stirring frequently, until edges begin to turn translucent, about 2 minutes. Add water and salt and bring to boil.

3. Cover, reduce heat to low, and simmer until liquid is absorbed and rice is tender, about 20 minutes. Off heat, remove lid and place kitchen towel over saucepan. Cover and let stand for 10 minutes. Fluff with fork. Serve.

☑ WHY THIS RECIPE WORKS

Unlike your standard bright green side dish, Southern green beans boast an army-green hue thanks to 4 or more hours of cooking. They also take on an irresistible salty, smoky flavor after their long simmer. We wanted to capture these elements within an hour. A two-pronged bacon approach was our secret weapon, imparting the dish's signature porky notes quickly. After crisping two slices of bacon, we used the rendered fat to cook the onion. We added three uncooked slices of bacon along with the green beans, water, salt, and a little sugar, which brought in a welcome touch of gentle sweetness. We simmered our ingredients for 45 minutes, just enough time to reduce the liquid and concentrate the flavors. After we removed the bacon slices and reduced the liquid further, our green beans were flavorful and perfectly cooked—almost but not quite falling apart. A sprinkling of crisped bacon added a crunchy finishing touch.

SOUTHERN-STYLE GREEN BEANS

SERVES 6 TO 8

The long-simmered beans will easily break apart; be sure to handle them gently.

5	slices bacon
1	large onion, halved and sliced thin
3	pounds green beans, trimmed
2½	cups water
	Salt and pepper
1	teaspoon sugar

1. Cook 2 slices bacon in Dutch oven over medium heat until crisp, 5 to 7 minutes. Using slotted spoon, transfer bacon to paper towel–lined plate, leaving fat in pot. Add onion to now-empty pot and cook until softened, about 6 minutes. Add green beans, water, 2 teaspoons salt, sugar, and remaining 3 slices bacon and bring to boil. Cover, reduce heat to medium-low, and simmer, stirring occasionally, until green beans are very tender, about 45 minutes.

2. Remove lid and discard bacon. Increase heat to medium-high and cook until liquid is reduced slightly, about 5 minutes. Season with salt and pepper to taste. (Stir carefully to avoid breaking apart green beans.) Transfer green beans to serving bowl. Crumble reserved bacon over top before serving.

TRIMMING GREEN BEANS

Line up several green beans in a row on cutting board. Trim about ½ inch from each end, then cut beans as directed in your favorite green bean recipes.

FREEZING BACON

Bacon is often sold by the pound or half-pound, but since many recipes call for just a few slices, you're bound to have some leftovers. But how can you freeze bacon so that you can use each slice as needed?

We have found that the best way is simply to roll up each slice (or two slices together) tightly, put the rolled bacon in a zipper-lock bag, and freeze it. Then you can pull out the desired number of slices as you need them.

✓ WHY THIS RECIPE WORKS

A versatile Southern specialty, grits are served at breakfast, lunch, and dinner and in its many forms, from simmered to deep fried, sweet to savory. We were looking to perfect baked cheese grits, aiming for a crisp browned crust, a creamy center, and a delicate balance of cheese and spice. We began building savory flavor by cooking chopped onion in butter, adding heavy cream for richness and piquant hot sauce for contrast. Along with water, we stirred in old-fashioned grits—preferred over instant for their creamy yet pleasingly coarse texture. Extra-sharp cheddar folded into the cooked grits complemented the subtle corn flavors (for a more assertive side at dinner time, we liked smoked cheddar). To create a dense, polenta-like texture, we stirred in three lightly beaten eggs. Once in the oven, our grits developed a gorgeous golden crust—helped along by an extra sprinkling of cheese added during baking—and their rich, hearty flavor made them perfect for pairing with everything from eggs and bacon to roast chicken.

BAKED CHEESE GRITS

SERVES 4 TO 6

Old-fashioned grits are well worth the extra 10 minutes of cooking; instant grits will bake up too smooth and have an overprocessed flavor. Grits are ready when they are creamy and smooth but retain a little fine-textured coarseness. We prefer a very sharp aged cheddar, but feel free to use any extra-sharp cheddar you like. Or, for a heartier flavor more suitable to brunch or a dinner side dish, substitute smoked cheddar or smoked gouda.

2	tablespoons plus 1 teaspoon unsalted butter
1	small onion, chopped fine
3	cups water
1	cup heavy cream
½	teaspoon hot sauce
	Salt and pepper
1⅛	cups old-fashioned grits
8	ounces extra-sharp cheddar cheese, shredded (about 2 cups)
3	large eggs, lightly beaten

1. Adjust oven rack to lower-middle position and heat oven to 350 degrees. Grease 9-inch square baking dish with 1 teaspoon butter.

2. Heat remaining 2 tablespoons butter in large saucepan over medium heat until foam begins to subside. Add onion and cook until softened but not browned, about 4 minutes.

3. Add water, cream, hot sauce, and ½ teaspoon salt and bring to boil. Whisk in grits and reduce heat to low. Cook, stirring frequently, until grits are thick and creamy, about 15 minutes.

4. Off heat, thoroughly stir in 1½ cups cheese, eggs, and pepper to taste. Pour mixture into greased baking dish, smooth top with rubber spatula, and place grits in oven.

5. Bake for 30 minutes. Remove dish from oven, sprinkle remaining ½ cup cheese evenly over top, and return to oven. Continue baking until top is browned, about 15 minutes. Let rest for 5 minutes and serve.

STAYING SHARP

So what is extra-sharp cheddar? It depends on whom you ask. The U.S. Department of Agriculture's only requirement regarding cheddar is that the final product contain at least 50 percent milk-fat solids and no more than 39 percent moisture by weight. As for what distinguishes different varieties of cheddar— mild, medium, sharp, extra-sharp, and beyond—that is left in the hands of the cheesemakers. Our research revealed that most extra-sharp cheddars are aged from nine to 18 months. This much we do know for sure: As cheddar ages, new flavor compounds are created, and the cheese gets firmer in texture and more concentrated in flavor—and it gets sharper.

✔ WHY THIS RECIPE WORKS

Southern cooks have long made the most of an unripe crop by dunking sliced green tomatoes in breading and frying them to a crisp, golden crust. For a coating that wouldn't slide off, we first drained tomato slices on paper towels to absorb excess moisture. Once patted dry, the tomatoes were ready for breading. We found processing cornmeal to a fine crumb minimized its grittiness; we mixed it with flour, cayenne, and more cornmeal. We dunked the slices in a mixture of egg and buttermilk and dredged them through our cornmeal blend before frying in peanut oil. The acid in the buttermilk helped the starchy coating absorb moisture, making it especially crisp when fried. After just a few minutes, these sweet-tart tomatoes developed a tasty golden-brown crust that was so good, we found ourselves looking forward to the first frost with its bonanza of green (never-to-ripen) tomatoes.

FRIED GREEN TOMATOES

SERVES 4

You'll need four to five green tomatoes for this recipe.

- 1½   **pounds green tomatoes, cored and sliced ¼ inch thick**
- ⅔   **cup cornmeal**
- ⅓   **cup all-purpose flour**
- 1½   **teaspoons salt**
- ½   **teaspoon pepper**
- ⅛   **teaspoon cayenne pepper**
- ⅔   **cup buttermilk**
- 1   **large egg**
- 2   **cups peanut or vegetable oil**

1. Place tomatoes on paper towel–lined rimmed baking sheet. Cover with more paper towels, let sit for 20 minutes, and pat dry. Meanwhile, process ⅓ cup cornmeal in blender until very finely ground, about 1 minute. Combine processed cornmeal, remaining ⅓ cup cornmeal, flour, salt, pepper, and cayenne in shallow dish. Whisk buttermilk and egg together in second shallow dish.

2. Working with 1 at a time, dip tomato slices in buttermilk mixture, then dredge in cornmeal mixture, pressing firmly to adhere; transfer to clean baking sheet.

3. Set wire rack in rimmed baking sheet. Heat oil in 12-inch skillet over medium-high heat to 350 degrees. Fry 4 tomato slices until golden brown on both sides, 4 to 6 minutes. Drain on prepared wire rack. Bring oil back to 350 degrees and repeat with remaining tomato slices. Serve.

DRY BEFORE YOU FRY

To keep tomatoes from weeping as they fry (which will loosen coating), let them sit between paper towels for 20 minutes and then press dry.

ALL ABOUT CORNMEAL

Cornmeal, or ground processed corn kernels, is available in all manner of sizes for use in different applications. In most cases, we recommend choosing stone-ground over commercially produced cornmeal on two counts: First of all, stone-ground cornmeal has a more rustic texture because of the stone's rough grinding surface (many companies use smooth steel rollers that produce very fine, uniform cornmeal). And second, stone-ground cornmeal has a fuller flavor because it contains both the hull and oil-rich germ of the corn kernel, which commercial producers extract for better storage.

✔ WHY THIS RECIPE WORKS

To make this Prohibition-era side dish a winner in today's kitchens, we modernized some key steps. Though peeling tomatoes may seem a tedious task, three simple steps were enough to avoid the alternative—papery skins. Working with firm tomatoes, scoring an X in the bottom, submerging them in boiling water for 30 to 60 seconds, and cooling in ice water before peeling with a paring knife made the process a breeze. Instead of baking the tomatoes at the beginning and end of the recipe, we started with our skillet in the oven before moving it to the stovetop. One cup of brown sugar perfectly balanced the tomatoes' acidity. Baking the peeled and cored tomatoes with butter, brown sugar, and their natural juice produced a concentrated savory-sweet syrup and tender browned tomatoes, which pair perfectly with roast chicken or steak.

CARAMEL TOMATOES

SERVES 8

Peeling tomatoes may seem fussy, but otherwise you'll be eating bits of skin. Firm tomatoes are easier to peel. Use caution when handling the skillet in step 3, as the handle will be very hot.

- 8   **large tomatoes, peeled and cored**
- 1   **cup packed light brown sugar**
- 1   **tablespoon salt**
- 1   **teaspoon pepper**
- 4   **tablespoons unsalted butter,**
       cut into ¼-inch pieces

1. Adjust oven rack to upper-middle position and heat oven to 400 degrees. Arrange tomatoes in large ovensafe skillet, cored side up. Sprinkle with sugar, salt, and pepper. Dot with butter.

2. Bake until tomatoes are tender and lightly browned, about 1 hour, basting with juice every 15 minutes.

3. Transfer skillet to stovetop (skillet handle will be hot). Simmer over medium-low heat, basting every 5 minutes, until sauce is thick and syrupy, 25 to 30 minutes. Serve.

FIT FOR A PRESIDENT

Caramel tomatoes? Sugar and tomatoes may seem an odd couple today, but there is a precedent, an 1886 baked tomato recipe from *The Woman Suffrage Cook Book*. It promised "a rich, luscious jelly" and cautioned the cook "not to be sparing of sugar."

Caramel tomatoes were also apparently a favorite of first lady Lou Henry Hoover's, as they are featured in *The First Ladies Cook Book*. Maryland's own Mary Rattley, the Hoovers' cook, is credited with inventing these sweet treats, which the Hoovers brought with them to the White House. In Hoover's day, which coincided with Prohibition, "everything sweeter was better," according to culinary historian Lynne Olver (swapping one vice for another, apparently!).

PEELING TOMATOES

1. Remove core of tomato using paring knife.

2. Score X at each tomato's base using paring knife.

3. Using slotted spoon, lower tomatoes into large pot of boiling water and boil for 30 to 60 seconds. Using slotted spoon, transfer tomatoes to prepared ice bath to cool for 1 minute.

4. Starting at X, use paring knife to remove loosened peel in strips.

✓ WHY THIS RECIPE WORKS

From its pale pink color to its distinct spicy flavor, Carolina red slaw is worlds away from cool, creamy cole-slaw. To re-create this Southern barbecue slaw at home, we started by microwaving vinegar and red pepper flakes. This blast of heat quickly married their flavors before we whisked in ketchup and salt, a zesty (and color-boosting) combination reminiscent of Lexington barbecue sauce. Turning to the cabbage, we easily shredded a head of green cabbage in the food processor. Tossing the cabbage with sugar and salt helped draw out excess moisture, and a minute or two in the microwave released even more water. (We found that slaws made with salted cabbage also keep longer.) We drained and pressed the cabbage before tossing it with our spicy dressing. After 30 minutes in the refrigerator, this bright, tangy red slaw was ready to kick bland coleslaw to the curb.

CAROLINA RED SLAW

SERVES 8 TO 10

If any large pieces of cabbage slip by the shredding blade of the food processor, chop them by hand.

- ½ **cup cider vinegar**
- ½ **teaspoon red pepper flakes**
- ⅔ **cup ketchup**
  Salt
- 1 **head green cabbage (2 pounds), cored and cut into 2-inch-thick wedges**
- ¼ **cup sugar**

1. Microwave vinegar and pepper flakes until mixture is bubbling around edges, 1 to 1½ minutes. Whisk ketchup and 1 teaspoon salt into vinegar mixture until combined.

2. In food processor fitted with shredding disk, process cabbage until shredded. Toss cabbage, sugar, and 1 teaspoon salt together in large bowl. Microwave, covered, until cabbage is just beginning to wilt, 1½ to 2 minutes, stirring halfway through microwaving. Transfer cabbage mixture to colander set over bowl. Let cool completely, about 15 minutes, stirring occasionally.

3. Press cabbage mixture to release excess moisture; discard liquid (it should measure about ⅓ cup). Toss cabbage mixture and ketchup mixture together in large bowl until combined. Cover and refrigerate for 30 minutes or up to 2 days. Serve.

FASTER SHREDDING AND DRAINING

To prevent soggy slaw, you could chop a head of cabbage by hand, salt it, and let it drain for an hour before rinsing and pressing it dry, or you could use this quicker method:

1. Push cabbage wedges through feed tube of food processor fitted with shredding disk.

2. Together, heat (from microwave), salt, and sugar quickly draw moisture from shredded cabbage.

EATING LOCAL ★ LEXINGTON, NC

The pulled-pork sandwich we ordered at **LEXINGTON BARBECUE** (known as Honey Monk's locally) in Lexington, North Carolina, came with a vinegary, red-tinged slaw, spicy but sweet and as good as any we'd ever tasted. Our waitress explained the cabbage was shredded in a food processor and dressed with the restaurant's vinegar-based barbecue sauce and a few secret ingredients. That was all we could get out of her. Back in Boston, we phoned the restaurant.

"Hi. I'd like to ask you about your coleslaw."

There was a long pause.

"We don't have coleslaw. We have barbecue slaw."

Not surprisingly, they weren't too interested in divulging their house secrets to a Northerner who didn't even know the dish's proper name.

LEXINGTON BARBECUE
100 Smokehouse Ln.
Lexington, NC

✓ WHY THIS RECIPE WORKS

Red rice is a hearty, comforting side popular along the coastal towns of South Carolina and Georgia. We wanted to bring a lighter version of this Lowcountry classic home, but without sacrificing its bold flavors. The red color comes from tomato, so we decided to let this key ingredient shine. We started by softening onion, green bell pepper, and celery in a saucepan, next adding the rice and toasting it for a few minutes to add flavor and ensure distinct, tender grains. For a concentrated dose of tomato taste, we turned to tomato paste, sautéing just 1 tablespoon with the cooked vegetables and plenty of garlic. To finish the rice and reinforce the tomato flavors, we added juicy diced tomatoes and chicken broth. A touch of cayenne added welcome heat, and a handful of chopped parsley freshened our fluffy, spicy rice.

LOWCOUNTRY RED RICE

SERVES 4 TO 6

To give the rice a slightly sweeter flavor, use a red bell pepper instead of green.

1	tablespoon vegetable oil
1	onion, chopped fine
1	green or red bell pepper, stemmed, seeded, and minced
1	celery rib, minced
1½	cups long-grain white rice
4	garlic cloves, minced
1	tablespoon tomato paste
2	cups chicken broth
1	(14.5-ounce) can diced tomatoes, drained
1½	teaspoons salt
¼	teaspoon cayenne pepper
¼	cup minced fresh parsley

1. Heat oil in large saucepan over medium-high heat until shimmering. Cook onion, bell pepper, and celery until softened, about 5 minutes. Add rice and cook, stirring frequently, until edges begin to turn translucent, about 2 minutes. Stir in garlic and tomato paste and cook until fragrant, about 30 seconds.

2. Stir in broth, tomatoes, salt, and cayenne and bring to boil. Cover, reduce heat to low, and cook until liquid is absorbed and rice is tender, about 20 minutes. Remove from heat and let stand, covered, for 10 minutes. Fluff rice with fork, stir in parsley, and serve.

THE SKINNY ON LONG-GRAIN RICE

Aside from its longer, slimmer grains, what distinguishes long-grain white rice from medium- or short-grain white rice (the kinds used in risotto and sushi, respectively) is that after cooking the grains remains fluffy and separate. Long-grain white rice contains less of a starch called amylopectin, which is what makes rice stick together.

White rice is neutral in flavor, providing a backdrop for other foods. Nonetheless, higher-quality white rice—like good white pasta, or a real French baguette—offers a pleasingly chewy "al dente" texture and a slightly buttery natural flavor of its own. The buttery notes are caused by a naturally occurring flavor compound, 2-acetyl-1-pyrroline, and higher levels lend an almost popcornlike taste. While most of this subtle variation comes from the varietal of rice that was planted, processing also affects flavor. All rice starts out brown; to become white, it is milled, a process that removes the husk, bran, and germ, which contain flavor compounds as well as nutrients. The longer the rice is milled, the whiter it becomes—and the more flavor is removed. (Many brands of rice are then enriched to replace lost nutrients.)

✓ WHY THIS RECIPE WORKS

Frugal Cajun cooks traditionally serve up "dirty" rice as a way of using up leftover chicken giblets—the gizzard, heart, kidneys, and liver. To replicate the meaty, rich flavors of this thrifty recipe while skipping most of the innards, we kept readily available chicken livers for their distinct taste and replaced the rest with ground pork. To spice up our rice, we turned to onion, sweet red bell pepper, thyme, and a bit of cayenne pepper. Cooking the meat and vegetables separately from the rice, and combining everything once the rice was cooked through, ensured that the rice cooked evenly and didn't taste muddy. Chopped scallions gave a clean finish to our perfectly dirty rice.

DIRTY RICE SERVES 4 TO 6

This dirty rice has a mild heat; for a spicier dish, add more cayenne or pass hot sauce at the table.

1	tablespoon vegetable oil
8	ounces ground pork
1	onion, chopped fine
1	red bell pepper, stemmed, seeded, and chopped fine
1	celery rib, minced
4	ounces chicken livers, rinsed, trimmed, and chopped fine
3	garlic cloves, minced
1	teaspoon salt
¼	teaspoon dried thyme
¼	teaspoon cayenne pepper
2¼	cups chicken broth
1½	cups long-grain white rice, rinsed
2	bay leaves
3	scallions, sliced thin

1. Heat oil in Dutch oven over medium heat until shimmering. Add pork and cook, breaking up meat with wooden spoon, until browned, about 5 minutes. Stir in onion, bell pepper, and celery and cook until softened, about 10 minutes. Add chicken livers, garlic, salt, thyme, and cayenne and cook until livers are browned, 3 to 5 minutes. Transfer meat mixture to fine-mesh strainer set over bowl and cover with aluminum foil.

2. Increase heat to high and add broth, rice, and bay leaves to now-empty pot, scraping up any browned bits. Bring to boil, reduce heat to low, cover, and cook until rice is tender, 15 to 17 minutes. Off heat, discard bay leaves and fluff rice with fork. Gently stir in drained meat mixture, discarding any accumulated juices. Sprinkle scallions over rice and serve.

RINSING RICE

For dirty rice with grains that won't clump together, it's important to rinse the rice before cooking. This washes away any excess starch and prevents the final dish from turning out sticky or gummy. (If you are using enriched white rice, note that this step will rinse away some of the added vitamins.)

Simply place the rice in a fine-mesh strainer and rinse under cool water until the water runs clear, occasionally stirring the rice around lightly with your hand. Set the strainer of rinsed rice over a bowl to drain until needed.

☑ WHY THIS RECIPE WORKS

In many Creole kitchens, red beans and rice was (and is) a Monday night dish. The hambone saved from Sunday dinner would simmer on the back burner, its marrow flavoring the red beans and thickening the broth. Today, however, most home cooks don't have leftover hambones readily available, so we set out to serve an equally flavorful, spicy dish with ingredients we could pick up at the supermarket. For porky, salty flavor, we cooked four strips of bacon and added onion, bell pepper, and celery to the rendered fat, then the garlic and spices. To ensure that our beans turned out tender and tasted meaty without a hambone, we simmered them in both water and chicken broth before adding smoky, spicy andouille sausage. Half an hour was just enough time for the sausage to impart great flavor to the beans without becoming too tough. We would be happy to serve this Louisiana classic, spooned over hot white rice, any night of the week.

RED BEANS AND RICE

SERVES 8 TO 10

Andouille sausage is traditional in this recipe. If you can't find andouille at your local market, use kielbasa. In order for the starch from the beans to thicken the cooking liquid, it's important to maintain a vigorous simmer in step 1.

BEANS

- 4 slices bacon, chopped
- 1 small onion, chopped fine
- 1 green bell pepper, stemmed, seeded, and chopped fine
- 1 celery rib, minced
- 4 garlic cloves, minced
- 7 cups chicken broth
- 7 cups water
- 1 pound (2½ cups) dried red kidney beans, picked over and rinsed
- 4 bay leaves
- 1 teaspoon minced fresh oregano
- 1 teaspoon minced fresh thyme
  Salt and pepper
- ½ teaspoon cayenne pepper
- 8 ounces andouille sausage, halved lengthwise and sliced ¼ inch thick

RICE

- 2 tablespoons vegetable oil
- 3 cups long-grain white rice
- 4½ cups water
- 1½ teaspoons salt

  Hot sauce

1. FOR THE BEANS: Cook bacon in Dutch oven over medium heat until crisp, about 7 minutes. Add onion, bell pepper, and celery and cook, stirring frequently, until softened, about 8 minutes. Stir in garlic and cook until fragrant, about 30 seconds. Add broth, water, beans, bay leaves, oregano, thyme, 1 teaspoon pepper, ½ teaspoon salt, and cayenne and bring to boil over high heat. Reduce heat and simmer vigorously, stirring occasionally, until beans are soft and liquid thickens, 2 to 2½ hours.

2. Stir in sausage and cook until liquid is thick and creamy, about 30 minutes.

3. FOR THE RICE: Heat oil in large saucepan over medium heat. Add rice; cook, stirring constantly, for 1 to 3 minutes, until rice is lightly toasted. Add water and salt; bring to boil, swirling pan to blend ingredients.

4. Reduce heat to low, place dish towel folded in half over pan, and cover pan. Cook until liquid is absorbed, about 15 minutes.

5. Turn off heat and let rice stand on burner, covered, to finish cooking, about 15 minutes longer.

6. Fluff rice with fork. Season beans with salt and pepper to taste. Serve over rice, passing hot sauce separately.

KIDNEY BEAN CONCERNS

There are rumors that dried red kidney beans must be boiled—not just simmered—to make them safe to eat. Is this true? And if so, for how long should they be boiled?

Many dried beans contain proteins called lectins that, if ingested raw or partially cooked, can produce symptoms similar to those of food poisoning. Red kidney beans are higher in lectins than other beans, but there's no need to fret: A 1985 research paper published in the *Journal of Food Science* reported that lectins are completely destroyed when beans are boiled for 10 minutes. To keep them from turning mushy, we suggest boiling the beans at the beginning of cooking (when they are at their sturdiest). After that, you can turn down the heat and simmer them until tender.

✔ WHY THIS RECIPE WORKS

In the Lowcountry of South Carolina and Georgia, eating hoppin' John—a humble slow-cooked dish of rice, black-eyed peas, and ham hocks—at the start of a new year is said to bring good luck. Hoping to turn out a quicker version of this hearty (and supposedly lucky) dish, we started by swapping ham hocks for more readily available (and still very flavorful) bacon and boneless ham. After browning the bacon, we used the rendered fat to brown slices of boneless ham. Since fresh black-eyed peas are not readily available outside the South, we turned to frozen ones, which, unlike canned varieties, held their shape and cooked much faster than dried beans. We cooked onion, celery, garlic, and thyme before adding the peas, broth, and browned ham. Rinsing the rice before adding it to the pot rid the grains of any excess starch, and covering the hoppin' John with aluminum foil contained the escaping steam—two steps that ensured tender, toothsome rice. We stirred in the reserved bacon and ham and served up a one-pot meal that, lucky for us, makes for delicious eating.

HOPPIN' JOHN   SERVES 8

Small boneless hams are available in the meat case at most supermarkets. If you can't find one, you can substitute an equal weight of ham steak. Covering the surface of the dish with aluminum foil after adding the rice helps ensure that the rice cooks evenly. Serve with hot sauce, if desired.

6   slices bacon, chopped
1   (1- to 1½-pound) boneless ham,
     cut into ¾-inch-thick planks
1   onion, chopped fine
2   celery ribs, minced
4   garlic cloves, minced
½   teaspoon dried thyme
4   cups chicken broth
2   pounds frozen black-eyed peas
2   bay leaves
1½   cups long-grain white rice
3   scallions, sliced thin

1. Cook bacon in Dutch oven over medium heat until crisp, 5 to 7 minutes. Using slotted spoon, transfer bacon to paper towel–lined plate. Pour off all but 1 tablespoon fat from pot and brown ham, about 3 minutes per side. Transfer ham to plate with bacon.

2. Add onion and celery to pot and cook until softened, about 5 minutes. Stir in garlic and thyme and cook until fragrant, about 30 seconds. Add broth, peas, bay leaves, and ham and bring to boil. Reduce heat to low and simmer, covered, until peas are just tender, about 20 minutes. Transfer ham to cutting board and cut into ½-inch pieces.

3. Place rice in fine-mesh strainer and rinse under cold running water until water runs clear, about 1 minute. Drain rice well and stir into pot. Place square of aluminum foil directly on surface of simmering liquid. Simmer, covered, until liquid is absorbed and rice is tender, about 20 minutes, stirring and repositioning foil twice during cooking. Remove from heat and let stand, covered, for 10 minutes. Discard bay leaves. Fluff rice with fork. Stir in scallions, bacon, and ham. Serve.

HURRYING HOPPIN' JOHN

Hoppin' John can take as long as 4 hours to make. We drastically reduce the cooking time by using boneless ham in place of a smoked ham hock and frozen peas instead of dried.

BONELESS HAM: Browned and simmered boneless ham adds smoky depth and meatiness to our hoppin' John in a quarter of the time.

FROZEN BLACK-EYED PEAS: Frozen black-eyed peas can be used straight from the freezer and simmered to the perfect creamy consistency in less than 1 hour.

✔ WHY THIS RECIPE WORKS

A dish of deliciously salty fried ham steaks in a bracing, coffee-based gravy is often served for breakfast in Southern kitchens. Up north, bone-in ham steaks were our most readily available option for making this dish. Compensating for this lean meat, we started with fatty bacon and used its flavorful rendered fat to fry the ham to a beautiful golden brown. Patting the ham dry before frying proved the key to maximum browning. For an eye-opening gravy, we browned a little onion and stirred in body-building flour. Using chicken broth as our base concentrated the gravy's meaty flavors, and maple syrup (an admittedly Northern ingredient) added mellow sweetness to balance the coffee's acidity. After thickening the gravy at a gentle simmer, we removed the skillet from the heat and stirred in the key eye-opening ingredient—espresso powder—as well as butter for a silky, rich final touch. Though it is traditionally a breakfast dish, we'd be more than happy to serve this crisp, browned ham in its red-eye gravy three times a day.

HAM STEAK WITH RED-EYE GRAVY SERVES 4

Pat the ham steak dry before cooking so it will brown well. Before pouring the gravy over the ham in step 3, discard any accumulated juices on the platter, as they will make the sauce too salty. A simple side of Short-Order Home Fries (recipe follows) pairs well with the salty ham.

HAM STEAK

- 1 (1¼-pound) bone-in ham steak
  Pepper
- 2 slices bacon

RED-EYE GRAVY

- 2 tablespoons finely chopped onion
- 1 teaspoon all-purpose flour
- 1½ cups chicken broth
- 1 tablespoon maple syrup
- 3 tablespoons unsalted butter, cut into 3 pieces and chilled
- 2 teaspoons instant espresso powder

1. FOR THE HAM STEAK: Pat ham dry with paper towels and season with pepper. Cook bacon in 12-inch skillet over medium heat until crisp, about 5 minutes. Remove bacon from skillet (leaving fat behind) and reserve for another use. Add ham to skillet with bacon fat and cook until well browned on first side, about 5 minutes. Flip ham and cook on second side until lightly browned, about 2 minutes. Transfer ham to platter and tent loosely with aluminum foil.

2. FOR THE RED-EYE GRAVY: Add onion to now-empty skillet and cook until just beginning to brown, about 1 minute. Stir in flour and cook for 15 seconds. Whisk in broth and maple syrup, scraping up any browned bits. Bring to simmer and cook until mixture is reduced to ¾ cup and slightly thickened, 5 to 7 minutes.

3. Off heat, whisk in butter and espresso powder. Season with pepper to taste. Discard any juices on ham platter. Carve ham steak into 4 equal portions. Pour red-eye gravy over ham. Serve.

SHORT-ORDER HOME FRIES
SERVES 4

Although we prefer the sweetness of Yukon Gold potatoes, other medium-starch or waxy potatoes, such as all-purpose or red-skinned potatoes, can be substituted. If you want to spice things up, add a pinch of cayenne pepper.

- 1½ pounds Yukon Gold potatoes (3 medium), unpeeled, cut into ¾-inch pieces
- 4 tablespoons unsalted butter
- 1 onion, chopped fine
- ½ teaspoon garlic salt
  Salt and pepper

1. Arrange potatoes in large microwave-safe bowl, top with 1 tablespoon butter, and cover tightly with plastic wrap. Microwave on high until edges of potatoes begin to soften, 5 to 7 minutes, shaking bowl (without removing plastic) to redistribute potatoes halfway through cooking.

2. Meanwhile, melt 1 tablespoon butter in 12-inch nonstick skillet over medium heat. Add onion and cook until softened and golden brown, about 8 minutes. Transfer to small bowl.

3. Melt remaining 2 tablespoons butter in now-empty skillet over medium heat. Add potatoes and pack down with spatula. Cook, without moving, until underside of potatoes is brown, 5 to 7 minutes. Turn potatoes, pack down again, and continue to cook until well browned and crisp, 5 to 7 minutes. Reduce heat to medium-low and continue cooking, stirring potatoes every few minutes, until crusty, 9 to 12 minutes. Stir in onion, garlic salt, ½ teaspoon salt, and pepper to taste. Serve.

BRINGING MAPLE SYRUP SOUTH

Pure maple syrup and pancake syrup are not the same. Real maple syrup is nothing but sap from the sugar maple tree that has been boiled down (from about 40 gallons to 1). In the process, the sap caramelizes and develops its characteristic flavor. We prefer stronger, less expensive Grade A Dark Amber to Grade A Light Amber; reserve the strongest syrup, Grade B, for cooking.

✔ WHY THIS RECIPE WORKS

Hushpuppies, bite-size fried cornmeal dumplings, are a habit-forming treat served throughout the South with fried fish and barbecue. We wanted ours to boast a crisp crust, tender center, and strong corn taste without any cornmeal grit or extra effort. A combination of ¾ cup of cornmeal and ½ cup of flour struck the perfect balance between being too soft and too dense with great corn flavor. To kick up the hushpuppies' flavor, we stirred in cayenne and finely chopped onion. Buttermilk contributed a nice tang, and baking soda's reaction with its acidity provided a light texture and a golden-brown crust. With all of our batter's components in place, we let the whisked mixture sit to thicken before dropping heaping tablespoons into hot oil. Within minutes, our hushpuppies fried into golden mini fritters we couldn't wait to devour.

HUSHPUPPIES

MAKES ABOUT 25

Avoid coarsely ground cornmeal for this recipe, as it will make the hushpuppies gritty. If you don't have buttermilk on hand, make clabbered milk by whisking 2¼ teaspoons of lemon juice into ¾ cup of milk and letting it stand at room temperature until slightly thickened, about 10 minutes. Use a Dutch oven that holds 6 quarts or more for this recipe.

¾	cup (3¾ ounces) fine-ground cornmeal
½	cup (2½ ounces) all-purpose flour
1½	teaspoons baking powder
½	teaspoon baking soda
¾	teaspoon salt
¼	teaspoon cayenne pepper
¾	cup buttermilk
2	large eggs
¼	cup finely chopped onion
2	quarts peanut or vegetable oil

1. Combine cornmeal, flour, baking powder, baking soda, salt, and cayenne in large bowl. Whisk in buttermilk, eggs, and onion until combined. Let batter sit at room temperature for 10 minutes or up to 1 hour.

2. Set wire rack in rimmed baking sheet. Heat oil in large Dutch oven over medium-high heat to 350 degrees. Working with half of batter at a time, drop heaping tablespoons into oil and fry until deep golden brown, 2 to 3 minutes, turning hushpuppies halfway through frying. Transfer to prepared wire rack. Return oil to 350 degrees and repeat with remaining batter. Serve.

TO MAKE AHEAD: Hushpuppies can be refrigerated for up to 2 days. Reheat in 450-degree oven for about 10 minutes before serving.

CORN AND RED PEPPER HUSHPUPPIES

Prepare Hushpuppies, adding 1 cup corn kernels (fresh or frozen, thawed), ½ red bell pepper, seeded and chopped fine, and 2 thinly sliced scallions to batter in step 1.

CRAB AND CHIVE HUSHPUPPIES

Prepare Hushpuppies, adding ½ pound crabmeat (picked over for shells), 2 tablespoons Dijon mustard, and 2 tablespoons minced fresh chives to batter in step 1.

HAM AND CHEDDAR HUSHPUPPIES

Prepare Hushpuppies, adding 4 ounces finely chopped deli ham, 1 cup shredded sharp cheddar cheese, 2 tablespoons Dijon mustard, and 2 thinly sliced scallions to batter in step 1.

✓ WHY THIS RECIPE WORKS

Buttermilk biscuits topped with sausage gravy are a quintessentially Southern breakfast. These indulgent biscuits should be big and fluffy, sturdy enough to stand tall while still absorbing the spicy gravy. We made an easy batter, using a 2-to-1 ratio of butter to shortening for rich flavor and tender texture. Extra baking powder and baking soda created maximum lift, and brief kneading yielded biscuits with even better structure. We stamped out 3-inch rounds, applying equal pressure on our cutter for biscuits that rose to lofty (and uniform) heights. For the gravy, we combined flour and pepper with ground fennel and sage, added to reinforce the sausage's flavor. We cooked bulk pork sausage through before stirring in the seasoned flour, which combined with the fat to form a thickening roux. After adding whole milk, we simmered the gravy until it was piping hot and thickened. Served together, our tender, buttery biscuits and creamy, meaty gravy made for a hearty, flavor-packed start to the day.

BISCUITS AND SAUSAGE GRAVY SERVES 8

If you don't have buttermilk on hand, whisk 1 tablespoon of lemon juice into 1¼ cups of milk and let it stand until slightly thickened, about 10 minutes.

BISCUITS

3	cups (15 ounces) all-purpose flour
1	tablespoon sugar
1	tablespoon baking powder
½	teaspoon baking soda
1	teaspoon salt
8	tablespoons unsalted butter, cut into ½-inch pieces and chilled
4	tablespoons vegetable shortening, cut into ½-inch pieces and chilled
1¼	cups buttermilk

SAUSAGE GRAVY

¼	cup all-purpose flour
1	teaspoon ground fennel
1	teaspoon ground sage
	Salt and pepper
1½	pounds bulk pork sausage
3	cups whole milk

1. FOR THE BISCUITS: Adjust oven rack to middle position and heat oven to 450 degrees. Line baking sheet with parchment paper. Pulse flour, sugar, baking powder, baking soda, salt, butter, and shortening in food processor until mixture resembles coarse meal, about 15 pulses. Transfer to large bowl. Stir in buttermilk until combined.

2. On lightly floured counter, knead dough until smooth, 8 to 10 times. Pat dough into 9-inch circle, about ¾ inch thick. Using 3-inch biscuit cutter dipped in flour, cut out rounds of dough and arrange on prepared baking sheet. Gather remaining dough, pat into ¾-inch-thick circle, and cut out remaining biscuits. (You should have 8 biscuits in total.)

3. Bake until biscuits begin to rise, about 5 minutes, then rotate pan and reduce oven temperature to 400 degrees. Bake until golden brown, 12 to 15 minutes, then transfer to wire rack and let cool. (Biscuits can be stored in zipper-lock bag for up to 2 days.)

4. FOR THE SAUSAGE GRAVY: Combine flour, fennel, sage, and 1½ teaspoons pepper in small bowl. Cook sausage in 12-inch nonstick skillet over medium heat, breaking up meat with wooden spoon, until no longer pink, about 8 minutes. Sprinkle flour mixture over sausage and cook, stirring constantly, until flour has been absorbed, about 1 minute. Slowly stir in milk and simmer until gravy has thickened, about 5 minutes. Season with salt to taste. Serve over split biscuits.

STAMP BUT DON'T TWIST

Twisting the cutter when stamping out biscuits pinches the dough, resulting in an uneven rise. Using a well-floured cutter and pressing down with equal pressure on all sides of the cutter (and not twisting) ensures that the biscuits will rise evenly.

☑ WHY THIS RECIPE WORKS

It was only a matter of time before sweet potato–loving Southern cooks combined the fluffy texture and pleasant tang of biscuits with the earthy sweetness of this popular tuber. To add this potato's natural sweetness without weighing down the dough, we microwaved the sweet potatoes, which eliminated their moisture while concentrating the flavor. After mashing the flesh, we stirred in cider vinegar to mimic buttermilk's tang and to create greater lift once combined with the dough's baking powder and baking soda. We maximized the biscuits' tender texture with low-protein cake flour and opted for the deep, molasses-like sweetness of brown sugar to complement the sweet potatoes. The dough took on a pretty deep orange color, and, once baked, the biscuits emerged tender and subtly sweet, perfect for a smear of butter or jam, or sliced and stuffed with ham and mustard.

SWEET POTATO BISCUITS

MAKES 16

You can substitute a combination of 3 cups of all-purpose flour and 6 tablespoons of cornstarch for the cake flour. If you halve the recipe, in step 1 reduce the microwave time to 10 to 15 minutes.

2½	**pounds sweet potatoes (3 to 4 medium)**
2	**tablespoons cider vinegar**
3¼	**cups (13 ounces) cake flour**
¼	**cup packed (1¾ ounces) dark brown sugar**
5	**teaspoons baking powder**
½	**teaspoon baking soda**
1½	**teaspoons salt**
8	**tablespoons unsalted butter, cut into ½-inch pieces and chilled, plus 2 tablespoons melted**
4	**tablespoons vegetable shortening, cut into ½-inch pieces and chilled**

1. Prick potatoes all over with fork. Microwave on large plate until potatoes are very soft and surface is wet, 15 to 20 minutes, flipping every 5 minutes. Immediately slice potatoes in half to release steam. When cool enough to handle, scoop flesh into bowl and mash until smooth. (You should have 2 cups. Reserve any extra for another purpose.) Stir in vinegar and refrigerate until cool, about 15 minutes.

2. Adjust oven rack to middle position and heat oven to 425 degrees. Line rimmed baking sheet with parchment paper. Pulse flour, sugar, baking powder, baking soda, salt, chilled butter, and shortening in food processor until mixture resembles coarse meal, about 15 pulses. Transfer to bowl with cooled potatoes and fold with rubber spatula until incorporated.

3. Turn out dough onto floured counter and knead until smooth, 8 to 10 times. Pat dough into 9-inch circle, about 1 inch thick. Using 2¼-inch biscuit cutter dipped in flour, cut out biscuits and arrange on prepared baking sheet. Pat remaining dough into 1-inch-thick circle and cut out remaining biscuits. (You should have 16 biscuits in total.)

4. Brush tops of biscuits with melted butter and bake until golden brown, 18 to 22 minutes. Let cool for 15 minutes. Serve. (Biscuits can be stored at room temperature for up to 2 days.)

PICKING OUT SWEET POTATOES

Choose firm sweet potatoes with skins that are taut, not wrinkled. Many varieties are available, and they can vary quite a bit in color, texture, and flavor. Beauregard (usually sold as a conventional sweet potato) and Jewel are sweet and moist and have the familiar sweet potato flavor. Red Garnet is more savory and has a looser texture. Nontraditional varieties that are lighter in color, like the Japanese White, White Sweet, Batata, and purple potatoes, tend to be starchier and drier. Store sweet potatoes in a dark, well ventilated spot (do not store them in a plastic bag); they will keep for about one week.

✓ WHY THIS RECIPE WORKS

Particularly popular in Charleston, South Carolina, cream cheese biscuits are known for their ethereally fluffy (not flaky) texture and distinctly moist crumb. Using frozen cream cheese and butter allowed both to thaw during baking, creating airy pockets when they melted and released steam. For added lightness, we used a blend of cake flour and all-purpose flour, which produced a tender crumb and some structure. Because of cream cheese's high water content, excess rolling would result in tough biscuits, so we skipped the biscuit cutter, instead rolling the dough into a rectangle and cutting it into 12 squares. Our cream cheese biscuits surpassed all expectations, turning out so tender and soft we hardly noticed their untraditional square shape.

CREAM CHEESE BISCUITS   MAKES 12

All biscuits taste great with butter, but these taste even better with sweet Chocolate Gravy (recipe follows) to complement their tang.

- 1½ **cups (7½ ounces) all-purpose flour**
- 1½ **cups (6 ounces) cake flour**
- 1 **tablespoon sugar**
- 1 **tablespoon baking powder**
- 1 **teaspoon salt**
- ¾ **teaspoon baking soda**
- 4 **ounces cream cheese, cut into ½-inch pieces and frozen for 30 minutes**
- 4 **tablespoons unsalted butter, cut into ½-inch pieces and frozen for 30 minutes**
- 1 **cup plus 1 tablespoon buttermilk**

1. Adjust oven rack to middle position and heat oven to 450 degrees. Line baking sheet with parchment paper. Pulse all-purpose flour, cake flour, sugar, baking powder, salt, baking soda, cream cheese, and butter in food processor until mixture resembles coarse meal, about 15 pulses. Transfer flour mixture to large bowl. Stir in buttermilk until combined (dough may appear slightly dry).

2. Turn out dough onto lightly floured counter and knead briefly until dough comes together. Roll dough into 8 by 6-inch rectangle, about ¾ inch thick. Cut into twelve 2-inch squares and transfer to prepared baking sheet. Bake until light brown, 12 to 15 minutes. Transfer to wire rack and let cool for 5 minutes. Serve warm.

TO MAKE AHEAD: Unbaked cut biscuits can be refrigerated on baking sheet, covered with plastic wrap, for up to 1 day. To finish, heat oven to 450 degrees and bake as directed.

CHOCOLATE GRAVY
MAKES ABOUT 4 CUPS

This chocolate sauce, a popular topping for biscuits in the South, is called "gravy" because it uses flour as a thickener.

- 1 **cup (7 ounces) sugar**
- ½ **cup (2½ ounces) all-purpose flour**
- 6 **tablespoons (1⅛ ounces) Dutch-processed cocoa**
- ¼ **teaspoon salt**
- 4 **cups whole milk**
- 1 **teaspoon vanilla extract**

Whisk sugar, flour, cocoa, and salt together in large saucepan. Slowly whisk in milk until smooth. Bring to simmer over medium heat, stirring constantly, and simmer until thickened, 2 to 3 minutes. Remove from heat and whisk in vanilla. Serve over biscuits.

SQUARE IS THE NEW ROUND

Instead of rolling the dough, cutting round biscuits, then rerolling the scraps to cut more, we roll the dough into a rectangle and cut 12 square biscuits.

WHY THIS RECIPE WORKS

Traditionally, what makes this savory Southern cornbread "crackle" are crispy bits of rendered pork skin stirred into the batter. To capture this satisfying salty element, we had two options: the time-consuming task of rendering pork skin ourselves, or downgrading the cornbread's taste with store-bought pork rind. Hoping to forge ahead without the cracklings, we looked to chopped bacon. We infused our favorite skillet cornbread batter with pork flavor by stirring in crisp bacon bits and using the rendered bacon fat instead of butter. To ensure that our cornbread released cleanly, we dolloped the batter into an oiled, hot cast-iron skillet, a trick that kept the oil evenly distributed under the batter as it baked. Turning the round loaf out of the pan minutes after it finished baking kept the bread from softening and steaming in the skillet. With its crisp, dark golden crust and flecks of chewy bacon, our finished cornbread really crackled.

CRACKLIN' CORNBREAD

SERVES 10

For the crunchiest crust, bake the cornbread in a cast-iron pan. Avoid coarsely ground cornmeal, which will make the cornbread too gritty.

6	slices bacon, chopped fine
2¼	cups (11¼ ounces) cornmeal
1	teaspoon baking powder
1	teaspoon baking soda
½	teaspoon salt
2	cups buttermilk
¼	cup vegetable oil
2	large eggs, lightly beaten

1. Adjust oven rack to middle position and heat oven to 450 degrees. Cook bacon in 10-inch ovenproof skillet over medium heat until crisp, about 8 minutes. Transfer bacon to paper towel–lined plate. Pour off fat from pan, reserving ¼ cup.

2. Combine cornmeal, baking powder, baking soda, and salt in large bowl. Whisk in buttermilk, 3 tablespoons oil, reserved bacon fat, eggs, and crisp bacon.

3. Heat remaining 1 tablespoon oil in now-empty skillet over medium-high heat until just smoking. Spoon cornmeal mixture, ½ cup at a time, into skillet and bake until top begins to crack and sides are golden brown, 12 to 16 minutes. Cool in pan for 5 minutes, then turn out onto wire rack. Serve.

DO THE DOLLOP

If you dump the batter in all at once, the hot oil that's greasing the skillet gets pushed to the edge. Dolloping the batter guarantees that the cornbread will release cleanly, even from an underseasoned skillet.

BAKING POWDER VS. BAKING SODA

Baking soda and baking powder are both leaveners that, when activated, form carbon dioxide; this gas, in turn, causes batters and doughs to rise. Baking soda is activated when mixed with a moist, acidic ingredient, such as sour cream. Baking powder already contains acid (as well as baking soda) so is activated by moisture alone (or, in the case of double-acting baking powder, first by moisture and then by heat).

In our tests, cornbread made with only baking soda turned deep brown and had a dense, heavy crumb; baking soda increases browning because it makes batters more alkaline. Cornbread made with baking powder alone was bright yellow with an open crumb, but it tasted sour and metallic. The combination of baking powder and soda worked best, producing a golden-brown bread with good height and an open crumb.

☑ WHY THIS RECIPE WORKS

To bring the warm, fruity sweetness of blackberry jam cake down from the Appalachian Mountains into our own kitchen, we focused on capturing its inviting flavors. Toasted cinnamon, allspice, and cloves gave the cake an aromatic and gently spicy quality without masking the key ingredient: a generous scoop of blackberry jam, which turns the cake a pretty plum color. Thinning the jam in the microwave and adding water to the batter created a lighter texture. We made a decadent but not overly sweet caramel frosting, straining it after whipping it together to eliminate lumps. Whisking over heat and then, once cooled, beating in softened butter transformed the pasty mixture into a silken, custardlike frosting. After coating the first layer in frosting, we spread on a layer of jam to reinforce the blackberry flavor before topping it with the second cake round. Though many recipes have walnuts in the batter, we saved them for last: We pressed toasted chopped nuts into the sides of the frosted cake for a crunchy and good-looking finish.

BLACKBERRY JAM CAKE SERVES 12

Whole milk makes the richest, tastiest frosting. Use a stand mixer; the frosting is too thick for a handheld mixer. And plan ahead, as the frosting needs time to cool.

CAKE

2	teaspoons ground cinnamon
¼	teaspoon ground allspice
⅛	teaspoon ground cloves
¾	cup seedless blackberry jam
1	cup buttermilk, room temperature
3	tablespoons water
1	teaspoon vanilla extract
3	cups (15 ounces) all-purpose flour
1	tablespoon baking powder
¾	teaspoon salt
20	tablespoons (2½ sticks) unsalted butter, softened
1⅓	cups (9⅓ ounces) granulated sugar
½	cup packed (3½ ounces) light brown sugar
4	large eggs, room temperature

FROSTING AND JAM LAYER

1½	cups packed (10½ ounces) dark brown sugar
¼	teaspoon baking soda
¼	cup (1¼ ounces) all-purpose flour
3	tablespoons cornstarch
½	teaspoon salt
1½	cups whole milk
2	teaspoons vanilla extract
24	tablespoons (3 sticks) unsalted butter, softened, cut into 24 pieces
¼	cup seedless blackberry jam
1½	cups (6 ounces) walnuts, toasted and chopped (optional)

1. FOR THE CAKE: Adjust oven rack to lower-middle position and heat oven to 350 degrees. Grease and flour two 9-inch round cake pans. Heat cinnamon, allspice, and cloves in small skillet over medium heat until fragrant, about 1 minute. Microwave jam in medium bowl until thin enough to pour, 35 to 45 seconds, carefully stirring halfway through cooking.

2. Whisk buttermilk, water, and vanilla into warm jam. Combine flour, baking powder, toasted spices, and salt in large bowl. Using stand mixer fitted with paddle, beat butter, granulated sugar, and brown sugar together on medium-high speed until light and fluffy, about 2 minutes. Reduce speed to medium-low and add eggs, 1 at a time, until incorporated. Add flour mixture in 3 additions, alternating with 2 additions of jam mixture, stopping occasionally to scrape down sides of bowl.

3. Divide batter evenly between prepared pans and smooth tops. Tap pans on counter to release air bubbles. Bake until deep golden brown and toothpick inserted in center comes out clean, 35 to 40 minutes. Let cakes cool in pans for 10 minutes, then turn out onto wire rack. Let cool completely, at least 1 hour.

4. FOR THE FROSTING AND JAM LAYER: Combine sugar, baking soda, flour, cornstarch, and salt in medium bowl. Slowly whisk in milk until smooth. Pour mixture through fine-mesh strainer into medium saucepan. Cook over medium heat, whisking constantly, until mixture boils and is very thick, 5 to 7 minutes. Transfer milk mixture to clean bowl and let cool to room temperature, about 2 hours.

5. Using stand mixer fitted with whisk, whip cooled milk mixture and vanilla together on low speed until combined, about 30 seconds. Add butter, 1 piece at a time, and whip until incorporated, about 2 minutes. Increase speed to medium-high and whip until frosting is light and fluffy, about 5 minutes. Let sit at room temperature until stiff, about 1 hour.

6. Whisk jam in bowl until smooth. Line edges of cake platter with 4 strips of parchment paper to keep platter clean. Place 1 cake layer on prepared platter. Place about 1½ cups frosting in center of cake layer and, using large spatula, spread in even layer right to edge of cake. Place jam on frosting layer and use spatula to spread over frosting, leaving ½-inch border. Place second cake layer on top, making sure layers are aligned, then frost top in same manner as first layer, this time spreading frosting until slightly over edge. Gather more frosting on tip of spatula and gently spread onto side of cake. Smooth frosting by gently running edge of spatula around cake and leveling ridge that forms around top edge, or create billows by pressing back of spoon into frosting and twirling spoon as you lift away. Garnish with walnuts, if using. Carefully pull out pieces of parchment from beneath cake and refrigerate until set, about 30 minutes. Serve. (Assembled cake can be refrigerated for up to 1 day. Bring to room temperature before serving.)

🥄 WHY THIS RECIPE WORKS

When it comes to coffee cake, the Moravians of Winston-Salem, North Carolina, have had it right for centuries. Their cakes stand out for their extra-tender crumb, signature sugary craters, and caramelized brown sugar topping. The cake's moist interior comes from a mashed potato–based dough. For a streamlined approach with the same results, we used instant potato flakes. We blended the flakes with a simple yeasted dough and let it rise before pressing it into a baking pan and letting it rise again in a warm oven. For the crunchy sugar topping, we created streusel-like crumbles with chilled butter, brown sugar, and cinnamon. Once the dough had risen, we pressed shallow indentations into the entire surface and sprinkled the crumbles over the cake, which melted into pockets during baking. After cooling, the topping and our sugar cake looked—and tasted—as good as any from down South.

MORAVIAN SUGAR CAKE   SERVES 12

Potato flakes and potato buds both work well here, but avoid potato granules, which can have off-flavors.

¾   cup warm milk (110 degrees)
1½   teaspoons instant or rapid-rise yeast
⅓   cup (2⅓ ounces) granulated sugar
¼   cup instant potato flakes
½   teaspoon salt
4   tablespoons unsalted butter, softened,
       plus 6 tablespoons cut into ½-inch pieces and
       chilled
1   large egg
2   cups (10 ounces) all-purpose flour
1½   cups packed (10½ ounces) light brown sugar
1   tablespoon ground cinnamon

1. Adjust oven rack to middle position and heat oven to 200 degrees. Maintain temperature for 10 minutes, then turn off oven. Grease medium bowl and 13 by 9-inch baking dish.

2. Stir milk and yeast together until yeast is dissolved. In bowl of stand mixer fitted with paddle, mix together yeast mixture, granulated sugar, potato flakes, salt, softened butter, egg, and flour on medium speed until smooth and shiny, about 2 minutes. Transfer dough to prepared bowl, cover with plastic wrap, and place in warm oven. Let rise until doubled in size, about 30 minutes.

3. Press dough into even layer in prepared dish. Cover dish with plastic and place in warm oven. Let rise until doubled in size, about 30 minutes. Meanwhile, using fingers, combine chilled butter, brown sugar, and cinnamon until mixture resembles coarse meal.

4. Remove dish from oven and heat oven to 375 degrees. With floured fingers, make shallow indentations in surface of dough and sprinkle with brown sugar mixture. Bake until topping is bubbling and deep brown, 18 to 22 minutes. Let cool for 30 minutes. Serve. (Cooled cake can be wrapped in plastic and stored at room temperature for up to 2 days.)

TO MAKE AHEAD: After pressing dough into dish and covering, dough can be refrigerated for up to 24 hours. When ready to bake, let sit at room temperature for 30 minutes before proceeding with step 4.

EATING LOCAL ★ WINSTON-SALEM, NC

The Moravians have a long history as bakers, and in 1808 Brother Christian Winkler took over the bakery that now bears his name. Today, **WINKLER BAKERY** is part of the Old Salem Museums & Gardens. Employees wear period costumes and bake an array of cookies, cakes, and breads using traditional Moravian recipes and techniques. You won't find any electric mixers here—everything is mixed by hand with long wooden paddles.

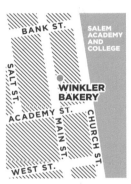

WINKLER BAKERY
521 S. Main St.
Winston-Salem, NC

HOW TO SHAPE SUGAR CAKE

1. Press dough into even layer in greased 13 by 9-inch baking dish and let rise.

2. Using fingers, work chilled butter into brown sugar and cinnamon until mixture resembles coarse meal.

3. Using floured fingertips, make shallow indentations over surface of risen dough.

4. Evenly sprinkle brown sugar mixture over indented dough.

✔ WHY THIS RECIPE WORKS

Jefferson Davis Pie, a brown sugar chess pie, named for the Confederate President Jefferson Davis, is known for its caramel-y custard with dried fruit and nuts. For a silky, thick texture, we used rich heavy cream as our custard's starting place. A cup of brown sugar contributed enough sweetness without masking the warm, spicy flavors of cinnamon and allspice. Egg yolks set more slowly than whole eggs, so we used five to draw out the pie's baking time. Rather than stir in the raisins, dates, and nuts, we ground them in a food processor and pressed them into an unbaked pie shell to provide a flavorful base for the custard layer above. This layered pie baked for about an hour in a gentle oven, allowing the crust to brown and the custard to set gradually. Dolloped with a spoonful of bourbon-fortified whipped cream, this pie was worthy of a national introduction.

JEFFERSON DAVIS PIE SERVES 8

Homemade crust tastes the best, but you can use store-bought pie dough in this recipe. We prefer golden raisins here, but regular raisins will also work. We like to serve this pie with Bourbon Whipped Cream (recipe follows) or vanilla ice cream.

CRUST

1¼	cups (6¼ ounces) all-purpose flour
1	tablespoon sugar
½	teaspoon salt
4	tablespoons vegetable shortening, cut into ¼-inch pieces and chilled
6	tablespoons unsalted butter, cut into ¼-inch pieces and chilled
3–4	tablespoons ice water

FILLING

½	cup golden raisins
3	ounces pitted dates, chopped (½ cup)
½	cup pecans, toasted and chopped
3	tablespoons all-purpose flour
1	teaspoon ground cinnamon
½	teaspoon salt
¼	teaspoon ground allspice
8	tablespoons unsalted butter, softened
1	cup packed (7 ounces) light brown sugar
5	large egg yolks
1¼	cups heavy cream

1. FOR THE CRUST: Process flour, sugar, and salt in food processor until combined, about 5 seconds. Scatter shortening over top and process until mixture resembles coarse cornmeal, about 10 seconds. Scatter butter over top and pulse until mixture resembles coarse crumbs, about 10 pulses. Transfer to bowl.

2. Sprinkle 3 tablespoons water over flour mixture. Using rubber spatula, stir and press dough until it sticks together. If dough does not come together, add remaining 1 tablespoon water. Turn out dough onto sheet of plastic wrap and form dough into 4-inch disk, wrap tightly in plastic wrap, and refrigerate for 1 hour.

3. Let chilled dough soften slightly, about 10 minutes, before rolling. (Wrapped dough can be refrigerated for up to 2 days or frozen for up to 1 month. If frozen, let dough thaw completely on counter before rolling.) Roll dough into 12-inch circle on lightly floured counter. Loosely roll dough around rolling pin and gently unroll it onto 9-inch pie plate, letting excess dough hang over edge. Ease dough into plate by gently lifting edge of dough with 1 hand while pressing into plate bottom with your other hand.

4. Trim overhang to ½ inch beyond lip of pie plate. Tuck overhang under itself; folded edge should be flush with edge of pie plate. Crimp dough evenly around edge of pie plate using your fingers. Wrap dough-lined pie plate loosely in plastic and freeze until dough is firm, about 30 minutes.

5. FOR THE FILLING: Adjust oven rack to lowest position and heat oven to 325 degrees. Process raisins, dates, and pecans in food processor until finely ground, 20 to 35 seconds. Transfer mixture to chilled pie shell. Using your fingers, gently press mixture into even layer. Combine flour, cinnamon, salt, and allspice in small bowl. Beat butter and sugar together with handheld mixer on medium-low speed until just combined, about 1 minute. Add yolks, 1 at a time, and continue to beat until incorporated. Add cream and flour mixture and continue to beat, scraping down sides of bowl as needed, until just combined.

6. Pour filling over raisin mixture and bake until surface is deep brown and center jiggles slightly when pie is gently shaken, 55 to 65 minutes, rotating plate halfway through baking. Let pie cool completely in plate on wire rack before serving. (Pie can be refrigerated for up to 2 days.)

BOURBON WHIPPED CREAM
MAKES ABOUT 2 CUPS

Though any style of whiskey will work here, we prefer the smoky sweetness of bourbon. For the most efficient whipping, make sure your heavy cream is as cold as possible.

1	cup heavy cream
2	tablespoons bourbon
1½	tablespoons light brown sugar
½	teaspoon vanilla extract

With handheld mixer on medium speed, beat cream, bourbon, sugar, and vanilla together until stiff peaks form, about 2 minutes. (Whipped cream can be refrigerated for up to 4 hours.)

✔ WHY THIS RECIPE WORKS

Some think the moniker "tar heel" comes from the Revolutionary War when North Carolinians poured tar into a river to slow British troops; others point to the Civil War when soldiers from that state threatened to tar the heels of retreating comrades. Whatever its origins, tar heel pie serves up the best of pie and gooey, fudgy brownies. To correct the brownie filling's cloying sweetness, we replaced granulated sugar with dark brown sugar, adding depth. For a rich chocolate filling, we combined melted semisweet chocolate and butter with cocoa powder and oil. Brown sugar's molasses notes bolstered the chocolate, and mixing it with vanilla, salt, and eggs developed an appealingly crackly top. A scoop of flour gave the filling structure and upped the fudgy texture. Parbaking the pie shell and toasting the pecans ensured that both stayed crisp. Sprinkling the nuts over the bottom of the prebaked pie shell kept the crust from getting soggy. For people who like brownies so fudgy that they are too messy to eat out of hand, this pie is a must.

FUDGY TAR HEEL PIE SERVES 8

Homemade crust tastes the best, but you can use store-bought pie dough in this recipe. Serve with ice cream.

CRUST

1¼	cups (6¼ ounces) all-purpose flour
1	tablespoon sugar
½	teaspoon salt
4	tablespoons vegetable shortening, cut into ¼-inch pieces and chilled
6	tablespoons unsalted butter, cut into ¼-inch pieces and chilled
3–4	tablespoons ice water

FILLING

1	cup (6 ounces) semisweet chocolate chips
4	tablespoons unsalted butter
¼	cup vegetable oil
2	tablespoons unsweetened cocoa powder
¾	cup packed (5¼ ounces) dark brown sugar
2	large eggs
1	tablespoon vanilla extract
¾	teaspoon salt
¼	cup (1¼ ounces) all-purpose flour
1¼	cups pecans, toasted and chopped coarse

1. FOR THE CRUST: Process flour, sugar, and salt in food processor until combined, about 5 seconds. Scatter shortening over top and process until mixture resembles coarse cornmeal, about 10 seconds. Scatter butter over top and pulse until mixture resembles coarse crumbs, about 10 pulses. Transfer to bowl.

2. Sprinkle 3 tablespoons ice water over flour mixture. Using rubber spatula, stir and press dough until it sticks together. If dough does not come together, add remaining 1 tablespoon water. Turn out dough onto sheet of plastic wrap and form into 4-inch disk, wrap tightly in plastic wrap, and refrigerate for 1 hour.

3. Let chilled dough soften slightly, about 10 minutes, before rolling. (Wrapped dough can be refrigerated for up to 2 days or frozen for up to 1 month. If frozen, let dough thaw completely on counter before rolling.) Roll dough into 12-inch circle on lightly floured counter. Loosely roll dough around rolling pin and gently unroll it onto 9-inch pie plate, letting excess dough hang over edge. Ease dough into plate by gently lifting edge of dough with 1 hand while pressing into plate bottom with your other hand.

4. Trim overhang to ½ inch beyond lip of pie plate. Tuck overhang under itself; folded edge should be flush with edge of pie plate. Crimp dough evenly around edge of pie plate using your fingers. Wrap dough-lined pie plate loosely in plastic and freeze until dough is firm, about 30 minutes. Adjust oven rack to lower-middle position and heat oven to 375 degrees.

5. Line chilled pie shell with two 12-inch squares of parchment paper or double layer of aluminum foil, covering edges to prevent burning, and fill with pie weights. Bake until lightly golden around edges, 18 to 25 minutes. Carefully remove weights and parchment, rotate pie shell, and continue to bake until center begins to look opaque and slightly drier, 3 to 6 minutes. Let cool completely.

6. FOR THE FILLING: Reduce oven temperature to 325 degrees. Microwave ⅔ cup chocolate chips and butter in bowl, stirring often, until melted, 60 to 90 seconds. Whisk in oil and cocoa until smooth.

7. In separate bowl, whisk sugar, eggs, vanilla, and salt together until smooth. Whisk chocolate mixture into sugar mixture until incorporated. Stir in flour and remaining ⅓ cup chocolate chips until just combined.

8. Spread pecans in bottom of pie shell, then pour batter over top, using spatula to level. Bake pie until toothpick inserted in center comes out with thin coating of batter attached, 30 to 35 minutes. Let pie cool on wire rack until barely warm, about 1½ hours. Serve. (Pie can be reheated, uncovered, in 300-degree oven until warm throughout, 10 to 15 minutes.)

NUT REGIMEN

After toasting nuts in 350-degree oven for about 5 minutes, sprinkle them in bottom of prebaked pie shell; don't mix them into filling. This way, pie shell won't get soggy and pie will be easy to slice.

✔ WHY THIS RECIPE WORKS

Smooth and creamy peanut butter pie is a tempting creation from down South. To transform peanut butter into a mousselike filling, we started by whipping it with cream cheese (for tang and sliceability), confectioners' sugar, and a touch of cream until it was light and fluffy. We folded airy whipped cream into this mixture, which turned the filling silky yet sturdy enough to slice cleanly. The caramel notes of brown sugar in the graham cracker crust complemented the peanut flavor. A cloud of whipped cream on top of the filling rounded out our pie's light texture, but we craved a little crunch in the finished product. Homemade candied peanuts were the answer. A layer of the peanuts on top of the cooled crust and the rest over the topping provided an irresistible salty-sweet flavor. Before resting on our laurels, we revisited the crust, trying it with chocolate grahams. The chocolate–peanut butter pairing was just as (if not more) appealing.

PEANUT BUTTER PIE SERVES 8

All-natural peanut butter will work in this recipe. You can use our Homemade Candied Peanuts (recipe follows) in place of the honey-roasted peanuts.

9	whole graham crackers, broken into 1-inch pieces
3	tablespoons packed light brown sugar
5	tablespoons unsalted butter, melted
½	cup honey-roasted peanuts, chopped
¾	cup (3 ounces) plus 2 tablespoons confectioners' sugar
¾	cup creamy peanut butter
6	ounces cream cheese, softened
1¾	cups heavy cream
1	teaspoon vanilla extract

1. Adjust oven rack to middle position and heat oven to 325 degrees. Grease 9-inch pie plate. Process graham crackers and brown sugar in food processor until finely ground, about 30 seconds. Add melted butter and pulse until combined, about 8 pulses.

2. Transfer crumbs to prepared plate. Using bottom of dry measuring cup, press crumbs into bottom and up sides of plate. Bake until crust is fragrant and beginning to brown, 12 to 14 minutes, rotating plate halfway through baking. Let crust cool completely on wire rack, about 30 minutes. Spread ⅓ cup peanuts evenly over bottom of cooled crust.

3. Using stand mixer fitted with whisk, mix ¾ cup confectioners' sugar, peanut butter, cream cheese, and 3 tablespoons cream on low speed until combined, about 1 minute. Increase speed to medium-high and whip until fluffy, about 1 minute. Transfer to large bowl; set aside.

4. In now-empty mixer bowl, whip ¾ cup cream on medium-low speed until foamy, about 1 minute. Increase speed to high and whip until stiff peaks form, 1 to 3 minutes. Gently fold whipped cream into peanut butter mixture in 2 additions until no white streaks remain. Spoon filling into crust and spread into even layer.

5. In now-empty mixer bowl, whip vanilla, remaining cream, and remaining 2 tablespoons confectioners' sugar on medium-low speed until foamy, about 1 minute. Increase speed to high and whip until stiff peaks form, 1 to 3 minutes. Spread whipped cream evenly over filling. Refrigerate until set, about 2 hours. Sprinkle with remaining peanuts. Serve.

PEANUT BUTTER PIE WITH CHOCOLATE GRAHAM CRUST

In step 1, substitute chocolate graham crackers for graham crackers.

HOMEMADE CANDIED PEANUTS
MAKES ABOUT ½ CUP

½	cup dry-roasted peanuts
2	tablespoons sugar
2	tablespoons water
¼	teaspoon salt

1. Line baking sheet with parchment paper. Bring all ingredients to boil in medium saucepan over medium heat. Cook, stirring constantly, until water evaporates and sugar appears dry, opaque, and somewhat crystallized and evenly coats peanuts, about 5 minutes.

2. Reduce heat to low and continue to stir peanuts until sugar turns amber color, about 2 minutes longer. Transfer peanuts to prepared sheet and spread in even layer. Let cool completely, about 10 minutes.

✓ WHY THIS RECIPE WORKS

The original recipe for Derby Pie—the chocolate-walnut-bourbon pie served at Kentucky Derby parties—is the closely guarded secret of the Kern family of Prospect, Kentucky. After tasting the real thing, we were jockeying to re-create this top-secret pie at home. We kept the filling's sweetness in check with a combination of brown and white sugars and used cornstarch for thickening. Browned butter added depth, and a hit of bourbon gave the filling a nutty, boozy flavor that paired well with the toasted walnuts. Parbaking the shell ensured a crisp crust under the filling, but the warm crust was an opportunity to sprinkle the bottom with chopped bittersweet chocolate chunks, which melted so we could spread them into an even layer. We knew we had a Triple Crown winner—a sweet, deeply nutty filling baked in a golden crust with an intense jolt of chocolate in every bite.

THOROUGHBRED PIE

SERVES 8

Homemade crust tastes the best, but you can use store-bought pie dough in this recipe. We like this pie served with a dollop of Bourbon Whipped Cream (page 157).

CRUST

1¼	cups (6¼ ounces) all-purpose flour
1	tablespoon sugar
½	teaspoon salt
4	tablespoons vegetable shortening, cut into ¼-inch pieces and chilled
6	tablespoons unsalted butter, cut into ¼-inch pieces and chilled
3–4	tablespoons ice water
3	ounces bittersweet chocolate, chopped

FILLING

8	tablespoons unsalted butter, cut into 8 pieces
3	tablespoons bourbon
¾	cup (5¼ ounces) granulated sugar
½	cup packed (3½ ounces) light brown sugar
2	tablespoons cornstarch
½	teaspoon salt
2	large eggs plus 1 large yolk, lightly beaten
1	teaspoon vanilla extract
1½	cups walnuts, toasted and chopped

1. FOR THE CRUST: Process flour, sugar, and salt in food processor until combined, about 5 seconds. Scatter shortening over top and process until mixture resembles coarse cornmeal, about 10 seconds. Scatter butter over top and pulse until mixture resembles coarse crumbs, about 10 pulses. Transfer to bowl.

2. Sprinkle 3 tablespoons ice water over flour mixture. Using rubber spatula, stir and press dough until it sticks together. If dough does not come together, add remaining 1 tablespoon water. Turn out dough onto sheet of plastic wrap and form dough into 4-inch disk, wrap tightly in plastic wrap, and refrigerate for 1 hour.

3. Let chilled dough soften slightly, about 10 minutes, before rolling. (Wrapped dough can be refrigerated for up to 2 days or frozen for up to 1 month. If frozen, let dough thaw completely on counter before rolling.) Roll dough into 12-inch circle on lightly floured counter. Loosely roll dough around rolling pin and gently unroll it onto 9-inch pie plate, letting excess dough hang over edge. Ease dough into plate by gently lifting edge of dough with 1 hand while pressing into plate bottom with your other hand.

4. Trim overhang to ½ inch beyond lip of pie plate. Tuck overhang under itself; folded edge should be flush with edge of pie plate. Crimp dough evenly around edge of pie plate using your fingers. Wrap dough-lined pie plate loosely in plastic and freeze until dough is firm, about 30 minutes. Adjust oven rack to lower-middle position and heat oven to 375 degrees.

5. Line chilled pie shell with two 12-inch squares of parchment paper or double layer of aluminum foil, covering edges to prevent burning, and fill with pie weights. Bake until surface of dough no longer looks wet, 20 to 25 minutes. Carefully remove crust from oven and reduce oven temperature to 325 degrees. Remove weights and parchment and sprinkle chocolate over bottom of hot crust. Let chocolate sit for 5 minutes to soften. Using offset spatula, spread chocolate into even layer; set aside crust.

6. FOR THE FILLING: Melt butter in small saucepan over medium-low heat. Cook, stirring constantly, until butter is dark golden brown and has nutty aroma, 5 to 7 minutes. Off heat, slowly stir in bourbon; let cool for 5 minutes.

7. Whisk granulated sugar, brown sugar, cornstarch, and salt together in large bowl until combined. Add eggs and yolk and vanilla, whisking until smooth. Slowly whisk in warm butter mixture until incorporated. Stir in walnuts, then pour filling into chocolate-lined crust. Bake until filling is puffed and center jiggles slightly when pie is gently shaken, 35 to 40 minutes, rotating plate halfway through baking. Let pie cool on wire rack for 4 hours. Slice and serve. (Pie can be covered with plastic and refrigerated for up to 2 days.)

✓ WHY THIS RECIPE WORKS

Named after the minty, creamy cocktail first shaken up in New Orleans, grasshopper pie should boast a billowy chiffon filling in a chocolate-cookie crust. While ice cream pie is what often comes to mind at the mention of this dessert, we wanted to add the original chiffon recipe to our repertoire. We started by softening gelatin in cream with sugar and salt before melting it over medium heat, then whisking the heated mixture into beaten egg yolks. We returned the gelatin-egg mixture to the stove to thicken and then incorporated the cordials: minty green crème de menthe and chocolaty white crème de cacao. After letting the filling firm up in the refrigerator, we doubled up on whipped cream for an ultrafluffy texture, carefully whisking in 1 cup before folding in the rest. A simple cookie crust of minty Oreos mirrored the filling's mint-chocolate flavors.

GRASSHOPPER PIE SERVES 8

Rather than a classic chocolate-cookie crumb crust, we like one made with minty Oreos. Chocolate curls add a professional touch and are easy to make.

CRUST

- 16 Mint Creme Oreo cookies (with filling), broken into rough pieces
- 3 tablespoons unsalted butter, melted and cooled

FILLING

- 3 large egg yolks
- 2 cups heavy cream
- ½ cup (3½ ounces) sugar
-    Pinch salt
- 2 teaspoons unflavored gelatin
- ¼ cup green crème de menthe
- ¼ cup white crème de cacao

   Shaved chocolate curls (optional)

1. FOR THE CRUST: Adjust oven rack to middle position and heat oven to 350 degrees. Process cookies in food processor to fine crumbs, about 45 seconds. Transfer to bowl, drizzle with butter, and toss. Press crumbs evenly into bottom and sides of 9-inch pie plate and refrigerate crust until firm, about 20 minutes. Bake until set, 8 to 10 minutes. Let cool completely on wire rack.

2. FOR THE FILLING: Beat egg yolks in medium bowl. Combine ½ cup cream, sugar, and salt in medium saucepan. Sprinkle gelatin over cream mixture and let sit until gelatin softens, about 5 minutes. Cook over medium heat until gelatin dissolves and mixture is very hot but not boiling, about 2 minutes. Whisking vigorously, slowly add gelatin mixture to egg yolks. Return mixture to saucepan and cook, stirring constantly, until slightly thickened, about 2 minutes. Remove from heat and add crème de menthe and crème de cacao. Pour into clean bowl and refrigerate, stirring occasionally, until filling is wobbly but not set, about 20 minutes.

3. Using stand mixer fitted with whisk, whip remaining 1½ cups cream until foamy, about 1 minute. Increase speed to high and whip until stiff peaks form, 1 to 3 minutes. Whisk 1 cup whipped cream into gelatin mixture until completely incorporated. Using rubber spatula, fold gelatin mixture into remaining whipped cream until no white streaks remain. Scrape mixture into cooled pie shell, smooth top, and refrigerate until firm, at least 6 hours or preferably overnight. (Pie will keep tightly wrapped in refrigerator for up to 2 days.) Serve, topped with chocolate curls if using.

MESS-FREE CRUMB CRUST

While it's easier to put together a crumb crust than to roll out traditional pie dough, that doesn't mean that crumb crusts are problem-free. The crust can be crumbly and loose, and it often sticks to everything but the pie plate. Here's how to make even, mess-free crumb crusts every time:

1. DISTRIBUTE AND PRESS: Use hands to distribute crumbs in even layer over bottom and up sides of pie plate. Press down lightly.

2. SMOOTH INTO PAN: Place plastic wrap on top of crust, then run back of spoon over crumbs, smoothing them into bottom, curves, and sides of pan.

CHOCOLATE CURLS

You'll need a block (not bar) of chocolate—semisweet and bittersweet both work well—that's at least 1 inch thick.

Soften chocolate by microwaving on lowest power setting for 1 minute. It should soften, not melt. Run blade of vegetable peeler along width of the softened chocolate, creating curl.

☑ WHY THIS RECIPE WORKS

Buttermilk pie is a Southern classic, holding its own against pecan, sweet potato, and peach pies with its creamy texture, tangy-sweet taste, and crunchy sugar top. To make ours stand out, we looked to the texture we love in flans and *pots de crème* for the filling. All custards get their richness from egg and heavy cream, so we whisked eggs, egg yolks, and cream together with the standard buttermilk pie components: sugar, vinegar, butter, vanilla, cornstarch, and, of course, plenty of buttermilk. The cornstarch and yolks provided a perfectly wobbly structure, and the vinegar backed up the buttermilk's tasty tang. To prevent a soggy crust, we parbaked the shell and brushed it with an egg white to protect it from the wet filling. Baking the pie at a gentle 300 degrees cooked the filling evenly, but we also wanted a crackly, lightly browned top. A sprinkling of sugar 10 minutes into baking got us on the right track, and increasing the temperature for the last few minutes sealed the deal—the almost-melted sugar caramelized quickly. From its delicate, crackly sugar crust to its rich, creamy filling, our buttermilk pie was simple but full of Southern charm.

BUTTERMILK PIE SERVES 8

Homemade crust tastes the best, but you can use store-bought pie dough in this recipe. Use commercial cultured buttermilk (avoid nonfat), as some locally produced, artisanal buttermilks that we tested were prone to curdling during baking.

CRUST

1¼	cups (6¼ ounces) all-purpose flour
1	tablespoon sugar
½	teaspoon salt
4	tablespoons vegetable shortening, cut into ¼-inch pieces and chilled
6	tablespoons unsalted butter, cut into ¼-inch pieces and chilled
3–4	tablespoons ice water
1	large egg white, lightly beaten

FILLING

¾	cup (5¼ ounces) plus 2 teaspoons sugar
1	tablespoon cornstarch
¾	teaspoon salt
2	large eggs plus 5 large yolks
1¾	cups buttermilk
¼	cup heavy cream
4	tablespoons unsalted butter, melted
2	teaspoons distilled white vinegar
1½	teaspoons vanilla extract

1. FOR THE CRUST: Process flour, sugar, and salt in food processor until combined, about 5 seconds. Scatter shortening over top and process until mixture resembles coarse cornmeal, about 10 seconds. Scatter butter over top and pulse until mixture resembles coarse crumbs, about 10 pulses. Transfer to bowl.

2. Sprinkle 3 tablespoons ice water over flour mixture. Using rubber spatula, stir and press dough until it sticks together. If dough does not come together, add remaining 1 tablespoon water. Turn out dough onto sheet of plastic wrap and form dough into 4-inch disk, wrap tightly in plastic wrap, and refrigerate for 1 hour.

3. Let chilled dough soften slightly, about 10 minutes, before rolling. (Wrapped dough can be refrigerated for up to 2 days or frozen for up to 1 month. If frozen, let dough thaw completely on counter before rolling.) Roll dough into 12-inch circle on lightly floured counter. Loosely roll dough around rolling pin and gently unroll it onto 9-inch pie plate, letting excess dough hang over edge. Ease dough into plate by gently lifting edge of dough with 1 hand while pressing into plate bottom with your other hand.

4. Trim overhang to ½ inch beyond lip of pie plate. Tuck overhang under itself; folded edge should be flush with edge of pie plate. Crimp dough evenly around edge of pie plate using your fingers. Wrap dough-lined pie plate loosely in plastic and freeze until dough is firm, about 30 minutes. Adjust oven racks to upper-middle and lower-middle positions and heat oven to 375 degrees.

5. Line chilled pie shell with two 12-inch squares of parchment paper or double layer of aluminum foil, covering edges to prevent burning, and fill with pie weights. Place pie plate on rimmed baking sheet and bake on lower-middle oven rack until lightly golden around edges, 20 to 25 minutes. Carefully remove weights and parchment, rotate sheet, and continue to bake until golden brown, 5 to 7 minutes. Brush surface of hot crust with egg white (you won't need all of it to coat crust) and bake for 1 minute longer.

6. FOR THE FILLING: Meanwhile, whisk ¾ cup sugar, cornstarch, and salt together in large bowl. Whisk eggs and yolks into sugar mixture until well combined. Whisk buttermilk, cream, melted butter, vinegar, and vanilla into sugar-egg mixture until incorporated.

7. Reduce oven temperature to 300 degrees. Whisk buttermilk mixture to recombine and, leaving pie shell in oven, carefully pour buttermilk mixture into hot pie shell. Bake for 10 minutes.

8. Sprinkle remaining 2 teaspoons sugar evenly over top of pie. Continue to bake until center jiggles slightly when pie is shaken, 30 to 40 minutes. Remove pie from oven and increase oven temperature to 450 degrees. Once oven comes to temperature, place pie on upper-middle oven rack and bake until golden brown on top, 5 to 7 minutes. Let pie cool for 30 minutes on wire rack. Transfer to refrigerator to chill, about 3 hours. Serve.

✔ WHY THIS RECIPE WORKS

From its funny name to its starring ingredient, the little-known sweet potato sonker baffles food historians to this day. One thing remains clear, though: This isn't your typical sweet potato pie. Where the more familiar pie delivers a creamy filling of mashed sweet potatoes in a single crust, sonker serves up sliced sweet potatoes tossed with brown sugar and spices, baked under a lattice-top crust, and drizzled with a sweet, spiced, custard "dip." For soft, flavorful sweet potatoes that held their shape, we steamed the slices over apple cider until almost tender, then reduced the cider and tossed the sweets with the concentrated liquid. A combination of cinnamon, allspice, lemon juice, and sugar boosted the filling's warm, homey flavors. Once cooled, we spread the slices in a parbaked crust and folded strips of the top crust into a lattice. Brushing the lattice with beaten egg and finishing with a sprinkling of cinnamon sugar gave it a spice-flecked, crunchy coating. For the creamy dip, we simmered milk, sugar, cinnamon, and cornstarch together, adding vanilla off the heat. After we took just one bite of this sweet and spiced sonker, its unusual name was no laughing matter.

CAROLINA SWEET POTATO SONKER   SERVES 12

It takes a big sheet of pie dough to line a 13 by 9-inch baking dish. We make it easy by using store-bought pie dough.

SONKER

- 2 packages store-bought pie dough
- 1 large egg, beaten
- 2 cups apple cider
- 4 pounds sweet potatoes, peeled, quartered lengthwise, and sliced ¼ inch thick
- 1 cup packed (7 ounces) light brown sugar
- 4 tablespoons unsalted butter, softened
- 2½ tablespoons all-purpose flour
- 2 tablespoons lemon juice
- 1 teaspoon vanilla extract
- ¾ teaspoon ground cinnamon
- ½ teaspoon ground allspice
- ¼ teaspoon salt
- 1 tablespoon granulated sugar

CUSTARD DIP

- 2 cups whole milk
- ¼ cup (1¾ ounces) granulated sugar
- 2 teaspoons cornstarch
- ¼ teaspoon ground cinnamon
- ⅛ teaspoon salt
- 1½ teaspoons vanilla extract

1. FOR THE SONKER: Unroll 2 dough rounds on lightly floured counter. Brush half of 1 round with egg. Overlap half of second round over egg-coated portion of first. Roll dough into 17 by 13-inch rectangle; fit dough into 13 by 9-inch baking dish. Cover with plastic wrap and refrigerate for 30 minutes. Line rimmed baking sheet with parchment paper. Repeat shaping and rolling with remaining 2 rounds; set aside egg. Trim dough into rectangle and cut into ten 1-inch strips. Transfer strips to prepared sheet, cover with plastic, and refrigerate for 30 minutes.

2. While dough chills, adjust oven rack to middle position and heat oven to 375 degrees. Bring cider to boil in Dutch oven. Place steamer basket in pot and fill with sweet potatoes. Reduce heat to medium and cook, covered, until potatoes are nearly tender, 20 to 30 minutes. Remove potatoes, leaving cider in pot.

3. Cook cider over high heat until reduced to ½ cup, about 5 minutes. Combine brown sugar, butter, flour, lemon juice, vanilla, ½ teaspoon cinnamon, allspice,

salt, drained potatoes, and reduced cider in large bowl. Spread potato mixture in rimmed baking sheet and let cool completely, about 20 minutes.

4. Transfer potato mixture to dough-lined dish and press into even layer. Brush edges of dough with reserved egg. With long side facing you, lay 4 dough strips lengthwise over potato mixture (strips will be longer than dish). Fold back first and third strips and lay perpendicular strip across second and fourth strips. Unfold first and third strips, covering perpendicular strip. Repeat with remaining 5 strips, alternating between folding back first and third strips and second and fourth strips. Press dough strips into edges of crust and trim excess. Fold dough sides inward under lip of baking dish and crimp with fork.

5. Combine granulated sugar and remaining ¼ teaspoon cinnamon in bowl. Brush dough with reserved egg and sprinkle with cinnamon sugar. Cover with foil and bake for 15 minutes. Uncover and bake until deep golden brown, 55 minutes to 1 hour, rotating dish halfway through baking. Let sonker cool on wire rack for at least 1½ hours before serving. (Sonker can be refrigerated for up to 24 hours. Bring sonker to room temperature before serving.)

6. FOR THE CUSTARD DIP: While sonker cools, bring milk, sugar, cornstarch, cinnamon, and salt to simmer in medium saucepan over medium heat. Reduce heat to medium-low and cook, whisking frequently, until slightly thickened, about 15 minutes. Off heat, add vanilla. Transfer dip to bowl and let cool completely, about 30 minutes. Serve sonker with dip.

WEAVING A LATTICE FOR SONKER

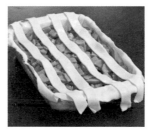 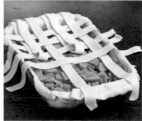

1. Evenly lay 4 dough strips of dough parallel to the long side of dish.

2. Fold first and third strips back; lay perpendicular strip across other 2. Unfold strips to cover. Continue, alternating sets of strips.

THE MIDWEST AND GREAT PLAINS

CANADA

KNOEPHLA SOUP
NORTH DAKOTA

IOWA SKINNIES
DES MOINES, IA

IRON RANGE PORKETTA
HIBBING, MN

GREEN BAY BOOYAH
GREEN BAY, WI

CHICKEN VESUVIO
CHICAGO, IL

NORTH DAKOTA

MINNESOTA

SOUTH DAKOTA

WISCONSIN

MICHIGAN

IOWA

NEBRASKA

ILLINOIS

OHIO

INDIANA

KANSAS

MISSOURI

BUCKEYES
COLUMBUS, OH

BIEROCKS
NEBRASKA AND KANSAS

THE BEST REUBEN SANDWICHES
OMAHA, NE

ST. LOUIS GOOEY BUTTER CAKE
ST. LOUIS, MO

173 **Cheese Frenchees**

175 **Iowa Loose Meat Sandwiches** ★

177 **Iowa Skinnies**

179 **Prosperity Sandwiches**

181 **The Best Reuben Sandwiches**

183 **Iron Range Porketta**

185 **Chicago-Style Italian Roast Beef**

187 **Chicago-Style Italian Beef Sandwiches** ★

Quick Jus

189 **Wisconsin Grilled Brats and Beer**

191 **Wisconsin Cheddar Beer Soup**

193 **Green Bay Booyah**

195 **Knoephla Soup**

197 **Barberton Fried Chicken** ★

Barberton Hot Sauce

199 **Chicken Vesuvio**

201 **Steak de Burgo**

203 **Bierocks**

205 **Kielbasa Casserole**

207 **Pork Chop Casserole**

209 **Kansas City Barbecued Brisket**

211 **Kansas City Sticky Ribs**

213 **Smoky Kansas City Barbecue Beans**

215 **Crumb-Coated Baked Ham**

Hot Mustard Sauce

217 **Hoppel Poppel**

219 **Goetta**

Perfect Fried Eggs

221 **Swedish Pancakes**

223 **Dilly Casserole Bread**

225 **Sand Tarts**

227 **Kringle**

229 **Blueberry Boy Bait**

231 **St. Louis Gooey Butter Cake**

Butterscotch Gooey Butter Cake

Chocolate Gooey Butter Cake

233 **Buckeyes**

★ FIND A LOCAL HOT SPOT

✔ WHY THIS RECIPE WORKS

The deep-fried grilled cheese sandwiches known as Frenchees won the now-closed Midwestern family restaurant King's Food Host hordes of fans in the 1960s. Long before folks were deep-frying everything from cookies to pickles, this Nebraska-based restaurant chain was making the grilled cheese sandwich even more irresistible by coating the buttery bread and gooey cheese filling in a golden, fried crust. To re-create the Frenchee at home, we began with a simple grilled cheese sandwich: American cheese between two slices of hearty white bread with a smear of mayo for extra richness. We sliced the sandwiches into triangles and dunked them in an egg-milk mixture before breading them in coarse Ritz cracker crumbs. Chilling the Frenchees in the refrigerator for about an hour set the crust. We heated oil in a Dutch oven to protect us from hot splatter and fried our chilled Frenchees until golden brown. These sandwiches were as temptingly crunchy and cheesy as we imagined, and a dip in ketchup sealed the deal.

CHEESE FRENCHEES SERVES 4

Though many recipes don't specify a brand of cracker, we like Ritz here. Try dipping the sandwiches in ketchup—a Frenchee fanatic told us that's how she ate them growing up in Oklahoma.

1½	sleeves Ritz crackers (50 crackers), pulsed in food processor to coarse crumbs
⅔	cup milk
2	large eggs
½	cup mayonnaise
8	slices hearty white sandwich bread
6	slices deli American cheese
3-4	quarts peanut or vegetable oil

1. Line rimmed baking sheet with parchment paper. Spread cracker crumbs in shallow dish. Whisk milk and eggs together in medium bowl. Spread mayonnaise on 1 side of each slice bread. Arrange 1½ slices cheese on 4 slices bread and top with remaining 4 slices bread, mayonnaise side facing cheese. Cut each sandwich diagonally into quarters. One at a time, dip sandwich quarters into egg mixture, then coat with cracker crumbs, pressing to adhere. Refrigerate on prepared baking sheet until set, about 1 hour.

2. Pour oil into large Dutch oven until it measures 2 inches deep. Heat oil to 375 degrees over medium-high heat. Fry half of chilled sandwich quarters until golden brown, 1 to 2 minutes per side. Transfer to paper towel–lined plate and repeat with remaining sandwich quarters. Serve.

FRYING SUCCESS

When done right, frying isn't difficult. It all comes down to the temperature of the oil. If the oil is too hot, the exterior of the food will burn before it cooks through. If it's not hot enough, the food won't release moisture and will fry up limp and soggy. Follow our tips for frying Frenchees and all your fried foods.

HAVE THE RIGHT THERMOMETER: A thermometer that can register high temperatures is essential. One that clips to the side of the pot, like a candy thermometer, saves you from dipping a thermometer in and out of a pot of hot oil.

USE A LARGE, HEAVY POT: A heavy pot or Dutch oven that is at least 6 quarts in capacity ensures even heating, helps to keep the oil hot, and gives the food plenty of room to fry.

FRY IN BATCHES: Add food to the hot oil in small portions. Adding too much food at once will make the temperature drop too much and will turn out soggy—rather than crisp—fried food.

LET THE FRIED FOOD DRAIN: Let the finished food drain on paper towels or a wire rack to minimize greasiness.

REUSE THE OIL: Unless you have used it to fry fish, don't throw away your fry oil—you can use it three or four more times. To save oil for another use, let the oil cool to room temperature, then filter it through a strainer lined with two or three layers of cheesecloth or paper coffee filters to remove any bits of food. For short-term storage, store oils (leftover or new) in a cool, dark spot, since exposure to air and light makes oil turn rancid faster. But for long-term storage (beyond one month), the cooler the storage temperature, the better—we recommend the freezer.

✔ WHY THIS RECIPE WORKS

At first glance, the Iowa loose meat sandwich looks like a Sloppy Joe gone wrong, but one taste of its savory, flavorful ground beef proves it's just right. For meat that stayed tasty and moist when cooked well done, we used 85 percent lean ground beef. We kept our seasoning simple, adding only salt, pepper, tangy yellow mustard, and a teaspoon of sugar to give the beef some subtle sweetness. Without a classic Maid-Rite steam box on hand, we used a skillet to simmer the beef and seasoning in water. Chopped onion added extra flavor, and covering the pan steamed the loose meat filling to perfection. A smear of mustard on the hamburger buns and a few dill pickle slices were all the condiments we needed. Though not much to look at, these juicy, crumbly loose meat sandwiches won us over with one bite.

IOWA LOOSE MEAT SANDWICHES   SERVES 4

Do not substitute leaner ground beef in this recipe or the sandwich will be dry.

- **1**   **pound 85 percent lean ground beef**
- **¼**   **cup water**
- **1**   **tablespoon yellow mustard, plus extra for serving**
- **1**   **teaspoon sugar**
- **1**   **teaspoon salt**
- **1**   **teaspoon pepper**
- **½**   **cup finely chopped onion**
- **4**   **hamburger buns**
-      **Sliced dill pickles**

1. Combine beef, water, mustard, sugar, salt, and pepper in 10-inch skillet. Bring to simmer over medium heat, breaking up meat with spoon. Reduce heat to medium-low to maintain gentle simmer and cook, stirring frequently, until meat is no longer pink, about 5 minutes. Stir in onion, cover, and remove from heat; keep warm while preparing buns.

2. Spread extra mustard on bun bottoms, then, using slotted spoon, mound beef mixture on top. Cap with pickles and bun tops. Serve.

EATING LOCAL ★ MARSHALLTOWN, IA

In earlier days, the loose meat sandwich was ubiquitous throughout the states of Iowa, Minnesota, Nebraska, Illinois, and Kansas. If you ask folks in central Iowa, this beloved sandwich is properly called a Maid-Rite, after the Maid-Rite chain that made it famous. In other states, though, you might find it sold under different aliases: a tavern, a steamer, a Big T, and a tastee, to name a few.

Whatever you call it, the sandwich can still be found in a handful of diners and small restaurants around the central Midwest, and Iowa claims some 30 remaining Maid-Rite franchises. John "Doc" Willoughby, *Cook's Country*'s editorial director and a native of Grundy Center, Iowa, helped us understand the beauty (and simplicity) of the sandwich. Doc was a regular at Hulne's Maid-Rite in his hometown until it closed some 40 years ago. After that, he had to get his loose meat fix at **TAYLOR'S MAID-RITE** in nearby Marshalltown, which is still open today. The recipe hasn't changed substantially since its debut there in 1928. As all Maid-Rites used to do, Taylor's grinds its meat daily and uses a large steam box to cook and hold the lightly seasoned meat. As for the seasonings, that's something of a mystery. Plenty of aficionados on the Internet claim to have nailed the formula, but there's little consensus. Most agree on the basics: salt and pepper. Beyond that, some call for sugar, Worcestershire sauce, mustard, beef bouillon, soy sauce, or paprika. The beef has no sauce, per se—nothing to really bind it together. In fact, the sandwich is served with a spoon to scoop up all the beef that escapes from the wax paper wrapping. We recommend napkins, too.

TAYLOR'S MAID-RITE
106 S. 3rd Ave.
Marshalltown, IA

✓ WHY THIS RECIPE WORKS

Don't let the name fool you—the crunchy, fried pork tenderloin sandwich known as the "skinny" is not light fare. All over Iowa, pork tenderloins are pounded thin, breaded, fried, and served on hamburger buns. A trimmed pork tenderloin was the key ingredient, sliced into four even pieces and pounded into almost comically oversize cutlets. For the breading, the cutlets were coated with flour, dipped in a tangy, rich mixture of egg and mayonnaise, and rolled in a crunchy blend of saltines and bread crumbs. With cutlets so thin, we were able to fry our skinnies to a crisp, deep golden color in under 5 minutes without overcooking. Following Iowa skinny custom, we served our crunchy cutlets on a soft bun with shredded iceberg lettuce, tomato slices, and mayonnaise.

IOWA SKINNIES SERVES 4

After the tenderloin is cut into pieces in step 1, each piece should weigh roughly 4 ounces.

- **1 (1-pound) pork tenderloin, trimmed**
  Salt and pepper
- **3 slices hearty white sandwich bread,**
  torn into quarters
- **16 square or 18 round saltines**
- **½ cup all-purpose flour**
- **2 large eggs**
- **¼ cup mayonnaise, plus extra for serving**
- **1 cup vegetable oil**
- **4 hamburger buns**
- **¼ head iceberg lettuce (2¼ ounces), shredded**
- **1 tomato, cored and sliced**

1. Adjust oven rack to middle position and heat oven to 200 degrees. Set wire rack in rimmed baking sheet. Cut tenderloin in half. Cut each half in half again, cutting tapered tail piece slightly thicker than middle medallions. Cover pork pieces, cut side up, with plastic wrap and pound to ¼-inch thickness with meat pounder. Pat cutlets dry with paper towels and season with salt and pepper.

2. Pulse bread and saltines in food processor to fine crumbs, about 12 pulses; transfer to shallow dish. Spread flour in second shallow dish. Whisk eggs and mayonnaise together in third shallow dish.

3. Working with 1 cutlet at a time, dredge cutlets in flour, dip in egg mixture, then coat with crumbs, pressing gently to adhere. Transfer cutlets to prepared wire rack and let dry for 5 minutes or refrigerate for up to 1 hour.

4. Heat ½ cup oil in 12-inch nonstick skillet over medium heat until shimmering. Working with 2 cutlets at a time, fry cutlets until deep golden brown and crisp, 2 to 3 minutes per side. Transfer to paper towel–lined plate and keep warm in oven. Discard oil, wipe out skillet, and repeat with remaining ½ cup oil and remaining 2 cutlets. Serve on hamburger buns with lettuce, tomato, and extra mayonnaise.

THE SKINNY ON PORK CUTLETS

1. Use paring knife to remove any silverskin or extraneous fat from tenderloin.

2. Cut trimmed tenderloin into 4 equal pieces.

3. Cover each piece of pork with plastic wrap and pound into ¼-inch-thick cutlets.

✓ WHY THIS RECIPE WORKS

Though this open-faced sandwich is a great way to use up leftover turkey, we wanted to make our version of this Midwestern melt a standout meal worth a trip to the deli counter. For prosperity sandwiches with a wealth of flavor, we paired slices of roast turkey and ham with a rich cheese sauce, earthy sautéed mushrooms, and sliced tomatoes—but the challenge would be protecting the crusty toasted bread. Starting with a roux of butter and flour, we whisked together a thick cheese sauce of milk, shredded cheddar, spicy Dijon, Worcestershire, and pepper. Sautéing white mushrooms with shallot and butter until the juice evaporated concentrated their flavor and dried them enough to prevent soggy toast. After layering the mushrooms, meat, and tomatoes on the bread, we finished with a generous helping of the cheese sauce and an extra sprinkling of cheddar. After a few minutes under the broiler our prosperity sandwiches emerged with melted, golden-brown cheese coating the warm toppings. The toast stayed crisp, crunchy, and dry, and with so much gooey cheese to enjoy, we felt prosperous indeed.

PROSPERITY SANDWICHES SERVES 4

Leftover roast turkey works great here.

- **5** **tablespoons unsalted butter**
- **8** **ounces white mushrooms, trimmed and sliced thin**
- **1** **shallot, minced**
- **½** **teaspoon salt**
- **¼** **cup all-purpose flour**
- **2** **cups whole milk**
- **8** **ounces sharp cheddar cheese, shredded (2 cups)**
- **2** **teaspoons Dijon mustard**
- **2** **teaspoons Worcestershire sauce**
- **½** **teaspoon pepper**
- **4** **(¾-inch-thick) slices rustic white bread**
- **8** **ounces thinly sliced roast turkey**
- **8** **ounces thinly sliced deli ham**
- **2** **tomatoes, cored, cut into 8 (¼-inch-thick) slices, and patted dry**

1. Melt 1 tablespoon butter in large saucepan over medium-high heat. Add mushrooms, shallot, and salt and cook, stirring occasionally, until well browned, 5 to 7 minutes. Transfer to bowl.

2. Melt remaining 4 tablespoons butter in now-empty saucepan over medium heat. Stir in flour and cook for 1 minute. Slowly whisk in milk and bring to simmer. Reduce heat to low and cook, stirring occasionally, until thickened, 4 to 6 minutes. Off heat, stir in ½ cup cheddar, mustard, Worcestershire, and pepper; set aside.

3. Adjust oven rack 5 inches from broiler element and heat broiler. Line rimmed baking sheet with aluminum foil and spray with vegetable oil spray. Arrange bread slices on prepared baking sheet and broil until toasted, 1 to 2 minutes per side.

4. Divide mushroom mixture among toasted bread slices. Arrange 2 ounces turkey, 2 ounces ham, and 2 slices tomato over mushrooms on each slice of toast. Spoon ½ cup cheese sauce evenly over each sandwich and sprinkle with remaining 1½ cups cheddar. Broil until cheddar is browned, 3 to 5 minutes. Let cool for 5 minutes. Serve.

BROILER HEAT

It's good to know if your broiler runs relatively hot, average, or cold. This information allows you to adjust the cooking time for recipes accordingly. To see how your broiler stacks up, heat it on high and place a slice of white sandwich bread directly under the heating element on the upper-middle rack. If the bread toasts to golden brown in 30 seconds or less, your broiler runs very hot, and you will need to reduce the cooking time by a minute or two. If the bread toasts perfectly in 1 minute, your broiler runs about average. If the bread takes 2 minutes or longer to toast, your broiler runs cool and you may need to increase the cooking time by a minute or two.

A SANDWICH IN EVERY POT?

During the Great Depression, Mayfair Hotel chef Edward Voegeli in St. Louis came up with the recipe for the knife-and fork "prosperity" sandwich. What's in the name? Apparently, an insult. The humble, albeit tasty, dish was intended as a dig at then-president Herbert Hoover and his (failed) promises that prosperity was just around the corner.

✅ WHY THIS RECIPE WORKS

The Nebraska-born Reuben is a deli counter staple, but at-home adaptations of this corned beef sandwich often yield wet rye with a chilly filling. To prevent waterlogged bread, we drained and quickly cooked the sauerkraut to remove excess moisture. Cider vinegar and brown sugar contributed great tang to the store-bought kraut, and our own hybrid of Russian and Thousand Island dressings added a zesty, creamy layer of flavor. To ensure gooey cheese and a warm center, we used quick-melting shredded Swiss cheese and cooked our sandwiches in a covered skillet. Our efforts paid off—our Reubens were warm and tangy, and the rye (and our hands) stayed nice and dry.

THE BEST REUBEN SANDWICHES SERVES 4

Corned beef is typically made from either the brisket or the round. We prefer the corned beef brisket. We find pouched sauerkraut, sold near the pickles in most supermarkets, more flavorful than jarred or canned varieties.

¼	**cup mayonnaise**
¼	**cup finely chopped sweet pickles plus 1 teaspoon sweet pickle juice**
2	**tablespoons cocktail sauce**
1	**cup sauerkraut, drained and rinsed**
2	**tablespoons cider vinegar**
1	**teaspoon brown sugar**
8	**slices rye bread**
1	**cup shredded Swiss cheese (4 ounces)**
12	**ounces thinly sliced deli corned beef**
4	**tablespoons unsalted butter**

1. Whisk mayonnaise, pickles, pickle juice, and cocktail sauce together in small bowl; set aside. Cook sauerkraut, vinegar, and sugar in 12-inch skillet over medium-high heat, stirring occasionally, until liquid evaporates, about 3 minutes. Transfer sauerkraut to bowl and wipe out skillet.

2. Spread dressing evenly on 1 side of each slice bread. Layer half of cheese on 4 slices bread, then top with half of corned beef. Divide sauerkraut evenly over meat, then top with remaining corned beef and remaining cheese. Arrange remaining 4 slices bread, dressing side down, over cheese.

3. Melt 2 tablespoons butter in now-empty skillet over medium heat. Place 2 sandwiches in pan and cook until golden brown on first side, 2 to 3 minutes. Flip sandwiches and cook, covered, over medium-low heat until second side is golden brown and cheese is melted, about 2 minutes longer. Transfer to wire rack and repeat with remaining 2 tablespoons butter and remaining 2 sandwiches. Serve.

REINVENTING REUBEN

Soggy rye bread and a cold interior are common problems for many homemade Reubens. To prevent a squishy situation, we quickly cook the sauerkraut to evaporate excess moisture. As an added bonus, the cooked 'kraut also helps to warm up the middle of the sandwich.

NOT SO FAST, NEW YORK

The grilled Reuben is the epitome of a New York deli sandwich, but even *The New York Times* reports that the Reuben was created in the 1920s at the Blackstone Hotel in Omaha, Nebraska, when a local grocer, Reuben Kulakofsky, concocted it for his poker buddies, then convinced the hotel owner to put it on the menu. A waitress there won a national contest with the sandwich in the 1950s and it soon swept the country. Good taste travels!

✔ WHY THIS RECIPE WORKS

Porketta sandwiches are as ubiquitous as hamburgers in Minnesota's Iron Range, but they are virtually unknown elsewhere. Hoping to introduce this heavily seasoned shredded pork specialty to a wider audience, we started by infusing a boneless pork butt roast with the signature porketta spices—fennel and garlic. To maximize the seasoning's penetration and to shorten the roast's cooking time, we butterflied the meat and cut a crosshatch pattern into both sides. We rubbed a mixture of cracked fennel seeds, salt, pepper, and granulated garlic into the meat before wrapping it in plastic wrap and refrigerating it for 6 hours. The pork butt's licorice flavor was reinforced when we spread chopped fresh fennel over its surface just before roasting. The roast was tender and ready for shredding in about 3 hours, and after we tossed the bite-size pieces of meat with some of the drippings, our flavor-packed porketta was fit to serve. This sandwich was almost too good to share—but we decided it was high time this Iron Range mainstay made its big debut.

IRON RANGE PORKETTA

SERVES 8

Pork butt roast is often labeled "Boston butt" in the supermarket. This recipe calls for granulated garlic, which has a well-rounded garlic flavor. It is golden and has the texture of table salt. Garlic powder is paler, with the texture of flour, and can be acrid. Don't confuse the two or substitute garlic powder in this recipe. To crack the fennel seeds, spread them on a cutting board, place a skillet on top, and press down firmly with both hands. The porketta tastes best when the raw meat sits in the refrigerator for a full 24 hours with the spices.

- 3 **tablespoons fennel seeds, cracked**
   Salt and pepper
- 2 **teaspoons granulated garlic**
- 1 **(5-pound) boneless pork butt roast, trimmed**
- 1 **fennel bulb, stalks discarded, bulb halved, cored, and chopped**
- 8 **crusty sandwich rolls**

1. Combine fennel seeds, 1 tablespoon salt, 2 teaspoons pepper, and granulated garlic in bowl. Slice through pork parallel to counter, stopping ½ inch from edge, then open meat flat like a book. Cut ¼-inch-deep slits, spaced 1 inch apart, in crosshatch pattern on both sides of roast. Rub roast all over with spice mixture, taking care to work spices into crosshatch. Wrap roast tightly with plastic wrap and refrigerate for at least 6 hours or up to 24 hours.

2. Adjust oven rack to middle position and heat oven to 325 degrees. Unwrap meat and place in roasting pan, fat side down. Spread chopped fennel evenly over top of roast. Cover roasting pan tightly with aluminum foil. Roast until meat registers 200 degrees and fork slips easily in and out of meat, 3 to 4 hours.

3. Transfer pork to carving board and let rest for 30 minutes. Strain liquid in roasting pan through fine-mesh strainer into fat separator; discard solids. Shred pork into bite-size pieces, return to pan, and toss with ½ cup defatted cooking liquid. Season with salt and pepper to taste. Divide meat among rolls and serve.

PREPPING THE PORKETTA

We butterfly and crosshatch the pork roast to expose maximum surface area to soak up seasoning.

1. BUTTERFLY: Slice through pork parallel to counter, stopping ½ inch from edge. Then open meat flat like a book.

2. CROSSHATCH: Use chef's knife to cut 1-inch crosshatch pattern ¼ inch deep on both sides of meat.

ITALIAN ROOTS IN MINNESOTA SOIL

If you follow food media, you'd think that porchetta has been popularized in recent years by Brooklyn's hipster food elite. Well, Hibbing, Minnesota, might have something on Park Slope. We went out to Minnesota to meet Mark Thune, president of Fraboni's, which has been making porketta (a cousin of porchetta) since 1968. The wholesale meat company was the offshoot of a grocery store that founder Leo Fraboni's parents opened at the turn of the last century. The locally famous recipe was his mom's and called for fresh fennel—easy to find in her native Italy but much harder to procure in Hibbing at that time. To ensure a steady supply, Leo grew his own, and one year, when the fennel crop failed, Fraboni's refused to make porketta at all. Today, they still grow their own fennel; it's harvested over the summer and frozen for use in porketta year-round. That's the kind of thrift we admire.

⊘ WHY THIS RECIPE WORKS

In Chicago, bold, flavorful Italian roast beef is served au jus after an overnight marinade and a lengthy oven braise. We wanted the same zesty, seasoned beef without the wait, so we turned to a spicy rub rather than a marinade. A blend of garlic powder, dried basil and oregano, and pepper did the trick, and browning the surface of the roast before applying the rub ensured a flavorful crust. Cooking chopped onion, minced garlic, flour, and some of our spice rub in the roast's rendered fat established our jus's base; chicken and beef broths boosted its savory flavors. With our sirloin roast nestled in a V-rack, we applied the spice rub, bolstered with salt, pepper flakes, and oil (added for easy adhering), and poured the jus into the roasting pan below. As the meat roasted in the oven, its drippings landed right in the jus, reinforcing its meaty flavor even further. With our juicy medium-rare beef, its garlicky herbed crust, and spicy jus all ready in record time, the Windy City's favorite Sunday dinner was now a dish we would happily serve any day of the week—making sure to leave some leftovers for Chicago-Style Italian Beef Sandwiches (page 187)!

CHICAGO-STYLE ITALIAN ROAST BEEF   SERVES 6 TO 8

If your roast is larger than 4 pounds, you may need to increase the cooking time slightly in step 4. Save leftover meat and jus for Chicago-Style Italian Beef Sandwiches (page 187).

4	teaspoons garlic powder
4	teaspoons dried basil
4	teaspoons dried oregano
1	tablespoon pepper
1	(4-pound) top sirloin roast, fat trimmed to ¼ inch
2	tablespoons vegetable oil
1	onion, chopped fine
3	garlic cloves, minced
1	tablespoon all-purpose flour
2	cups beef broth
2	cups chicken broth
1½	cups water
2	teaspoons salt
1	teaspoon red pepper flakes

1. Adjust oven rack to lower-middle position and heat oven to 300 degrees. Set V-rack in roasting pan.

Combine garlic powder, basil, oregano, and pepper in small bowl; set aside.

2. Pat roast dry with paper towels. Heat 1 tablespoon oil in 12-inch skillet over medium-high heat until just smoking. Brown roast on all sides, about 10 minutes; transfer to V-rack.

3. Add onion to now-empty skillet and cook over medium heat until softened, about 5 minutes. Stir in garlic, flour, and 1 teaspoon reserved spice mixture until fragrant, about 1 minute. Stir in beef broth, chicken broth, and water, scraping up any browned bits. Bring mixture to boil, then pour into roasting pan.

4. Stir salt, pepper flakes, and remaining 1 tablespoon oil into remaining spice mixture. Rub mixture all over roast, transfer to oven, and cook until meat registers 120 to 125 degrees (for medium-rare), 1¼ to 1½ hours. Transfer roast to carving board, tent loosely with aluminum foil, and let rest for 20 minutes.

5. Pour jus from roasting pan through fine-mesh strainer and keep warm. Slice roast crosswise against grain into ¼-inch-thick slices. Serve with jus.

BUILDING BETTER FLAVOR

1. Brown meat before roasting to create flavorful crust on exterior. Transfer roast to V-rack in roasting pan and begin work on jus.

2. Keep browned bits left behind in pan as base for jus. Cook onion, garlic, and seasonings in empty skillet, then add broths and water to help loosen browned bits.

3. Pour jus into roasting pan below elevated roast so it can catch flavorful drippings and cook down to desired consistency while meat cooks.

4. Apply rub, mixed with oil to help it adhere, after browning to prevent dried herbs from burning.

✓ WHY THIS RECIPE WORKS

Italian beef sandwiches are a Chicago specialty that you simply won't find anywhere else. From the spicy giardiniera to the jus-soaked roll, the flavors are bright, bold, and well equipped to stand up to juicy, generously seasoned Chicago-Style Italian Roast Beef (page 185). To quickly marry the sandwich's bold flavors, we simmered the meat, jus, and jarred giardiniera brine until the beef was no longer pink. For a rich, spicy relish that stayed put and didn't turn our bread soggy, we used the drained giardiniera and pulsed the vegetables in the food processor with mayonnaise and red pepper flakes. Brushing the sub rolls with oil and toasting them under the broiler made for a sturdy sandwich, ready to sop up the flavorful jus. Our kitchen may not have the same charm as the Little Italy eateries that made these sandwiches famous, but our take on their spicy claim to fame tasted like the real deal.

CHICAGO-STYLE ITALIAN BEEF SANDWICHES SERVES 4

If you don't have enough leftover jus, make our Quick Jus (recipe follows).

- 4 (6-inch) sub rolls, partially split lengthwise
- 1 tablespoon vegetable oil
- 4 cups thinly sliced leftover roast beef
- 1½ cups leftover jus
- 1 (16-ounce) bottle giardiniera, drained, 1 tablespoon brine reserved
- 1 tablespoon mayonnaise
- ¼ teaspoon red pepper flakes

1. Adjust oven rack to upper-middle position and heat broiler. Brush interior of rolls with oil and arrange, oiled side up, on baking sheet. Broil until golden brown, about 1 minute.

2. Combine beef, jus, and giardiniera brine in 12-inch skillet and simmer over medium heat until meat is no longer pink, about 6 minutes. Meanwhile, pulse giardiniera, mayonnaise, and pepper flakes in food processor until finely chopped.

3. Arrange beef on toasted rolls, drizzle with jus, and top with giardiniera mixture. Serve.

QUICK JUS MAKES 1 CUP

For this Quick Jus recipe, we enriched canned beef broth with browned scraps of beef, then thickened the broth with a little flour.

- 1 teaspoon olive oil
- 1 cup leftover roast beef trimmings
- ¼ cup finely chopped onion
- 1 teaspoon all-purpose flour
- 2 cups beef broth

Heat oil in 10-inch skillet over medium-high heat until just smoking. Add beef and cook until dark brown, about 1 minute. Reduce heat to medium, add onion, and cook until slightly softened, about 1 minute. Add flour and cook, stirring constantly, until fragrant and toasty, about 1 minute. Whisk in broth, scraping up browned bits. Simmer until liquid is reduced by half, about 10 minutes. Pour through fine-mesh strainer and serve.

EATING LOCAL ★ CHICAGO, IL

Ask Chicago transplants what they miss most about their home city, and it's a good bet the list will include spicy Italian beef sandwiches, which originated with street vendors outside the Union Stock Yards. Unlike deep-dish pizza, this local favorite is almost impossible to find outside the Chicago city limits. Before we developed a recipe for this iconic sandwich, we had to go to the source and eat the real thing.

We stopped in at AL's, a roadside sandwich stand on Taylor Street in Chicago's Little Italy. The ambience wasn't much to speak of, but Al's Italian beef sandwich definitely was. The meat was seasoned with Italian spices (oregano, basil, garlic, and red pepper flakes), sliced thin, and bathed in a tangy jus before being piled high onto a jus-soaked roll and topped with a peppery giardiniera (a spicy relish of pickled vegetables)—a perfect starting point for our own recipe.

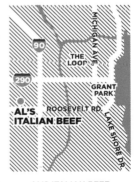

AL'S ITALIAN BEEF
1079 W. Taylor St., Chicago, IL

✔ WHY THIS RECIPE WORKS

Wisconsin tailgate parties are just not complete without grilled bratwurst, and every tailgate cook seems to prepare this game-day staple a little differently. Grilling and then braising the brats made them soggy, so we reversed the order and put them directly into a beer-filled disposable pan right on the grill. Grilling the onions before stirring them into the beer gave the braise serious flavor, and Dijon mustard lent brightness and body to the liquid. Before we nestled them into sub rolls, our flavorful braised bratwurst got some time on the grill to char and crisp. To take the beer braise's flavors a step further, we took a few minutes to reduce the cooking liquid into a tangy sauce to spoon over our full-flavored, kickoff-ready grilled brats.

WISCONSIN GRILLED BRATS AND BEER SERVES 6 TO 8

Light-bodied lagers work best here; Budweiser's mellow sweetness made it our top pick. Standard hot dog buns will be too small for the bulky brats.

- 2 **pounds onions, sliced into ½-inch-thick rounds (do not separate rings)**
- 3 **tablespoons vegetable oil**
  Pepper
- 3 **cups beer**
- ⅔ **cup Dijon mustard**
- 1 **teaspoon sugar**
- 1 **teaspoon caraway seeds**
- 1 **(13 by 9-inch) disposable aluminum roasting pan**
- 2 **pounds bratwurst (8 to 12 sausages)**
- 8–12 **(6-inch) sub rolls**

1. Brush onion rounds with oil and season with pepper; set aside. Combine beer, mustard, sugar, caraway seeds, and 1 teaspoon pepper in disposable pan, then add sausages in single layer.

2A. FOR A CHARCOAL GRILL: Open bottom vent completely. Light large chimney starter filled with charcoal briquettes (6 quarts). When top coals are partially covered with ash, pour evenly over grill. Set cooking grate in place, cover, and open lid vent completely. Heat grill until hot, about 5 minutes.

2B. FOR A GAS GRILL: Turn all burners to high, cover, and heat grill until hot, about 15 minutes. Leave all burners on high.

3. Clean and oil cooking grate. Place onions on grill and cook, turning as needed, until lightly charred on both sides, 6 to 10 minutes. Transfer onions to pan, put pan on cooking grate, cover grill, and cook for 15 minutes.

4. Move pan to 1 side of grill. Transfer sausages directly to grill and brown on all sides, about 5 minutes. Transfer sausages to platter and tent with aluminum foil. Continue to cook onion mixture in pan until sauce is slightly thickened, about 5 minutes. Serve sausages and onions on rolls and spoons sauce over.

GRILLING BETTER BRATWURST

Whether you're tailgating before the game or just grilling in your backyard, here's how to get great grilled brats and perfectly cooked onions every time.

1. Grill sliced onions and transfer to pan.

2. After braising, transfer sausages to grill to crisp while sauce reduces.

☑ WHY THIS RECIPE WORKS

Wisconsin is famous for its beers and cheeses, so it comes as no surprise that residents of the Badger State have long enjoyed a rich combination of the two in creamy, hearty, and often popcorn-garnished cheddar beer soup. We aimed to give ours a pureed texture and balanced, tangy flavor. A mix of onion, carrots, and garlic formed the base, to which we added chicken broth and beer. Wisconsin's own Miller High Life offered honest beer flavor without any bitterness. Milk paired well with the beer broth, keeping the soup creamy but not heavy. Pureeing the soup produced a smooth texture, but simply stirring in shredded cheddar led to lumps. To fix this, we mixed clump-preventing cornstarch into a blend of hand-shredded American cheese (which contains emulsifiers for smooth melting) and cheddar cheese, ensuring a creamy, even texture and sharp cheese flavor. When the cheese was stirred into our blended base, the soup finally took on the velvety quality we were expecting with enough warm cheddar and beer flavors to get us through a Wisconsin-caliber winter.

WISCONSIN CHEDDAR BEER SOUP SERVES 6

Any domestic lager will work in this soup, but it didn't seem authentic without a Wisconsin beer; our favorite is Miller High Life. You will need one 4-ounce chunk of American cheese from the deli counter for this recipe; do not use presliced or packaged shredded cheese here. Freeze the American cheese for 15 minutes to make shredding easier.

4	tablespoons unsalted butter
1	onion, chopped fine
2	carrots, peeled and chopped fine
2	garlic cloves, minced
⅓	cup all-purpose flour
2	cups whole or 2 percent low-fat milk
1¾	cups chicken broth
1½	cups beer
12	ounces sharp cheddar cheese, shredded (3 cups)
4	ounces American cheese, shredded (1 cup)
2	teaspoons cornstarch
	Salt and pepper
	Popcorn (optional)

1. Melt butter in Dutch oven over medium heat. Add onion and carrots and cook until lightly browned, 8 to 10 minutes. Add garlic and cook until fragrant, about 30 seconds. Stir in flour and cook until golden, about 1 minute. Slowly whisk in milk, broth, and beer. Bring mixture to simmer, then reduce heat to low and simmer gently (do not boil) until carrots are very soft, 20 to 25 minutes.

2. Meanwhile, toss cheeses and cornstarch together in large bowl until well combined. Working in batches, process soup in blender until smooth, 1 to 2 minutes. Return soup to clean pot and simmer over medium-low heat. Whisk in cheese mixture, 1 handful at a time, until smooth. Season with salt and pepper to taste; garnish with popcorn, if using; and serve. (Soup can be refrigerated for up to 3 days.)

THE COLOR OF CHEDDAR

Is there really a difference in flavor between yellow and white cheddar cheese? We donned blindfolds to find out.

If you live in the Midwest, your cheddar is probably orange. If you live in the Northeast, your cheddar is definitely white (it's the color of butter). Our test cooks have strong opinions about which color cheese tastes better (predictably lining up with where they grew up). To settle the matter once and for all, we blindfolded 10 cooks and editors and had them taste two national brands of sharp white and orange (sometimes labeled yellow) cheddar, plain and in macaroni and cheese. What did we learn?

Only one taster was able to distinguish flavor differences between the two colors of cheddar (and was that just blind luck?); most wondered, "Is this a trick? Are you sure we're not tasting just one cheese?" Orange cheddars are colored with ground annatto seeds. These seeds, which are called *achiote* in Latin cooking, are used to color butter and margarine, too. Don't let regionalism color your perception: Color has no flavor.

WHICH BEER IS BEST?

Although any domestic lager will work in this soup, Wisconsin Cheddar Beer Soup just didn't seem authentic without a Wisconsin beer. We tasted five widely available Wisconsin brands—Miller, Miller High Life, Miller Genuine Draft, Schlitz, and Pabst Blue Ribbon—both in soup and on their own. After some heated debate, tasters selected Miller High Life for its hoppy character and balanced flavor, praising it as the "perfect complement to the tanginess of the cheddar."

WHY THIS RECIPE WORKS

Booyah is a stick-to-your-ribs chicken and beef soup that draws crowds all across northeast Wisconsin. For a soup loaded with meaty flavors and hearty vegetables, we needed to scale down Green Bay's big-batch recipes. We browned beef short ribs and bone-in chicken thighs first to develop their flavor and to capture their renderings. Trimming the ribs of fat before browning eliminated excess grease, and removing the chicken's skin after browning also kept the booyah light. We used some of the flavorful fat to cook the onions and celery before pouring in chicken broth. With the soup's broth in place, we brought back the chicken and beef, this time adding the beef bones for the full-bodied, silken quality their gelatin adds. We removed the chicken first, deboning and refrigerating it while the beef continued to simmer. Once that, too, was cooked, we shredded the beef. After defatting the broth, we added the remaining vegetables in stages. Our small-scale booyah was rich, hearty, and loaded with tender chunks of meat and vegetables, and we were happy to welcome (small) crowds over for a bowl.

GREEN BAY BOOYAH SERVES 8 TO 10

The bone side of a short rib is especially fatty and requires the most trimming.

2½ pounds bone-in, English-style short ribs, trimmed, meat and bones separated
2½ pounds bone-in chicken thighs, trimmed
    Salt and pepper
1 tablespoon vegetable oil
2 onions, chopped fine
2 celery ribs, minced
8 cups chicken broth
2 bay leaves
½ small head green cabbage, cored and shredded (4 cups)
1 (28-ounce) can diced tomatoes
8 ounces rutabaga, peeled and cut into ½-inch pieces
1 pound russet potatoes, peeled and cut into ½-inch pieces
3 carrots, peeled and sliced ¼ inch thick
1 cup frozen peas
1 tablespoon lemon juice

1. Pat beef and chicken dry with paper towels and season with salt and pepper. Heat oil in Dutch oven over medium-high heat until just smoking. Brown beef on all sides, about 10 minutes; transfer to plate. Cook chicken until browned all over, about 10 minutes; transfer to plate. When chicken is cool enough to handle, remove and discard skin.

2. Pour off all but 1½ teaspoons fat from pot. Add onions and celery and cook over medium heat until softened, about 5 minutes. Stir in broth and bay leaves, scraping up any browned bits. Add beef, beef bones, and chicken and bring to boil.

3. Reduce heat to low and simmer, covered, until chicken registers 175 degrees, about 30 minutes. Transfer chicken to bowl. When chicken is cool enough to handle, shred into bite-size pieces, discarding bones. Cover chicken and refrigerate. Continue to simmer stew until beef is tender, about 1¼ hours longer. Transfer beef to plate. When cool enough to handle, shred into bite-size pieces, discarding fat. Remove beef bones and bay leaves. Strain broth through fine-mesh strainer; discard solids. Allow liquid to settle, about 5 minutes, then skim off fat and return liquid to pot.

4. Add shredded beef, cabbage, tomatoes, rutabaga, 1¼ teaspoons salt, and 1 teaspoon pepper to liquid and bring to boil. Reduce heat to medium-low and simmer until rutabaga is translucent around edges, about 15 minutes. Stir in potatoes and carrots and cook until all vegetables are tender, about 20 minutes. Add chicken and peas and simmer until heated through, 2 to 3 minutes. Off heat, stir in lemon juice. Season with salt and pepper to taste. Serve.

SOUP FOR EVERYONE

Booyah just may be the richest, heartiest chicken and beef soup you've never heard of—unless you happen to be from Green Bay, Wisconsin, that is. Little known even in the rest of the state, booyah is both a soup and an event in Green Bay, made in huge batches in outdoor kettles for fairs, fundraisers, and family gatherings. One cold, slushy morning at the Suamico United Methodist Church, just north of Green Bay, we found people were lining up for bowls of booyah at 7:30 a.m., never mind the 10:00 a.m. start time or the discouraging weather. Clearly, the soup is a celebration all by itself and worth being enjoyed outside of Green Bay—and without the early-morning wait.

✔ WHY THIS RECIPE WORKS

Knoephla (pronounced NEF-la) might not be a word you recognize, but this chicken and dumpling soup is loaded with the warming, hearty flavors that see North Dakotans through the region's bitter winters year after year. For a rich, meaty broth, we browned bone-in chicken thighs and then set the chicken aside. We cooked chopped onion in the rendered fat, creating a flavorful fond at the bottom of the pot, and poured in chicken broth. We removed the skin from the browned thighs, added the chicken to the broth, and let our "double stock" simmer until the meat was ready for shredding. For tender dumplings, we boosted our standard recipe of flour, eggs, and water with creamy half-and-half and aerating baking powder. We dropped dozens of mini dumplings into the pot using a makeshift pastry bag: We chilled the dough in a zipper-lock bag, snipped off a corner, then piped and cut the dumplings into the broth. We stirred the shredded chicken and some extra half-and-half into our full-flavored broth for a creamy, homey finish to a soup we were happy to get to know.

KNOEPHLA SOUP   SERVES 6

Let the batter chill for at least 30 minutes before forming the dumplings. Chicken and broth can be made through step 2 and refrigerated; reheat before proceeding with step 3.

- 4 **(5- to 7-ounce) bone-in chicken thighs, trimmed**
  Salt and pepper
- 1 **teaspoon vegetable oil**
- 1 **onion, chopped fine**
- 8 **cups chicken broth**
- 2½ **cups (12½ ounces) all-purpose flour**
- ¼ **teaspoon baking powder**
- 3 **large eggs, lightly beaten**
- 1 **cup half-and-half**
- ½ **cup water**
- 2 **pounds Yukon Gold potatoes, peeled and cut into ½-inch pieces**

1. Pat chicken dry with paper towels and season with salt and pepper. Heat oil in Dutch oven over medium heat until just smoking. Cook chicken, skin side down, until well browned, 6 to 8 minutes; transfer chicken to plate. Remove and discard skin.

2. Pour off all but 1 teaspoon fat and return pot to medium heat. Add onion and cook until just beginning to brown, 3 to 5 minutes. Add broth, chicken, and 1¼ teaspoons salt and bring to boil. Reduce heat to medium-low, cover, and simmer until chicken is tender, about 30 minutes. (At this point, cooled chicken and broth can be refrigerated separately for up to 3 days; reheat together before proceeding with step 3.)

3. Meanwhile, whisk flour, baking powder, 1 teaspoon salt, and ½ teaspoon pepper together in large bowl. Whisk eggs, ½ cup half-and-half, and water into flour mixture until thick batter forms. Transfer batter to gallon-size zipper-lock bag and refrigerate until ready to use.

4. Remove chicken from pot and set aside. Add potatoes to broth and simmer for 10 minutes. Cut ¼ inch off corner of bag of batter. Pipe batter into simmering broth, snipping dumplings with moistened kitchen shears every ½ to ¾ inch as extruded. Simmer until dumplings float to surface, 10 to 15 minutes, stirring occasionally.

5. Shred chicken into bite-size pieces, discarding bones, and add to soup. Off heat, stir in remaining ½ cup half-and-half. Season with salt and pepper to taste and serve.

DUMPLINGS ON THE DOUBLE

Spooning 100 individual dumplings into the soup was tedious. We figured out how to streamline their production.

1. LOAD: Pour batter into zipper-lock bag. (It's easier if you prop it open in measuring cup.) Press batter toward corner.

2. SNIP: After batter has chilled, snip ¼ inch—no larger or dumplings will be too big—off corner of bag.

3. SQUEEZE: As you squeeze batter from bag, use kitchen shears to snip every ½ to ¾ inch to form dumplings (taking care not to cut into plastic).

✔ WHY THIS RECIPE WORKS

You may never have heard of Barberton, Ohio, but fried chicken fanatics flock there for a taste of the town's famous fried chicken. There, small whole chickens are cut into parts, breaded, and chilled for two days to ensure that the shaggy coating stays put. For distinct Barberton crunch without the extended wait, we began by brining bone-in chicken pieces, which gave us moist, seasoned meat in only 30 minutes. For a craggy, deeply browned coating, we pulverized coarse panko bread crumbs in the food processor. After dredging the chicken in flour, egg, and the now-fine panko crumbs, we found that a 30-minute rest was just enough time for the breading to set. True to Barberton tradition, we used lard (as well as oil) because of the great meaty flavor it gave our fried chicken. Served up with a bowl of mild, chunky Barberton Hot Sauce, our take on this Akron suburb's signature dish was juicy, crunchy, and as good as—if not better than—the chicken that put Barberton on the map.

BARBERTON FRIED CHICKEN SERVES 4 TO 6

You can use wings here, but they will require only about 10 minutes of frying. Two cups of peanut or vegetable oil can be substituted for the lard. Use a Dutch oven that holds 6 quarts or more. Serve with Barberton Hot Sauce (recipe follows).

Salt and pepper
3   pounds bone-in chicken pieces, breasts halved crosswise and leg quarters separated into drumsticks and thighs, trimmed
3   cups panko bread crumbs
1   cup all-purpose flour
3   large eggs
2   quarts peanut or vegetable oil
1   pound lard

1. Dissolve ½ cup salt in 2 quarts cold water in large container. Submerge chicken in brine, cover, and refrigerate for 30 minutes to 1 hour.

2. Pulse panko in food processor until finely ground, about 5 pulses. Combine 2 teaspoons pepper, ½ teaspoon salt, and ground panko in shallow dish. Combine flour, 1 teaspoon pepper, and ½ teaspoon salt in second shallow dish. Beat eggs in third shallow dish.

3. Set wire rack in rimmed baking sheet. Remove chicken from brine and pat dry with paper towels. Working with 2 pieces at a time, dredge chicken in flour mixture, dip in egg, then coat with panko mixture, pressing gently to adhere. Transfer chicken to prepared wire rack and refrigerate, uncovered, for at least 30 minutes or up to 2 hours.

4. Adjust oven rack to middle position and heat oven to 200 degrees. Set second wire rack in second rimmed baking sheet. Heat oil and lard in large Dutch oven over medium-high heat to 325 degrees. Fry half of chicken, adjusting burner if necessary to maintain oil temperature between 275 and 300 degrees, until deep golden brown and breasts register 160 degrees and thighs/drumsticks register 175 degrees, 14 to 18 minutes. Transfer chicken to prepared wire rack and keep warm in oven. Return oil to 325 degrees and repeat with remaining chicken. Serve.

BARBERTON HOT SAUCE MAKES 2½ CUPS

3   tablespoons olive oil
1   onion, chopped fine
1   red bell pepper, stemmed, seeded, and chopped fine
2   jalapeño chiles, stemmed, seeded, and minced
2   teaspoons paprika
1   garlic clove, minced
1½ cups water
1   (14.5-ounce) can diced tomatoes
1   tablespoon long-grain white rice
2   teaspoons packed brown sugar
¼   teaspoon red pepper flakes

1. Heat oil in medium saucepan over medium heat until shimmering. Add onion, bell pepper, and jalapeños and cook until softened, about 5 minutes. Stir in paprika and garlic and cook until fragrant, about 30 seconds. Add water, tomatoes and their juice, rice, sugar, and pepper flakes and bring to boil.

2. Reduce heat to low, cover, and simmer, stirring occasionally, until thickened and vegetables are completely softened, about 45 minutes. Serve. (Hot sauce can be refrigerated for up to 3 days.)

EATING LOCAL ★ BARBERTON, OH

The Akron suburb of Barberton, Ohio, is known as the state's "fried chicken capital." For fried chicken lovers like us, that reputation was an irresistible lure. Once there, we ate our way through chicken dinners with bowls of chunky "hot sauce" at Barberton's famous chicken joints, including the original chicken house, **BELGRADE GARDENS**. Conceived by Serbian immigrants, it opened on July 4, 1933, and has been handed down for generations since. We couldn't wait to create our own version.

BELGRADE GARDENS
401 E. State St.
Barberton, OH

✔ WHY THIS RECIPE WORKS

The list of Chicago restaurants serving to-die-for chicken Vesuvio is long, and everyone has a favorite. To easily enjoy this meal at home, we made it a one-skillet supper. Streamlining this dish meant starting with easy-to-cook boneless, skinless chicken breasts. After browning the chicken in a skillet, we set it aside and added potatoes. Since we had broken a few traditions already, we went with baby red potatoes over the standard russets, because the waxy, firm potatoes would maintain their shape and texture during cooking. We added the spuds to the skillet cut side down and built the sauce around them as they browned. Garlic, oregano, and white wine reflected the dish's Italian American roots, fresh rosemary gave our sauce its assertive herbal flavor, and chicken broth added a meaty boost. While the potatoes finished browning, we returned the chicken to the skillet to continue cooking in the simmering sauce. Once the chicken and potatoes were cooked, we finished the sauce with some butter, a squeeze of lemon, and peas. Our simplified take on this restaurant specialty was as good as the real thing—check, please!

CHICKEN VESUVIO   SERVES 4

We prefer to use small red potatoes measuring 1 to 1½ inches in diameter for this recipe. If you can't find small red potatoes, you can substitute larger red potatoes that have been quartered. For a spicier dish, stir in ¼ teaspoon of red pepper flakes with the garlic in step 2.

- 4 (6-ounce) boneless, skinless chicken breasts, trimmed
  Salt and pepper
- 2 tablespoons olive oil
- 1½ pounds small red potatoes, unpeeled, halved
- 2 garlic cloves, minced
- 1 teaspoon minced fresh rosemary
- ½ teaspoon dried oregano
- 1½ cups chicken broth
- ½ cup white wine
- 1 cup frozen peas, thawed
- 2 tablespoons unsalted butter
- 2 teaspoons lemon juice

1. Pat chicken dry with paper towels and season with salt and pepper. Heat 1 tablespoon oil in 12-inch nonstick skillet over medium-high heat until just smoking. Brown chicken well, 3 to 4 minutes per side; transfer to plate.

2. Add remaining 1 tablespoon oil to skillet and heat until shimmering. Add potatoes, cut side down, and cook until golden brown, about 7 minutes. Stir in garlic, rosemary, oregano, and ½ teaspoon salt and cook until fragrant, about 30 seconds. Add broth and wine, scraping up any browned bits, and bring to boil. Return chicken to skillet on top of potatoes. Reduce heat to medium-low and simmer, covered, until potatoes are tender and chicken registers 160 degrees, about 12 minutes. Using slotted spoon, transfer chicken and potatoes to serving platter and tent loosely with aluminum foil.

3. Increase heat to medium-high and cook, uncovered, until sauce is reduced to 1 cup, about 5 minutes. Stir in peas and cook until heated through, about 1 minute. Off heat, whisk in butter and lemon juice and season with salt and pepper to taste. Pour sauce over chicken and potatoes and serve.

FROZEN PEAS, PLEASE!

In developing our Chicken Vesuvio recipe, we came to depend on frozen peas. Not only are they more convenient than their fresh, in-the-pod comrades, but they taste better. In test after test, we found frozen peas to be tender and sweet while fresh peas tasted starchy and bland. Trying to understand this curious finding, we looked to the frozen food industry for some answers.

Green peas are one of the oldest vegetables known to humankind. Yet despite this long history, they are relatively delicate; fresh peas have little stamina. Green peas lose a substantial portion of their nutrients within 24 hours of being picked. This rapid deterioration is the reason for the starchy, bland flavor of most "fresh" peas found at the grocery store. These not-so-fresh peas might be several days old, depending on where they came from and how long they were kept in the cooler. Frozen peas, on the other hand, are picked, cleaned, sorted, and frozen within several hours of harvest, which helps to preserve their delicate sugars and flavors. When commercially frozen vegetables began to appear in the 1920s and 1930s, green peas were one of the first among them.

Finding good frozen peas is not hard. All of the frozen peas we tried were sweet and fresh, with a bright green color. So unless you grow your own or can stop by your local farm stand for fresh picked, you're better off cruising up the frozen food aisle for a bag of frozen peas.

✔ WHY THIS RECIPE WORKS

In the 1950s, Vic's Tally-Ho was Des Moines, Iowa's, spot to see and be seen, and their steak de burgo was just as hot as the restaurant's jazz scene. The seared fillet was served in a bold garlic-herb-butter sauce, a winning combination that appears on Des Moines menus to this day. The dish seemed simple—tender, browned beef smothered in a garlicky butter sauce—but for ours to stand out, the steak needed a seasoned crust, and our sauce had to have bright, rich flavors. Working with inch-thick fillets, we rubbed the meat with a blend of dried oregano, garlic powder, salt, and pepper. Once in the hot skillet, the spices toasted and created an exceptional sear in minutes. Heating halved garlic cloves in the skillet jump-started the sauce's robust flavors. The acidity of white wine balanced out what came next: butter and rich heavy cream. Fresh basil and oregano livened up the lush sauce. Our juicy Steak de Burgo in its signature sauce was bursting with the flavors diners fell for decades ago—and we were just as happy to see and be seen enjoying it at home.

STEAK DE BURGO SERVES 4

For even cooking, avoid pieces from the tapered end of the meat. You can substitute rib-eye or strip steak of similar thickness for the filets mignons.

- 1 teaspoon dried oregano
- ½ teaspoon garlic powder
- Salt and pepper
- 4 (4- to 5-ounce) center-cut filets mignons, about 1 inch thick, trimmed
- 1 tablespoon vegetable oil
- 2 garlic cloves, peeled and halved
- ¼ cup white wine
- 5 tablespoons unsalted butter, cut into 5 pieces and chilled
- 1 tablespoon heavy cream
- 1 tablespoon chopped fresh basil
- 1 tablespoon chopped fresh oregano

1. Combine dried oregano, garlic powder, ½ teaspoon salt, and ½ teaspoon pepper in small bowl. Pat steaks dry with paper towels and rub evenly with oregano mixture. Heat oil in 12-inch skillet over medium-high heat until just smoking. Cook steaks until well browned and meat registers 120 to 125 degrees (for medium-rare), 3 to 5 minutes per side. Transfer steaks to serving platter and tent loosely with aluminum foil.

2. Add garlic to now-empty skillet and cook until fragrant, about 30 seconds. Stir in wine, scraping up any browned bits, and cook until reduced to about 1 tablespoon, about 1 minute. Whisk in butter, cream, basil, and fresh oregano and cook for about 1 minute. Discard garlic. Season with salt and pepper to taste, pour sauce over steaks, and serve.

FAUX FILLET

If beef tenderloin fillets exceed your budget, two 1-inch-thick rib-eye or strip steaks fashioned into smaller "fillets" keep this dish somewhat wallet-friendly.

1. Cut 2 steaks in half crosswise, creating 4 "fillets" of equal size.

2. Tie steaks to create evenly rounded "fillets" similar to ones cut from beef tenderloin.

NO WINE? NO WORRIES.

Since few of us want to open a bottle of white wine just to use ¼ cup for a sauce, vermouth—which is much more shelf-stable—seemed as though it might be a good alternative. To find out, we replaced white wine with dry vermouth in sauces—an idea made famous by Julia Child. Our tasters found the sauces made with dry vermouth to be a little sweeter and "more herbal" than the same sauces made with white wine, but the difference was subtle. Refrigerated vermouth will continue to taste good for three to nine months, whereas white wine goes south in just days. Even if you store the bottle in the refrigerator, though, expect the flavor of vermouth to slowly deteriorate (it will lose aroma and complexity) long before it actually goes bad.

✅ WHY THIS RECIPE WORKS

Popular on-the-go food throughout Nebraska and Kansas, bierocks (also called runsas) are faintly sweet buns filled with seasoned ground beef, onion, and cabbage. Hoping to have these buns in hand without the road trip, we started with the filling. Lean ground beef was a must, as grease would compromise the dough. We browned the beef and let it drain while we sautéed chopped onion. We returned the beef to the skillet, also stirring in chopped cabbage and adding a cup of chicken broth to speed the vegetables' cooking time. Simmering evaporated the liquid and left the beef infused with the broth's savory flavor. Shredded Colby Jack cheese added a creamy dimension to the beef while also gently binding it for easy forming. Bierocks' buttery, yeasted bread is similar to brioche, so we used plenty of butter and an egg to turn out a soft, sturdy bun. After letting the dough rise, we divided it into balls, flattened them, formed small mounds of filling on each, and pinched them closed. The buns rose one last time before we brushed on an egg wash and baked them. These golden-brown buns may be meant for eating on the run, but we stayed put to savor every bite.

BIEROCKS MAKES 12

The filling for the buns can be made (and refrigerated) up to one day in advance. For quicker assembly, portion the filling into 12 (½-cup) mounds before rolling out the dough. Serve warm or at room temperature.

FILLING

- 4 teaspoons vegetable oil
- 2 pounds 90 percent lean ground beef
  Salt and pepper
- 1 onion, chopped fine
- ½ small head green cabbage, cored and chopped fine (4 cups)
- 1 cup chicken broth
- 8 ounces Colby Jack cheese, shredded (2 cups)

DOUGH

- ½ cup whole milk
- ½ cup water
- 6 tablespoons unsalted butter
- ¼ cup (1¾ ounces) sugar
- 3½–3¾ cups (17½ to 18¾ ounces) all-purpose flour
- 1 tablespoon instant or rapid-rise yeast
- ½ teaspoon salt
- 1 large egg, lightly beaten, plus 1 large egg beaten with 1 tablespoon water

1. FOR THE FILLING: Heat 2 teaspoons oil in Dutch oven over medium-high heat until just smoking. Add beef, 1 teaspoon salt, and 1 teaspoon pepper and cook, breaking up pieces with spoon, until liquid evaporates and meat begins to sizzle, 10 to 15 minutes. Drain meat in colander and set aside.

2. Add remaining 2 teaspoons oil to now-empty Dutch oven and heat over medium-high heat until shimmering. Add onion and cook, stirring occasionally, until just beginning to brown, about 2 minutes. Stir in drained beef, cabbage, and broth. Bring to simmer, cover, and cook until cabbage is tender, about 5 minutes. Uncover and continue to cook until liquid evaporates and mixture begins to sizzle, 5 to 7 minutes. Season with salt and pepper to taste. Transfer to bowl and let cool for 15 minutes. Stir in Colby Jack and let cool to room temperature. Refrigerate until ready to assemble bierocks.

3. FOR THE DOUGH: Meanwhile, grease large bowl. Line 2 rimmed baking sheets with parchment paper. Combine milk, water, butter, and sugar in 2-cup liquid measuring cup. Microwave until temperature registers 110 degrees, 1 to 2 minutes. Using stand mixer fitted with dough hook, mix 3½ cups flour, yeast, and salt on low speed until combined, about 30 seconds. With mixer running, slowly add milk mixture and single beaten egg until incorporated and dough comes together, about 3 minutes. Increase speed to medium-low and continue to mix until dough is smooth and pulls away from sides of bowl, about 8 minutes. If after 4 minutes dough looks wet, add remaining ¼ cup flour, 1 tablespoon at a time, until dough clears sides of bowl but sticks to bottom. Transfer dough to greased bowl, cover with plastic wrap, and let rise in warm place until doubled in size, 50 to 60 minutes.

4. Transfer dough to lightly floured counter and divide into 12 equal (½-cup) portions. Form dough pieces into balls, cover with plastic, and let rest for 5 minutes.

5. Working with 1 dough ball at a time (keep remaining balls covered with plastic), roll out into 5½-inch round. Transfer ½ cup lightly packed filling (3 ounces) to center of round. Use hands to press filling into compact mound. Stretch edges of dough over filling and pinch together to form bun. Arrange 6 bierocks, seam side down, on each prepared baking sheet, 2 inches apart. Cover with plastic and let rise until doubled in size, 45 to 60 minutes.

6. Adjust oven racks to upper-middle and lower-middle positions and heat oven to 375 degrees. Discard plastic, brush bierocks with egg wash, and bake until golden brown, 22 to 25 minutes, switching and rotating sheets halfway through baking. Transfer sheets to wire rack and let cool for 15 minutes. Serve.

TO MAKE AHEAD: Baked, cooled bierocks can be tightly wrapped in aluminum foil, placed in zipper-lock bag, and refrigerated for up to 3 days or frozen for up to 1 month. To reheat, adjust oven rack to middle position and heat oven to 350 degrees. Place foil-wrapped bierocks directly on oven rack until heated through, about 10 minutes if refrigerated or 60 minutes if frozen.

✔ WHY THIS RECIPE WORKS

In the home kitchens of Chicago and farther afield, kielbasa casserole is a go-to Polish American dish. Most recipes call for condensed cream of potato soup, but we knew using fresh ingredients would make this casserole even better. We browned sliced kielbasa, heightening its smoky notes, and used its renderings to start our sauce. Sautéing onions and caraway seeds in the fat before stirring in flour, chicken broth, and half-and-half created a rich, lush upgrade from canned soup. We simmered cut russet potatoes in the sauce, letting them soften before adding sauerkraut, yellow mustard, and fresh dill to round out the savory flavors. We stirred in the browned kielbasa and moved our mixture to a baking dish, finishing it off with coarse homemade bread crumbs for a crunchy, golden crust. With each of our ingredients partially cooked, 15 minutes in the oven was all we needed to crisp up the casserole's topping. With an extra sprinkling of dill, we were happy to call our from-scratch version of this popular meal an easy victory.

KIELBASA CASSEROLE

SERVES 8 TO 10

Use russet potatoes here for the best texture. We prefer pouched sauerkraut, sold near the pickles in most supermarkets, to jarred or canned varieties.

3	tablespoons vegetable oil
1½	pounds kielbasa sausage, halved lengthwise and sliced crosswise ½ inch thick
1	onion, chopped fine
	Salt and pepper
⅛	teaspoon caraway seeds
¼	cup all-purpose flour
3½	cups chicken broth
½	cup half-and-half
2	pounds russet potatoes, peeled and cut into ½-inch pieces
3	slices hearty white sandwich bread, torn into 1-inch pieces
1	pound sauerkraut, squeezed dry (1½ cups)
2	tablespoons yellow mustard
1	tablespoon chopped fresh dill

1. Adjust oven rack to middle position and heat oven to 400 degrees. Heat 2 tablespoons oil in Dutch oven over medium heat until just smoking. Add kielbasa and cook, stirring occasionally, until spotty brown, about 5 minutes. Using slotted spoon, transfer kielbasa to paper towel–lined plate, leaving fat in pot.

2. Add onion, 1¼ teaspoons salt, ½ teaspoon pepper, and caraway seeds to fat in pot and cook until onion is just softened, about 3 minutes. Stir in flour to coat onion and cook for 1 minute. Slowly whisk in broth and half-and-half until incorporated. Add potatoes and bring to boil. Reduce heat to medium-low and simmer, stirring occasionally, until potatoes are just tender, about 15 minutes.

3. Meanwhile, pulse bread, remaining 1 tablespoon oil, ½ teaspoon salt, and ¼ teaspoon pepper in food processor until coarsely ground, about 7 pulses; set aside.

4. Off heat, stir sauerkraut, mustard, 2 teaspoons dill, and kielbasa into pot. Transfer mixture to 13 by 9-inch baking dish and sprinkle bread crumbs evenly over top. Bake until crumbs are golden brown and edges of casserole are bubbling, 12 to 15 minutes. Sprinkle with remaining 1 teaspoon dill. Let cool for 15 minutes. Serve.

FREEZING BROTH

Inevitably, recipes like Kielbasa Casserole will leave you with some leftover chicken broth, but there's no need to let it go to waste. Here are three ideas for freezing different amounts of leftover broth; all can be stored for up to three months.

SMALL AMOUNTS: Pour broth into ice cube trays. After cubes have frozen, remove and store them in zipper-lock bag. Use cubes for pan sauces, stir-fry sauces, and vegetable braises.

MEDIUM AMOUNTS: Nonstick muffin tins create slightly larger portions. After broth has frozen, store "cups" in large zipper-lock bag. "Cups" are good for casseroles and braising/steaming/poaching liquid.

LARGE AMOUNTS: Line 4-cup measuring cup with zipper-lock bag (it holds bag open so you can use both hands to pour) and pour in broth. Seal bag (double up if you wish) and lay it flat to freeze. Good for rice, gravies, soups, or stews.

KILLER KRAUT IS IN THE BAG

Briny, salty sauerkraut is an essential component of our kielbasa casserole. To see which variety of sauerkraut is best, we tasted it from jars, cans, and vacuum-sealed bags. Right off the bat, tasters panned the heavily processed (and long-cooked) canned brands as "flaccid and flavorless" and "flat." Jarred and bagged brands are cooked less; these generally had more crunch and flavor. Our favorite sauerkraut is the bagged variety, with its chewy-crisp texture and fresh, vinegary kick.

✔ WHY THIS RECIPE WORKS

Every Midwestern home cook worth his or her salt has a host of casserole recipes on hand, ready to turn out a crowd-pleasing meal at a moment's notice. Pork chop casserole has all the trappings of a rustic, stick-to-your-bones feast, but with the ease of a weeknight meal. Bone-in blade-cut pork chops were our chop of choice for their flavor-building fat. We removed the bones, browned the chops, sliced them in half, and arranged them in a baking dish. We wanted a rich, roux-based sauce, so we sautéed sliced cabbage, carrots, and onion to drive away moisture. Robust herbs, flour, white wine, and heavy cream finished the thick sauce, which thinned in the oven as the chops and vegetables shed liquid. For a crunchy, savory crumb topping, we processed hearty white bread with Parmesan, butter, and sage. We kept the crumbs on standby as the casserole baked, covered with aluminum foil, for an hour. We then ramped up the heat, removed the foil, and let the surface dry out, adding the crumbs with 15 minutes left in the oven. Our herb-flecked casserole boasted flavorful chops surrounded by tender vegetables and a full-bodied sauce that tied the whole dish together.

PORK CHOP CASSEROLE   SERVES 6

The chops can fit in the pot in one batch.

- 4 slices hearty white sandwich bread, torn into 1-inch pieces
- 1 ounce Parmesan cheese, grated (½ cup)
- 4 tablespoons unsalted butter
- 2 tablespoons chopped fresh sage
  Salt and pepper
- 4 (8- to 10-ounce) bone-in blade-cut pork chops, about 1 inch thick, bones removed, trimmed
- 1 head green cabbage (2 pounds), cored and sliced ½ inch thick
- 4 carrots, peeled and cut into ½-inch pieces
- 1 onion, halved and sliced thin
- 4 garlic cloves, minced
- 1 tablespoon minced fresh thyme
- 2 tablespoons all-purpose flour
- ½ cup dry white wine
- ½ cup heavy cream

1. Adjust oven rack to middle position and heat oven to 300 degrees. Pulse bread, Parmesan, 2 tablespoons butter, 1 tablespoon sage, ½ teaspoon salt, and ½ teaspoon pepper in food processor until coarsely ground, about 8 pulses; set aside. Pat chops dry with paper towels and season with salt and pepper. Melt remaining 2 tablespoons butter in Dutch oven over medium-high heat. Add chops and cook until well browned, about 4 minutes per side. Transfer chops to cutting board, halve crosswise, and place in 13 by 9-inch baking dish.

2. Add cabbage, carrots, onion, ½ teaspoon salt, and ½ teaspoon pepper to now-empty pot and cook, covered, until cabbage is wilted, 7 to 10 minutes. Remove lid and continue to cook until onion is browned and moisture has evaporated, about 5 minutes.

3. Add garlic, thyme, and remaining 1 tablespoon sage and cook until fragrant, about 30 seconds. Add flour and cook for 1 minute. Add wine and cream, bring to boil, and cook until thickened, about 1 minute. Pour cabbage mixture over chops and cover dish with aluminum foil. Bake until chops are tender, about 1 hour.

4. Remove foil, increase oven temperature to 425 degrees, and continue to cook until top of casserole is browned, about 15 minutes. Top casserole with bread-crumb mixture and continue to bake until golden brown, about 15 minutes. Let casserole cool for 15 minutes. Serve.

CHOP SHOP(PING)

Many recipes calling for pork chops simply specify "loin" chops—a vague and unhelpful term, since all pork chops are cut from the loin of the pig. Butchers further break down the loin into four different types of chop—blade, rib, center cut, and sirloin—each of which cooks differently, depending on the muscles they contain. Here's what you need to know to buy the right chop for the job.

BLADE: Cut near the fatty shoulder end, this chop's high content of marbled dark meat and connective tissue makes it ideal for braising.

RIB: Featuring one large eye of loin muscle, this chop is very tender as well as flavorful and a good choice for grilling and pan searing.

CENTER CUT: Because the loin and tenderloin muscles in these chops are bisected by bulky bone or cartilage, they don't lie flat and thus make a poor choice for pan searing. Save them for the grill, but position the ultralean tenderloin away from the fire to keep it from drying out.

SIRLOIN: These muscle mosaics contain the loin, the tenderloin, and part of the hip section. Because they're generally tough and dry, we don't recommend them.

✔ WHY THIS RECIPE WORKS

Kansas City's pit masters are widely hailed for their smoky, fork-tender, and abundantly spiced brisket. Traditional briskets require a full day of minding the grill, which is why most KC barbecue fans leave this dish to the experts. To make it a reality for home cooks, we looked to a hybrid technique that captured the grill's smoky flavor before finishing in the oven. A vibrant combination of spices nailed the trademark red hue and heavily seasoned flavors we wanted in our rub. A disposable roasting pan protected our spice-rubbed meat from charring while it smoked on the grill. A simple mixture of ketchup, water, molasses, and hot sauce served as our sauce, which we poured into the roasting pan before moving the brisket into the oven. Once the brisket registered 195 degrees, we turned off the oven and let the meat absorb some of the surrounding liquid, creating a perfectly tender texture as the oven gradually cooled. This forgiving cooking technique seemed tailor-made for entertaining—perfect, since we couldn't wait to share our juicy brisket with everyone we know.

KANSAS CITY BARBECUED BRISKET SERVES 8 TO 10

To use wood chunks when using a charcoal grill, substitute two medium chunks, soaked in water for 1 hour, for the wood chip packet.

- 1½   **tablespoons paprika**
- 1½   **tablespoons packed brown sugar**
- 1   **tablespoon chili powder**
- 1   **tablespoon pepper**
- 2   **teaspoons salt**
- 1   **teaspoon granulated garlic**
- 1   **teaspoon onion powder**
- 1   **(5- to 6-pound) beef brisket, flat cut, fat trimmed to ¼ inch**
- 2   **cups wood chips, soaked in water for 15 minutes and drained**
- 1   **(13 by 9-inch) disposable aluminum roasting pan**
- 1   **cup ketchup**
- 1   **cup water**
- 3   **tablespoons molasses**
- 1   **tablespoon hot sauce**

1. Combine paprika, sugar, chili powder, pepper, salt, granulated garlic, and onion powder in small bowl. Cut ½-inch crosshatch pattern through brisket fat cap, ¼ inch deep. Rub brisket with spice mixture. Wrap brisket in plastic wrap and refrigerate for at least 6 hours or up to 24 hours. Using large piece of heavy-duty aluminum foil, wrap soaked chips in foil packet and cut several vent holes in top.

2A. FOR A CHARCOAL GRILL: Open bottom vent halfway. Light large chimney starter filled with charcoal briquettes (6 quarts). When top coals are partially covered with ash, pour evenly over half of grill. Place wood chip packet on coals. Set cooking grate in place, cover, and open lid vent halfway. Heat grill until hot and wood chips are smoking, about 5 minutes.

2B. FOR A GAS GRILL: Place wood chip packet over primary burner. Turn all burners to high, cover, and heat grill until hot and wood chips are smoking, about 15 minutes. Leave primary burner on high and turn off other burners.

3. Pat brisket dry with paper towels and transfer to disposable pan. Set pan with brisket on cooler side of grill and cook, covered (position lid vent over brisket if using charcoal), for 2 hours.

4. Adjust oven rack to lower-middle position and heat oven to 300 degrees. Whisk ketchup, water, molasses, and hot sauce together in bowl and pour over brisket. Cover pan tightly with foil and transfer to oven. Cook until brisket registers 195 degrees, 2½ to 3 hours. Turn off heat and let brisket rest in oven for 1 hour.

5. Transfer brisket to carving board. Skim fat from sauce. Slice brisket against grain into ¼-inch-thick slices. Serve with sauce.

SMOKE, BRAISE, REST

To turn this notoriously tough cut into juicy, tender barbecue, we devised a hybrid barbecue-braising method that ended with an hour of resting in the oven.

1. Place wood chip packet over hot coals (or gas grill's primary burner) to impart smoky flavor. Use disposable aluminum roasting pan, which catches cooking juices yet lets brisket develop smoky char.

2. Add sauce, cover pan, and put it in oven. The moist cooking environment efficiently tenderizes brisket.

3. After braising brisket, leave meat in turned-off oven to relax and fully tenderize.

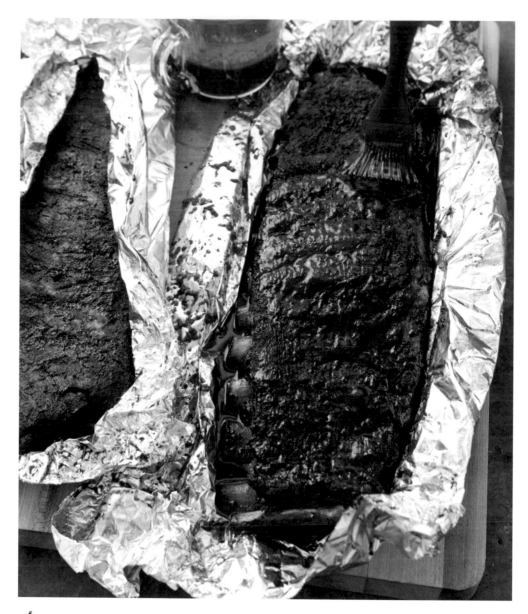

✔ WHY THIS RECIPE WORKS

For barbecue fans who like to get their hands dirty, Kansas City sticky ribs are just the ticket. Hoping to bring the smoky flavor, tender meat, and signature sticky barbecue sauce home without hours by the grill, we focused on keeping the ribs moist while speeding up their cooking time. After rubbing a rack of St. Louis–style spareribs with a spicy blend of paprika, brown sugar, salt, pepper, and cayenne, we readied our grill. Wood chips gave the ribs great smoky flavor, and we kept the meat moist by capturing the escaping steam with a sheet of aluminum foil placed directly on top of the ribs. Even on the cooler side of the grill, the ribs still developed a nice crusty exterior. After spreading on a thick coating of our homemade barbecue sauce, we wrapped the ribs tightly in foil to prevent the sauce from charring, added more hot coals and wood chips, and let the ribs cook for a final hour. More sauce brushed on before serving added a final layer of flavor. Smothered in finger-licking, sticky barbecue sauce and tender as can be, our ribs had all the qualities of great Kansas City barbecue, but in our own backyard.

KANSAS CITY STICKY RIBS SERVES 4 TO 6

We like St. Louis–style racks, but if you can't find them, baby back ribs will work fine. If you want to pair the ribs with a side of Smoky Kansas City Barbecue Beans, see page 213.

RIBS

- 3 tablespoons paprika
- 2 tablespoons brown sugar
- 1 tablespoon salt
- 1 tablespoon pepper
- ¼ teaspoon cayenne pepper
- 2 (2½- to 3-pound) full racks pork spareribs, trimmed of any large pieces of fat and membrane removed
- 2 cups wood chips, soaked in water for 15 minutes and drained
- 1 (13 by 9-inch) disposable aluminum roasting pan (if using charcoal)

SAUCE

- 1 tablespoon vegetable oil
- 1 onion, chopped fine
  Salt and pepper
- 4 cups chicken broth
- 1 cup root beer
- 1 cup cider vinegar
- 1 cup dark corn syrup
- ½ cup molasses
- ½ cup tomato paste
- ½ cup ketchup
- 2 tablespoons brown mustard
- 1 tablespoon hot sauce
- ½ teaspoon garlic powder
- ¼ teaspoon liquid smoke

1. FOR THE RIBS: Combine paprika, sugar, salt, pepper, and cayenne in bowl. Pat ribs dry with paper towels and rub evenly with spice mixture. Wrap ribs in plastic wrap and let sit at room temperature for at least 1 hour, or refrigerate for up to 24 hours. (If refrigerated, let sit at room temperature for 1 hour before grilling.) Using 2 large pieces of heavy-duty aluminum foil, wrap soaked chips in 2 foil packets and cut several vent holes in top.

2. FOR THE SAUCE: Meanwhile, heat oil in large saucepan over medium heat until shimmering. Add onion and pinch salt and cook until softened, 5 to 7 minutes.

Whisk in broth, root beer, vinegar, corn syrup, molasses, tomato paste, ketchup, mustard, hot sauce, and garlic powder. Bring sauce to simmer and cook, stirring occasionally, until reduced to 4 cups, about 1 hour. Off heat, stir in liquid smoke. Let sauce cool to room temperature. Season with salt and pepper to taste. Measure out 1 cup barbecue sauce for cooking; set aside remaining sauce for serving. (Sauce can be refrigerated for up to 4 days.)

3A. FOR A CHARCOAL GRILL: Open bottom vent halfway and place disposable pan on 1 side of grill. Light large chimney starter three-quarters full with charcoal briquettes (4½ quarts). When top coals are partially covered with ash, pour into steeply banked pile against side of grill (opposite disposable pan). Place 1 wood chip packet on coals. Set cooking grate in place, cover, and open lid vent halfway. Heat grill until hot and wood chips are smoking, about 5 minutes.

3B. FOR A GAS GRILL: Remove cooking grate and place wood chip packet directly on primary burner. Set cooking grate in place, turn all burners to high, cover, and heat grill until hot and wood chips are smoking, about 15 minutes. Turn primary burner to medium-high and turn off other burner(s). (Adjust primary burner as needed to maintain grill temperature around 325 degrees.)

4. Clean and oil cooking grate. Unwrap ribs and place, meat side down, on cooler side of grill; ribs may overlap slightly. Place sheet of foil directly on top of ribs. Cover (position lid vent over meat if using charcoal) and cook until ribs are deep red and smoky, about 2 hours, flipping and rotating racks halfway through cooking. During final 20 minutes of grilling, if using charcoal, light another large chimney starter three-quarters full with charcoal (4½ quarts). When top coals are partially covered with ash, pour hot coals on top of spent coals and top with remaining wood chip packet. Flip and rotate ribs and cook, covered, for 1 hour.

5. Remove ribs from grill, brush evenly with 1 cup sauce, and wrap tightly with foil. Lay foil-wrapped ribs on grill and cook until tender, about 1 hour longer.

6. Transfer ribs (still in foil) to cutting board and let rest for 30 minutes. Unwrap ribs and brush with additional sauce. Slice ribs between bones and serve with remaining sauce.

✓ WHY THIS RECIPE WORKS

Slow-cooked beans studded with smoky bits of barbecued meat are a signature side at Kansas City bar-becue eateries, but few home cooks have leftover burnt ends on hand. While we were setting up the grill for our Kansas City Sticky Ribs (page 211), an old insider trick came to mind: We could cook the beans on the bottom of the grill while the ribs cooked above, their drippings contributing the porky, smoky taste we were looking for. We started on the stove, establishing a base of flavor with crisp bacon, onion, and garlic. Once these ingredients were cooked and fragrant, we added the beans and water. Midway through cooking, we stirred in even more flavor with brown sugar, mustard, hot sauce, and barbecue sauce, letting the liquid thicken. When the ribs had just a few hours left on the grill, we poured the beans into a disposable aluminum pan, covered it with foil, poked holes in the foil, and nestled the container on the coals. As the ribs finished cooking, the beans' Kansas City flavors deepened. With perfect timing, our barbecue beans finished tender and loaded with meaty, smoky taste just as the ribs were ready to serve.

SMOKY KANSAS CITY BARBECUE BEANS SERVES 4 TO 6

This recipe accompanies Kansas City Sticky Ribs (page 211) and is meant for a charcoal grill. If you're cooking on a gas grill, omit step 3 and finish cooking the beans in a 300-degree oven for 2 to 2½ hours.

4	slices bacon, chopped fine
1	onion, chopped fine
4	garlic cloves, minced
1	pound dried pinto beans, picked over and rinsed, soaked overnight and drained
6	cups water
1	cup barbecue sauce
⅓	cup packed light brown sugar
2	tablespoons brown mustard
1	teaspoon hot sauce
	Salt
1	(13 by 9-inch) disposable aluminum roasting pan

1. Cook bacon in Dutch oven over medium heat until beginning to crisp, about 5 minutes. Stir in onion and cook until softened, about 5 minutes. Add garlic and cook until fragrant, about 30 seconds. Add beans and water and bring to simmer. Reduce heat to medium-low, cover, and cook until beans are just soft, about 1 hour.

2. Stir in ½ cup barbecue sauce, sugar, mustard, hot sauce, and 2 teaspoons salt and simmer, uncovered, over medium-low heat until beans are tender and sauce is slightly thickened, about 1 hour. (If mixture becomes too thick, add water.) Transfer beans to 13 by 9-inch disposable aluminum pan and wrap tightly with aluminum foil. Using paring knife or skewer, poke holes in foil.

3. See step 4 of Kansas City Sticky Ribs (page 211). When new coals are added, nestle pan with beans inside disposable pan already in grill. Replace cooking grate and position ribs directly above beans. Cover grill and cook until beans are smoky and completely tender, about 2 hours. Discard foil, stir in remaining ½ cup barbecue sauce, and season with salt. Serve.

BEANS ON THE GRILL

Our beans finish cooking on the grill, where they pick up smoke and pork flavors. Here's how to let the flavors in and keep the grease out.

1. When beans are tender and sauce is slightly thickened, transfer beans to 13 by 9-inch disposable aluminum roasting pan. Wrap tightly in aluminum foil and poke several holes in foil so juices from ribs can flavor beans.

2. When you're ready to add more coals, nestle pan of beans into pan already on bottom of grill. Replace cooking grate, making sure to position ribs directly above beans.

✔ WHY THIS RECIPE WORKS

Crunchy, moist crumb-coated ham is a Christmas tradition among Swedish American families across the Midwest, but getting the coating to stay put without turning soggy can be as challenging as assembling Ikea furniture. Hoping to slice up a ham loaded with zesty seasoning and a crunchy bread-crumb crust, we started with a room-temperature spiral-sliced ham. Setting the ham on a piece of foil and tucking an oven bag around it contained the moisture, and baking it on a wire rack set inside a rimmed baking sheet left all sides of the ham accessible for glazing and crumbing. For a glaze with great cling, we combined brown sugar, spicy brown mustard, and balsamic vinegar. Dry mustard, ginger, and cloves are classic baked ham flavorings, so we added those too. We kept a blend of panko bread crumbs, minced fresh parsley, oil, salt, and pepper at the ready as we coated the ham with our sticky glaze. The seasoned crumbs, pressed onto the surface, clung nicely. While the ham baked to a lovely golden brown, we stirred together a no-cook hot mustard sauce. One taste said it all: This ham was so good we didn't want to wait until Christmas to enjoy it.

CRUMB-COATED BAKED HAM
SERVES 12 TO 14

This recipe requires a turkey-size oven bag. Serve the ham with Hot Mustard Sauce (recipe follows). Leftover ham works perfectly in Hawaiian Fried Rice (page 273).

1	(8- to 9-pound) bone-in spiral-sliced ham
1	turkey-size oven bag
1	cup packed brown sugar
½	cup spicy brown mustard
½	cup balsamic vinegar
2	tablespoons dry mustard
2	teaspoons ground ginger
¼	teaspoon ground cloves
1½	cups panko bread crumbs
½	cup minced fresh parsley
3	tablespoons vegetable oil
¼	teaspoon salt
¼	teaspoon pepper

1. Set wire rack in aluminum foil–lined rimmed baking sheet. Place 12-inch square of foil in center of wire rack. Set ham on foil, flat side down, and cover with oven bag, tucking bag under ham to secure it. Let ham sit at room temperature for 1½ hours.

2. Adjust oven rack to lowest position and heat oven to 325 degrees. Bake ham until it registers 100 degrees, about 2 hours. (Lift bag to take temperature; do not puncture.)

3. Meanwhile, combine sugar, brown mustard, vinegar, dry mustard, ginger, and cloves in medium saucepan and bring to boil over medium-high heat. Reduce heat to medium-low and simmer until reduced to ¾ cup, 15 to 20 minutes. Let cool while ham cooks.

4. Combine panko, parsley, oil, salt, and pepper in bowl. Remove ham from oven, remove and discard oven bag, and let ham cool for 5 minutes. Increase oven temperature to 400 degrees.

5. Brush ham all over with sugar-mustard glaze. Press panko mixture against sides of ham to coat evenly. Bake until crumbs are deep golden brown, 20 to 30 minutes. Transfer ham, flat side down, to carving board and let rest for 30 minutes. Carve and serve.

HOT MUSTARD SAUCE
MAKES ABOUT 1 CUP

The longer this sauce sits, the milder it becomes.

3	tablespoons cold water
2	tablespoons dry mustard
½	teaspoon salt
½	cup Dijon mustard
2	tablespoons honey

Whisk water, dry mustard, and salt together in bowl until smooth; let sit for 15 minutes. Whisk in Dijon mustard and honey. Cover and let sit at room temperature for at least 2 hours. Use immediately or transfer sauce to glass jar with tight-fitting lid and refrigerate for up to 2 months.

PREPARING A CRUMB-COATED HAM

1. BAG IT: Cover ham with oven bag, tucking it under ham to prevent meat from drying out. Bake bagged ham for about 2 hours.

2. GLAZE IT: Remove ham from oven, lift off oven bag, and brush warm ham with brown sugar–mustard glaze.

3. CRUMB IT: Sprinkle seasoned crumbs on ham and press them on to coat. Bake until golden.

✔ WHY THIS RECIPE WORKS

Hoppel poppel frequently appears on Midwestern diner menus, and though we knew it was fun to say, we wondered: What would it taste like? Roughly translated from the German word for "hodgepodge," hoppel poppel is a hearty one-skillet meal, calling for a combination of browned potatoes, chopped vegetables, and various meats, all bound together with soft-set scrambled eggs and cheese. Cooking the eggs and mix-ins all at once made the vegetables steam, preventing browning, so we cooked our vegetables and potatoes first. We softened chopped onion and bell pepper, sautéing them in butter with garlic. For the potatoes, we went for frozen diced hash browns, finding that they cooked up quickly and browned deeply. We browned the meat—leftover pork and deli salami—last. We left the meat and potatoes in the skillet and whisked the eggs, onion, bell pepper, parsley, and cheddar cheese together in a bowl before setting the mixture in a hot skillet. Transferring the skillet to the broiler allowed the eggs to cook evenly for a perfectly set and easily sliceable, delicious egg pie.

HOPPEL POPPEL

SERVES 6 TO 8

Use diced frozen hash brown potatoes here (you don't need to thaw them); shredded hash browns will turn mushy. Rather than individual thin slices, this recipe calls for one ½-inch-thick slice of salami, which you can ask for at the supermarket deli counter.

12	**large eggs**
3	**tablespoons half-and-half**
	Salt and pepper
4	**tablespoons unsalted butter**
1	**onion, chopped**
1	**red bell pepper, stemmed, seeded, and chopped**
2	**garlic cloves, minced**
2	**cups frozen diced hash brown potatoes**
2	**cups cooked pork, ham, or sausage, cut into ½-inch pieces**
1	**(½-inch-thick) slice salami (2¼ ounces), cut into ½-inch pieces**
8	**ounces sharp cheddar cheese, shredded (2 cups)**
2	**tablespoons minced fresh parsley**

1. Adjust oven rack 8 inches from broiler element and heat broiler. Whisk eggs, half-and-half, ½ teaspoon salt, and ½ teaspoon pepper together in large bowl.

2. Melt 2 tablespoons butter in nonstick broiler-safe 12-inch skillet over medium heat. Add onion and bell pepper and cook until softened, about 5 minutes. Add garlic and cook until fragrant, about 30 seconds; transfer vegetable mixture to plate. Melt remaining 2 tablespoons butter in now-empty skillet, then add potatoes, ¼ teaspoon salt, and ¼ teaspoon pepper and cook until potatoes are golden brown, 5 to 7 minutes. Add pork and salami and cook until browned, about 3 minutes.

3. Whisk cheddar, parsley, and vegetable mixture into egg mixture. Add egg mixture to skillet and cook, using rubber spatula to stir and scrape bottom of skillet, until large curds form but egg mixture is still wet, about 2 minutes. Shake skillet to distribute egg mixture evenly and cook, without stirring, until bottom is set, about 30 seconds.

4. Transfer skillet to oven and broil until surface is spotty brown, 3 to 4 minutes. Carefully remove skillet from oven (skillet handle will be hot) and let rest on wire rack for 5 minutes. Slide hoppel poppel onto cutting board, cut into wedges, and serve.

FINISHING HOPPEL POPPEL

1. UNDER THE BROILER: When eggs form large curds but top is still wet, slide skillet under broiler.

2. TURN IT OUT: Once top browns, move skillet to wire rack, where residual heat gently completes cooking center of hoppel poppel. After 5-minute rest, slide onto cutting board.

✓ WHY THIS RECIPE WORKS

Some things just go together: peas and carrots, peanut butter and jelly, eggs and...goetta? This German American breakfast item combines oats and meat and is the companion to morning eggs for folks all across Ohio, Indiana, and Kentucky. We just had to give goetta (pronounced GET-ta) a try, using ground breakfast sausage to streamline our version. To jump-start the savory flavor, we browned chopped onion in butter, next adding ground seasonings—sage, fennel, and allspice. We poured in water and then used a potato masher to incorporate the sausage into the flavorful liquid. We added quick-cooking steel-cut oats once the pot reached a boil, which thickened the mixture to a nubby consistency. We transferred the goetta to a loaf pan, chilled it for a few hours, and turned it onto a cutting board. Sliced and fried in oil for a few minutes per side, our meaty goetta had a crisp crust to contrast with its creamy interior. We tried ours with all of the usual goetta fixings—from applesauce to maple syrup to ketchup—and knew our supersavory side could compete with any breakfast meat on the menu.

GOETTA SERVES 6 TO 8

Quick-cooking steel-cut oats (aka pinhead oats) are essential; don't substitute rolled oats. Chill the goetta for at least 3 hours before you slice it. Goetta is a great make-ahead dish: Fry as much as you want, and save the rest for another day. Goetta is often served with eggs, and we like Perfect Fried Eggs (recipe follows) in particular.

1	tablespoon unsalted butter
1	onion, chopped fine
1½	teaspoons ground sage
1	teaspoon ground fennel
¼	teaspoon ground allspice
4¼	cups water
1	pound bulk breakfast sausage
1¾	cups quick-cooking steel-cut oats
	Salt and pepper
2	tablespoons vegetable oil, plus extra as needed

1. Grease 8½ by 4½-inch nonstick loaf pan. Melt butter in Dutch oven over medium-high heat. Add onion and cook until lightly browned, about 5 minutes. Stir in sage, fennel, and allspice and cook until fragrant, about 30 seconds. Add water and sausage and mash with potato masher until water and sausage are fully combined. Bring to boil and stir in oats. Cover, reduce heat to low, and simmer gently, stirring occasionally, for 15 minutes.

2. Uncover and maintain gentle simmer, stirring frequently, until mixture is very thick and rubber spatula dragged across bottom of pot leaves trail for about 3 seconds, 15 to 18 minutes. Season with salt and pepper to taste.

3. Transfer mixture to prepared pan. Smooth top and tap firmly on counter. Let cool completely, then cover with plastic wrap and refrigerate until fully chilled and firm, at least 3 hours or up to 2 days.

4. Run thin knife around edges of goetta, then briefly set bottom of pan in hot water to loosen goetta from pan. Turn out goetta onto cutting board. Cut desired number of ½-inch-thick slices from loaf. Heat oil in 12-inch nonstick skillet over medium heat until shimmering. Add up to 4 slices goetta and cook until well browned, about 5 minutes per side. Transfer to wire rack and let drain. Repeat as needed. Serve. (Wrap any remaining goetta in plastic wrap and refrigerate for up to 3 days, or slice, wrap, and freeze for up to 1 month. To cook from frozen, reduce heat to medium-low and increase cooking time to 7 to 9 minutes per side.)

PERFECT FRIED EGGS SERVES 2

While you can pair Goetta with any style of eggs, we like to serve fried. When checking the eggs for doneness, lift the lid just a crack to prevent loss of steam should they need further cooking. When cooked, the thin layer of white surrounding the yolk will turn opaque, but the yolk should remain runny. To cook two eggs, use an 8- or 9-inch nonstick skillet and halve the amounts of oil and butter. You can use this method with extra-large or jumbo eggs without altering the timing.

2	teaspoons vegetable oil
4	large eggs
	Salt and pepper
2	teaspoons unsalted butter, cut into 4 pieces and chilled

1. Heat oil in 12- or 14-inch nonstick skillet over low heat for 5 minutes. Meanwhile, crack 2 eggs into small bowl and season with salt and pepper. Repeat with remaining 2 eggs and second small bowl.

2. Increase heat to medium-high and heat until oil is shimmering. Add butter to skillet and quickly swirl to coat pan. Working quickly, pour 1 bowl of eggs in 1 side of pan and second bowl of eggs in other side. Cover and cook for 1 minute. Remove skillet from burner and let stand, covered, for 15 to 45 seconds for runny yolks (white around edge of yolk will be barely opaque), 45 to 60 seconds for soft but set yolks, and about 2 minutes for medium-set yolks. Slide eggs onto plates and serve.

✔ WHY THIS RECIPE WORKS

When thousands of Swedish immigrants settled in the Midwest over a century ago, they brought more than their cultural and religious traditions—they also brought their pancakes. Worlds away from their American counterparts, these crêpe-like pancakes are delicate, with lacy, buttery edges and a barely custardy middle. Without a traditional Swedish pancake pan in our cabinet, we turned to a hot skillet. Taking a tip from Julia Child's crêpe recipe, we used instant flour for our base, as its ability to "instantly" dissolve meant less whisking, and therefore less gluten formation and no need to rest the batter before cooking. Equal parts half-and-half and club soda created rich flavor and just enough lift. Two eggs plus two extra yolks upped the richness further without any distracting eggy flavor, and ¼ cup of sugar added enough sweetness for these pancakes to be enjoyed plain. With our skillet at the ready, we slowly poured batter into a tilted pan, swirling until it coated the surface evenly. Cooked only a minute or two per side, these dainty pancakes were perfectly browned. For a quintessentially Swedish experience, we served our pancakes with lingonberry jam.

SWEDISH PANCAKES

MAKES 15; SERVES 4 TO 6

This recipe requires instant flour, like Wondra. Keep the pancakes warm, covered, in a 200-degree oven. Serve with lingonberry jam, as the Swedes do, or your favorite jam.

2	cups (10 ounces) instant flour
¼	cup (1¾ ounces) sugar
1	teaspoon salt
1½	cups half-and-half
1½	cups club soda
9	tablespoons unsalted butter, melted and cooled
2	large eggs plus 2 large yolks, lightly beaten

1. Combine flour, sugar, and salt in large bowl. Slowly whisk half-and-half, club soda, 4 tablespoons butter, eggs, and yolks into flour mixture until smooth.

2. Brush surface and sides of 10-inch nonstick skillet with 1 teaspoon butter and heat over medium heat. When butter stops sizzling, pour ⅓ cup batter into skillet, tilting pan to evenly coat bottom with batter. Cook until golden brown, 1 to 2 minutes per side. Transfer to plate and cover tightly with aluminum foil. Repeat with remaining butter and remaining batter. Serve.

TO MAKE AHEAD: Swedish pancakes can be refrigerated for up to 3 days or frozen for up to 1 month. Layer cooled pancakes between sheets of parchment paper, wrap in plastic wrap, and transfer to zipper-lock bag. To serve, microwave stack of 3 pancakes on 50 percent power until heated through, 10 to 20 seconds.

PANCAKE PRIMER

Like crêpes, our Swedish pancakes are made one at a time.

1. Tilt hot, buttered skillet and pour in ⅓ cup batter in slow, steady stream.

2. Swirl batter to evenly cover bottom of skillet. Cook until pancake appears dry.

3. Loosen edge with rubber spatula, grab it, and flip pancake.

PANCAKES IN AN INSTANT

In spite of its name, all-purpose flour isn't the best choice for every task. Instant flour (Wondra is the most common brand) is finely ground, low-protein flour that dissolves instantly (with very few lumps) in hot or cold liquids like sauces, gravies, soups, and, of course, crêpes. This is due to pregelatinization, a process in which the flour is effectively precooked and then dried. Instant flour is also used as a coating for fried chicken or fish, as the tiny particles distribute evenly into thin crusts.

WHY THIS RECIPE WORKS

The pride of Crab Orchard, Nebraska, Leona Schnuelle took home the grand prize at the 1960 Pillsbury Bake-Off for this homey loaf of chewy, herb-flecked bread. Dilly Casserole Bread owes its supremely soft and airy texture to one unusual ingredient: cottage cheese. For our own version, we began by mashing cottage cheese to remove its large lumps, preventing large air pockets from forming during baking. Microwaving the mashed curds with onion, water, butter, and sugar helped mellow the onion's bite and united the ingredients' distinct flavors. After adding an egg to this mixture, we slowly incorporated the wet ingredients into a combination of flour, yeast, minced fresh dill, salt, and baking soda. We let our dill and onion–studded dough rise, stirred it to remove the air bubbles, and transferred it to a soufflé dish to rise again. After this second rest, we baked our bread to a deep golden brown, then reinforced its bright herbal flavor with a final brush of dill butter. We had to thank our old friend from Crab Orchard—our fresh take on her winning recipe was irresistible.

DILLY CASSEROLE BREAD   SERVES 8

Either small- or large-curd cottage cheese will work in this recipe. If you don't own a 1½-quart soufflé dish, you can use a loaf pan instead.

8	ounces (1 cup) cottage cheese
¼	cup water
2	tablespoons sugar
1	tablespoon plus 1 teaspoon unsalted butter, softened
1	tablespoon grated onion
1	large egg, room temperature
2¼	cups (11¼ ounces) all-purpose flour
2¼	teaspoons instant or rapid-rise yeast
2½	tablespoons minced fresh dill
1	teaspoon salt
¼	teaspoon baking soda

1. Grease large bowl and 1½-quart soufflé dish. Using potato masher, mash cottage cheese until no large lumps remain. Combine cottage cheese, water, sugar, 1 tablespoon butter, and onion in 2-cup liquid measuring cup. Microwave until mixture registers 110 degrees, about 30 seconds. Whisk in egg until combined.

2. Using stand mixer fitted with paddle, mix 1¼ cups flour, yeast, 2 tablespoons dill, salt, and baking soda together on low speed until combined. Slowly add cottage cheese mixture and mix until dough just comes together, about 1 minute. Using rubber spatula, stir in remaining 1 cup flour until just combined.

3. Transfer dough to prepared bowl. Cover with plastic wrap and let rise at room temperature until doubled in size, about 45 minutes. Adjust oven rack to lower-middle position and heat oven to 350 degrees. Stir dough to remove air bubbles and transfer to prepared soufflé dish. Cover loosely with plastic and let rise at room temperature until doubled in size, about 20 minutes. Discard plastic.

4. Combine remaining 1½ teaspoons dill and remaining 1 teaspoon butter in bowl. Bake loaf until deep golden brown, about 25 minutes, rotating dish halfway through baking. Brush bread with dill butter and let cool in dish on wire rack for 20 minutes. Remove bread from dish and let cool completely, about 2 hours. Serve.

YEAST 101

Yeast is commonly available in two forms: instant and active dry. We prefer instant yeast, also called rapid-rise, because it's faster-acting and easy to use. It does not need to be "proofed" in warm water; it can simply be added to dry ingredients. Both types of yeast come in packets of 2¼ teaspoons. Active dry yeast can be substituted for instant yeast, although you will need to use more. To compensate for the greater quantity of inactive yeast cells in active dry, simply use 25 percent more of it (for example, if the recipe calls for 1 teaspoon of instant, use 1¼ teaspoons of active dry). The inverse also applies—use about 25 percent less instant yeast in a recipe that calls for active dry. Don't forget to dissolve active dry yeast in a portion of the liquid (heated to 110 degrees) from the recipe. Then let it stand for 5 minutes before adding it to the remaining wet ingredients. Yeast begins to die at 130 degrees, so make sure the liquid is not too hot.

Yeast should be stored in a cool environment, in either the fridge or the freezer. Because yeast is a living organism, the expiration date on the package should be observed.

☙ WHY THIS RECIPE WORKS

Once one of America's favorite cookies, sand tarts were introduced to the United States by German immigrants in the 19th century and were especially popular across Ohio. It's quite possible they fell out of favor because rolling out this cookie's firm dough takes a lot of muscle. We decided to find a way to turn out these buttery, crisp cookies without the workout. For cookies that baked flat and crisp, we cut the butter into the flour and sugar (a technique called reverse creaming) and used a food processor for mixing—two steps that eliminated excess air in the dough. Switching from two eggs to one whole egg plus an extra yolk also helped prevent the cookies from doming. Bypassing cookie cutters and rolling pins altogether, we found that the rich, sticky dough was easily formed into balls, rolled in cinnamon sugar, and flattened with the bottom of a greased measuring cup. After a final sprinkle of cinnamon sugar, we carefully arranged sliced almonds in the dough to give our cookies their signature sand dollar look.

SAND TARTS   MAKES ABOUT 3 DOZEN

Both sliced natural almonds and blanched slices work well here.

2	cups (10 ounces) all-purpose flour
1¾	cups (12¼ ounces) sugar
¾	teaspoon salt
16	tablespoons unsalted butter, softened
1	large egg plus 1 large yolk
1½	teaspoons ground cinnamon
¼	cup sliced almonds

1. Adjust oven racks to upper-middle and lower-middle positions and heat oven to 350 degrees. Line 2 baking sheets with parchment paper. Process flour, 1½ cups sugar, and salt in food processor until combined. Add butter, 1 tablespoon at a time, and pulse until just incorporated. Add egg and yolk and pulse until soft dough forms.

2. Wrap dough in plastic wrap and flatten into 1-inch-thick disk. Transfer to freezer until firm, about 15 minutes. Combine cinnamon and remaining ¼ cup sugar in small bowl. Break disk of chilled dough into 2 pieces and return 1 piece to freezer. Working with floured hands, roll 1½ tablespoons chilled dough into 1½-inch ball, then roll in cinnamon-sugar mixture to coat. Place balls 3 inches apart on prepared baking sheets. Press balls into 2½-inch disks with greased measuring cup, sprinkle with cinnamon sugar, and garnish with almonds.

3. Bake cookies until edges are lightly browned, 10 to 12 minutes, switching and rotating sheets halfway through baking. Let cool for 5 minutes on sheets, then transfer to wire rack and cool completely. Repeat rolling, shaping, and garnishing process with remaining dough and bake as directed. Serve. (Cookies can be stored at room temperature for up to 3 days.)

SHAPING SAND TARTS

Rolling and cutting out this soft, butter-rich dough can be frustratingly messy. Pressing the individual balls of dough into thin cookies works much better. Here's how we do it.

1. Roll each 1½-inch ball of dough in cinnamon sugar.

2. Spray bottom of measuring cup with vegetable oil spray, then use it to press each ball into 2½-inch disk.

3. Sprinkle each cookie with more cinnamon sugar before decorating with sliced almonds and baking.

✓ WHY THIS RECIPE WORKS

Wisconsin's prized beers and dairy are no secret, but in the city of Racine, kringle—a buttery, flaky, oval-shaped Danish pastry—is king. There, bakers follow traditional kringle-making to the letter, spending three days folding, refolding, chilling, and relaxing the delicate dough. We wondered if we could shorten this process. A dough of flour, sugar, yeast, salt, butter, shortening, and sour cream was just the ticket—the shortening created tenderness, and the sour cream's acidity weakened the dough's gluten for a flaky texture. We rolled the dough into a rectangle, wrapped it, and refrigerated it for only 30 minutes before the real kringle construction began. After rolling out the chilled dough, we spread a buttery filling of pecans, brown sugar, and cinnamon (easily made in the food processor) along the bottom half of the dough. We folded the strip in half, sealing in the filling, and then we tucked one end of the strip into the other, forming an oval. Rather than wait overnight to bake, we found that 4 hours was just enough chilling time. With hours (if not days) to spare, our kringle baked to a beautifully flaky golden brown, making it a pastry we couldn't wait to share.

KRINGLE   MAKES 2; SERVES 16

If your food processor holds less than 11 cups, pulse the butter and shortening into the dry mixture in two batches in step 2.

FILLING

- 1 **cup pecans, toasted**
- ¾ **cup packed (5¼ ounces) light brown sugar**
- ¼ **teaspoon ground cinnamon**
- ⅛ **teaspoon salt**
- 4 **tablespoons unsalted butter, cut into ½-inch pieces and chilled**

DOUGH

- 4 **cups (20 ounces) all-purpose flour**
- 16 **tablespoons unsalted butter, cut into ½-inch pieces and chilled**
- 4 **tablespoons vegetable shortening, cut into ½-inch pieces and chilled**
- 2 **tablespoons confectioners' sugar**
- 2¼ **teaspoons instant or rapid-rise yeast**
- ¾ **teaspoon salt**
- 2 **cups sour cream**
- 1–2 **tablespoons ice water (optional)**
- 1 **large egg, lightly beaten**

GLAZE

- 1 **cup (4 ounces) confectioners' sugar**
- 2 **tablespoons whole or low-fat milk**
- ½ **teaspoon vanilla extract**

1. FOR THE FILLING: Process pecans, sugar, cinnamon, and salt in food processor until pecans are coarsely ground, about 5 seconds. Add butter and pulse until mixture resembles coarse meal, about 9 pulses. Transfer to bowl.

2. FOR THE DOUGH: Add flour, butter, shortening, sugar, yeast, and salt to now-empty food processor and pulse until mixture resembles coarse meal, 15 to 20 pulses. Transfer to bowl and stir in sour cream until dough forms. (If dough appears shaggy and dry, stir in up to 2 tablespoons ice water as needed.) Turn out dough onto lightly floured counter and divide in half. Pat each piece of dough into 7 by 3-inch rectangle and wrap in plastic wrap. Refrigerate dough for 30 minutes, then freeze until firm, about 15 minutes.

3. Line 2 rimmed baking sheets with parchment paper. Roll 1 piece of dough into 28 by 5-inch rectangle on lightly floured counter, about ¼ inch thick. Leaving ½-inch border around bottom and side edges, cover bottom half of strip with half of filling. Brush edge of uncovered dough with water, fold dough over filling, and pinch seams closed. Shape folded dough into oval, tuck 1 end inside other, and pinch to seal. Repeat with remaining dough and filling. Transfer to prepared sheets, cover with plastic, and refrigerate for at least 4 hours or up to 12 hours.

4. Adjust oven racks to upper-middle and lower-middle positions and heat oven to 350 degrees. Remove plastic, brush kringles with egg, and bake until golden brown, 40 to 50 minutes, switching and rotating sheets halfway through baking. Transfer kringles to wire rack and let cool for 30 minutes.

5. FOR THE GLAZE: Whisk sugar, milk, and vanilla in bowl until smooth. Drizzle glaze over kringles and let set for 10 minutes. Serve warm or at room temperature. (Kringles can be stored at room temperature for 2 days.)

KRINGLE CONSTRUCTION

1. Leave ½-inch border around edges of 28 by 5-inch strip of dough. Spread half of filling over bottom half.

2. Brush edge of uncovered dough with water and fold dough over filling. Pinch to close long seam.

3. Fit 1 end of folded dough inside other to make oval. Press together to seal.

✔ WHY THIS RECIPE WORKS

There are endless ways to make good use of summer's fresh blueberries, but Blueberry Boy Bait takes the cake all year long. Named for the tasty treat's habit-forming effect on young men, this coffee cake won second place in a Pillsbury baking contest, and we were sure its balance of tart berries, tender cake, and sweet cinnamon-sugar topping would win hearts all over again today. For a rich, flavorful cake, we combined flour, baking powder, and salt in one bowl, then beat together brown sugar, granulated sugar, and butter in another bowl until fluffy. To form the batter, we alternated beating the flour mixture and milk into the butter-sugar mixture. Tossing the blueberries with a teaspoon of flour before folding them into the batter ensured that they stayed suspended throughout the cake, promising berries in every bite. We sprinkled an extra helping of berries over the cake just before baking and followed with cinnamon sugar for a crunchy, sweet topping. Our boy bait emerged golden brown and packed with blueberries from top to bottom. Forget teenage boys—we were all hooked.

BLUEBERRY BOY BAIT

SERVES 12

If using frozen blueberries, do not let them thaw, as they will turn the batter a blue-green color.

CAKE

2	cups (10 ounces) plus 1 teaspoon all-purpose flour
1	tablespoon baking powder
1	teaspoon salt
16	tablespoons unsalted butter, softened
¾	cup packed (5¼ ounces) light brown sugar
½	cup (3½ ounces) granulated sugar
3	large eggs
1	cup whole milk
2½	ounces (½ cup) fresh or frozen blueberries

TOPPING

2½	ounces (½ cup) fresh or frozen blueberries
¼	cup (1¾ ounces) granulated sugar
½	teaspoon ground cinnamon

1. FOR THE CAKE: Adjust oven rack to middle position and heat oven to 350 degrees. Grease and flour 13 by 9-inch baking pan.

2. Whisk 2 cups flour, baking powder, and salt together in medium bowl. With electric mixer, beat butter and sugars on medium-high speed until fluffy, about 2 minutes. Add eggs, 1 at a time, beating until just incorporated. Reduce speed to medium and beat in one-third of flour mixture until incorporated; beat in half of milk. Beat in half of remaining flour mixture, then remaining milk, and finally remaining flour mixture. Toss blueberries with remaining 1 teaspoon flour. Using rubber spatula, gently fold blueberries into batter. Spread batter in prepared pan.

3. FOR THE TOPPING: Scatter blueberries over top of batter. Stir sugar and cinnamon together in small bowl and sprinkle over batter. Bake until toothpick inserted in center of cake comes out clean, 45 to 50 minutes. Let cake cool in pan for 20 minutes, then turn out and place on serving platter or cutting board (topping side up). Cut into squares and serve warm or at room temperature. (Cake can be stored at room temperature for up to 3 days.)

THE NAME SAYS IT ALL

We found the source of this recipe in a 1954 edition of the *Chicago Tribune*. A 15-year-old girl named Adrienne (aka Renny) Powell of Chicago entered her dessert—Blueberry Boy Bait—in the junior division of the Pillsbury Grand National Recipe and Baking Contest. She won second place, which included a $2,000 cash prize plus a promise to print her recipe in Pillsbury's *5th Grand National Recipes* cookbook. Renny named the cake (a family recipe) for the effect it had on teenage boys—one bite and they were hooked.

BLUEBERRIES: FRESH OR FROZEN?

There are two types of fresh blueberries: tiny field-grown berries such as the wild Maine blueberries available for a few weeks in the summer, and the larger cultivated berries. Buy fresh local berries for the best flavor. When not in season, you can buy berries from South America, but they do not have the flavor of fresh-picked berries.

Frozen blueberries, which are picked when fully ripe and immediately individually quick-frozen, make a good stand-in for fresh in many recipes, and they cost far less. In fact, a cake or pie made out of season will taste better (and be much cheaper) if you use frozen berries.

TOP-TO-BOTTOM BERRIES

For Blueberry Boy Bait to work its charm, the berries need to be evenly distributed. To keep blueberries from sinking to the bottom, we toss them with a teaspoon of flour.

✓ WHY THIS RECIPE WORKS

Gooey butter cake is a coffeehouse favorite across St. Louis, featuring rich coffee cake under a layer of indulgent, silky topping. Missouri's best melt-in-your-mouth squares strike the perfect balance between sturdy cake and sweet custard—a balance we wanted to replicate in our kitchen. We began with a yeasted dough, gradually adding butter to the dry ingredients and letting the dough rise in a warm oven. For a rich, gooey topping with enough body for clean slicing, we discovered that a little flour, some cream cheese, and a few tablespoons of instant pudding mix did the trick. We whipped sugar, butter, and cream cheese together before adding corn syrup, egg, and vanilla. Structure-boosting flour and the pudding mix were added last. We pressed the risen dough into a pan, then spread the topping into an even layer. Our finished cake was tender but held up nicely below our perfectly sticky, custardlike topping. Eyeing the other instant pudding flavors in our pantry, we made a few tweaks and turned out two more batches of gooey butter cake—butterscotch and chocolate—proving this lush St. Louis snack is a treat to suit every sweet tooth.

ST. LOUIS GOOEY BUTTER CAKE SERVES 8 TO 10

Be sure to remove the cake from the oven when the perimeter is golden brown and the center is still slightly loose; the topping will continue to set as the cake cools.

DOUGH

¼	cup warm whole milk (110 degrees)
1½	teaspoons instant or rapid-rise yeast
1½	cups (7½ ounces) all-purpose flour
2	large eggs, room temperature
¼	cup (1¾ ounces) granulated sugar
½	teaspoon vanilla extract
½	teaspoon salt
6	tablespoons unsalted butter, cut into 6 pieces and softened

TOPPING

½	cup (3½ ounces) granulated sugar
4	tablespoons unsalted butter, softened
2	ounces cream cheese, softened
1	large egg, room temperature
2	tablespoons light corn syrup
1	teaspoon vanilla extract
⅓	cup (1⅔ ounces) all-purpose flour
3	tablespoons instant vanilla pudding mix
2	tablespoons confectioners' sugar

1. FOR THE DOUGH: Adjust oven rack to lower-middle position and heat oven to 200 degrees. When oven temperature reaches 200 degrees, turn off oven. Make foil sling for 8-inch square baking pan by folding 2 long sheets of aluminum foil so each is 8 inches wide. Lay sheets of foil in pan perpendicular to each other, with extra foil hanging over edges of pan. Push foil into corners and up sides of pan, smoothing foil flush to pan. Grease foil, then grease medium bowl.

2. Using stand mixer fitted with paddle, mix together milk and yeast on low speed until yeast dissolves. Add flour, eggs, sugar, vanilla, and salt and mix until combined, about 30 seconds. Increase speed to medium-low and add butter, 1 piece at a time, until incorporated. Beat batter for 5 minutes, then transfer to prepared bowl, cover with plastic wrap, and place in warm oven. Let rise until doubled in size, about 30 minutes. Spread batter evenly in prepared pan. Heat oven to 350 degrees.

3. FOR THE TOPPING: Using clean, dry mixer bowl and paddle attachment, beat granulated sugar, butter, and cream cheese on medium speed until fluffy, about 2 minutes. Reduce speed to low; add egg, corn syrup, and vanilla; and beat until combined. Add flour and pudding mix and mix until incorporated. Portion topping evenly over batter, then spread into even layer.

4. Bake until exterior is golden and center of topping is just beginning to color (center should jiggle slightly when you shake pan), about 25 minutes, rotating pan halfway through baking. Let cake cool in pan on wire rack for at least 3 hours. Using foil overhang, lift cake out of pan. Dust cake with confectioners' sugar and serve. (Cake can be wrapped tightly in plastic and refrigerated for up to 2 days.)

BUTTERSCOTCH GOOEY BUTTER CAKE

For dough, substitute ¼ cup packed (1¾ ounces) light brown sugar for granulated sugar in step 2. For topping, substitute 3 tablespoons instant butterscotch pudding mix for vanilla pudding mix in step 3.

CHOCOLATE GOOEY BUTTER CAKE

For dough, replace 3 tablespoons flour with equal amount of Dutch-processed cocoa in step 2. For topping, substitute 3 tablespoons instant chocolate pudding mix for vanilla pudding mix in step 3.

MEET ME IN ST. LOUIS...FOR BUTTER CAKE

As any St. Louis native will tell you, there are actually two distinct styles of gooey butter cake—and everyone we talked to during a recent two-day visit had a favorite. Many bakeries and coffee shops sell squares of gooey butter cake that are more like a chewy (and messy) bar cookie than a cake. The base is cake batter and the topping is like cheesecake. The second style is more like an old-fashioned coffee cake, with a rich yeast dough and custardy topping.

☑ WHY THIS RECIPE WORKS

In Ohio, the buckeye is everywhere. It's the state tree, so named because its nuts resemble a deer's eyes; the Ohio State University's beloved mascot, Brutus Buckeye; and—our personal favorite—an irresistible chocolate-dipped peanut butter candy made to resemble the nut. For a rich peanut butter ball that would hold its shape when dipped in chocolate, we beat together peanut butter, melted white chocolate, confectioners' sugar, and vanilla. This combination turned soft peanut butter into a moldable dough, easily rolled into bite-size balls. Once frozen, the peanut butter balls were ready for their chocolate coating. Melted semisweet chocolate chips were all we needed for the buckeyes' sturdy shell. Using a toothpick, we picked up and dipped each ball in the melted chocolate, leaving some of the peanut butter exposed for candies that looked like real buckeye nuts. An hour in the refrigerator set the chocolate, forming a crisp chocolate shell to pair with the buckeyes' big peanut butter flavor. Turns out you don't need to live in Ohio to be a buckeye fan.

BUCKEYES

MAKES 4 DOZEN

Do not use natural peanut butter here.

- 1½ ounces white chocolate chips
- 2¾ cups creamy peanut butter
- 4 tablespoons unsalted butter, softened
- 3 cups (12 ounces) confectioners' sugar
- 1 teaspoon vanilla extract
- ⅛ teaspoon salt
- 2 cups (12 ounces) semisweet chocolate chips

1. Line rimmed baking sheet with parchment paper. Microwave white chocolate chips in bowl on 50 percent power, stirring occasionally, until melted, about 1 minute. Let cool for 5 minutes. Using stand mixer fitted with paddle, beat peanut butter, melted white chocolate, butter, sugar, vanilla, and salt on medium-high speed until just combined, about 1 minute. Roll dough into 1¼-inch balls and place on prepared sheet. Freeze until firm, about 30 minutes.

2. Microwave semisweet chocolate chips in bowl on 50 percent power, stirring occasionally, until melted, 1½ to 2 minutes. Using toothpick, dip chilled balls into melted chocolate, leaving top quarter of balls uncovered. Return balls to prepared sheet and refrigerate until chocolate is set, about 1 hour. Serve. (Buckeyes can be refrigerated for up to 1 week or frozen for up to 1 month.)

DO THE DIP

Pick up chilled peanut butter balls with toothpick. Dip them into melted chocolate, leaving small portion of peanut butter exposed. Let chocolate set in refrigerator.

SEMISWEET VERSUS BITTERSWEET

What's the difference between semisweet and bittersweet chocolates? Legally speaking, there is no difference. In order for a chocolate to be called "bittersweet" or "semisweet," the U.S. Food and Drug Administration mandates that it contain at least 35 percent cacao, and manufacturers may use either term for chocolate that meets that minimum. That said, most manufacturers use "bittersweet" for chocolates that are higher in cacao (and hence less sweet) than their "semisweet" offering. Thus, "bittersweet" and "semisweet" can be useful terms for comparing products within one brand but are imprecise across different brands.

TEXAS AND THE WEST

FUNERAL POTATOES
UTAH

CANADA

JO JO POTATOES
PACIFIC
NORTHWEST

WASHINGTON

MONTANA

MILLIONAIRE PIE
HOBBS, NM

OREGON

IDAHO

WYOMING

HEAVENLY HOTS
BERKELEY, CA

NEVADA

UTAH

COLORADO

CALIFORNIA

TICK TOCK ORANGE
STICKY ROLLS
HOLLYWOOD, CA

ARIZONA

NEW
MEXICO

OKLAHOMA

TEXAS

PACIFIC OCEAN

HAWAII

KALUA PORK
OAHU, HI

OKLAHOMA BARBECUED
CHOPPED PORK
MARIETTA, OK

MEXICO

TEXAS CAVIAR
DALLAS, TX

237	**Crispy Beef Taquitos**		269	**Texas Caviar**
239	**Baked Jalapeño Poppers**		271	**Wild Rice Dressing**
241	**Monterey Chicken**			Dried Fruit and Nut Wild
	Pico de Gallo			Rice Dressing
243	**Monte Cristo Sandwiches** ⭐			Leek and Mushroom Wild
245	**Oklahoma Barbecued Chopped Pork**			Rice Dressing
	Oklahoma Barbecue Relish		273	**Hawaiian Fried Rice**
247	**Kalua Pork**			Faux Leftover Rice
249	**Country-Fried Pork with Gravy**		275	**Tex-Mex Rice**
251	**Oven-Barbecued Beef Brisket**		277	**Cornflake Stuffing**
253	**Indoor Barbecue Beef Short Ribs** ⭐		279	**Jo Jo Potatoes**
				Ranch Dressing
255	**Texas Chicken-Fried Steak**		281	**Funeral Potatoes**
257	**Mulligan Stew**		283	**Heavenly Hots**
259	**New Mexican Pork Stew (Posole)**		285	**Tick Tock Orange Sticky Rolls**
261	**Carne Adovada**		287	**Harvey House Chocolate Puffs**
263	**Hollywood Chili**		289	**Millionaire Pie**
265	**Chiles Rellenos Casserole**		291	**Black-Bottom Pie**
267	**King Ranch Casserole**		293	**Texas Blueberry Cobbler**

⭐ FIND A LOCAL HOT SPOT

✔ WHY THIS RECIPE WORKS

If you don't live in the Southwest, it's likely that the only *taquitos* you've had came from the freezer, which are nothing like the real thing: deep-fried rolled tacos filled with spicy, well-seasoned meat. For our "from scratch" version, we needed the beef filling to be loaded with Tex-Mex flavor and the tortilla to stay closed for tidy frying and hand-held eating. Browned ground beef mixed with sautéed onion, jalapeños, garlic, cumin, and chili powder went into our filling, and mashed pinto beans, tomato sauce, and cilantro rounded out the authentic flavors. Steaming the tortillas in the microwave made folding a cinch. Before spooning the filling onto the now-pliable shells, we brushed egg on the top edge to seal. We folded and rolled the bottom of the tortilla over the beef into a tight cylinder. While we assembled the remaining taquitos, we kept the finished ones under a damp towel to prevent cracking. Shallow-frying with their seams against the bottom of the skillet crisped the tortillas and kept the filling sealed in. For a creamy companion to these beefy taquitos, we mashed avocados with cilantro, lime juice, and sour cream for a cool, fresh dipping sauce.

CRISPY BEEF TAQUITOS

MAKES 12

Keep the seam side in contact with the bottom of the pan while frying to prevent the taquitos from unrolling.

TAQUITOS

1	cup plus 4 teaspoons vegetable oil
8	ounces 90 percent lean ground beef
1	cup canned pinto beans, rinsed
1	onion, halved and sliced thin
2	jalapeño chiles, stemmed, seeded, and minced
3	garlic cloves, minced
1	teaspoon ground cumin
1	teaspoon chili powder
1	(8-ounce) can tomato sauce
½	cup water
3	tablespoons minced fresh cilantro
	Salt and pepper
12	(6-inch) corn tortillas
1	large egg, lightly beaten

AVOCADO SAUCE

2	avocados, halved, pitted, and chopped coarse
½	cup sour cream
¼	cup water
3	tablespoons lime juice (2 limes)
2	tablespoons minced fresh cilantro
	Salt and pepper

1. FOR THE TAQUITOS: Heat 1 teaspoon oil in 12-inch nonstick skillet over medium-high heat until just smoking. Add beef and cook, breaking up pieces with spoon, until no longer pink, about 5 minutes. Drain beef in colander; set aside. Mash beans to paste with potato masher or fork; set aside.

2. Heat 1 tablespoon oil in now-empty skillet over medium heat until shimmering. Add onion and cook until lightly browned, about 5 minutes. Stir in jalapeños, garlic, cumin, and chili powder and cook until fragrant, about 30 seconds. Stir in mashed beans, tomato sauce, water, cilantro, ½ teaspoon salt, and ½ teaspoon pepper. Stir in drained beef and cook, stirring occasionally, until mixture has thickened and begins to sizzle, about 10 minutes. Season with salt and pepper to taste. Transfer to bowl; set aside to cool, about 20 minutes.

3. Line rimmed baking sheet with parchment paper. Set wire rack inside second rimmed baking sheet. Wrap 6 tortillas in clean damp dish towel, place on plate, and cover plate. Microwave until hot and pliable, about 90 seconds. Working with 1 tortilla at a time, brush edge of top half with egg. Place row of 3 level tablespoons filling across lower half of tortilla. Fold bottom of tortilla up and over filling, then pull back on tortilla to tighten it around filling. Roll tightly and place seam side down on lined baking sheet. Cover with second clean damp towel. Microwave remaining 6 tortillas and repeat with remaining filling. (Taquitos can be made up to 24 hours ahead, covered with damp towel, wrapped tightly in plastic wrap, and refrigerated.)

4. Adjust oven rack to middle position and heat oven to 200 degrees. Heat remaining 1 cup oil in 12-inch nonstick skillet over medium-high heat to 350 degrees. Using tongs, place 6 taquitos, seam side down, in oil and fry until golden, about 5 minutes. Flip and fry until second side is golden, about 3 minutes longer. Transfer to wire rack and place in oven to keep warm. Repeat with remaining 6 taquitos.

5. FOR THE AVOCADO SAUCE: Meanwhile, combine avocados, sour cream, water, lime juice, and cilantro in bowl and mash with potato masher or fork until smooth. Season with salt and pepper to taste. Cover with plastic until ready to serve. Serve taquitos with sauce.

TRICKS TO TIDY TAQUITOS

1. Place line of filling on bottom half of each tortilla, fold over, pull tortilla taut, and roll.

2. Shallow-fry rolled taquitos, pressing seams against bottom of skillet to seal.

✅ WHY THIS RECIPE WORKS

Jalapeño poppers are an addictive bar snack with a one-two punch: intense jalapeño heat and a cool, cheesy filling. Poppers are usually deep-fried, but to make this rich, crunchy appetizer at home, baking was our best bet. A brief blast of heat in the oven softened the halved, seeded jalapeños. An egg yolk and panko bread crumbs gave the filling—a flavor-packed blend of cream cheese, cheddar, and Monterey Jack—some stability. Scallions, cilantro, lime juice, cumin, and bacon added contrasting smoke and bright citrus notes. We spooned the filling into the softened jalapeño halves and baked them for about 10 minutes, just enough time for them to develop a tender texture and lightly browned crust. In no time at all, we had spicy, creamy poppers that put their deep-fried brethren to shame.

BAKED JALAPEÑO POPPERS   MAKES 24

Use a teaspoon to scrape the seeds and ribs from the halved chiles.

- **6** slices bacon
- **12** jalapeño chiles, halved lengthwise with stems left intact, seeds and ribs removed
- Salt
- **4** ounces mild cheddar cheese, shredded (1 cup)
- **4** ounces Monterey Jack cheese, shredded (1 cup)
- **4** ounces cream cheese, softened
- **2** scallions, sliced thin
- **3** tablespoons minced fresh cilantro
- **2** tablespoons panko bread crumbs
- **1** large egg yolk
- **2** teaspoons lime juice
- **1** teaspoon ground cumin

1. Adjust oven rack to upper-middle position and heat oven to 500 degrees. Set wire rack in rimmed baking sheet. Cook bacon in 12-inch nonstick skillet over medium heat until crisp, 7 to 9 minutes. Transfer to paper towel–lined plate. When bacon is cool enough to handle, chop fine and set aside.

2. Season jalapeños with salt and place cut side down on wire rack. Bake until just beginning to soften, about 5 minutes. Remove jalapeños from oven and reduce oven temperature to 450 degrees. When cool enough to handle, flip jalapeños cut side up.

3. Mix cheddar, Monterey Jack, cream cheese, scallions, cilantro, panko, egg yolk, lime juice, cumin, and bacon together in bowl until thoroughly combined. Divide cheese mixture among jalapeños, pressing into cavities. Bake until jalapeños are tender and filling is lightly browned, 9 to 11 minutes. Let cool for 5 minutes. Serve.

TO MAKE AHEAD: Filled and unbaked jalapeños can be covered and refrigerated for up to 1 day. Add 3 minutes to baking time.

PICK A COLOR

A red jalapeño is simply a jalapeño that has been allowed to ripen before harvest. To determine if color would make a difference in our Baked Jalapeño Poppers, we grilled a few of each and had tasters try them plain. Some found the red jalapeños more "fruity" and the green more "vegetal." Still, all tasters felt that the jalapeños would make fine substitutes for each other. The factors responsible for a chile's heat are genetic makeup and growing conditions (hot, dry conditions usually make for spicier chiles), not color.

But maybe our tasters were influenced by what they saw, not what they tasted. To correct for that possibility, we devised a third test: We pureed equal weights of each type of chile with equal weights of water and then added food coloring to make the green chile mixture appear red and the red chile mixture appear green. (Sneaky, huh?) This time, the results split down the middle: Half of the tasters found the disguised red chile mixture slightly fruitier and "spicier," but the other half, perhaps influenced by its apparent color, called it "green-tasting" and "flatter."

Our consensus? You may use red and green jalapeños interchangeably. Heat is not determined by color.

✔ WHY THIS RECIPE WORKS

Actor Dan Blocker was famous for playing Hoss Cartwright on the TV Western *Bonanza*, but he also left a tastier legacy when he established Bonanza Steakhouse. A mainstay on the menu, chicken Monterey features flame-broiled chicken breasts bursting with "exclusive Monterey marinade" flavors and topped with bacon and Monterey Jack cheese. For our version, we butterflied chicken breasts and marinated them in a tangy mixture of Dijon, honey, salt, and pepper. We tossed cooked bacon pieces with pepper Jack cheese (a livelier alternative to Monterey Jack) for the melted cheese topping. The chicken developed a nice char on the hotter side of the grill while the onion slices, brushed with the bacon's rendered fat, softened and took on great smoky flavor on the cooler side. Before the chicken finished cooking, we moved the breasts to the cooler side and topped them with the charred onion rings and bacon-cheese mixture. A few minutes on the covered grill melted the cheese to perfection. A spoonful or two of pico de gallo gave the dish a bright, zesty finish, making Monterey chicken a recipe we certainly wanted to keep in syndication.

MONTEREY CHICKEN SERVES 4

We skewer the onion slices with a toothpick to keep them from falling apart on the grill. You won't need an entire red onion for this recipe; you can use the remainder to make Pico de Gallo (recipe follows).

- ½ **cup Dijon mustard**
- ¼ **cup honey**
  Salt and pepper
- 4 **(6- to 8-ounce) boneless, skinless chicken breasts, trimmed**
- 4 **slices bacon, cut into ½-inch pieces**
- 6 **ounces pepper Jack cheese, shredded (1½ cups)**
- 4 **(½-inch-thick) slices red onion**
  Lime wedges

1. Whisk mustard, honey, 1 teaspoon salt, and ½ teaspoon pepper together in bowl. Reserve ¼ cup honey-mustard mixture for basting chicken. Transfer remaining honey-mustard mixture to 1-gallon zipper-lock bag.

2. Working with 1 breast at a time, starting on thick side, cut chicken in half horizontally, stopping ½ inch from edge so halves remain attached. Open up breast like book, creating single flat piece. Place chicken in bag with honey-mustard mixture, toss to coat, and refrigerate for at least 30 minutes or up to 1 hour.

3. Meanwhile, cook bacon in 10-inch skillet over medium heat until crisp, 5 to 7 minutes. Using slotted spoon, transfer bacon to paper towel–lined plate. Reserve bacon fat. Once cool, toss bacon with pepper Jack.

4A. FOR A CHARCOAL GRILL: Open bottom vent completely. Light large chimney starter filled with charcoal briquettes (6 quarts). When top coals are partially covered with ash, pour two-thirds evenly over half of grill, then pour remaining coals over other half of grill. Set cooking grate in place, cover, and open lid vent completely. Heat grill until hot, about 5 minutes.

4B. FOR A GAS GRILL: Turn all burners to high, cover, and heat grill until hot, about 15 minutes. Leave primary burner on high and turn other burner(s) to medium. (Adjust primary burner as needed to maintain grill temperature of 350 to 400 degrees.)

5. Clean and oil cooking grate. Push toothpick horizontally through each onion slice to keep rings intact while grilling. Brush onion slices lightly with reserved bacon fat and place on cooler side of grill. Place chicken on hotter side of grill, cover, and cook until lightly charred, about 5 minutes. Flip onion slices and chicken. Brush chicken with reserved honey-mustard mixture, cover, and cook until lightly charred on second side, about 5 minutes.

6. Remove onion slices from grill and move chicken to cooler side of grill. Quickly remove toothpicks and separate onion rings. Divide onion rings evenly among chicken breasts. Divide bacon–pepper Jack mixture evenly over onion rings. Cover and cook until pepper Jack is melted and chicken registers 160 degrees, about 2 minutes. Transfer chicken to platter, tent loosely with aluminum foil, and let rest for 5 to 10 minutes. Serve with lime wedges.

PICO DE GALLO SERVES 4

While pico de gallo is not part of the original Bonanza Steakhouse recipe, we did find it in a few copycat recipes. It's delicious spooned over our Monterey Chicken. To make it spicier, include the jalapeño seeds.

- 3 **tomatoes, cored and chopped**
  Salt and pepper
- ¼ **cup finely chopped red onion**
- ¼ **cup chopped fresh cilantro**
- 1 **jalapeño chile, stemmed, seeded, and minced**
- 1 **tablespoon lime juice**
- 1 **garlic clove, minced**

Toss tomatoes with ¼ teaspoon salt in bowl. Transfer to colander and let drain for 30 minutes. Combine drained tomatoes, onion, cilantro, jalapeño, lime juice, and garlic in bowl. Season with salt and pepper to taste. Serve.

✓ WHY THIS RECIPE WORKS

Monte Cristo sandwiches are a sweet-and-savory, crisp-yet-tender take on grilled cheese, loaded with all the familiar, cozy flavors of a grilled ham, turkey, and cheese sandwich—but with a twist. A batter of eggs, heavy cream, sugar, dry mustard, and cayenne established our Monte Cristo coating, giving the bread a browned, caramelized exterior with a hint of heat. Toasting the bread first dried it out enough to stay crisp after the batter dunk. These sandwiches are served with a sweet dip, and strawberry jam stirred with Dijon mustard was the perfect blend. Spreading some of the jam-Dijon sauce on the bread carried its contrasting flavors into every bite. After we layered the ham, turkey, and Swiss on the bread and coated each sandwich with batter, arranging the Monte Cristos on a preheated oiled baking sheet kick-started their sizzle. Ten minutes in a hot oven (with a flip halfway through for even browning) was all it took to turn out hot, crisp sandwiches to please everyone at the table. With a dusting of confectioners' sugar and the extra jam-mustard sauce on the side, this grilled-cheese-meets-French-toast sandwich was ready for brunch.

MONTE CRISTO SANDWICHES   SERVES 6

Trim the slices of meat and cheese as necessary to fit neatly on the bread.

4	large eggs
¼	cup heavy cream
2	teaspoons sugar
½	teaspoon salt
½	teaspoon dry mustard
⅛	teaspoon cayenne pepper
6	tablespoons strawberry or raspberry jam
2	tablespoons Dijon mustard
12	slices hearty white sandwich bread, lightly toasted
18	thin slices deli Swiss or Gruyère cheese
12	thin slices deli ham, preferably Black Forest
12	thin slices deli turkey
3	tablespoons vegetable oil
	Confectioners' sugar

1. Adjust oven rack to upper-middle position and heat oven to 450 degrees. Whisk together eggs, cream, sugar, salt, dry mustard, and cayenne in shallow dish until combined. Stir jam and Dijon mustard together in small bowl.

2. Spread 1 teaspoon jam mixture on 1 side of each slice of toast. Layer slices of cheese, ham, and turkey over jam on 6 slices of toast. Repeat with second layer of cheese, ham, and turkey. Add final layer of cheese and top with remaining toast, with jam side facing cheese. Using hands, lightly press down on sandwiches.

3. Pour oil into rimmed baking sheet and heat in oven until just smoking, about 7 minutes. Meanwhile, using 2 hands, coat each sandwich with egg mixture and transfer to large plate. Transfer sandwiches to preheated baking sheet and bake until golden brown on both sides, 4 to 5 minutes per side, using spatula to flip. Sprinkle with confectioners' sugar and serve immediately with remaining jam mixture.

NO-FRY CRISP MONTE CRISTOS

1. TOASTED BREAD: Toasting bread jump-starts browning and helps keep it from turning soggy when coated with batter.

2. SWEET BATTER: Coating sandwiches in egg batter that contains a bit of sugar encourages browning and crispness.

3. HOT PAN: Preheating oil and baking sheet makes sandwiches sizzle when they hit pan; they begin to crisp right away.

EATING LOCAL ★ ANAHEIM, CA

The Monte Cristo earned national recognition when it appeared on the menus of Disneyland's **BLUE BAYOU** and Tahitian Terrace restaurants in 1966. Though the Terrace has since closed, the Monte Cristo remains a favorite at Blue Bayou. But before Disneyland, this sandwich was being enjoyed as far back as the 1920s. No one is certain of the story behind the name, but some think there is a connection between the sandwich and film adaptations of Alexander Dumas's *The Count of Monte Cristo*. We'll bite.

BLUE BAYOU RESTAURANT
New Orleans Square
Disneyland Park
Anaheim, CA

✓ WHY THIS RECIPE WORKS

Oklahomans have a no-frills approach to barbecue. As one Sooner State pit master confided, "If your pork is smothered in sauce, it means you're trying to cover something up." A hybrid grill-oven technique promised tender, full-flavored chopped pork with nothing to hide—and in half the time. Weighing in at a manageable 7 pounds or so, a bone-in pork butt was our roast of choice. We rubbed its surface with a classic Oklahoma blend of brown sugar, paprika, salt, and black and white peppers. For staggered smoking, we made two wood chip packets and layered them—packet, unlit coals, packet, lit coals. (For a gas grill, we added ice cubes to one of the packets to slow its release of smoke.) With our grill equipped for extended smoking, we placed our rubbed pork on the cooler side of the grill and covered it. Once the char and signature smoky flavor were established, moving the pork to a hot oven turned the meat tender. Chopped into hearty chunks, the pork was juicy, loaded with flavor, and, as promised, had nothing to be ashamed of. (A little Oklahoma Barbecue Relish never hurt, though.)

OKLAHOMA BARBECUED CHOPPED PORK

SERVES 8

Pork butt roast is often labeled "Boston butt"; do not use a picnic roast. If you can't find a bone-in roast, use a 4- to 5-pound boneless roast and begin checking for doneness after 1 hour in step 5. We like hickory wood chips for this recipe; avoid mesquite. Serve with Oklahoma Barbecue Relish (recipe follows) and your favorite barbecue sauce, if desired.

- 2 **tablespoons packed brown sugar**
- 2 **tablespoons paprika**
  Salt and pepper
- 1 **tablespoon white pepper**
- 1 **(6- to 8-pound) bone-in pork butt roast, trimmed**
- 4 **cups wood chips, soaked in water for 15 minutes and drained**

1. Combine sugar, paprika, 2 tablespoons pepper, 1 tablespoon salt, and white pepper in small bowl. Pat pork dry with paper towels and rub spice mixture all over pork. (Pork can be wrapped in plastic wrap and refrigerated for up to 24 hours.)

2. Using large piece of heavy-duty aluminum foil, wrap 2 cups soaked wood chips in foil packet and cut several vent holes in top. Repeat with remaining chips (if using gas grill, add ½ cup ice cubes to remaining packet).

3A. FOR A CHARCOAL GRILL: Open bottom vent halfway. Place foil packet on 1 side of grill and cover packet and half of grill with 3 quarts unlit charcoal. Place second foil packet on top of unlit coals. Light chimney starter three-quarters filled with charcoal briquettes (4½ quarts). When top coals are partially covered with ash, pour evenly on top of second foil packet. Set cooking grate in place, cover, and open lid vent halfway. Heat grill until hot, about 5 minutes.

3B. FOR A GAS GRILL: Place both foil packets over primary burner. Turn all burners to high, cover, and heat grill until hot and wood chips are smoking, about 15 minutes. Turn primary burner to medium-high and turn off other burner(s). (Adjust primary burner as needed to maintain grill temperature of 275 to 300 degrees.)

4. Clean and oil cooking grate. Place pork on cooler side of grill and cook, covered, until pork is lightly charred and smoky, about 4 hours.

5. Adjust oven rack to middle position and heat oven to 325 degrees. Transfer smoked pork to roasting pan and cover pan tightly with foil. Bake until pork is tender and pulls away from bone and meat near (but not touching) bone registers 190 degrees, 2 to 3 hours. Remove from oven and let rest, covered, for 30 minutes.

6. Uncover pork and place on carving board. If desired, strain contents of pan through fine-mesh strainer into fat separator. Let liquid settle, then return defatted juices to chopped pork. When meat is cool enough to handle, pull into large chunks. Roughly chop pork and transfer to large bowl. Season with salt and pepper to taste and serve. (Pork can be refrigerated for up to 3 days.)

OKLAHOMA BARBECUE RELISH
MAKES ABOUT 4 CUPS

Since the relish must be refrigerated until it is well chilled, we recommend making it while the pork is cooking in the oven.

- ½ **head green cabbage, cored and chopped fine (6 cups)**
- 1½ **cups sweet pickle relish**
- ½ **cup cider vinegar**
- 3 **tablespoons yellow mustard**
- ¾ **teaspoon celery salt**
- ¼ **teaspoon white pepper**

Combine all ingredients in large bowl. Cover with plastic wrap and refrigerate until chilled, at least 30 minutes. (Relish can be refrigerated for up to 5 days.)

✅ WHY THIS RECIPE WORKS

Beyond the beaches of Oahu, you'd be hard-pressed to find anyone serving kalua pork, the shredded smoked suckling pig that's the centerpiece at Hawaiian luaus. There, a whole pig is cooked over a fire of Hawaiian kiawe wood in a pit lined with rocks and banana leaves. Without easy access to most of those flavor builders, we tried to re-create the smoky, tropical notes with common supermarket items. Pork butt's balance of muscle and fat would stay moist and flavorful during low, slow cooking. Mesquite is related to kiawe, so we created a foil packet of mesquite wood chips for similar smoke. To replicate the earthy, grassy flavor given off by banana leaves, we rubbed the roast with a blend of green tea, brown sugar, salt, and pepper. Using both the grill and the oven gave us all the smoke and tenderness of pit cooking without the wait (or the digging). Placing the pork in an aluminum pan and covering the pan with foil collected the juices and contained the steam. After capturing the mesquite's flavorful smoke on the grill, we moved the roast to the oven. Soon enough, the pork was tender as can be, and its bright flavor brought the luau home.

KALUA PORK SERVES 8

You'll need 10 to 15 green tea bags. Pork butt roast is often labeled "Boston butt" in the supermarket. If your pork butt comes with an elastic netting, remove it before you rub the pork with the tea. When using a charcoal grill, we prefer wood chunks to wood chips whenever possible; substitute six medium wood chunks, soaked in water for 1 hour, for the wood chip packets.

- 3 **tablespoons green tea leaves**
- 4 **teaspoons kosher salt**
- 1 **tablespoon packed brown sugar**
- 2 **teaspoons pepper**
- 1 **(4- to 5-pound) boneless pork butt roast, trimmed**
- 1 **(13 by 9-inch) disposable aluminum roasting pan**
- 6 **cups mesquite wood chips, soaked in water for 15 minutes and drained**

1. Combine tea, salt, sugar, and pepper in bowl. Pat pork dry with paper towels and rub with tea mixture. Wrap meat tightly with plastic wrap and refrigerate for 6 to 24 hours. Place pork in disposable pan and cover pan loosely with aluminum foil. Poke about twenty ¼-inch holes in foil. Using large piece of heavy-duty foil, wrap 2 cups wood chips in foil packet and cut several vent holes in top. Make 2 more packets with additional foil and remaining 4 cups chips.

2A. FOR A CHARCOAL GRILL: Open bottom vent halfway. Light large chimney starter three-quarters filled with charcoal briquettes (4½ quarts). When top coals are partially covered with ash, pour into steeply banked pile against side of grill. Place wood chip packets on coals. Set cooking grate in place, cover, and open lid vent halfway. Heat grill until hot and wood chips are smoking, about 5 minutes.

2B. FOR A GAS GRILL: Place wood chip packets over primary burner. Turn all burners to high, cover, and heat grill until hot and wood chips are smoking, about 15 minutes. Turn primary burner to medium-high and turn off other burner(s). (Adjust primary burner as needed to maintain grill temperature around 300 degrees.)

3. Place pan on cool side of grill. Cover (positioning lid vent over meat if using charcoal) and cook for 2 hours. During last 20 minutes of grilling, adjust oven rack to lower-middle position and heat oven to 325 degrees.

4. Remove pan from grill. Cover pan tightly with new sheet of foil, transfer to oven, and bake until tender and fork inserted in meat meets no resistance, 2 to 3 hours. Let pork rest, covered, for 30 minutes. Unwrap and, when meat is cool enough to handle, shred into bite-size pieces, discarding fat. Strain contents of pan through fine-mesh strainer into fat separator. Let liquid settle, then return ¼ cup defatted pan juices to pork. Serve. (Pork can be refrigerated for up to 3 days.)

SOAKING WOOD CHIPS

Wood chips are soaked for smoking because they produce much more smoke than dry chips do. To investigate the effects of soaking time, we soaked batches of relatively mild oak chips for 15 minutes, 1 hour, 4 hours, and 24 hours before smoking halved chickens for 1 hour and large pork shoulders for 2 hours (we finished cooking the pork in the oven) in a standard kettle grill.

We noticed something interesting right away: After about 2 hours of soaking, the chips started to saturate and sink. At the 4-hour mark, all lay at the bottom of the bowl. And whether the chips were saturated or not made a big difference in flavor. The meat we smoked using chips soaked for 15 and 60 minutes tasted nice and smoky, but the meat smoked using chips that had soaked for 4 and 24 hours tasted like "a wet ashtray," in the words of one taster. What was going on here?

Saturated chips produce steam until they dry out, at which point they begin smoking. The culprit here is not the smoke but the steam, which carries malodorous molecules from the wood to the surface of the food. When smoking for a short period, saturated chips produce impure steam for a greater proportion of the total smoking time, so the off-flavors dominate. In longer-smoked pulled pork, however, tasters couldn't detect a difference between pork that was smoked with short-soaked versus saturated chips. When food is left on the grill long after the soaked chips stop producing impure steam, any off-flavors are covered up by the additional smoke.

The bottom line: 15 minutes is sufficient for soaking wood chips—and longer soaking can be a problem.

✔ WHY THIS RECIPE WORKS

Good country-fried pork ought to be a thin, tender cut of pork coated with a crisp, craggy shell. First things first, we needed an assertive, creamy gravy on hand. Onion softened in butter kicked off its flavor, followed by garlic, dried sage, and paprika for an intense, seasoned jolt. Flour added body, and milk and chicken broth imparted creamy, meaty taste to complement the pork. A generous amount of Worcestershire and pepper gave our gravy a bold finish. Turning to the pork, we began with a single tenderloin split into four pieces, scoring the uncut sides' surfaces and dredging the pork in flour bolstered with cornstarch (to create a supercrisp crust), baking powder (for lightness), and bold seasonings—garlic powder, onion powder, and cayenne. We pounded the pork thin and dredged it again, this time following the flour with a dip in an egg-milk solution and a pasty mixture of the flour blend and milk. Resting our breaded pork in the refrigerator set the coating. It took just a few minutes for the crust to turn golden when frying two pieces at a time in a skillet. With its crunchy crust and bold, creamy gravy, this basic piece of pork had serious country cred.

COUNTRY-FRIED PORK WITH GRAVY SERVES 4

Avoid using low-fat or skim milk in the gravy. Make the gravy first so the crisp pork doesn't turn soggy while waiting for it.

GRAVY

3	tablespoons unsalted butter
¼	cup finely chopped onion
3	tablespoons all-purpose flour
1	garlic clove, minced
1	teaspoon dried sage
½	teaspoon paprika
2	cups chicken broth
1	cup whole milk
4	teaspoons Worcestershire sauce
	Salt and pepper

PORK

2	cups all-purpose flour
½	cup cornstarch
2	teaspoons garlic powder
2	teaspoons onion powder
	Salt and pepper
1½	teaspoons baking powder
¼	teaspoon cayenne pepper
½	cup whole milk
2	large eggs
1	(1-pound) pork tenderloin, trimmed, cut crosswise into 4 pieces
1	cup peanut or vegetable oil

1. FOR THE GRAVY: Melt butter in medium saucepan over medium heat. Add onion and cook until softened, about 5 minutes. Stir in flour, garlic, sage, and paprika and cook, whisking constantly, until golden and fragrant, about 1 minute. Slowly whisk in broth and milk and bring to boil. Reduce heat to medium-low and simmer until thickened, about 10 minutes. Off heat, stir in Worcestershire and season with salt and pepper to taste. Cover and set aside. (Gravy can be refrigerated for up to 2 days.)

2. FOR THE PORK: Meanwhile, combine flour, cornstarch, garlic powder, onion powder, 2 teaspoons pepper, 1 teaspoon salt, baking powder, and cayenne in bowl. Transfer 1 cup seasoned flour to shallow dish. Whisk 6 tablespoons milk and eggs together in second shallow dish. Stir remaining 2 tablespoons milk into remaining seasoned flour, rub with fingers until mixture resembles coarse meal, and transfer to third shallow dish.

3. Pat pork dry with paper towels and season with salt and pepper. Lightly score both uncut sides of pork pieces in ¼-inch crosshatch pattern. Working with 1 piece at a time, coat pork lightly with seasoned flour. Place pork between 2 sheets of plastic wrap and pound to ¼-inch thickness; remove plastic. Coat pork again with seasoned flour, dip into egg mixture, and dredge in milk-flour mixture, pressing firmly to adhere. Arrange pork on wire rack set in rimmed baking sheet and refrigerate for 15 minutes or up to 4 hours.

4. Adjust oven rack to middle position and heat oven to 200 degrees. Warm gravy over medium-low heat, stirring occasionally. Heat oil in 12-inch skillet over medium heat until shimmering. Fry 2 pieces of pork until deep golden brown and crisp, 2 to 3 minutes per side. Drain on clean wire rack set in rimmed baking sheet and place in oven. Fry remaining 2 pieces of pork. Serve with gravy.

BETTER BREADING

1. SCORE: Use chef's knife to mark meat in crosshatch pattern on both sides. This helps flour adhere.

2. FLOUR AND POUND: Dredge scored tenderloin pieces in seasoned flour, wrap in plastic wrap, and pound to ¼-inch thickness.

3. COAT: Dredge pounded pork in flour again, dip in egg mixture, and coat with moistened, seasoned flour.

☑ WHY THIS RECIPE WORKS

Texas pit masters will tell you that the secret to blue-ribbon barbecued brisket is hours and hours of low, smoky heat penetrating the beef. Since our hunger for barbecue doesn't waver come winter, we wanted to re-create those signature flavors indoors. After we rubbed a spicy-sweet blend of brown sugar and seasonings onto a brisket roast, poking its surface with a fork readied the meat to absorb flavor. Wrapping the brisket in smoky-sweet bacon mimicked the flavors imparted by wood chips on the grill. Wrapped in aluminum foil, the brisket cooked to a fully tender texture in 4 hours. Rather than letting the brisket's flavorful renderings and cooked bacon go to waste, we incorporated them into a quick barbecue sauce, brushed it over the brisket, and put the meat under the broiler. The sauce glazed the top, turning the brisket a rich mahogany color. Now, with its authentic appearance and robust smoky, seasoned flavor, we had an indoor brisket that screamed barbecue, even in the dead of winter.

OVEN-BARBECUED BEEF BRISKET SERVES 8 TO 10

You can substitute 3½ cups of bottled barbecue sauce, if desired. You will need a broiler-safe baking dish here; glass (such as Pyrex) may crack under the high heat.

BARBECUE RUB

- 4 teaspoons packed brown sugar
- 4 teaspoons paprika
- 2 teaspoons dry mustard
- 2 teaspoons pepper
- 2 teaspoons salt
- 1 teaspoon onion powder
- 1 teaspoon garlic powder
- 1 teaspoon ground cumin
- ¼ teaspoon cayenne pepper

BRISKET

- 1 (4- to 5-pound) beef brisket, flat cut, fat trimmed to ¼ inch
- 1 pound bacon

BARBECUE SAUCE

- 1 onion, chopped fine
- ½ cup cider vinegar
- ⅓ cup packed dark brown sugar
- 1–2 cups chicken broth
- ½ cup ketchup
- 4 teaspoons minced canned chipotle chile in adobo sauce

1. FOR THE BARBECUE RUB: Combine all ingredients in bowl, breaking up any lumps of sugar.

2. FOR THE BRISKET: Adjust oven rack to upper-middle position and heat oven to 275 degrees. Massage rub into brisket and prick all over with fork. Arrange half of bacon strips, overlapping slightly, crosswise on bottom of broiler-safe 13 by 9-inch baking dish. Place brisket fat side down in bacon-lined dish and place remaining bacon strips on top, tucking ends of strips underneath brisket. Cover dish with aluminum foil and roast until fork slips easily in and out of beef, about 4 hours.

3. Remove dish from oven and carefully flip brisket fat side up. Replace foil and return brisket to oven. Turn off oven and let brisket rest in warm oven for 1 hour.

4. FOR THE BARBECUE SAUCE: Pour any accumulated juices from baking dish into 4-cup liquid measuring cup and set aside. Remove bacon from brisket and chop into small pieces. Cook bacon in medium saucepan over medium heat until fat has rendered, about 5 minutes. Add onion and cook until softened, about 5 minutes. Off heat, add vinegar and sugar and stir to combine. Return to medium heat and reduce to syrupy consistency, about 5 minutes.

5. Meanwhile, skim fat from reserved juices and discard. Add broth to juices as needed to equal 3 cups, then add to saucepan and reduce until mixture measures 3 cups, about 8 minutes. Off heat, stir in ketchup and chipotle. Strain sauce through fine-mesh strainer, if desired.

6. Heat broiler. Brush brisket with 1 cup sauce and broil until top is lightly charred and fat is crisped, 5 to 7 minutes. Transfer to carving board and slice against grain into ¼-inch-thick slices. Serve, passing remaining sauce separately.

TO MAKE AHEAD: Rub can be stored for up to 1 month. Uncarved brisket can be refrigerated for up to 1 day. To reheat, place brisket in baking dish covered with foil in 300-degree oven until warmed through, about 30 minutes.

BARBECUE FLAVOR FROM YOUR OVEN

1. To contain spices, place brisket on rimmed baking sheet. Massage dry rub into meat and poke all over with fork.

2. Arrange half of bacon strips, overlapping slightly, crosswise on bottom of baking dish. Place brisket, fat side down, on bacon, and place remaining strips on top.

✔️ WHY THIS RECIPE WORKS

In Central Texas, barbecue beef reigns supreme, and meaty English-style short ribs take to the pit like ducks to water. These blocky hunks of meat turn succulent and become infused with smokiness. Hoping to turn out tender short ribs with a Texas-style thick, peppery "bark" straight from the oven, we began with a flavor-packed braising liquid. Liquid smoke and a few tablespoons of instant espresso, Worcestershire, barbecue sauce, and brown sugar created a deeply smoky braise. We poured the hot liquid over the ribs and roasted them, tightly covered with foil. Once the beef was ultratender, a spicy rub of chili powder, pepper, salt, and brown sugar delivered the baked-on crust Texans crave. A coating of barbecue sauce mixed with a little more liquid smoke helped the rub cling while also doubling up on flavor. After 30 minutes in a 425-degree oven, the ribs emerged deeply browned, crisp, and loaded with bold barbecue flavor. In less than 4 hours, our short ribs had all the trappings of daylong pit-smoked Texas beef, but with minimal hands-on effort.

INDOOR BARBECUE BEEF SHORT RIBS

SERVES 4 TO 6

The meat on a short rib shrinks a lot during cooking, so make sure to buy ribs that are 4 to 5 inches long when raw.

4	cups water
¾	cup barbecue sauce, plus extra for serving
¼	cup plus ½ teaspoon liquid smoke
¼	cup Worcestershire sauce
5	tablespoons packed brown sugar
2	tablespoons instant espresso powder
	Salt and pepper
¼	teaspoon ground cloves
6	pounds bone-in English-style short ribs, bones 4 to 5 inches long, 1 to 1½ inches of meat on top of bone, trimmed
2	teaspoons chili powder
¼	teaspoon cayenne pepper (optional)

1. Adjust oven rack to middle position and heat oven to 300 degrees. Bring water, ¼ cup barbecue sauce, ¼ cup liquid smoke, Worcestershire, 3 tablespoons sugar, espresso powder, 1 teaspoon salt, and cloves to boil in medium saucepan over medium-high heat. Remove from heat once boiling.

2. Arrange ribs meat side down in large roasting pan. Pour hot water mixture over ribs. Wrap pan tightly with aluminum foil and transfer to oven. Roast until ribs are easily pierced with paring knife, about 3 hours.

3. Remove pan from oven and increase oven temperature to 425 degrees. Line rimmed baking sheet with foil. Combine remaining ½ cup barbecue sauce and remaining ½ teaspoon liquid smoke in small bowl. In separate bowl, combine chili powder; cayenne, if using; 2 teaspoons pepper; 1½ teaspoons salt; and remaining 2 tablespoons sugar.

4. Place ribs meat side up on prepared sheet. Brush ribs liberally with barbecue sauce mixture, then sprinkle tops and sides with spice mixture. Roast until ribs are crisp and dark brown, about 30 minutes. Let ribs rest for 15 minutes. Serve, passing extra barbecue sauce separately.

SMOKE WITHOUT FIRE

Anyone who is passionate about barbecue knows nothing beats the real smoke flavor that comes from slowly smoldering chunks of hickory or mesquite. To mimic that flavor indoors, we used liquid smoke. Most people assume that the process of making liquid smoke involves distasteful chemical shenanigans, but that's not the case. Liquid smoke is made by collecting smoke from smoldering wood chips in a condenser that quickly cools the vapors, causing them to liquefy. The droplets are captured and filtered twice before being bottled. Be forewarned, this stuff is extremely concentrated—a few drops go a long way!

ENGLISH-STYLE WITH A TEXAS ACCENT

Short ribs are full of collagen, which converts to gelatin during cooking and produces a tender texture. Boneless ribs will shrivel in the time it takes the collagen to break down, so bone-in English-style ribs are the clear choice for long cooking.

EATING LOCAL ★ CENTRAL TEXAS

To get our bearings on Texas barbecue beef ribs, we went straight to the source—Central Texas. What did we learn? You will pay top dollar for smoked short ribs at such vaunted Texas barbecue haunts as **LOUIE MUELLER BARBECUE** and **FRANKLIN BARBECUE**—and they are worth every penny. The lines are long, too, but as the adage goes, good things will come to those who wait.

LOUIE MUELLER BARBECUE 206 W. 2nd St., Taylor, TX
FRANKLIN BARBECUE 900 E. 11th St., Austin, TX

✓ WHY THIS RECIPE WORKS

Chicken-fried steak—a cheap cut of steak pounded to tenderness, coated, fried, and served with a peppery gravy—was once described by Dallas newspaper columnist Jerry Flemmons as the food that best "defines the Texas character." For CFS (its nickname in Texas diners) with great fried texture and seasoned heat, beef flap meat was our cut of choice. Pounding flour seasoned with garlic powder, onion powder, and cayenne into the scored meat brought its moisture to the surface, preventing a soggy crust. Baking powder lightened the coating's texture, and cornstarch maximized its crispness. Dredging the now-thin steaks through the seasoned flour, beaten eggs, and an adhesive paste of the flour blend mixed with milk promised a surface that clung and stayed crunchy. Just 15 minutes in the refrigerator set the crust, and after a reinforcing dredge in the milk-flour mixture, a shallow fry produced the Texas-caliber CFS we were hoping for. A creamy, butter-based gravy perfectly complemented the crunchy, salty chicken-fried steaks.

TEXAS CHICKEN-FRIED STEAK SERVES 4

Avoid using low-fat or skim milk in the gravy. Sirloin steak tips are often sold as flap meat. We prefer to buy a whole 1-pound steak and cut our own steak tips.

GRAVY

3	tablespoons unsalted butter
3	tablespoons all-purpose flour
½	teaspoon garlic powder
1½	cups chicken broth
1½	cups whole milk
¾	teaspoon salt
½	teaspoon pepper

STEAK

3½	cups all-purpose flour
½	cup cornstarch
1	tablespoon garlic powder
1	tablespoon onion powder
2	teaspoons baking powder
	Salt and pepper
½	teaspoon cayenne pepper
4	large eggs
¼	cup whole milk
4	(4-ounce) sirloin steak tips
1½	cups peanut or vegetable oil

1. FOR THE GRAVY: Melt butter in 12-inch skillet over medium heat. Stir in flour and garlic powder and cook until golden, about 2 minutes. Slowly whisk in broth, milk, salt, and pepper and simmer until thickened, about 5 minutes. Cover and set aside. (Cooled gravy can be refrigerated for up to 2 days.)

2. FOR THE STEAK: Whisk flour, cornstarch, garlic powder, onion powder, baking powder, 2 teaspoons pepper, 1 teaspoon salt, and cayenne together in bowl. Transfer 1 cup seasoned flour mixture to shallow dish. Beat eggs in second shallow dish. Stir milk into remaining flour mixture, rub with your fingers until mixture resembles coarse meal, and transfer to third shallow dish.

3. Set wire rack in rimmed baking sheet. Pat steaks dry with paper towels and season with salt and pepper. Lightly score both sides of steaks in ¼-inch crosshatch pattern. Working with 1 piece at a time, coat steaks lightly with seasoned flour and pound to ⅛- to ¼-inch thickness with meat pounder. Coat steaks again with seasoned flour, dip in egg, and dredge in milk-flour mixture,

pressing firmly to adhere. Transfer steaks to prepared wire rack and refrigerate for 15 minutes; do not discard milk-flour mixture.

4. Adjust oven rack to middle position and heat oven to 200 degrees. Set clean wire rack in rimmed baking sheet. Heat oil in Dutch oven over medium-high heat until just smoking. Working with 2 steaks at a time, return steaks to milk-flour mixture and turn to coat. Fry steaks until deep golden brown and crisp, 2 to 3 minutes per side. Transfer to prepared wire rack and keep warm in oven. Warm gravy over medium-low heat, stirring occasionally. Repeat with remaining 2 steaks. Serve, passing gravy separately.

KEYS TO CHICKEN-FRIED STEAK

Pounding seasoned flour into the scored steaks is the first step to an ultracrunchy coating. To finish the process, the steaks go back into the flour, into beaten egg, and finally into a flour-and-milk mixture. Resting the steaks gives the coating time to adhere.

1. Tenderize meat by scoring at ¼-inch intervals in cross-hatch pattern. Repeat on other side.

2. Dredge each steak in seasoned flour, then use meat pounder to flatten. Flour helps coating stick.

3. After final dredge, fry 2 steaks at a time in Dutch oven to minimize splatter and mess.

✓ WHY THIS RECIPE WORKS

Mulligan stew falls squarely in the category of "kitchen sink" recipes for its higgledy-piggledy collection of on-hand ingredients piled into a single pot. Hoping to bring order to the mishmash of vegetables, meats, and grains used in this hearty, highly practical stew, we focused on superflavorful ingredients. Beef chuck-eye roast promised moist, tender meat loaded with flavor. We browned it, leaving behind the fond (the flavorful browned bits) to boost the beefy flavor as we added oil, carrots, onion, and allspice. Canned diced tomatoes contributed subtle sweetness, and a smoked ham hock brought incredible flavor and richness to the water-based broth. We added chewy, malty barley before bringing the pot to a simmer and moving it to the oven. We channeled the not-so-subtle Irish "mulligan" moniker, adding potatoes and mustardy turnips with fresh green beans, and left the pot in the oven for another 45 minutes. When the potatoes and turnips were almost tender and the broth was loaded with rich, meaty flavors, chopped cabbage added some hearty texture. After cooking for 15 more minutes, our mulligan stew was ready to go.

MULLIGAN STEW SERVES 8

Be sure to use a smoked ham hock for this recipe. You should have about 2¾ pounds of beef after trimming.

- 1 **(4-pound) boneless beef chuck-eye roast, pulled apart at seams, trimmed, and cut into 1½-inch pieces**
  Salt and pepper
- 3 **tablespoons vegetable oil**
- 4 **carrots, peeled and cut into 1½-inch lengths (2 cups)**
- 1 **large onion, chopped**
- ½ **teaspoon ground allspice**
- 1 **(14.5-ounce) can diced tomatoes**
- 5½ **cups water**
- 1 **(12-ounce) smoked ham hock**
- ½ **cup pearl barley**
- 2 **teaspoons minced fresh thyme**
- 1 **pound Yukon Gold potatoes, unpeeled, cut into 1-inch pieces**
- 1 **(8-ounce) turnip, unpeeled, cut into 1-inch pieces**
- 8 **ounces green beans, trimmed and cut into 1-inch lengths**
- 1½ **cups coarsely chopped green cabbage**

1. Adjust oven rack to lower-middle position and heat oven to 300 degrees. Pat beef dry with paper towels and season with salt and pepper. Heat 1 tablespoon oil in large Dutch oven over medium-high heat until just smoking. Add half of beef and cook until well browned on all sides, about 8 minutes, reducing heat if pot bottom becomes too dark. Transfer beef to plate. Repeat with 1 tablespoon oil and remaining beef.

2. Add remaining 1 tablespoon oil, carrots, onion, and allspice to now-empty pot. Cook over medium heat, scraping up any browned bits, until onion is just softened, about 2 minutes. Add tomatoes and their juice and cook until nearly dry, about 8 minutes. Add water, ham hock, barley, thyme, beef and any accumulated juices, and 1 teaspoon salt. Increase heat to high and bring to simmer. Cover, transfer to oven, and cook for 1¾ hours.

3. Remove pot from oven; stir in potatoes, turnip, and green beans. Cover, return to oven, and cook until potatoes and turnip are nearly tender, about 45 minutes. Remove pot from oven, then remove ham hock from stew and let cool for 5 minutes. Using 2 forks, shred meat from ham hock, discarding skin and bones.

4. Stir cabbage and ham hock meat into stew. Cover, return to oven, and cook until all vegetables are tender, about 15 minutes longer. Season with salt and pepper to taste. Serve.

DIVIDING A CHUCK-EYE ROAST

The best tool for separating an eye roast at its natural seams (so you can trim away the excess fat) isn't a knife—it's your hands. Carefully work your fingers into the seams and ease the sides apart before cutting the roast into 1½-inch pieces.

BARLEY WORKS BEST

While barley might be most familiar as a key ingredient in beer, it is a nutritious high-fiber, high-protein, and low-fat cereal grain with a nutty flavor that is similar to that of brown rice. It is great in soups and in salads, as risotto, and as a simple side dish. Barley is available in multiple forms. Hulled barley, which is sold with the hull removed and the fiber-rich bran intact, is considered a whole grain and is higher in nutrients than pearl barley, which is hulled barley that has been polished to remove the bran. There is also quick-cooking barley, which is available as kernels or flakes. Hulled barley takes a long time to cook and should be soaked prior to cooking. Pearl barley cooks much more quickly, making it the best choice for Mulligan Stew, barley risotto, or a simple pilaf. You can also use it as a stand-in for dishes where you might ordinarily use rice, such as stir-fries or curries.

✔ WHY THIS RECIPE WORKS

New Mexican posole is one of those wonderful Southwestern stews that emerged when Mexican and European cooking traditions collided in the New World. Recipes for this warming, mildly spicy stew range from oversimplified afterthoughts to over-the-top opuses; we wanted to streamline the process while maintaining posole's complex flavor. Baking dried ancho chiles deepened their flavor, and steeping them in hot chicken broth produced an extra boost. We browned boneless pork ribs before adding them to the pot to up their porky flavor. "Posole" is Spanish for "hominy," so using this canned dried corn was a must. Browning drained hominy in the ribs' rendered fat turned it sweet, toasty, and chewy, and reserving the cooked hominy until the end preserved these qualities. Sautéed onions and garlic pureed with the chiles created a gentle, caramelized sweetness. We combined the chile puree, broth, and pork, cooking the ribs to tenderness in about an hour. We shredded the pork and added it back to the stew just before serving, along with the hominy and some lime juice. Our recipe made quick work of serving a flavor-packed posole.

NEW MEXICAN PORK STEW (POSOLE)

SERVES 6 TO 8

Do not use store-bought chili powder: Dried ancho chiles make all the difference. Serve posole with sliced radishes and green cabbage, chopped avocado, hot sauce, and lime wedges.

¾	ounce dried ancho chiles (about 3 chiles)
8	cups chicken broth
2	pounds boneless country-style pork ribs
	Salt and pepper
3	tablespoons vegetable oil
3	(15-ounce) cans white hominy, rinsed and drained well
2	onions, chopped
5	garlic cloves, minced
1	tablespoon minced fresh oregano
1	tablespoon lime juice

1. Adjust oven rack to middle position and heat oven to 350 degrees. Place chiles on baking sheet and bake until puffed and fragrant, about 6 minutes. When chiles are cool enough to handle, remove stems and seeds. Combine chiles and 1 cup broth in medium bowl. Cover and microwave until bubbling, about 2 minutes. Let stand until softened, 10 to 15 minutes.

2. Pat pork dry with paper towels and season with salt and pepper. Heat 2 tablespoons oil in Dutch oven over medium-high heat until just smoking. Cook pork until well browned all over, about 10 minutes. Transfer pork to plate. Add hominy to now-empty pot and cook, stirring frequently, until fragrant and hominy begins to darken, 2 to 3 minutes. Transfer hominy to medium bowl.

3. Heat remaining 1 tablespoon oil in now-empty pot over medium heat until shimmering. Add onions and cook until softened, about 5 minutes. Stir in garlic and cook until fragrant, about 30 seconds. Puree onion mixture with softened chile mixture in blender. Combine remaining 7 cups broth, pureed onion-chile mixture, pork, oregano, ½ teaspoon salt, and ½ teaspoon pepper in now-empty pot and bring to boil. Reduce heat to low and simmer, covered, until meat is tender, 1 to 1½ hours.

4. Transfer pork to clean plate. Add hominy to pot and simmer, covered, until tender, about 30 minutes. Skim fat from broth. When meat is cool enough to handle, shred into bite-size pieces, discarding fat. Return pork to pot and cook until heated through, about 1 minute. Off heat, add lime juice. Season with salt and pepper to taste. Serve. (Posole can be refrigerated for up to 3 days.)

PREPPING DRIED CHILES

Whole dried chiles require some advance preparation but contribute mightily to this stew's flavor (and that of other Southwestern and south-of-the-border dishes).

1. Toast dried chiles to enhance their earthy flavor.

2. Steep stemmed, seeded ancho chiles in hot broth to soften their tough skin.

3. Puree softened chiles with onion and garlic to add depth of flavor to posole.

✔ WHY THIS RECIPE WORKS

Texas chili might get more hype, but we thought that rich, under-the-radar *carne adovada* deserved our attention. Making this New Mexican pork chili, with its tender chunks of pork butt bathed in a soulful, spiced sauce, is a challenge without access to the chiles native to the Southwest. We set out to mimic their flavors using supermarket staples. Browning the pork in a Dutch oven expelled some of its fat, which we used to build the sauce. We softened chopped onion in the fat before adding chili powder, canned chipotle chile in adobo sauce, and minced garlic. Flour thickened the mixture, and although oregano is included in most chili powder blends, we included this authentic ingredient for noticeable herbal flavor. To replicate the fruity, bitter quality of dried chiles, we plumped raisins in coffee and added them along with chicken broth. We pureed this mixture into a rich, earthy sauce and returned it to the pot with the pork. After 2 hours in the oven, the carne adovada emerged tender and smothered in bold, seasoned sauce. Lime zest and juice and cilantro added a bright finish to this extraordinary chili that you can make no matter where you live.

CARNE ADOVADA SERVES 6 TO 8

Pork butt roast is often labeled "Boston butt" in the super-market—and comes either boneless or on the bone. If using bone-in pork butt, buy a 6- to 6½-pound roast. When trimming excess fat, leave at least a ⅛-inch thickness on the exterior. Serve the finished dish over rice or with warm corn tortillas.

¼	cup raisins
½	cup brewed coffee
1	(4- to 5-pound) boneless pork butt roast, trimmed of excess fat and cut into 1½-inch chunks
	Salt and pepper
1	tablespoon vegetable oil
2	onions, chopped
¼	cup all-purpose flour
½	cup chili powder
1	teaspoon dried oregano
1	tablespoon minced canned chipotle chile in adobo sauce
6	garlic cloves, minced
2½	cups chicken broth
1	teaspoon grated lime zest plus 1 tablespoon juice
¼	cup chopped fresh cilantro

1. Adjust oven rack to lower-middle position and heat oven to 350 degrees. Combine raisins and coffee in small bowl. Wrap tightly with plastic wrap and microwave until liquid begins to boil, 1 to 3 minutes; let stand for 5 minutes, until raisins are plump.

2. Pat pork dry with paper towels and season with salt and pepper. Heat oil in Dutch oven over medium-high heat until just smoking. Brown half of pork, about 10 minutes. Transfer to plate and repeat with remaining pork.

3. Pour off all but 1 tablespoon fat from Dutch oven. Add onions and cook until softened, about 5 minutes. Add flour, chili powder, oregano, chipotle, and garlic and cook until fragrant, about 1 minute. Add broth and raisin mixture, scraping up any browned bits, and bring to boil. Working in 2 batches, transfer mixture to blender or food processor and puree until smooth. Return sauce to pot.

4. Add browned pork to sauce in pot and transfer to oven. Cook, covered, until pork is fork-tender, about 2 hours. Skim fat from sauce, then stir in lime zest, lime juice, and cilantro. Season with salt and pepper to taste. Serve. (Pork can be refrigerated for up to 3 days.)

CHILES: A LOVE STORY

New Mexicans love their chiles. Need proof? Read this 2005 joint memorial requesting that the secretary of state list the chile as the state vegetable—never mind that scientists classify them as a fruit. We quote in small part: "WHEREAS, mass immigration to New Mexico in the past four hundred years has been rumored to be a result of the addictive qualities of chile…; and WHEREAS, New Mexicans are more proud of this magical vegetable than they are of the Lobos basketball team, the roadrunner state bird, the biscochito, the state's sunsets or its blue skies, combined…" The official state question is "Red or green?" This refers to chile preference, and if you're dining out in New Mexico, you'll be asked it when you place your order.

BUILDING COMPLEX CHILE FLAVOR

Our goal was to develop complexity and subtle heat in our carne adovada—without having to toast and grind a heap of hard-to-find dried chiles. In the end, we replicated the taste of dried chiles by enhancing supermarket chili powder with a few common ingredients.

BITTERSWEET: A surprising combination of raisins and brewed coffee mimics the bittersweet complexity of dried chiles.

HOT AND SAUCY: Just 1 tablespoon of minced canned chipotle chile in adobo sauce gives the sauce smokiness and subtle heat.

☑ WHY THIS RECIPE WORKS

Though Chasen's Restaurant was well known for its A-list clientele—from Frank Sinatra to Elizabeth Taylor—the Hollywood landmark's rich, gently spiced chili was its main draw. Every bowl was loaded with green peppers, hand-ground beef chuck and pork butt, and plenty of butter. Without a meat grinder handy, we looked for workable cuts that would impart the same strong pork and beef flavors. Ground beef was an easy swap, and for pork that stayed moist and meaty, we browned pork chops in butter. Peppers, onions, and spices cooked in butter created a seasoned, flavorful base, and canned chipotle chile and adobo sauce added depth and heat. Using canned crushed tomatoes and tomato sauce sped up our prep, and we used the simmering tomato mixture to finish cooking the browned pork chops and the beef. The chops were perfectly tender in an hour, so we removed the bones, chopped the pork, and stirred it into the pot along with canned pinto beans. Our chili was ready to serve, its warm flavors immediately transporting us back to the red-boothed restaurant of Hollywood's bygone days.

HOLLYWOOD CHILI SERVES 6 TO 8

Use a Dutch oven that holds 6 quarts or more for this recipe. Chipotle chiles can be very hot: We wear rubber gloves when handling them. To freeze leftover chile in adobo sauce, transfer the contents of the can to a zipper-lock bag and freeze for up to 3 months.

3   **pounds bone-in blade-cut pork chops, about 1½ inches thick, trimmed**
      Salt and pepper
4   **tablespoons unsalted butter**
2   **pounds 85 percent lean ground beef**
3   **green bell peppers, stemmed, seeded, and chopped fine**
2   **onions, chopped fine**
¼   **cup chili powder**
4   **garlic cloves, minced**
2   **teaspoons ground cumin**
1   **teaspoon minced canned chipotle chile in adobo sauce plus 2 teaspoons adobo sauce**
2   **(28-ounce) cans crushed tomatoes**
1   **(29-ounce) can tomato sauce**
1   **cup water**
3   **(15-ounce) cans pinto beans, rinsed**

1. Pat pork dry with paper towels and season with salt and pepper. Melt 1 tablespoon butter in Dutch oven over medium-high heat. Add pork and brown well, about 5 minutes per side. Transfer pork to plate. Add beef to pot and cook over medium-high heat, stirring occasionally, until no longer pink, about 5 minutes. Drain beef and set aside.

2. Return pot to medium heat and melt remaining 3 tablespoons butter. Add peppers and onions and cook until softened, about 5 minutes. Stir in chili powder, garlic, and cumin and cook until fragrant, about 30 seconds.

3. Stir in chipotle, adobo sauce, crushed tomatoes, tomato sauce, and water and bring to boil. Return pork and beef to pot, along with any accumulated juices. Reduce heat to low and simmer, covered, stirring occasionally, until pork is tender, about 1 hour.

4. Transfer pork to cutting board. When cool enough to handle, remove meat from bones, discard fat, and chop coarse. Skim any fat from surface of chili using large spoon. Stir chopped pork and beans into pot, return to simmer, and cook, uncovered, stirring occasionally, for 30 minutes. Season with salt and pepper to taste and serve. (Chili can be refrigerated for up to 3 days.)

WHAT'S A PORK CHOP DOING IN MY CHILI?

For his legendary chili, Hollywood restaurateur Dave Chasen used a custom grinder on a mix of beef chuck and pork butt. Since most of us haven't got a fancy grinder, we paired supermarket ground beef with pork blade chops for the same meaty impact.

1. Brown bone-in pork chops in butter and remove from pan. Reserve rendered fat to brown ground meat.

2. After building chili's base, stir in ground meat and reserved chops; pork bones help flavor sauce.

3. One hour later, remove cooked chops, separate meat from bones, coarsely chop meat, and stir into chili.

✓ WHY THIS RECIPE WORKS

Making traditional *chiles rellenos* is truly a labor of love. From roasting chiles to preparing the filling to stuffing to frying—*ay, caramba*, it's a lot of work! To make this Tex-Mex specialty a more doable dish, we converted its roasted chile flavor, hearty beef filling, and crisp fried shell into a casserole. Lean ground beef sautéed with chopped onion kicked off the filling, and browning the smoky poblanos in some of the rendered fat gave them nice meaty flavor. We seasoned the filling with garlic, cumin, oregano, and cayenne to finish it off. Canned diced tomatoes studded with spicy chiles mimicked the traditional spicy sauce, and Monterey Jack contributed a creamy dimension. A simple mixture of flour, skim milk, and whipped egg whites served as the shell, creating a puffed browned top to the casserole. A sprinkling of cheese added with 10 minutes left in the oven browned the surface and reinforced the filling's cheese flavors. Boasting all the elements of our beloved chiles rellenos but without the time-consuming prep, this casserole was a clear winner.

CHILES RELLENOS CASSEROLE   SERVES 6 TO 8

If you can't find Ro-tel tomatoes, use 1 cup of diced tomatoes combined with 1 finely chopped, stemmed, and seeded jalapeño chile.

1	tablespoon vegetable oil
1	onion, chopped fine
2	pounds 90 percent lean ground beef
4	poblano (or 6 Anaheim) chiles, stemmed, seeded, and chopped
2	garlic cloves, minced
2	teaspoons ground cumin
1	teaspoon dried oregano
	Salt and pepper
¼	teaspoon cayenne pepper
1	(10-ounce) can Ro-tel Diced Tomatoes & Green Chilies, drained
10	ounces Monterey Jack cheese, shredded (2½ cups)
½	cup all-purpose flour
¾	cup skim milk
2	large egg whites

1. Adjust oven rack to upper-middle position and heat oven to 450 degrees. Heat oil in 12-inch nonstick skillet over medium heat until shimmering. Add onion and cook until softened, about 5 minutes. Stir in beef, breaking up meat into small pieces, and cook until no longer pink, 8 to 10 minutes. Using slotted spoon, transfer beef mixture to paper towel–lined plate. Pour off all but 2 tablespoons fat from skillet.

2. Add poblanos and cook over medium-high heat until browned, 8 to 10 minutes. Stir in beef mixture, garlic, cumin, oregano, ¾ teaspoon salt, ½ teaspoon pepper, and cayenne and cook until fragrant, about 30 seconds. Add tomatoes and cook until beef mixture is dry, about 1 minute. Off heat, stir in 2 cups Monterey Jack. Scrape mixture into 13 by 9-inch baking dish, pressing into even layer.

3. Combine flour, ½ teaspoon salt, and ¼ teaspoon pepper in bowl. Slowly whisk milk into flour mixture until smooth; set aside. Using stand mixer fitted with whisk, whip egg whites on medium-low speed until foamy, about 1 minute. Increase speed to medium-high and whip until stiff peaks form, about 3 minutes. Whisk one-third of whipped egg whites into batter, then gently fold in remaining whites, 1 scoop at a time, until combined.

4. Pour batter over beef mixture. Bake until topping is light golden and puffed, about 15 minutes. Sprinkle with remaining ½ cup Monterey Jack and bake until golden brown, about 10 minutes. Let cool on wire rack for 10 minutes. Serve.

A TASTE OF THE SOUTHWEST

Carl Roettele opened a small canning plant in Elsa, Texas, in the early 1940s. By the 1950s, his blend of tomatoes, green chiles, and spices had become popular throughout the state and beyond. His spicy, tangy tomatoes are used in countless local recipes, including Chiles Rellenos Casserole, King Ranch Casserole (page 267), and a mixture of Velveeta and Ro-tel tomatoes known locally as Ro-tel dip (a no-frills version of chili con queso).

✓ WHY THIS RECIPE WORKS

King Ranch just might be the most famous casserole in Texas, so we had to do it justice. Keeping its mildly spicy Southwestern flavors intact without relying on canned cream of chicken soup for body was an easy (and tasty) decision. After crisping tortillas in the oven, we started the sauce with sautéed chopped onions, minced jalapeños, and cumin. We used canned diced tomatoes and let their juices reduce, intensifying the tomato flavor, and green chiles bolstered the jalapeños' heat. Flour thickened the sauce, and heavy cream and chicken broth amped up its flavor, giving it a lush texture. We poached sliced chicken breasts in the sauce, stirring in cilantro and cheese off the heat to finish. This casserole is layered with tortillas scattered on the bottom of the pan, followed by filling, more tortillas, and the rest of the filling. The tortillas stayed crisp during baking, but this casserole needed something extra to top it off. As a nod to this dish's convenience item roots, we sprinkled crushed Fritos over the surface before removing the casserole from the oven, crowning this Texas classic with crunchy corn flavor.

KING RANCH CASSEROLE SERVES 6 TO 8

If you can't find Ro-tel tomatoes, use 2 cups of diced tomatoes combined with 2 finely chopped, stemmed, and seeded jalapeño chiles. Monterey Jack can be substituted for the Colby Jack here.

12	(6-inch) corn tortillas
	Vegetable oil spray
1	tablespoon unsalted butter
2	onions, chopped fine
2	jalapeño chiles, stemmed, seeded, and minced
2	teaspoons ground cumin
2	(10-ounce) cans Ro-tel Diced Tomatoes & Green Chilies
5	tablespoons all-purpose flour
3	cups chicken broth
1	cup heavy cream
4	(6-ounce) boneless, skinless chicken breasts, trimmed, halved lengthwise, and cut crosswise into ½-inch-thick slices
1	pound Colby Jack cheese, shredded (4 cups)
2	tablespoons minced fresh cilantro
	Salt and pepper
6	ounces Fritos corn chips, crushed (2¼ cups)

1. Adjust oven racks to upper-middle and lower-middle positions and heat oven to 450 degrees. Arrange tortillas on 2 baking sheets and lightly spray both sides of tortillas with oil spray. Bake until slightly crisp and browned, about 12 minutes. Let tortillas cool slightly, then break into bite-size pieces. Adjust upper oven rack to middle position (oven rack will be hot).

2. Heat butter in Dutch oven over medium-high heat. Add onions, jalapeños, and cumin and cook until lightly browned, about 8 minutes. Add tomatoes and their juice and cook until most of liquid has evaporated, about 10 minutes. Stir in flour and cook for 1 minute. Add broth and cream, bring to simmer, and cook until thickened, 2 to 3 minutes. Stir in chicken and cook until no longer pink, about 4 minutes. Off heat, add Colby Jack and cilantro and stir until cheese is melted. Season with salt and pepper.

3. Scatter half of tortilla pieces in 13 by 9-inch baking dish set in rimmed baking sheet. Spoon half of filling evenly over tortilla pieces. Scatter remaining tortilla pieces over filling, then top with remaining filling. (Unbaked casserole can be wrapped tightly in aluminum foil and refrigerated for up to 24 hours; increase covered baking time to 30 minutes.)

4. Cover dish with foil and bake until filling is bubbling, about 15 minutes. Remove foil, sprinkle with Fritos, and bake until lightly browned, about 10 minutes. Let casserole cool for 10 minutes before serving.

PREDICTING A CHILE'S BURN

Many cooks claim that the smaller the chile, the bigger the burn. To see if this was true, we gathered a dozen jalapeños of varying size and started sampling. A flood of tears later, we learned that there is no correlation between the size of the jalapeño and its heat level.

Not willing to take the pain in vain, we chose a more quantitative approach and sent a handful of similarly sized jalapeños to a lab to test their levels of capsaicin, the chemical compound responsible for their heat. Shockingly, some chiles had as much as 10 times the kick as seemingly identical chiles. Unfortunately, the only way to gauge a chile's burn is to try a small piece. If you want to preserve the flavor of the chile but lose some of the heat, cut away the white ribs and seeds (we like to wear gloves when handling any hot chile), which is where the capsaicin is located; the flesh of a jalapeño has just a fraction of the heat of the interior.

✓ WHY THIS RECIPE WORKS

You won't find any roe in Texas caviar, but that doesn't make it any less delectable. This black-eyed pea salad was created in 1940 by Helen Corbitt, the "mother of modern Texas cooking," during her stint as director of food services at the Zodiac Room in Dallas. Then, her "pickled" black-eyed peas were marinated in a simple vinaigrette and tossed with onion and garlic. We wanted to brighten the flavors while keeping things fuss-free. A highly acidic dressing was key, so we used a heavy hand with red wine vinegar and balanced it with oil, adding some sugar to soften the burn and garlic for flavor. Canned black-eyed peas saved us hours of soaking and cooking dried beans without sacrificing texture. Bypassing onions altogether, we created a crunchy, savory, earthy mélange by tossing the black-eyed peas with sliced scallions, red and green bell pepper, chopped celery, and two jalapeños (leave the seeds in for folks who like things on the spicy side). Mixed together, the salad tasted good, but it was even better after sitting for an hour (and great the next day). Though it was not real caviar, we felt pretty privileged to serve up this tasty Texas picnic dish.

TEXAS CAVIAR SERVES 6

If you prefer a spicier salad, reserve and stir in some of the jalapeño seeds. Note that the salad needs to sit for at least an hour prior to serving. It will keep in the refrigerator for at least five days.

- ⅓ **cup red wine vinegar**
- 3 **tablespoons vegetable oil**
- 1 **tablespoon sugar**
- 2 **garlic cloves, minced**
- **Salt and pepper**
- 2 **(15.5-ounce) cans black-eyed peas, rinsed**
- 6 **scallions, sliced thin**
- 1 **red bell pepper, stemmed, seeded, and chopped**
- 1 **green bell pepper, stemmed, seeded, and chopped**
- 2 **jalapeño chiles, stemmed, seeded, and minced**
- 1 **celery rib, chopped fine**
- ¼ **cup chopped fresh cilantro**
- ¼ **cup chopped fresh parsley**

1. Whisk vinegar, oil, sugar, garlic, 1 teaspoon salt, and ½ teaspoon pepper together in large bowl.

2. Add peas, scallions, bell peppers, jalapeños, celery, cilantro, and parsley and toss to combine. Season with salt and pepper to taste. Let sit for at least 1 hour before serving.

TOSSING THE STEMS: DO OR DON'T?

Recently, we heard a wild rumor that the stems of flat-leaf parsley and cilantro hold more flavor than the leaves. We decided to put this notion to the test. After cleaning and drying several bunches of parsley and cilantro, we asked tasters to eat the herbs by the sprig, from the tender leaf to the fat tip of the stem. What did we find? Well, the stems do have more flavor, but that's not always good news. While the parsley leaves were fresh and herbal, we were surprised by how intense the flavor became as we traveled down the stems. By the time we reached the stem ends, tasters were complaining (loudly) about bitterness.

Cilantro, however, was another story. Sure, the leaves were tasty, but the great flavor found in the stems caught us all off guard. Sweet, fresh, and potent, the flavor intensified as we traveled down the stem but never became bitter. The moral? If a recipe calls for cilantro and a crunchy texture isn't an issue (as in our Texas Caviar), feel free to use the stems as well as the leaves. But when it comes to parsley—unless you'll be using the herb in a soup or stew where its strong flavor won't be out of place—be picky and use just the leaves.

RINSING CANNED BEANS

Canned beans are made by pressure-cooking dried beans directly in the can with water, salt, and preservatives. As the beans cook, starches and proteins leach into the liquid, thickening it. We generally call for canned beans to be rinsed to remove this starchy liquid, but is the extra step really necessary? We noticed that salads made with rinsed black-eyed peas were brighter in flavor and less pasty than the versions with unrinsed beans. We found that the thick, salty bean liquid does have the potential to throw a simpler recipe off-kilter. And since rinsing beans takes only a few seconds, we recommend doing so.

✓ WHY THIS RECIPE WORKS

Combining the best of bread stuffing with wild rice's nutty, earthy flavors, wild rice dressing should be rich and buttery, but not heavy—the best dressings leave room for turkey, of course. Different varieties of wild rice absorb varying amounts of liquid, so we boiled the grains in water and chicken broth before draining them, reserving the cooking liquid. Pea-size bread crumbs kept the bread from overshadowing the small grains of rice, and baking them for a few minutes added color and crunch. We sautéed onions and celery in butter, next adding garlic, sage, and thyme for their savory herbal flavors. A custardy blend of eggs and cream enriched the dressing and bound it together. Adding some of the starchy cooking liquid lightened the dish and enhanced the nutty flavor of the rice. Our dressing was loaded with distinct wild rice taste and toasty crunch, making it just the savory, wholly delicious change of pace we were looking for.

WILD RICE DRESSING

SERVES 10 TO 12

Depending on the brand, wild rice absorbs varying quantities of liquid. If you have less than 1½ cups of leftover rice cooking liquid, make up the difference with additional chicken broth.

2	cups chicken broth
2	cups water
1	bay leaf
2	cups wild rice
10	slices hearty white sandwich bread, torn into pieces
8	tablespoons unsalted butter
2	onions, chopped fine
3	celery ribs, minced
4	garlic cloves, minced
1½	teaspoons dried sage
1½	teaspoons dried thyme
1½	cups heavy cream
2	large eggs
¾	teaspoon salt
½	teaspoon pepper

1. Bring broth, water, and bay leaf to boil in medium saucepan over medium-high heat. Add rice, reduce heat to low, and simmer, covered, until rice is tender, 35 to 45 minutes. Strain contents of pan through fine-mesh strainer into 4-cup liquid measuring cup. Transfer rice to bowl; discard bay leaf. Measure out and reserve 1½ cups cooking liquid.

2. Adjust oven racks to upper-middle and lower-middle positions and heat oven to 325 degrees. Pulse half of bread in food processor into pea-size pieces, about 6 pulses; transfer to rimmed baking sheet. Repeat with remaining bread and second rimmed baking sheet. Bake bread crumbs until golden, about 20 minutes, stirring occasionally and switching and rotating sheets halfway through baking. Cool completely, about 10 minutes.

3. Melt 4 tablespoons butter in 12-inch skillet over medium heat. Cook onions and celery until softened and golden, 8 to 10 minutes. Add garlic, sage, and thyme and cook until fragrant, about 30 seconds. Stir in reserved cooking liquid, remove from heat, and let cool for 5 minutes.

4. Whisk cream, eggs, salt, and pepper together in large bowl. Slowly whisk in warm broth-vegetable mixture. Stir in rice and toasted bread crumbs and transfer to 13 by 9-inch baking dish. (Dressing can be refrigerated for up to 1 day; increase baking time to 65 to 75 minutes.)

5. Melt remaining 4 tablespoons butter in now-empty skillet and drizzle evenly over dressing. Cover dish with aluminum foil and bake on lower-middle rack until set, 45 to 55 minutes. Remove foil and let cool for 15 minutes. Serve.

DRIED FRUIT AND NUT WILD RICE DRESSING

Add 1½ cups chopped dried apricots, cranberries, or cherries and 1½ cups chopped toasted pecans with bread crumbs in step 4.

LEEK AND MUSHROOM WILD RICE DRESSING

Substitute 4 leeks (white and light green parts only), halved lengthwise and sliced thin, and 10 ounces cremini mushrooms, sliced thin, for onions and celery.

HARVESTING RICE WATER

We cook wild rice more like pasta than like traditional steamed rice, boiling the rice in extra water (and chicken broth) and then draining it. We then use the flavorful, starchy liquid to help the dressing cohere.

✓ WHY THIS RECIPE WORKS

Crammed with salty ham and juicy pineapple chunks, a bowl of Hawaiian fried rice is hard to beat. Boasting the same star ingredients as Hawaiian pizza, this salty-sweet dish starts with sautéed vegetables—red bell pepper, scallions, and onion—and browned chopped ham. To boost our rice's flavor, we added minced garlic and ginger for a 30-second turn, just enough time to become fragrant, and then set the ham mixture aside. Cold precooked rice holds its shape when fried, so we cooked it in a little oil just long enough to heat it before pushing it to one side, adding more oil, and pouring in beaten eggs. Once the eggs were set, we added the ham mixture and mixed everything together. We stirred in a zesty blend of soy sauce, sesame oil, and fiery Sriracha and then, off the heat, added pineapple and scallion greens for bright, fresh island flavor. This dangerously delicious fried rice was a breeze to make—and it disappeared just as easily.

HAWAIIAN FRIED RICE SERVES 4

You can use 6 ounces of chopped leftover ham, ham steak, or deli ham for this recipe. Crumb-Coated Baked Ham (page 215) works well in this recipe. Cold leftover rice stays firm during frying, but if you don't have any on hand, Faux Leftover Rice (recipe follows) is just as good.

- 3 tablespoons soy sauce
- 2 tablespoons toasted sesame oil
- 1 tablespoon Sriracha sauce
- 2 tablespoons plus 1 teaspoon peanut oil
- 1 cup (6 ounces) chopped ham
- 1 red bell pepper, stemmed, seeded, and cut into ½-inch pieces
- 6 scallions, white parts minced, green parts cut into ½-inch pieces
- 1 small onion, halved and sliced thin
- 3 garlic cloves, minced
- 1 tablespoon grated fresh ginger
- 4 cups cooked long-grain white rice, cold
- 2 large eggs, lightly beaten
- 1 cup ½-inch pineapple pieces

1. Combine soy sauce, sesame oil, and Sriracha in bowl and set aside. Heat 1 tablespoon peanut oil in 12-inch nonstick skillet over medium-high heat until just smoking. Add ham, bell pepper, scallion whites, and onion and cook, stirring occasionally, until lightly browned, 7 to 9 minutes. Stir in garlic and ginger and cook until fragrant, about 30 seconds. Transfer to plate.

2. Heat 1 tablespoon peanut oil in now-empty skillet over medium-high heat until shimmering. Add rice and cook, breaking up clumps with spoon, until heated through, about 3 minutes.

3. Push rice to 1 side of skillet and add remaining 1 teaspoon peanut oil to empty side of skillet. Add eggs to oiled side of skillet and cook, stirring, until set, about 30 seconds. Stir eggs and ham mixture into rice. Stir soy sauce mixture into rice until thoroughly combined. Off heat, stir in pineapple and scallion greens. Serve.

FAUX LEFTOVER RICE MAKES 6 CUPS

- 2 tablespoons vegetable oil
- 2 cups long-grain white rice, rinsed
- 2⅔ cups water

Heat oil in large saucepan over medium heat until shimmering. Add rice and stir to coat grains with oil, about 30 seconds. Add water, increase heat to high, and bring to boil. Reduce heat to low, cover, and simmer until all liquid is absorbed, about 18 minutes. Off heat, remove lid and place clean dish towel folded in half over saucepan; replace lid. Let stand until rice is just tender, about 8 minutes. Spread rice in rimmed baking sheet set on wire rack and cool for 10 minutes. Transfer to refrigerator and chill for 20 minutes.

PREPPING PINEAPPLE

1. Trim off bottom and top of pineapple so it sits flat on counter.

2. Rest pineapple on trimmed bottom and cut off skin in thin strips from top to bottom, using sharp paring, chef's, or serrated knife.

3. Quarter pineapple lengthwise, then cut through tough core from each quarter. Slice pineapple into ½-inch pieces.

✔ WHY THIS RECIPE WORKS

Tex-Mex rice is a gutsy, spicy, sunset-orange pilaf—nothing like the bland rice often stuffed into burritos. For grains with great tomato flavor and enough heat to keep us interested, we didn't cut any corners when cooking the rice. Rinsing long-grain white rice under running water removed excess starch, promising fluffier texture. After sautéing onion, poblano, and jalapeños in oil, we left some of the aromatic vegetables in the pot and added the rice along with cumin and oregano. Though rice is typically sautéed for about 3 minutes, a few more minutes on the stove imparted great toasty flavor. Canned diced tomatoes, pureed ahead of time and added to the pot along with chicken broth, gave the rice its signature color and sweet tomato flavor. We let the rice simmer, covered, until the liquid was absorbed, at which point we removed the pot from the heat and stirred in some of the reserved chile mixture. With a final fluffing before serving, this rice had bold flavor to back up its bold hue.

TEX-MEX RICE   SERVES 4 TO 6

If you can't find poblano chiles (sometimes labeled "pasilla chiles"), substitute an Anaheim chile or a green bell pepper combined with an extra jalapeño chile. For more heat, include the ribs and seeds of the jalapeño chiles.

1	**(14.5-ounce) can diced tomatoes**
¼	**cup vegetable oil**
1	**onion, chopped fine**
1	**poblano chile, stemmed, seeded, and minced**
2	**jalapeño chiles, stemmed, seeded, and minced**
1½	**cups long-grain white rice, rinsed**
1	**teaspoon ground cumin**
1	**teaspoon dried oregano**
1½	**cups chicken broth**
	Salt

1. Process tomatoes and their juice in food processor until smooth; set aside.

2. Heat oil in Dutch oven over medium-high heat until shimmering. Add onion, poblano, and jalapeños and cook until softened, about 5 minutes; reserve ¼ cup chile mixture. Stir rice, cumin, and oregano into pot and cook, stirring frequently, until rice is deep golden, 5 to 6 minutes.

3. Add broth, processed tomatoes, and 1 teaspoon salt and bring to boil. Cover, reduce heat to low, and simmer until liquid is absorbed and rice is tender, about 25 minutes. Remove from heat and stir in reserved chile mixture. Cover and let stand for 10 minutes. Fluff with fork and season with salt. Serve.

TALKING TEX-MEX RICE
Tex-Mex rice can be gloppy and bland. Ours repairs its texture and turns up the flavor.

1. Don't skip this step. Rinse rice to rid it of starches and prevent gummy texture.

2. Toast rice on stovetop for about 5 minutes, nearly twice as long as usual, to create deep, nutty flavor.

3. Puree canned diced tomatoes thinned with chicken broth to give rice bright tomato flavor.

✔ WHY THIS RECIPE WORKS

Hoping to mix things up on our Thanksgiving table this year, we couldn't wait to give the texture and savory flavors of cornflake stuffing a try. To kick-start the base, we softened chopped onion and celery in melted butter (though rendered chicken fat also tastes great). Once the chopped vegetables were cool, we tossed them with cornflakes before adding chicken broth, parsley, beaten eggs, salt, and pepper. A sheet of aluminum foil covering the baking pan contained the escaping steam while the stuffing set; removing the foil for the last 10 minutes allowed the top to turn appealingly brown and crisp. Served alongside turkey or chicken, this unusual stuffing was good enough to eat well beyond the fourth Thursday of November.

CORNFLAKE STUFFING

You can find rendered chicken fat with the kosher foods in the freezer section of most supermarkets. You will need 14 cups of cornflakes.

6   **tablespoons unsalted butter or rendered chicken fat**
4   **onions, chopped fine**
2   **celery ribs, chopped fine**
1   **(18-ounce) box cornflakes**
4   **cups chicken broth**
½   **cup chopped fresh parsley**
3   **large eggs, lightly beaten**
1   **teaspoon salt**
1   **teaspoon pepper**

1. Adjust oven rack to middle position and heat oven to 400 degrees. Grease 3-quart baking dish. Melt butter in 12-inch skillet over medium heat. Add onions and celery and cook until softened and beginning to brown, 10 to 15 minutes. Remove from heat and let cool for 5 minutes.

2. Combine cornflakes and warm onion mixture in large bowl. Stir in broth, parsley, eggs, salt, and pepper until combined. Transfer mixture to prepared baking dish and cover tightly with aluminum foil. Bake until set, about 30 minutes. Remove foil and continue to bake until surface is golden and crisp, about 10 minutes. Let cool for 15 minutes. Serve.

CHOPPING WITHOUT TEARS

Cornflake Stuffing is nothing to cry about, but the four chopped onions in this recipe might make it unavoidable. Over the years, we've collected ideas from readers, books, and colleagues all aimed at reducing tears while cutting onions. We decided to put those ideas to the test. They ranged from the commonsense (work underneath an exhaust fan or freeze the onions for 30 minutes before slicing) to the comical (wear ski goggles or hold a toothpick in your teeth).

Overall, the methods that worked best were to protect our eyes by covering them with goggles or contact lenses or to introduce a flame near the cut onions. The flame, which can be produced by either a candle or a gas burner, changes the activity of the thiopropanal sulfoxide by completing its oxidization. Contact lenses and goggles form a physical barrier that the thiopropanal cannot penetrate. So if you want to keep tears at bay when handling onions, light a candle or gas burner or put on some ski goggles.

LAYING ON THE SCHMALTZ

While Cornflake Stuffing is delicious made with butter, chicken fat (or schmaltz) adds richness and depth. How else can you use this flavor-booster? If you're making soup, use the fat instead of oil to sauté the aromatics. You can also use it in place of butter when making a roux for gravy or stew. Chicken fat will keep in the refrigerator and it also freezes well.

✔ WHY THIS RECIPE WORKS

Shaggy, crunchy Jo Jo potatoes are a mainstay in taverns and roadside eateries throughout the Pacific Northwest. Hoping to bring these heavily seasoned potatoes to prominence in home kitchens everywhere, we began by slicing russets into thick wedges. Simply baking them would yield uncooked centers, so we parcooked the potatoes in the microwave to jump-start their fluffy interior. For deep-fried crunch right out of the oven, we added vegetable oil to the microwaved wedges and stirred them for a full minute, causing the potatoes to emit an even film of starch. For the breading, a blend of crunchy panko, grated Parmesan, dry mustard, garlic powder, thyme, and cayenne clung nicely, creating the texture and seasoning we were looking for. A layer of oil brushed on a preheated baking sheet made for great crisping, and flipping the wedges halfway through baking ensured even cooking. Happy with our take on this takeout favorite, we served our homemade Jo Jo potatoes like the locals do: with cool homemade ranch dressing.

JO JO POTATOES SERVES 4 TO 6

Do not substitute standard store-bought bread crumbs for the panko here. These potatoes are perfect dipped in ranch dressing.

3	russet potatoes, unpeeled
5	tablespoons vegetable oil
⅔	cup panko bread crumbs
1⅓	ounces Parmesan cheese, grated (⅔ cup)
1	tablespoon paprika
2	teaspoons dry mustard
1	teaspoon salt
¾	teaspoon garlic powder
¾	teaspoon dried thyme
⅛	teaspoon cayenne pepper

1. Adjust oven rack to middle position, place rimmed baking sheet on rack, and heat oven to 400 degrees. Cut each potato lengthwise into 6 wedges. Place potatoes in large bowl and cover. Microwave until edges of potatoes are translucent but centers remain slightly firm, 6 to 8 minutes, shaking bowl (without uncovering) to redistribute potatoes halfway through microwaving. Carefully uncover and drain potatoes well. Return potatoes to bowl, add 3 tablespoons oil, and stir until potatoes are coated with starchy film, about 1 minute.

2. Combine panko, Parmesan, paprika, dry mustard, salt, garlic powder, thyme, and cayenne in shallow dish. Dredge one-quarter of potatoes in panko mixture, pressing gently to adhere. Transfer to platter and repeat with remaining potatoes. Let sit for 15 minutes.

3. Remove hot sheet from oven and brush with remaining 2 tablespoons oil. Arrange potatoes cut side down in single layer. Bake until crisp and golden brown, 25 to 30 minutes, flipping wedges halfway through baking. Serve immediately.

RANCH DRESSING MAKES 1 CUP

⅔	cup sour cream
¼	cup buttermilk
2	tablespoons minced fresh cilantro (or dill, tarragon, or parsley)
1	tablespoon minced shallot
2	teaspoons white wine vinegar
½	teaspoon granulated garlic
¼	teaspoon salt
¼	teaspoon pepper
	Sugar

Whisk sour cream, buttermilk, cilantro, shallot, vinegar, garlic, salt, and pepper together until smooth. Season with sugar to taste.

STIR OUT THE STARCH

Stir the parcooked potato wedges for a full minute to create a starchy glue on their exterior that can grab onto the panko coating.

PERFECT PARMESAN

Grating Parmesan yourself is an extra step that makes a big impact on Jo Jo potatoes. To start, always buy a wedge with a piece of the rind attached; this way, you can see the signature imprint stamped on the rind and know that you are getting what you're paying for. A rasp-style grater produces light, feathery strands of cheese with very little work. The small holes of a box grater work well, too. You can store any extra grated Parmesan in the freezer or refrigerator for about 3 weeks; for cooking applications, there is little difference between freshly grated and pregrated Parmesan that has been properly stored.

WHY THIS RECIPE WORKS

This cheesy potato casserole is commonly attributed to the Mormons, though versions of it have popped up all over the country. Most recipes rely on the convenience of condensed soup, but we were sure that swapping the can for fresh flavors would yield an ultrasatisfying casserole in no time. After softening chopped onions in butter, we added flour to create a golden roux. Chicken broth, half-and-half, and some seasoning gave our homemade take on the standard base plenty of body. Using frozen shredded hash browns for the potatoes cut hours out of our prep time without sacrificing the dish's flavor or texture. After we stirred in some shredded cheddar, cooking the frozen potatoes in the sauce thawed them in only 10 minutes. Sour cream gives funeral potatoes their signature tang, so we stirred some in off the heat to finish. Crushed sour-cream-and-onion potato chips sprinkled over the surface backed up the casserole's flavors and added irresistible crunch. At last, we had lush, homemade flavor alongside the convenience of store-bought hash browns and potato chips—these funeral potatoes proved a delicious compromise.

FUNERAL POTATOES SERVES 8 TO 10

You'll need one 30-ounce bag of frozen shredded (not diced) hash brown potatoes for this recipe.

- **3 tablespoons unsalted butter**
- **2 onions, chopped fine**
- **¼ cup all-purpose flour**
- **1½ cups chicken broth**
- **1 cup half-and-half**
- **1¾ teaspoons salt**
- **½ teaspoon dried thyme**
- **¼ teaspoon pepper**
- **8 ounces sharp cheddar cheese, shredded (2 cups)**
- **8 cups frozen shredded hash brown potatoes**
- **½ cup sour cream**
- **4 ounces sour-cream-and-onion potato chips, crushed**

1. Adjust oven rack to middle position and heat oven to 350 degrees. Melt butter in Dutch oven over medium-high heat. Add onions and cook until softened, about 5 minutes. Add flour and cook, stirring constantly, until golden, about 1 minute. Slowly whisk in broth, half-and-half, salt, thyme, and pepper and bring to boil. Reduce heat to medium-low and simmer, stirring occasionally, until slightly thickened, 3 to 5 minutes. Off heat, whisk in cheddar until smooth.

2. Stir potatoes into sauce, cover, and cook, stirring occasionally, over low heat until thawed, about 10 minutes. Off heat, stir in sour cream until combined.

3. Transfer mixture to 13 by 9-inch baking dish and top with potato chips. Bake until golden brown, 45 to 50 minutes. Let cool for 10 minutes before serving.

TO MAKE AHEAD: Potato mixture can be refrigerated in baking dish, covered with aluminum foil, for up to 2 days. To serve, bake potatoes, still covered with foil, for 20 minutes. Remove dish from oven and uncover. Top with potato chips and bake until golden brown, 45 to 50 minutes.

BEREAVEMENT BISCUITS

Mormons have their funeral potatoes, but for many of the first American colonists, respectable funerals were unthinkable without a stash of "funeral biscuits" to distribute to mourners. Unrelated to modern baking powder biscuits, these were basically large, flat cookies, usually round and stamped in molds with hearts or other decorative motifs. With a texture that resembled dry, slightly crisp ladyfingers, they were meant to be consumed with wine. Families that could afford them ordered many dozens from specialty confectioners and received them ready to hand out, handsomely wrapped in white paper—an expensive luxury at the time—and sealed with black wax. Funeral biscuits (the Dutch called them *dootcoekjes*, literally "death cookies") probably reached their height of popularity in the early 19th century and faded out after the Civil War.

CRUSHING ON CRUNCH

To crush potato chips, put them in zipper-lock bag, seal, and roll over them with rolling pin.

✔ WHY THIS RECIPE WORKS

The little pancakes known as Heavenly Hots, beloved for their tang and delicate, tender texture, were once the crowning item on the menu at Berkeley, California's Bridge Creek Restaurant. The secret lies in their unconventional ingredients: sour cream, a few eggs, and a mere ¼ cup of cake flour to (barely) hold the batter together. Using the original measurements, we found that the hots' ethereal texture also made them hard to flip. To strengthen the batter without turning our hots into plain old flapjacks, sturdier all-purpose flour, bolstered with cornstarch, baking powder, and baking soda, did the trick. We whisked the sour cream and eggs together, adding vanilla to subtly mellow the sour cream's tang. After folding the dry ingredients into the wet, we scooped the batter into a buttered skillet to cook for just over a minute before flipping the hots to finish them. In no time, we had our plates stacked with tender, golden-brown Heavenly Hots, and after a dusting of confectioners' sugar, one taste proved these little pancakes were truly sent from above.

HEAVENLY HOTS

MAKES 32; SERVES 4

Serve these pancakes plain or dusted with a bit of confectioners' sugar.

¼   cup (1¼ ounces) all-purpose flour
3   tablespoons sugar
1   teaspoon cornstarch
1   teaspoon baking powder
¼   teaspoon baking soda
½   teaspoon salt
2   cups sour cream
3   large eggs, lightly beaten
½   teaspoon vanilla extract
3   tablespoons unsalted butter

1. Adjust oven rack to middle position and heat oven to 200 degrees. Set wire rack in rimmed baking sheet. Whisk flour, sugar, cornstarch, baking powder, baking soda, and salt together in bowl. Whisk sour cream, eggs, and vanilla together in large bowl until smooth. Gently fold flour mixture into sour cream mixture until incorporated.

2. Heat 2 teaspoons butter in 12-inch nonstick skillet over medium-low heat until butter begins to sizzle. Using 1-tablespoon measure, portion batter into pan in 5 places, cover, and cook pancakes until tops appear dry and bottoms are golden brown, 1½ to 2 minutes.

3. Using thin spatula, gently flip pancakes and cook, uncovered, until golden brown, about 30 seconds. Transfer to prepared wire rack and keep warm in oven. Repeat with remaining batter, using remaining 7 teaspoons butter as needed. Serve.

CONFECTIONERS' SUGAR SUBSTITUTE

A dusting of confectioners' sugar gives Heavenly Hots a professional look, but if you have only granulated sugar on hand, you can still have the perfect finish. For 1 cup of confectioners' sugar, grind 1 cup of granulated sugar and 1 teaspoon of cornstarch in a blender (not a food processor).

THE PERFECT FINISH

For attractive, evenly coated results, the lightest possible touch is a must when dusting desserts with confectioners' sugar.

Hold fine-mesh strainer in 1 hand and gently tap its side with finger from opposite hand. (Do not shake strainer itself; this will produce heavy spots.) Move sieve over next area to be covered and repeat.

SOUR CREAM REIGNS SUPREME

The secret behind the unique tang and texture of Heavenly Hots is sour cream. Sour cream is simply cream fermented with a specific type of bacteria in order to thicken and sour it. We use full-fat sour cream here in the test kitchen; however light sour cream (made with part cream, part milk) is also fine. Avoid nonfat sour cream, which will adversely affect your baked goods. In a pinch, an equal amount of whole milk yogurt can be substituted for sour cream in baking.

✓ WHY THIS RECIPE WORKS

Between 1930 and 1988, Hollywood's Tick Tock Tea Room served up hearty platters of meatloaf, roast turkey, and fried chicken, but the restaurant's defining touch was the basket of hot sticky rolls served before each meal. The Tick Tock's rolls boasted a biscuitlike dough gleaming with a gooey orange glaze—a combination we wanted to bring to our own tables. For a thick, sticky glaze that wouldn't seep into the rolls, we reduced orange juice concentrate, brown sugar, granulated sugar, and butter. We let the glaze harden in a greased cake pan while we turned to the dough. The rolls needed to be sturdy but tender, so we stirred together a biscuit dough made with buttermilk and melted butter that became firmer after 5 minutes of kneading. We rolled the dough into a rectangle and pressed on a zesty orange-cinnamon filling before rolling it into a long, tight cylinder. After cutting the cylinder into eight even slices, we arranged the rolls on top of the hardened glaze. After about 20 minutes in the oven, the glaze melted into a gooey, citrusy topping. Our remake of Hollywood's long-lost sticky rolls was ready for its big premiere.

TICK TOCK ORANGE STICKY ROLLS   SERVES 8

Don't let the buns sit in the pan for more than 5 minutes after baking. The glaze will begin to harden and the buns will stick.

ORANGE GLAZE

- ½ cup frozen orange juice concentrate, thawed
- ¼ cup packed (1¾ ounces) light brown sugar
- ¼ cup (1¾ ounces) granulated sugar
- 3 tablespoons unsalted butter

ORANGE-CINNAMON FILLING

- ½ cup packed (3½ ounces) light brown sugar
- ¼ cup (1¾ ounces) granulated sugar
- 2 teaspoons ground cinnamon
- 1 teaspoon grated orange zest
- ⅛ teaspoon ground cloves
- ⅛ teaspoon salt
- 1 tablespoon unsalted butter, melted

BISCUIT DOUGH

- 2¾ cups (13¾ ounces) all-purpose flour, plus extra for counter
- 2 tablespoons granulated sugar
- 2 teaspoons baking powder
- ½ teaspoon baking soda
- ½ teaspoon salt
- 1¼ cups buttermilk
- 6 tablespoons unsalted butter, melted

1. FOR THE GLAZE: Grease 9-inch cake pan with vegetable oil spray. Bring all ingredients to simmer in small saucepan over medium heat. Cook until mixture thickens and clings to back of spoon, about 5 minutes. Pour mixture into prepared pan. Cool until glaze hardens, at least 20 minutes.

2. FOR THE FILLING: Adjust oven rack to lower-middle position and heat oven to 350 degrees. Combine all ingredients except butter in bowl. Using fork, stir in butter until mixture resembles wet sand.

3. FOR THE DOUGH: Whisk flour, sugar, baking powder, baking soda, and salt together in bowl. Whisk buttermilk and butter together in small bowl (mixture will clump), then stir into flour mixture until combined. Knead dough on lightly floured counter until smooth, about 5 minutes.

4. Roll dough into 12 by 9-inch rectangle. Pat filling into dough, leaving ½-inch border around edges. Starting at 1 long end, roll dough into tight cylinder and pinch seam together. Cut log into 8 pieces and arrange cut side down on cooled glaze, placing 1 roll in center and remaining rolls around edge of pan.

5. Bake until rolls are golden and glaze is darkened and bubbling, 18 to 25 minutes. Cool in pan for 5 minutes, then turn out onto platter. Let rolls sit for 10 minutes before serving.

TEAROOMS OF YESTERDAY

Tearooms in and around Los Angeles proliferated during the Depression when there was an influx of new residents in search of work. These tearooms weren't of the British High Tea sort but more like unpretentious cafés where one could order simple food at affordable prices—family joints. One such establishment, the Tick Tock Tea Room, opened in 1930, when Norwegian immigrants Arthur and Helen Johnson bought a rundown home on North Cahuenga Boulevard in Hollywood and converted it into a restaurant. They hung their most prized possession, an antique clock, on the wall and the rest was history; soon there were 48 clocks decorating the restaurant. The Johnsons would serve more than 2,000 three-course meals on busy days. The Tick Tock was such a success, thanks in part to the sweet rolls that came with every meal, that the family opened up two more locations in the Los Angeles area. The last Tick Tock closed for good in 1988.

✓ WHY THIS RECIPE WORKS

Before there was a fully stocked snack car on every train, Harvey House restaurants provided quick meals to travelers on the Atchison, Topeka & Santa Fe Railway, and their chocolate puffs made a lasting impact. Hoping to give this treat new life, we started with a *pâte à choux* dough (used for profiteroles and éclairs), and as it took shape in the food processor, we added cocoa for rich chocolate flavor. For perfect puffs, we piped the dough onto a baking sheet using a zipper-lock bag and set the oven to 425 degrees but reduced it to 350 after the puffs had baked for 15 minutes. Cutting slits into the puffs and letting them dry as the propped-open oven cooled crisped the puffs. For a lush, fruity filling, we mashed cooked frozen strawberries into a concentrated sauce. Whipped cream thickened with cream cheese provided a stable structure into which to fold the strawberry puree. We sliced the puffs, filled them with cream, and spooned an easy chocolate glaze over the tops to double up on chocolate. Historians credit Harvey House with civilizing the West, but with this much chocolate flavor surrounding lush strawberry cream, we felt anything but tamed.

HARVEY HOUSE CHOCOLATE PUFFS SERVES 8

An accurate oven temperature is essential for the puffs to puff. We recommend that you keep an oven thermometer in your oven. To prevent lumps in the whipped cream filling, be sure to sift the confectioners' sugar. The assembled puffs will hold in the refrigerator for up to 1 hour.

CHOCOLATE PUFFS
- 2 large eggs plus 1 large white
- 1 teaspoon vanilla extract
- ½ cup water
- 5 tablespoons unsalted butter, cut into ½-inch pieces
- 2 teaspoons granulated sugar
- ¼ teaspoon salt
- ½ cup (2½ ounces) all-purpose flour
- 3 tablespoons Dutch-processed cocoa powder

STRAWBERRY FILLING
- 8 ounces frozen strawberries, thawed
- 1 cup heavy cream, chilled
- 6 tablespoons (1½ ounces) confectioners' sugar, sifted
- 1 teaspoon vanilla extract
- 1½ ounces cream cheese, cut into 1-inch pieces and softened

CHOCOLATE GLAZE
- 1 cup (4 ounces) confectioners' sugar, sifted
- 3 tablespoons Dutch-processed cocoa powder
- 2 tablespoons water
- 1 teaspoon vanilla extract

1. FOR THE CHOCOLATE PUFFS: Adjust oven rack to upper-middle position and heat oven to 425 degrees. Line rimmed baking sheet with parchment paper. Whisk eggs, egg white, and vanilla together in bowl. Bring water, butter, sugar, and salt to boil in medium saucepan over medium-high heat. When butter is melted, remove pan from heat. Using rubber spatula, stir in flour until smooth. Return saucepan to low heat and cook, constantly stirring and smearing mixture against bottom of saucepan, until mixture is slightly shiny and registers 170 degrees, 2 to 3 minutes.

2. Transfer flour mixture to food processor and process until slightly cool, about 30 seconds. Remove feed tube insert from food processor. With food processor running, slowly add egg mixture through feed tube until incorporated. Scrape down sides of bowl and process until smooth, thick paste forms, about 30 seconds. Sprinkle cocoa over paste and process until combined, about 15 seconds, scraping down bowl as needed.

3. Cut ½ inch from corner of large zipper-lock bag. Transfer cocoa paste to bag and pipe eight 2-inch-wide and 1¼-inch-high mounds 2 inches apart on prepared baking sheet. Dip small spoon in water and smooth exterior of mounds.

4. Bake puffs for 15 minutes (do not open oven door), then reduce oven temperature to 350 degrees and continue to bake until firm, 20 minutes. Remove baking sheet from oven and turn off oven. Using tip of paring knife, carefully cut ½-inch slit into side of each puff. Return puffs to oven, prop door open with wooden spoon, and let puffs dry for 30 minutes. Transfer puffs to wire rack to cool completely, about 30 minutes. (Puffs can be stored at room temperature for up to 1 day or frozen in single layer for up to 1 month. Let frozen puffs come to room temperature before filling.)

5. FOR THE STRAWBERRY FILLING: Meanwhile, cook strawberries in medium saucepan over medium-low heat, mashing occasionally with potato masher, until thickened and reduced to ½ cup, 10 to 12 minutes. Transfer to large bowl and refrigerate until cool, about 1 hour.

6. Using stand mixer fitted with whisk, whip cream, sugar, and vanilla together on medium-low speed until foamy, about 1 minute. Increase speed to high and whip until soft peaks form, 1 to 3 minutes. Add cream cheese and whip until stiff peaks form, about 30 seconds. Gently fold chilled strawberries into whipped cream, return mixture to large bowl, and refrigerate until firm, about 1 hour. (Filling can be refrigerated for up to 1 day.)

7. FOR THE CHOCOLATE GLAZE: Set wire rack in rimmed baking sheet. Using serrated knife, cut puffs crosswise into 2 pieces, ½ inch from bottom. Top puff bottoms with strawberry whipped cream and replace tops; transfer to rack. Combine sugar and cocoa in bowl. Whisk in water and vanilla until smooth. Spoon 1 tablespoon glaze over each puff and let sit for 15 minutes until set. Serve.

✓ WHY THIS RECIPE WORKS

Millionaire pie, so named for its rich flavor and golden hue, is a New Mexico–born no-bake pineapple chiffon pie that makes a real impact. While most recipes call for off-the-shelf ingredients like whipped topping and cream cheese, we knew that boosting this dessert's texture and flavor was worth a little extra effort. Rather than marring the creamy filling with the requisite pecans, we incorporated their flavor and crunch into a pecan-studded cookie crust. For top-to-bottom pineapple flavor in our filling, we cooked canned crushed pineapple until lightly browned and fragrant, turning it into a smooth puree with a whirl in the food processor. Pineapple-flavored gelatin would make slicing easy while reinforcing the puree's flavor, so we dissolved it in pineapple juice and whisked it into egg yolks, sugar, and salt. While the punched-up pineapple filling set in the refrigerator, we whisked heavy cream and sugar into an airy whipped cream. We folded some of the whipped cream into the pineapple filling and spread it in the cookie crust, topping it with the remaining whipped cream. With full pineapple flavor and lush, creamy texture, this pie tasted like a million bucks.

MILLIONAIRE PIE SERVES 8

Pecan Sandies are the brand name of a cookie made by Keebler; any pecan shortbread cookie will work in this recipe. If desired, top the finished pie with ¼ cup of toasted and chopped pecans or ½ cup of toasted sweetened flaked coconut.

CRUST

- 12 **Pecan Sandies, broken into rough pieces (about 2½ cups)**
- ½ **cup pecans, chopped**
- 2 **tablespoons unsalted butter, melted**

FILLING

- 1 **(20-ounce) can crushed pineapple packed in juice**
- ½ **cup (3½ ounces) plus 1 tablespoon sugar Salt**
- 3 **large egg yolks**
- 1 **(3-ounce) box pineapple-flavored gelatin**
- 1 **cup frozen pineapple juice concentrate, thawed**
- 2 **cups heavy cream, chilled**

1. FOR THE CRUST: Adjust oven rack to middle position and heat oven to 350 degrees. Process cookies and pecans in food processor to fine crumbs, about 30 seconds. Add butter and pulse until combined, about 5 pulses. Press crumbs into bottom and sides of 9-inch pie plate and refrigerate until firm, about 20 minutes. Bake until lightly browned and set, about 15 minutes. Cool completely.

2. FOR THE FILLING: Cook crushed pineapple, ¼ cup sugar, and pinch salt in 12-inch nonstick skillet over medium-high heat, stirring occasionally, until liquid evaporates and pineapple is lightly browned, about 15 minutes. Scrape mixture into bowl of food processor and process until very smooth, about 1 minute; set aside.

3. Whisk egg yolks, ¼ cup sugar, and ¼ teaspoon salt together in medium bowl. Combine gelatin and ½ cup pineapple juice concentrate in medium saucepan and let sit until gelatin softens, about 5 minutes. Cook over medium heat until gelatin dissolves and mixture is very hot but not boiling, about 2 minutes. Whisking vigorously, slowly add gelatin mixture to egg yolks. Return mixture to saucepan and cook, stirring constantly, until slightly thickened, about 2 minutes. Off heat, stir in remaining ½ cup pineapple juice concentrate and processed pineapple mixture. Pour into clean large bowl and refrigerate until set, about 1½ hours.

4. With electric mixer on medium-high speed, whip cream and remaining 1 tablespoon sugar to stiff peaks, about 3 minutes. Whisk 1 cup whipped cream into gelatin mixture until completely incorporated. Using rubber spatula, fold 1 cup whipped cream into gelatin mixture until no streaks of white remain. Scrape mixture into cooled pie shell and smooth top. Spread remaining whipped cream evenly over filling and refrigerate until firm, at least 4 hours. Serve.

TOASTED (NOT BURNT) COCONUT

If you choose to top off Millionaire Pie with a sprinkling of toasted coconut, skip the oven (where it can easily burn) and use your microwave instead.

Spread coconut evenly on large microwave-safe plate and cook on high power until golden brown. It takes a couple of minutes and you need to stir it a few times (at about 30-second intervals).

✓ WHY THIS RECIPE WORKS

Restaurant critic Duncan Hines (yes, *that* Duncan Hines) had his first slice of black-bottom pie at an Oklahoma diner, and his rave review of that decadent trifecta of chocolate custard, rum chiffon, and whipped cream immediately put this luscious pie on the map. Most black-bottom pie recipes take hours to make and leave a mountain of bowls in the sink—could we serve up this dreamy dessert without the fuss? A chocolate cookie crust came together easily; we ground chocolate cookies in the food processor, added butter, and pressed the crumbs into a pie plate. We made a large batch of custard and whisked chopped semisweet chocolate into half of it for the chocolate layer. The rum chiffon required stability, and a mixture of gelatin, rum, and water got us on track. Once set and whisked into the rest of the custard, it emerged from the refrigerator with a perfectly wobbly texture. For even more structure, we made a frosting of sugar, egg white, water, and cream of tartar and folded it into the rum custard. It was easy to see why Duncan Hines was impressed with this pie: lush chocolate and rum layers topped with a cloud of sweetened whipped cream.

BLACK-BOTTOM PIE   SERVES 8 TO 10

To prevent the filling from overflowing the crust, add the final ½ cup of the rum layer after the filling has set for 20 minutes.

CRUST

32	chocolate cookies, broken into rough pieces (about 2½ cups)
4	tablespoons unsalted butter, melted

FILLING

⅔	cup (4⅔ ounces) plus 2 tablespoons sugar
2	cups half-and-half
4	teaspoons cornstarch
4	large egg yolks plus 1 large white
6	ounces semisweet chocolate, chopped fine
3	tablespoons golden or light rum
2	tablespoons water
1	teaspoon unflavored gelatin
¼	teaspoon cream of tartar
1½	cups heavy cream, chilled

1. FOR THE CRUST: Adjust oven rack to middle position and heat oven to 350 degrees. Process cookies in food processor to fine crumbs, about 45 seconds. Add butter and pulse until combined, about 8 pulses. Press crumbs into bottom and sides of 9-inch pie plate and refrigerate until firm, about 20 minutes. Bake until set, about 10 minutes. Cool completely.

2. FOR THE FILLING: Whisk ⅓ cup sugar, half-and-half, cornstarch, and egg yolks together in saucepan. Cook over medium heat, stirring constantly, until mixture comes to boil, about 8 minutes.

3. Divide hot custard evenly between 2 bowls. Whisk chocolate into custard in 1 bowl until smooth, then pour into cooled pie crust; refrigerate. Whisk rum, 1 tablespoon water, and gelatin together in third bowl and let sit for 5 minutes; stir into bowl with plain custard and refrigerate, stirring occasionally, until mixture is wobbly but not set, about 20 minutes.

4. Combine ⅓ cup sugar, egg white, remaining 1 tablespoon water, and cream of tartar in large heatproof bowl set over medium saucepan filled with ½ inch of barely simmering water (don't let bowl touch water). With electric mixer on medium-high speed, beat egg white mixture to soft peaks, about 2 minutes; remove bowl from heat and beat egg white mixture until very thick and glossy and cooled to room temperature, about 3 minutes.

5. Whisk cooled egg white mixture into chilled rum custard until smooth. Pour all but ½ cup rum custard into chocolate custard–filled pie crust. Refrigerate for 20 minutes, then top with remaining rum custard. Refrigerate until completely set, 3 hours or up to 24 hours.

6. To serve, whip cream and remaining 2 tablespoons sugar together with electric mixer on medium-low speed until frothy, about 1 minute. Increase speed to high and whip until soft peaks form, 1 to 3 minutes. Spread whipped cream over top of pie. Serve.

SILKY CHIFFON

Whipped egg whites and sugar couldn't support the whipped cream layer, but a seven-minute frosting turned things around:

1. Using electric mixer on medium-high speed, beat egg white mixture over pot of barely simmering water to soft peaks, about 2 minutes.

2. Remove bowl from heat and beat until egg white mixture becomes very thick and glossy and cools to room temperature, about 3 minutes.

A HOUSEHOLD NAME

Duncan Hines crisscrossed the country as a traveling salesman during the early 20th century. Displeased by many of the restaurants he visited, Hines began compiling a list of acceptable establishments. After receiving a positive response to his list of recommended restaurants in 1935, Hines began critiquing restaurants full time, leaving "Recommended by Duncan Hines" plaques along the way. Several books and cookbooks followed, but it was Hines's decision to license his name for packaged foods, including box cake mixes, that guaranteed his fame for generations to come.

✓ WHY THIS RECIPE WORKS

In the Hill Country region of Texas, cobblers take on a very different look from the fruit-and-biscuit desserts served elsewhere in America. There, a thick, pancakelike batter forms a craggy surface studded with fruit. Melting butter in the baking pan promised rich, deliciously crisp edges. Flour, sugar, baking powder, salt, milk, and cool melted butter created a thick batter, which we poured over the melted butter in our baking pan. Lemon brightens blueberry desserts, so we pulsed sugar and lemon zest in a food processor and mashed some of the citrusy sugar with blueberries to add some light acidity while also breaking down the berries. After we scattered the mashed berries over the batter and sprinkled extra lemon sugar over the surface, the cobbler was ready to bake. In about 45 minutes the batter rose and the fruit sank, creating the signature pocketed surface. It was a cobbler like we'd never seen before—and its bright fruit flavor and buttery crust tasted out of this world.

TEXAS BLUEBERRY COBBLER SERVES 8 TO 10

Keep a close eye on the butter as it melts in the oven so that it doesn't scorch. Place the hot baking dish with butter on a wire rack after removing it from the oven. Avoid untreated aluminum pans here. If using frozen blueberries, thaw them first.

4	tablespoons unsalted butter, cut into 4 pieces, plus 8 tablespoons melted and cooled
1½	cups (10½ ounces) sugar
1½	teaspoons grated lemon zest
15	ounces (3 cups) blueberries
1½	cups (7½ ounces) all-purpose flour
2½	teaspoons baking powder
¾	teaspoon salt
1½	cups milk

1. Adjust oven rack to upper-middle position and heat oven to 350 degrees. Place 4 tablespoons cut-up butter in 13 by 9-inch baking dish and transfer to oven. Heat until butter is melted, 8 to 10 minutes.

2. Meanwhile, pulse ¼ cup sugar and lemon zest together in food processor until combined, about 5 pulses; set aside. Using potato masher, mash blueberries and 1 tablespoon lemon sugar together in bowl until berries are coarsely mashed.

3. Combine flour, remaining 1¼ cups sugar, baking powder, and salt in large bowl. Whisk in milk and 8 tablespoons melted, cooled butter until smooth. Remove baking dish from oven, transfer to wire rack, and pour batter into prepared pan.

4. Dollop mashed blueberry mixture evenly over batter, sprinkle with remaining lemon sugar, and bake until golden brown and edges are crisp, 45 to 50 minutes, rotating pan halfway through baking. Let cobbler cool on wire rack for 30 minutes. Serve warm.

A DIFFERENT KIND OF COBBLER

Many of us know cobbler as a jammy fruit base with a baked biscuit topping. In the Lone Star State, they start with the batter on the bottom and the fruit on top.

1. Melt butter right in baking pan for rich, crisp cobbler edges.

2. Pour batter into baking pan over melted butter.

3. Scatter on mashed berries. Batter will rise over berries during baking.

⊛ DINING DESTINATIONS

Throughout this book we highlighted the communities and eateries whose dishes inspired our recipes. Here is more information on where you can try the original dishes today.

NEW ENGLAND AND THE MID-ATLANTIC

Connecticut Steamed Cheeseburgers (page 3)	Ted's Restaurant	1046 Broad Street, Meriden, CT 06450
Chicken Spiedies (page 5)	Spiedie Fest	spiediefest.com, Binghamton, NY
Philadelphia Cheesesteaks (page 9)	Pat's King of Steaks	1237 E. Passyunk Avenue, Philadelphia, PA 19147
	Geno's Steaks	1219 S. 9th Street, Philadelphia, PA 19147
Chicken Riggies (page 13)	Chesterfield Restaurant	1713 Bleeker Street, Utica, NY 13501
	Georgio's Village Café	60 Genesee Street, New Hartford, NY 13413
	Teddy's Restaurant	851 Black River Boulevard, Rome, NY 13440
New England Bar Pizza (page 19)	Lynwood Café	320 Center Street, Randolph, MA 02368
Bialys (page 43)	Kossar's Bialys	367 Grand Street, New York, NY 10002
Rhode Island Johnnycakes (page 47)	Johnny Cake Festival	johnnycakefestival.com, Richmond, RI

APPALACHIA AND THE SOUTH

New Orleans Muffulettas (page 81)	Central Grocery and Deli	923 Decatur Street, New Orleans, LA 70116
West Virginia Pepperoni Rolls (page 85)	Country Club Bakery	1211 Country Club Road, Fairmont, WV 26554
Kentucky Burgoo (page 95)	International Bar-B-Q Festival	bbqfest.com, Owensboro, KY
	Moonlite Bar-B-Q Inn	2840 W. Parrish Avenue, Owensboro, KY 42301
Carolina Chicken Bog (page 99)	Loris Bog-Off Festival	lorischambersc.com, Loris, SC
Fried Catfish (page 113)	Taylor Grocery	4-A Depot Street, Taylor, MS 38673
South Carolina Shrimp Burgers (page 115)	Shrimp Shack	1929 Sea Island Parkway St. Helena Island, SC 29920

Carolina Red Slaw (page 131)	Lexington Barbecue	100 Smokehouse Lane, Lexington, NC 27295
Moravian Sugar Cake (page 155)	Winkler Bakery	521 S. Main Street, Winston-Salem, NC 27101
Thoroughbred Pie (page 163)	Kern's Kitchen	*Mail order and retail outlet information* derbypie.com, Louisville, KY
Carolina Sweet Potato Sonker (page 169)	Sonker Festival	sonkertrail.org, Lowgap, NC

THE MIDWEST AND GREAT PLAINS

Iowa Loose Meat Sandwiches (page 175)	Taylor's Maid-Rite	106 S. 3rd Avenue, Marshalltown, IA 50158
Iron Range Porketta (page 183)	Fraboni Sausage	*Mail order and retail outlet information* frabonis.com, Hibbing, MN
	Cobb Cook Grocery	3817 1st Avenue, Hibbing, MN 55746
Chicago-Style Italian Beef Sandwiches (page 187)	Al's Italian Beef	1079 W. Taylor Street, Chicago, IL 60607
Barberton Fried Chicken (page 197)	Belgrade Gardens	401 E. State Street, Barberton, OH 44203
Chicken Vesuvio (page 199)	Harry Caray's Italian Steakhouse	33 W. Kinzie Street, Chicago, IL 60654
Bierocks (page 203)	Runza Restaurant	*Locations throughout Iowa, Kansas, and Nebraska* runza.com
Hoppel Poppel (page 217)	Benji's Deli	4156 N. Oakland Avenue, Milwaukee, WI 53211 8683 N. Port Washington Road Milwaukee, WI 53217
Kringle (page 227)	O&H Danish Bakery	1841 Douglas Avenue, Racine, WI 53402 4006 Durand Avenue, Racine, WI 53405

TEXAS AND THE WEST

Monte Cristo Sandwiches (page 243)	Blue Bayou Restaurant	New Orleans Square, Disneyland Park, Anaheim, CA 92802
Oklahoma Barbecued Chopped Pork (page 245)	Lotta Bull BBQ	*Mail order and retail outlet information* lottabullbbq.com, Marietta, OK
Indoor Barbecue Beef Short Ribs (page 253)	Louie Mueller Barbecue	206 W. 2nd Street, Taylor, TX 76574
	Franklin Barbecue	900 E. 11th Street, Austin, TX 78702

CONVERSIONS AND EQUIVALENTS

SOME SAY COOKING IS A SCIENCE AND AN ART. WE would say that geography has a hand in it, too. Flour milled in the United Kingdom and elsewhere will feel and taste different from flour milled in the United States. So we cannot promise that the loaf of bread you bake in Canada or England will taste the same as a loaf baked in the States, but we can offer guidelines for converting weights and measures. We also recommend that you rely on your instincts when making our recipes. Refer to the visual cues provided. If the bread dough hasn't "come together in a ball," as described, you may need to add more flour—even if the recipe doesn't tell you to. You be the judge.

The recipes in this book were developed using standard U.S. measures following U.S. government guidelines. The charts below offer equivalents for U.S., metric, and imperial (U.K.) measures. All conversions are approximate and have been rounded up or down to the nearest whole number.

EXAMPLE:

1 teaspoon	=	4.9292 milliliters, rounded up to 5 milliliters
1 ounce	=	28.3495 grams, rounded down to 28 grams

VOLUME CONVERSIONS

U.S.	METRIC
1 teaspoon	5 milliliters
2 teaspoons	10 milliliters
1 tablespoon	15 milliliters
2 tablespoons	30 milliliters
¼ cup	59 milliliters
⅓ cup	79 milliliters
½ cup	118 milliliters
¾ cup	177 milliliters
1 cup	237 milliliters
1¼ cups	296 milliliters
1½ cups	355 milliliters
2 cups (1 pint)	473 milliliters
2½ cups	591 milliliters
3 cups	710 milliliters
4 cups (1 quart)	0.946 liter
1.06 quarts	1 liter
4 quarts (1 gallon)	3.8 liters

WEIGHT CONVERSIONS

OUNCES	GRAMS
½	14
¾	21
1	28
1½	43
2	57
2½	71
3	85
3½	99
4	113
4½	128
5	142
6	170
7	198
8	227
9	255
10	283
12	340
16 (1 pound)	454

CONVERSIONS FOR INGREDIENTS COMMONLY USED IN BAKING

Baking is an exacting science. Because measuring by weight is far more accurate than measuring by volume, and thus more likely to achieve reliable results, in our recipes we provide ounce measures in addition to cup measures for many ingredients. Refer to the chart below to convert these measures into grams.

INGREDIENT	OUNCES	GRAMS
1 cup all-purpose flour*	5	142
1 cup whole-wheat flour	5½	156
1 cup granulated (white) sugar	7	198
1 cup packed brown sugar (light or dark)	7	198
1 cup confectioners' sugar	4	113
1 cup cocoa powder	3	85
4 tablespoons butter† (½ stick, or ¼ cup)	2	57
8 tablespoons butter† (1 stick, or ½ cup)	4	113
16 tablespoons butter† (2 sticks, or 1 cup)	8	227

* U.S. all-purpose flour, the most frequently used flour in this book, does not contain leaveners, as some European flours do. These leavened flours are called self-rising or self-raising. If you are using self-rising flour, take this into consideration before adding leavening to a recipe.

† In the United States, butter is sold both salted and unsalted. We generally recommend unsalted butter. If you are using salted butter, take this into consideration before adding salt to a recipe.

OVEN TEMPERATURES

FAHRENHEIT	CELSIUS	GAS MARK (IMPERIAL)
225	105	¼
250	120	½
275	135	1
300	150	2
325	165	3
350	180	4
375	190	5
400	200	6
425	220	7
450	230	8
475	245	9

CONVERTING TEMPERATURES FROM AN INSTANT-READ THERMOMETER

We include doneness temperatures in many of the recipes in this book. We recommend an instant-read thermometer for the job. Refer to the above table to convert Fahrenheit degrees to Celsius. Or, for temperatures not represented in the chart, use this simple formula:

Subtract 32 degrees from the Fahrenheit reading, then divide the result by 1.8 to find the Celsius reading.

EXAMPLE:

"Roast chicken until thighs register 175 degrees."
To convert:

175°F − 32 = 143°
143° ÷ 1.8 = 79.44°C, rounded down to 79°C

INDEX

Note: Page references in *italics* indicate photographs.

A

Almonds
   Bee Sting Cake, *64,* 65
   Cranberry Upside-Down Cake, *66,* 67
   and Red Grapes, Waldorf Salad with, 35
   Sand Tarts, *224,* 225
Anadama Bread, *52,* 53
Andouille
   and Bell Pepper, Corn Chowder with, 29
   Maque Choux, *90,* 91
   Maque Choux with Shrimp, 91
   Perfect Shrimp Jambalaya, *116,* 117
   Red Beans and Rice, *136,* 137
   South Carolina Shrimp Boil, *118,* 119
Appetizers
   Baked Jalapeño Poppers, *238,* 239
   Boneless Buffalo Chicken, *6,* 7
   Crispy Beef Taquitos, *236,* 237
   Maryland Crab Fluff, *86,* 87
Apple(s)
   Country Captain Chicken, *100,* 101
   Curried Waldorf Salad with Green Grapes and
      Peanuts, 35
   Pie, Marlborough, *70,* 71
   Waldorf Salad, *34,* 35
   Waldorf Salad with Dried Cherries and Pecans, 35
   Waldorf Salad with Red Grapes and Almonds, 35
Authentic Maryland Fried Chicken and Gravy, *96,* 97
Avocado Sauce, 237

B

Babka, *54,* 55
Bacon
   Baked Jalapeño Poppers, *238,* 239
   Cracklin' Cornbread, *150,* 151
   Monterey Chicken, *240,* 241
   Oven-Barbecued Beef Brisket, *250,* 251
   Potato Biscuits with, 49
   raw, freezing, 123
   Southern-Style Green Beans, *122,* 123
Baked Cheese Grits, *124,* 125
Baking powder vs. baking soda, 151
Ballpark Pretzels, *44,* 45
Barbecue Sauce, 251

Barberton Fried Chicken, *196,* 197
Barberton Hot Sauce, 197
Barley
   about, 257
   Mulligan Stew, *256,* 257
Bean(s)
   Barbecue, Smoky Kansas City, *212,* 213
   Boston Baked, Quicker, *38,* 39
   canned, rinsing, 269
   Crispy Beef Taquitos, *236,* 237
   Green, Southern-Style, *122,* 123
   green, trimming ends of, 123
   Hollywood Chili, *262,* 263
   Hoppin' John, *138,* 139
   Kentucky Burgoo, *94,* 95
   Mulligan Stew, *256,* 257
   Navy, Soup, Senate, *92,* 93
   Red, and Rice, *136,* 137
   red, food safety concerns about, 137
   Texas Caviar, *268,* 269
Beef
   The Best Reuben Sandwiches, *180,* 181
   Bierocks, *202,* 203
   Brisket, Oven-Barbecued, *250,* 251
   Chiles Rellenos Casserole, *264,* 265
   chuck-eye roast, dividing, 257
   Connecticut Steamed Cheeseburgers, *2,* 3
   Corned, and Cabbage, *20,* 21
   Green Bay Booyah, *192,* 193
   Hollywood Chili, *262,* 263
   Iowa Loose Meat Sandwiches, *174,* 175
   Joe Booker Stew, *30,* 31
   Kansas City Barbecued Brisket, *208,* 209
   Mulligan Stew, *256,* 257
   Pastrami and Swiss Football Sandwiches, 83
   Philadelphia Cheesesteaks, *8,* 9
   Pimento Cheeseburgers, *78,* 79
   Pittsburgh Wedding Soup, *32,* 33
   Quick Jus, 187
   Roast, Chicago-Style Italian, *184,* 185
   Sandwiches, Chicago-Style Italian, *186,* 187
   Short Ribs, Indoor Barbecue, *252,* 253
   Steak de Burgo, *200,* 201
   Taquitos, Crispy, *236,* 237
   Texas Chicken-Fried Steak, *254,* 255

Beer
    and Brats, Grilled, Wisconsin, *188,* 189
    Cheddar Soup, Wisconsin, *190,* 191
Bee Sting Cake, *64,* 65
Berries
    Cranberry Upside-Down Cake, *66,* 67
    Harvey House Chocolate Puffs, *286,* 287
    see also Blueberry(ies)
Betty, description of, 73
Bialys, *42,* 43
Bierocks, *202,* 203
Biscuit(s)
    Cream Cheese, *148,* 149
    Dressing, *110,* 111
    Potato, with Bacon, 49
    Potato, with Cheddar and Scallions, 49
    Potato, with Chives, *48,* 49
    and Sausage Gravy, *144,* 145
    Sweet Potato, *146,* 147
Blackberry Jam Cake, *152,* 153
Black-Bottom Pie, *290,* 291
Black-eyed peas
    Hoppin' John, *138,* 139
    Texas Caviar, *268,* 269
Blueberry(ies)
    Boy Bait, *228,* 229
    Cobbler, Texas, *292,* 293
    Crumble, Summer, *72,* 73
    Crumble without a Food Processor, 73
    fresh, types of, 229
    frozen, baking with, 229
Blue cheese
    Dressing for Boneless Buffalo Chicken, *6,* 7
Boneless Buffalo Chicken, *6,* 7
Booyah, Green Bay, *192,* 193
Boston Cream Cupcakes, *60,* 61
Bourbon
    Thoroughbred Pie, *162,* 163
    Whipped Cream, *156,* 157
Brats and Beer, Wisconsin Grilled, *188,* 189
Breads
    Anadama, *52,* 53
    Babka, *54,* 55
    Ballpark Pretzels, *44,* 45
    Bialys, *42,* 43
    Common Crackers, *22,* 23
    Cracklin' Cornbread, *150,* 151
    Dilly Casserole, *222,* 223

Breads *(cont.)*
    Garlic Knots, *50,* 51
    Garlic Toasts, 25
    Italian, Toasted, 11
    Tick Tock Orange Sticky Rolls, *284,* 285
    West Virginia Pepperoni Rolls, *84,* 85
    see also Biscuit(s)
Broth, freezing, 205
Buckeyes, *232,* 233
Buckle, description of, 73
Burgers
    Connecticut Steamed Cheeseburgers, *2,* 3
    Pimento Cheeseburgers, *78,* 79
    Shrimp, South Carolina, *114,* 115
Burgoo, Kentucky, *94,* 95
Butter, Maple, *46,* 47
Buttermilk Pie, *166,* 167
Butterscotch Gooey Butter Cake, 231

C

Cabbage
    Bierocks, *202,* 203
    Carolina Red Slaw, *130,* 131
    Corned Beef and, *20,* 21
    cutting into wedges, 21
    Green Bay Booyah, *192,* 193
    Mulligan Stew, *256,* 257
    Oklahoma Barbecue Relish, 245
    Pork Chop Casserole, *206,* 207
    shredding and draining, 131
    see also Sauerkraut
Cakes
    Bee Sting, *64,* 65
    Blackberry Jam, *152,* 153
    Blueberry Boy Bait, *228,* 229
    Boston Cream Cupcakes, *60,* 61
    Cranberry Upside-Down, *66,* 67
    Gooey Butter, Butterscotch, 231
    Gooey Butter, Chocolate, 231
    Gooey Butter, St. Louis, *230,* 231
    Moravian Sugar, *154,* 155
    Wellesley Fudge, *62,* 63
Caramel Tomatoes, *128,* 129
Carne Adovada, *260,* 261
Carolina Chicken Bog, *98,* 99
Carolina Red Slaw, *130,* 131
Carolina Sweet Potato Sonker, *168,* 169

Carrots
    Cider-Glazed Root Vegetables, *36, 37*
    Cider-Glazed Root Vegetables with Pomegranate and
        Cilantro, **37**
    Corned Beef and Cabbage, *20, 21*
    Joe Booker Stew, *30, 31*
    Mulligan Stew, *256, 257*
    Pork Chop Casserole, *206, 207*
Casseroles
    Chiles Rellenos, *264, 265*
    Kielbasa, *204, 205*
    King Ranch, *266, 267*
    Pork Chop, *206, 207*
Catfish, Fried, *112, 113*
Cheddar (Cheese)
    Baked Cheese Grits, *124, 125*
    Baked Jalapeño Poppers, *238, 239*
    Beer Soup, Wisconsin, *190, 191*
    color and taste, **191**
    Connecticut Steamed Cheeseburgers, *2, 3*
    extra-sharp, about, **125**
    Funeral Potatoes, *280, 281*
    and Ham Hushpuppies, **143**
    Hoppel Poppel, *216, 217*
    New England Bar Pizza, *18, 19*
    Pimento Cheeseburgers, *78, 79*
    Prosperity Sandwiches, *178, 179*
    and Scallions, Potato Biscuits with, **49**
Cheese
    Baked Jalapeño Poppers, *238, 239*
    The Best Reuben Sandwiches, *180, 181*
    Bierocks, *202, 203*
    cheddar, color and taste, **191**
    cheddar, extra-sharp, about, **125**
    Chicken Riggies, *12, 13*
    Chiles Rellenos Casserole, *264, 265*
    Connecticut Steamed Cheeseburgers, *2, 3*
    Cream, Biscuits, *148, 149*
    Dilly Casserole Bread, *222, 223*
    Dressing for Boneless Buffalo Chicken, *6, 7*
    Football Sandwiches, *82, 83*
    Frenchees, *172, 173*
    Funeral Potatoes, *280, 281*
    Grits, Baked, *124, 125*
    Ham and Cheddar Hushpuppies, **143**
    Hoppel Poppel, *216, 217*
    Jo Jo Potatoes, *278, 279*
    King Ranch Casserole, *266, 267*
    Monte Cristo Sandwiches, *242, 243*

Cheese *(cont.)*
    Monterey Chicken, *240, 241*
    New England Bar Pizza, *18, 19*
    New Orleans Muffulettas, *80, 81*
    Parmesan, grating, **279**
    Pastrami and Swiss Football Sandwiches, **83**
    Philadelphia Cheesesteaks, *8,* **9**
    Pimento Cheeseburgers, *78, 79*
    Potato Biscuits with Cheddar and Scallions, **49**
    Prosperity Sandwiches, *178, 179*
    Utica Greens, *14, 15*
    Wisconsin Cheddar Beer Soup, *190, 191*
Cherries, Dried, and Pecans, Waldorf Salad with, **35**
Chicago-Style Italian Beef Sandwiches, *186, 187*
Chicago-Style Italian Roast Beef, *184, 185*
Chicken
    à la King, *10, 11*
    Bog, Carolina, *98, 99*
    Boneless Buffalo, *6, 7*
    Bonne Femme, *102, 103*
    Country Captain, *100, 101*
    Fried, Barberton, *196, 197*
    Green Bay Booyah, *192, 193*
    Kentucky Burgoo, *94, 95*
    King Ranch Casserole, *266, 267*
    Knoephla Soup, *194, 195*
    Maryland Fried, and Gravy, Authentic, *96, 97*
    Monterey, *240, 241*
    raw, rinsing, **99**
    Riggies, *12, 13*
    Spiedies, *4, 5*
    Vesuvio, *198, 199*
Chicken livers
    Dirty Rice, *134, 135*
Chiles
    Baked Jalapeño Poppers, *238, 239*
    Barberton Hot Sauce, **197**
    and Chorizo, Corn Chowder with, **29**
    dried, prepping, **259**
    jalapeños, gauging heat in, **267**
    King Ranch Casserole, *266, 267*
    New Mexican Pork Stew (Posole), *258, 259*
    in New Mexico, **261**
    Rellenos Casserole, *264, 265*
    Texas Caviar, *268, 269*
    Tex-Mex Rice, *274, 275*
Chili
    Carne Adovada, *260, 261*
    Hollywood, *262, 263*

Chives, Potato Biscuits with, *48,* 49
Chocolate
    Black-Bottom Pie, *290,* 291
    Boston Cream Cupcakes, *60,* 61
    Buckeyes, *232,* 233
    -Dipped Potato Chip Cookies, **59**
    Fudgy Tar Heel Pie, *158,* 159
    Gooey Butter Cake, **231**
    Graham Crust, Peanut Butter Pie with, **161**
    Grasshopper Pie, *164,* 165
    Gravy, **149**
    Puffs, Harvey House, *286,* 287
    semisweet vs. bittersweet, **233**
    Thoroughbred Pie, *162,* 163
    Wellesley Fudge Cake, *62,* 63
Chorizo and Chiles, Corn Chowder with, **29**
Chowder
    Clam, Easy New England, *22,* 23
    Clam, Rhode Island Red, *24,* 25
    Corn, Classic, *28,* 29
    Corn, with Andouille and Bell Pepper, **29**
    Corn, with Chorizo and Chiles, **29**
    Corn, with Prosciutto and Sage, **29**
    Corn, with Sweet Potatoes and Cayenne, **29**
    Fish, New England, *26,* 27
Cider
    -Glazed Root Vegetables, *36,* 37
    -Glazed Root Vegetables with Pomegranate and
        Cilantro, **37**
    hard, revival of, **37**
    origins of, **37**
Cilantro stems, note about, **269**
Cinnamon
    Babka, *54,* 55
    Moravian Sugar Cake, *154,* 155
    Tick Tock Orange Sticky Rolls, *284,* 285
City Chicken, *16,* 17
Clam Chowder
    Easy New England, *22,* 23
    Rhode Island Red, *24,* 25
Classic Corn Chowder, *28,* 29
Cobbler
    Blueberry, Texas, *292,* 293
    description of, **73**
Cocktail Sauce, **87**
Colby Jack cheese
    Bierocks, *202,* 203
    King Ranch Casserole, *266,* 267
Comeback Sauce, *112,* 113

Common Crackers, *22,* 23
Connecticut Steamed Cheeseburgers, *2,* 3
Cookies
    Hermit, *56,* 57
    Potato Chip, *58,* 59
    Potato Chip, Chocolate-Dipped, **59**
    Sand Tarts, *224,* 225
Corn
    Chowder, Classic, *28,* 29
    Chowder with Andouille and Bell Pepper, **29**
    Chowder with Chorizo and Chiles, **29**
    Chowder with Prosciutto and Sage, **29**
    Chowder with Sweet Potatoes and Cayenne, **29**
    cutting kernels from, **29**
    Kentucky Burgoo, *94,* 95
    Maque Choux, *90,* 91
    Maque Choux with Shrimp, **91**
    and Red Pepper Hushpuppies, **143**
    shopping for and storing, **91**
    South Carolina Shrimp Boil, *118,* 119
Corned Beef and Cabbage, *20,* 21
Cornflake Stuffing, *276,* 277
Cornmeal
    about, **127**
    Anadama Bread, *52,* 53
    Corn and Red Pepper Hushpuppies, **143**
    Crab and Chive Hushpuppies, **143**
    Cracklin' Cornbread, *150,* 151
    Fried Catfish, *112,* 113
    Fried Green Tomatoes, *126,* 127
    Ham and Cheddar Hushpuppies, **143**
    Hushpuppies, *142,* 143
    Rhode Island Johnnycakes, *46,* 47
Cottage cheese
    Dilly Casserole Bread, *222,* 223
Country Captain Chicken, *100,* 101
Country-Fried Pork with Gravy, *248,* 249
Country Ham, *108,* 109
Crab
    and Chive Hushpuppies, **143**
    Fluff, Maryland, *86,* 87
Crackers, Common, *22,* 23
Cracklin' Cornbread, *150,* 151
Cranberry Upside-Down Cake, *66,* 67
Cream Cheese
    Baked Jalapeño Poppers, *238,* 239
    Biscuits, *148,* 149
Crème Fraîche, *68,* 69
Crumb-Coated Baked Ham, *214,* 215

Crumble
    description of, **73**
    Summer Blueberry, *72,* **73**
    without a Food Processor, **73**
Cupcakes, Boston Cream, *60,* **61**
Curried Waldorf Salad with Green Grapes and Peanuts, **35**

D

Dates
    Jefferson Davis Pie, *156,* **157**
Desserts
    Bee Sting Cake, *64,* **65**
    Blackberry Jam Cake, *152,* **153**
    Black-Bottom Pie, *290,* **291**
    Blueberry Boy Bait, *228,* **229**
    Boston Cream Cupcakes, *60,* **61**
    Buckeyes, *232,* **233**
    Buttermilk Pie, *166,* **167**
    Butterscotch Gooey Butter Cake, **231**
    Carolina Sweet Potato Sonker, *168,* **169**
    Chocolate-Dipped Potato Chip Cookies, **59**
    Chocolate Gooey Butter Cake, **231**
    Cranberry Upside-Down Cake, *66,* **67**
    Crumble without a Food Processor, **73**
    Fudgy Tar Heel Pie, *158,* **159**
    Grasshopper Pie, *164,* **165**
    Harvey House Chocolate Puffs, *286,* **287**
    Hermit Cookies, *56,* **57**
    Jefferson Davis Pie, *156,* **157**
    Kringle, *226,* **227**
    Lemon Snow, *74,* **75**
    Maple Syrup Pie, *68,* **69**
    Marlborough Apple Pie, *70,* **71**
    Millionaire Pie, *288,* **289**
    Moravian Sugar Cake, *154,* **155**
    old-fashioned fruit, types of, **73**
    Peanut Butter Pie, *160,* **161**
    Peanut Butter Pie with Chocolate Graham Crust, **161**
    Potato Chip Cookies, *58,* **59**
    Sand Tarts, *224,* **225**
    St. Louis Gooey Butter Cake, *230,* **231**
    Summer Blueberry Crumble, *72,* **73**
    Swedish Pancakes, *220,* **221**
    Texas Blueberry Cobbler, *292,* **293**
    Thoroughbred Pie, *162,* **163**
    Wellesley Fudge Cake, *62,* **63**
Dill–Sour Cream Sauce, **17**
Dilly Casserole Bread, *222,* **223**

Dirty Rice, *134,* **135**
Dressing (dips)
    for Boneless Buffalo Chicken, *6,* **7**
    Ranch, **279**
Dressing (side dishes)
    Biscuit, *110,* **111**
    Dried Fruit and Nut Wild Rice, **271**
    Leek and Mushroom Wild Rice, **271**
    Wild Rice, *270,* **271**
Dried Fruit and Nut Wild Rice Dressing, **271**

E

Easy New England Clam Chowder, *22,* **23**
Eating local
    Al's Italian Beef (Chicago, IL), **187**
    Belgrade Gardens (Barberton, OH), **197**
    Benji's Deli (Milwaukee, WI), **295**
    Blue Bayou Restaurant (Anaheim, CA), **243**
    Central Grocery (New Orleans, LA), **81**
    Chesterfield Restaurant (Utica, NY), **13**
    Cobb Cook Grocery (Hibbing, MN), **295**
    Country Club Bakery (Fairmont, WV), **294**
    Fraboni's (Hibbing, MN), **183**
    Franklin Barbecue (Austin, TX), **253**
    Geno's Steaks (Philadelphia, PA), **9**
    Georgio's Village (New Hartford, NY), **13**
    Harry Caray's Italian Steakhouse (Chicago, IL), **295**
    International Bar-B-Q Festival (Owensboro, KY), **95**
    Johnny Cake Festival (Richmond, RI), **294**
    Kossar's Bialys (New York, NY), **294**
    Lexington Barbecue (Lexington, NC), **131**
    Loris Bog-Off Festival (Loris, SC), **99**
    Lotta Bull BBQ (Marietta, OK), **295**
    Louie Mueller Barbecue (Taylor, TX), **253**
    Lynwood Café (Randolph, MA), **19**
    Moonlite Bar-B-Q Inn (Owensboro, KY), **294**
    O&H Danish Bakery (Racine, WI), **295**
    Pat's King of Steaks (Philadelphia, PA), **9**
    Runza Restaurant (Lincoln, NE), **295**
    Shrimp Shack (St. Helena Island, SC), **294**
    Sonker Festival (Lowgap, NC), **295**
    Spiedie Fest (Binghamton, NY), **294**
    Taylor Grocery (Taylor, MS), **113**
    Taylor's Maid-Rite (Marshalltown, IA), **175**
    Teddy's Restaurant (Rome, NY), **13**
    Ted's Restaurant (Meriden, CT), **3**
    Winkler Bakery (Winston-Salem, NC), **155**

Eggs
    Fried, Perfect, *218,* 219
    Hawaiian Fried Rice, *272, 273*
    Hoppel Poppel, *216,* 217
Escarole
    Utica Greens, *14,* 15

F

Fatback, about, 27
Faux Leftover Rice, 273
Fish
    Chowder, New England, *26,* 27
    Fried Catfish, *112,* 113
Football Sandwiches, *82,* 83
Frenchees, Cheese, *172, 173*
Fried Catfish, *112,* 113
Fried Green Tomatoes, *126,* 127
Fritos corn chips
    King Ranch Casserole, *266, 267*
Fruit
    Dried, and Nut Wild Rice Dressing, 271
    see also specific fruits
Frying foods, tips for, 173
Fudgy Tar Heel Pie, *158,* 159
Funeral Potatoes, *280,* 281

G

Garlic
    Knots, *50,* 51
    Toasts, 25
Giardiniera, jarred
    Chicago-Style Italian Beef Sandwiches, *186,* 187
    New Orleans Muffulettas, *80,* 81
Ginger
    Hermit Cookies, *56,* 57
Goetta, *218,* 219
Gooey Butter Cake
    Butterscotch, 231
    Chocolate, 231
    St. Louis, *230,* 231
Graham crackers
    Peanut Butter Pie, *160,* 161
    Peanut Butter Pie with Chocolate Graham Crust, 161
Grains
    Baked Cheese Grits, *124,* 125
    barley, about, 257
    Crumble without a Food Processor, 73

Grains *(cont.)*
    Goetta, *218,* 219
    Mulligan Stew, *256, 257*
    Summer Blueberry Crumble, *72, 73*
    see also Cornmeal; Rice
Grapes
    Green, and Peanuts, Curried Waldorf Salad with, 35
    Red, and Almonds, Waldorf Salad with, 35
Grasshopper Pie, *164,* 165
Gravy
    Authentic Maryland Fried Chicken and, *96,* 97
    Chocolate, 149
    Country-Fried Pork with, *248,* 249
    Red-Eye, Ham Steak with, *140,* 141
    Sausage, Biscuits and, *144,* 145
Green Bay Booyah, *192,* 193
Green Beans
    Mulligan Stew, *256, 257*
    Southern-Style, *122,* 123
    trimming ends of, 123
Greens
    Pittsburgh Wedding Soup, *32,* 33
    prepping kale, 33
    Utica, *14,* 15
    see also Cabbage, Kale
Grilled dishes
    Chicken Spiedies, *4, 5*
    Kalua Pork, *246,* 247
    Kansas City Barbecued Brisket, *208,* 209
    Kansas City Sticky Ribs, *210,* 211
    Memphis Spareribs, *104,* 105
    Monterey Chicken, *240,* 241
    Oklahoma Barbecued Chopped Pork, *244,* 245
    Pimento Cheeseburgers, *78,* 79
    Smoky Kansas City Barbecue Beans, *212,* 213
    Wisconsin Grilled Brats and Beer, *188,* 189
Grits, Baked Cheese, *124,* 125
Grunt, description of, 73

H

Ham
    Baked, Crumb-Coated, *214,* 215
    and Cheddar Hushpuppies, 143
    Corn Chowder with Prosciutto and Sage, 29
    Country, *108,* 109
    country, about, 109
    Football Sandwiches, *82,* 83
    Hawaiian Fried Rice, *272, 273*

Ham *(cont.)*
    Hoppel Poppel, *216,* 217
    Hoppin' John, *138,* 139
    Monte Cristo Sandwiches, *242,* 243
    Mulligan Stew, *256,* 257
    Prosperity Sandwiches, *178,* 179
    Senate Navy Bean Soup, *92,* 93
    Steak with Red-Eye Gravy, *140,* 141
Harvey House Chocolate Puffs, *286,* 287
Hawaiian Fried Rice, *272,* 273
Heavenly Hots, *282,* 283
Hermit Cookies, *56,* 57
Hollywood Chili, *262,* 263
Home Fries, Short-Order, *140,* 141
Homemade Candied Peanuts, 161
Hominy
    New Mexican Pork Stew (Posole), *258,* 259
Hoppel Poppel, *216,* 217
Hoppin' John, *138,* 139
Horseradish
    Jezebel Sauce, 109
Hot Mustard Sauce, 215
Hushpuppies, *142,* 143
    Corn and Red Pepper, 143
    Crab and Chive, 143
    Ham and Cheddar, 143

I

Indoor Barbecue Beef Short Ribs, *252,* 253
Iowa Loose Meat Sandwiches, *174,* 175
Iowa Skinnies, *176,* 177
Iron Range Porketta, *182,* 183

J

Jambalaya, Perfect Shrimp, *116,* 117
Jefferson Davis Pie, *156,* 157
Jezebel Sauce, 109
Joe Booker Stew, *30,* 31
Johnnycakes, Rhode Island, *46,* 47
Jo Jo Potatoes, *278,* 279

K

Kale
    Pittsburgh Wedding Soup, *32,* 33
    prepping, 33
Kalua Pork, *246,* 247

Kansas City Barbecued Brisket, *208,* 209
Kentucky Burgoo, *94,* 95
Kielbasa
    Carolina Chicken Bog, *98,* 99
    Casserole, *204,* 205
King Ranch Casserole, *266,* 267
Knishes, Potato, *40,* 41
Knoephla Soup, *194,* 195
Kringle, *226,* 227

L

Lamb
    Kentucky Burgoo, *94,* 95
Leek and Mushroom Wild Rice Dressing, 271
Lemon Snow, *74,* 75
Livers
    Dirty Rice, *134,* 135
Lowcountry Red Rice, *132,* 133

M

Main dishes
    Authentic Maryland Fried Chicken and Gravy, *96,* 97
    Barberton Fried Chicken, *196,* 197
    Biscuits and Sausage Gravy, *144,* 145
    Carne Adovada, *260,* 261
    Carolina Chicken Bog, *98,* 99
    Chicago-Style Italian Roast Beef, *184,* 185
    Chicken à la King, *10,* 11
    Chicken Bonne Femme, *102,* 103
    Chicken Riggies, *12,* 13
    Chicken Vesuvio, *198,* 199
    Chiles Rellenos Casserole, *264,* 265
    City Chicken, *16,* 17
    Corned Beef and Cabbage, *20,* 21
    Country Captain Chicken, *100,* 101
    Country-Fried Pork with Gravy, *248,* 249
    Country Ham, *108,* 109
    Crumb-Coated Baked Ham, *214,* 215
    Fried Catfish, *112,* 113
    Goetta, *218,* 219
    Ham Steak with Red-Eye Gravy, *140,* 141
    Hollywood Chili, *262,* 263
    Hoppel Poppel, *216,* 217
    Hoppin' John, *138,* 139
    Indoor Barbecue Beef Short Ribs, *252,* 253
    Joe Booker Stew, *30,* 31
    Kalua Pork, *246,* 247

Main dishes *(cont.)*

    Kansas City Barbecued Brisket, *208,* 209

    Kansas City Sticky Ribs, *210,* 211

    Kentucky Burgoo, *94,* 95

    Kielbasa Casserole, *204,* 205

    King Ranch Casserole, *266,* 267

    Maque Choux with Shrimp, *91*

    Memphis Spareribs, *104,* 105

    Monterey Chicken, *240,* 241

    Mulligan Stew, *256,* 257

    New England Bar Pizza, *18,* 19

    New Mexican Pork Stew (Posole), *258,* 259

    Oven-Barbecued Beef Brisket, *250,* 251

    Perfect Fried Eggs, *218,* 219

    Perfect Shrimp Jambalaya, *116,* 117

    Pork Chop Casserole, *206,* 207

    Pork Chops with Tomato Gravy, *106,* 107

    Red Beans and Rice, *136,* 137

    Shrimp Étouffée, *120,* 121

    South Carolina Shrimp Boil, *118,* 119

    Steak de Burgo, *200,* 201

    Texas Chicken-Fried Steak, *254,* 255

    see also Burgers; Sandwiches; Soups

Maple (Syrup)

    Butter, *46,* 47

    Pie, *68,* 69

    pure, about, **141**

Maque Choux, *90,* 91

Maque Choux with Shrimp, **91**

Marlborough Apple Pie, *70,* 71

Maryland Crab Fluff, *86,* 87

Meat. *See* Beef; Lamb; Pork

Meatloaf mix

    Pittsburgh Wedding Soup, *32,* 33

Memphis Spareribs, *104,* 105

Millionaire Pie, *288,* 289

Molasses

    Anadama Bread, *52,* 53

    Hermit Cookies, *56,* 57

Monte Cristo Sandwiches, *242,* 243

Monterey Chicken, *240,* 241

Monterey Jack cheese

    Baked Jalapeño Poppers, *238,* 239

    Chiles Rellenos Casserole, *264,* 265

Moravian Sugar Cake, *154,* 155

Mozzarella cheese

    New England Bar Pizza, *18,* 19

Muffulettas, New Orleans, *80,* 81

Mulligan Stew, *256,* 257

Mushroom(s)

    Chicken à la King, *10,* 11

    Chicken Riggies, *12,* 13

    and Leek Wild Rice Dressing, **271**

    Prosperity Sandwiches, *178,* 179

Mustard

    Jezebel Sauce, **109**

    Sauce, Hot, **215**

    yellow, about, **83**

N

New England Bar Pizza, *18,* 19

New England Fish Chowder, *26,* 27

New Orleans Muffulettas, *80,* 81

Nuts

    Curried Waldorf Salad with Green Grapes and Peanuts, **35**

    Homemade Candied Peanuts, **161**

    Peanut Butter Pie, *160,* 161

    Peanut Butter Pie with Chocolate Graham Crust, **161**

    Thoroughbred Pie, *162,* 163

    toasting, **35**

    Waldorf Salad, *34,* 35

    see also Almonds; Pecans

O

Oats

    Crumble without a Food Processor, *73*

    Goetta, *218,* 219

    Summer Blueberry Crumble, *72,* 73

Oklahoma Barbecued Chopped Pork, *244,* 245

Oklahoma Barbecue Relish, **245**

Old Bay seasoning, about, **119**

Olives

    Chicken Riggies, *12,* 13

    New Orleans Muffulettas, *80,* 81

Onions

    Bialys, *42,* 43

    Cornflake Stuffing, *276,* 277

    cutting, avoiding tears when, **277**

    Philadelphia Cheesesteaks, *8,* 9

    Potato Knishes, *40,* 41

    Southern-Style Green Beans, *122,* 123

    Wisconsin Grilled Brats and Beer, *188,* 189

Orange Sticky Rolls, Tick Tock, *284,* 285

Oven-Barbecued Beef Brisket, *250,* 251

Oyster(s)
  Po' Boys, *88,* 89
  shucking, 89

P

Pancakes
  Heavenly Hots, *282,* 283
  Rhode Island Johnnycakes, *46,* 47
  Swedish, *220,* 221
Pandowdy, description of, 73
Parmesan
  grating, 279
  Jo Jo Potatoes, *278,* 279
Parsley stems, note about, 269
Parsnips
  Cider-Glazed Root Vegetables, *36,* 37
  Cider-Glazed Root Vegetables with Pomegranate and
    Cilantro, 37
Pasta
  Chicken Riggies, *12,* 13
Pastrami and Swiss Football Sandwiches, 83
Pastries
  Kringle, *226,* 227
  Potato Knishes, *40,* 41
Peanut Butter
  Buckeyes, *232,* 233
  Pie, *160,* 161
  Pie with Chocolate Graham Crust, 161
Peanuts
  Candied, Homemade, 161
  and Green Grapes, Curried Waldorf Salad with, 35
  Peanut Butter Pie, *160,* 161
  Peanut Butter Pie with Chocolate Graham Crust, 161
Peas
  Chicken Vesuvio, *198,* 199
  frozen, flavor of, 199
Peas, black-eyed
  Hoppin' John, *138,* 139
  Texas Caviar, *268,* 269
Pecans
  Chocolate-Dipped Potato Chip Cookies, 59
  and Dried Cherries, Waldorf Salad with, 35
  Dried Fruit and Nut Wild Rice Dressing, 271
  Fudgy Tar Heel Pie, *158,* 159
  Jefferson Davis Pie, *156,* 157
  Kringle, *226,* 227
  Millionaire Pie, *288,* 289
  Potato Chip Cookies, *58,* 59

Pecorino Romano cheese
  Chicken Riggies, *12,* 13
  Utica Greens, *14,* 15
Pepper Jack cheese
  Monterey Chicken, *240,* 241
Pepperoni Rolls, West Virginia, *84,* 85
Pepper(s)
  Barberton Hot Sauce, 197
  Bell, and Andouille, Corn Chowder with, 29
  Chicken à la King, *10,* 11
  Chicken Riggies, *12,* 13
  Country Captain Chicken, *100,* 101
  Dirty Rice, *134,* 135
  Hawaiian Fried Rice, *272,* 273
  Hollywood Chili, *262,* 263
  Hoppel Poppel, *216,* 217
  Lowcountry Red Rice, *132,* 133
  Maque Choux, *90,* 91
  Maque Choux with Shrimp, 91
  Perfect Shrimp Jambalaya, *116,* 117
  Pimento Cheeseburgers, *78,* 79
  Red, and Corn Hushpuppies, 143
  Red Beans and Rice, *136,* 137
  Shrimp Étouffée, *120,* 121
  Texas Caviar, *268,* 269
  Utica Greens, *14,* 15
  see also Chiles
Perfect Fried Eggs, *218,* 219
Perfect Shrimp Jambalaya, *116,* 117
Philadelphia Cheesesteaks, *8,* 9
Pico de Gallo, *240,* 241
Pies
  Apple, Marlborough, *70,* 71
  Black-Bottom, *290,* 291
  Buttermilk, *166,* 167
  Carolina Sweet Potato Sonker, *168,* 169
  Fudgy Tar Heel, *158,* 159
  Grasshopper, *164,* 165
  Jefferson Davis, *156,* 157
  Maple Syrup, *68,* 69
  Millionaire, *288,* 289
  Peanut Butter, *160,* 161
  Peanut Butter, with Chocolate Graham Crust, 161
  Thoroughbred, *162,* 163
Pimento Cheeseburgers, *78,* 79
Pineapple
  Hawaiian Fried Rice, *272,* 273
  Jezebel Sauce, 109
  Millionaire Pie, *288,* 289

Pineapple *(cont.)*
> prepping, **273**

Pittsburgh Wedding Soup, *32,* **33**

Pizza, New England Bar, *18,* **19**

Po' Boys, Oyster, *88,* **89**

Pomegranate and Cilantro, Cider-Glazed Root Vegetables
> with, **37**

Pork
> Carne Adovada, *260,* **261**
> Chop Casserole, *206,* **207**
> Chopped, Oklahoma Barbecued, *244,* **245**
> chops, types of, **207**
> Chops with Tomato Gravy, *106,* **107**
> City Chicken, *16,* **17**
> Country-Fried, with Gravy, *248,* **249**
> cutlets, preparing, **177**
> Dirty Rice, *134,* **135**
> enhanced, about, **107**
> fatback, about, **27**
> Hollywood Chili, *262,* **263**
> Hoppel Poppel, *216,* **217**
> internal cooking temperatures, **107**
> Iowa Skinnies, *176,* **177**
> Iron Range Porketta, *182,* **183**
> Kalua, *246,* **247**
> Kansas City Sticky Ribs, *210,* **211**
> Memphis Spareribs, *104,* **105**
> Pittsburgh Wedding Soup, *32,* **33**
> salt, about, **27**
> Stew, New Mexican (Posole), *258,* **259**
> Utica Greens, *14,* **15**
> *see also* Bacon; Ham; Sausage(s)

Posole (New Mexican Pork Stew), *258,* **259**

Potato Chip(s)
> Cookies, *58,* **59**
> Cookies, Chocolate-Dipped, **59**
> history of, **59**

Potato(es)
> Biscuits with Bacon, **49**
> Biscuits with Cheddar and Scallions, **49**
> Biscuits with Chives, *48,* **49**
> Chicken Bonne Femme, *102,* **103**
> Chicken Vesuvio, *198,* **199**
> Classic Corn Chowder, *28,* **29**
> Corn Chowder with Andouille and Bell Pepper, **29**
> Corn Chowder with Chorizo and Chiles, **29**
> Corn Chowder with Prosciutto and Sage, **29**
> Corned Beef and Cabbage, *20,* **21**
> Easy New England Clam Chowder, *22,* **23**

Potato(es) *(cont.)*
> Funeral, *280,* **281**
> Green Bay Booyah, *192,* **193**
> Hoppel Poppel, *216,* **217**
> Joe Booker Stew, *30,* **31**
> Jo Jo, *278,* **279**
> Kentucky Burgoo, *94,* **95**
> Kielbasa Casserole, *204,* **205**
> Knishes, *40,* **41**
> Knoephla Soup, *194,* **195**
> Mulligan Stew, *256,* **257**
> New England Fish Chowder, *26,* **27**
> Rhode Island Red Clam Chowder, *24,* **25**
> Senate Navy Bean Soup, *92,* **93**
> Short-Order Home Fries, *140,* **141**
> South Carolina Shrimp Boil, *118,* **119**
> *see also* Sweet Potato(es)

Poultry. *See* Chicken; Turkey

Pretzels, Ballpark, *44,* **45**

Prosciutto and Sage, Corn Chowder with, **29**

Prosperity Sandwiches, *178,* **179**

Provolone cheese
> New Orleans Muffulettas, *80,* **81**
> Philadelphia Cheesesteaks, *8,* **9**

Q

Quicker Boston Baked Beans, *38,* **39**

Quick Jus, **187**

R

Raisins
> Country Captain Chicken, *100,* **101**
> Hermit Cookies, *56,* **57**
> Jefferson Davis Pie, *156,* **157**
> Waldorf Salad, *34,* **35**

Ranch Dressing, **279**

Red Beans and Rice, *136,* **137**

Relish, Oklahoma Barbecue, **245**

Reuben Sandwiches, The Best, *180,* **181**

Rhode Island Johnnycakes, *46,* **47**

Rhode Island Red Clam Chowder, *24,* **25**

Rice
> Carolina Chicken Bog, *98,* **99**
> Dirty, *134,* **135**
> Faux Leftover, **273**
> Hawaiian Fried, *272,* **273**
> Hoppin' John, *138,* **139**

Rice *(cont.)*
  long-grain, about, **133**
  Lowcountry Red, *132,* **133**
  Perfect Shrimp Jambalaya, *116,* **117**
  Red Beans and, *136,* **137**
  rinsing, **135**
  Tex-Mex, *274,* **275**
  White, *120,* **121**
  Wild, Dressing, *270,* **271**
  Wild, Dressing, Dried Fruit and Nut, **271**
  Wild, Dressing, Leek and Mushroom, **271**
Rutabaga
  Green Bay Booyah, *192,* **193**
  Joe Booker Stew, *30,* **31**

S

Salads
  Carolina Red Slaw, *130,* **131**
  Texas Caviar, *268,* **269**
  Waldorf, *34,* **35**
  Waldorf, Curried, with Green Grapes and Peanuts, **35**
  Waldorf, with Dried Cherries and Pecans, **35**
  Waldorf, with Red Grapes and Almonds, **35**
Salt pork, about, **27**
Sand Tarts, *224,* **225**
Sandwiches
  Beef, Chicago-Style Italian, *186,* **187**
  Bierocks, *202,* **203**
  Cheese Frenchees, *172,* **173**
  Chicken Spiedies, *4,* **5**
  Football, *82,* **83**
  Iowa Loose Meat, *174,* **175**
  Iowa Skinnies, *176,* **177**
  Iron Range Porketta, *182,* **183**
  Monte Cristo, *242,* **243**
  New Orleans Muffulettas, *80,* **81**
  Oklahoma Barbecued Chopped Pork, *244,* **245**
  Oyster Po' Boys, *88,* **89**
  Pastrami and Swiss Football Sandwiches, **83**
  Philadelphia Cheesesteaks, *8,* **9**
  Prosperity, *178,* **179**
  Reuben, The Best, *180,* **181**
  Wisconsin Grilled Brats and Beer, *188,* **189**
  see also Burgers
Sauces
  Avocado, **237**
  Barbecue, **251**

Sauces *(cont.)*
  Cocktail, **87**
  Comeback, *112,* **113**
  Hot, Barberton, **197**
  Hot Mustard, **215**
  Jezebel, **109**
  Pico de Gallo, *240,* **241**
  Quick Jus, **187**
  Sour Cream–Dill, **17**
  Tartar, *114,* **115**
  see also Gravy
Sauerkraut
  The Best Reuben Sandwiches, *180,* **181**
  buying, **205**
  Kielbasa Casserole, *204,* **205**
  Pastrami and Swiss Football Sandwiches, **83**
Sausage(s)
  Carolina Chicken Bog, *98,* **99**
  Corn Chowder with Andouille and Bell Pepper, **29**
  Corn Chowder with Chorizo and Chiles, **29**
  Goetta, *218,* **219**
  Gravy, Biscuits and, *144,* **145**
  Hoppel Poppel, *216,* **217**
  Kielbasa Casserole, *204,* **205**
  Maque Choux, *90,* **91**
  Maque Choux with Shrimp, **91**
  New Orleans Muffulettas, *80,* **81**
  Perfect Shrimp Jambalaya, *116,* **117**
  Red Beans and Rice, *136,* **137**
  South Carolina Shrimp Boil, *118,* **119**
  West Virginia Pepperoni Rolls, *84,* **85**
  Wisconsin Grilled Brats and Beer, *188,* **189**
Seafood. *See* Fish; Shellfish
Senate Navy Bean Soup, *92,* **93**
Shellfish
  Crab and Chive Hushpuppies, **143**
  Easy New England Clam Chowder, *22,* **23**
  Maque Choux with Shrimp, **91**
  Maryland Crab Fluff, *86,* **87**
  Oyster Po' Boys, *88,* **89**
  oysters, shucking, **89**
  Perfect Shrimp Jambalaya, *116,* **117**
  Rhode Island Red Clam Chowder, *24,* **25**
  shrimp, peeling and deveining, **115**
  Shrimp Étouffée, *120,* **121**
  South Carolina Shrimp Boil, *118,* **119**
  South Carolina Shrimp Burgers, *114,* **115**

Short-Order Home Fries, *140,* 141
Shrimp
    Boil, South Carolina, *118,* 119
    Burgers, South Carolina, *114,* 115
    Étouffée, *120,* 121
    Jambalaya, Perfect, *116,* 117
    Maque Choux with, *91*
    peeling and deveining, *115*
Sides
    Baked Cheese Grits, *124,* 125
    Bialys, *42,* 43
    Biscuit Dressing, *110,* 111
    Caramel Tomatoes, *128,* 129
    Carolina Red Slaw, *130,* 131
    Cider-Glazed Root Vegetables, *36,* 37
    Cider-Glazed Root Vegetables with Pomegranate and
        Cilantro, *37*
    Corn and Red Pepper Hushpuppies, *143*
    Cornflake Stuffing, *276,* 277
    Crab and Chive Hushpuppies, *143*
    Curried Waldorf Salad with Green Grapes and
        Peanuts, *35*
    Dirty Rice, *134,* 135
    Dried Fruit and Nut Wild Rice Dressing, *271*
    Fried Green Tomatoes, *126,* 127
    Funeral Potatoes, *280,* 281
    Garlic Toasts, *25*
    Ham and Cheddar Hushpuppies, *143*
    Hawaiian Fried Rice, *272,* 273
    Hushpuppies, *142,* 143
    Jo Jo Potatoes, *278,* 279
    Leek and Mushroom Wild Rice Dressing, *271*
    Lowcountry Red Rice, *132,* 133
    Maque Choux, *90,* 91
    Potato Knishes, *40,* 41
    Quicker Boston Baked Beans, *38,* 39
    Red Beans and Rice, *136,* 137
    Rhode Island Johnnycakes, *46,* 47
    Short-Order Home Fries, *140,* 141
    Smoky Kansas City Barbecue Beans, *212,* 213
    Texas Caviar, *268,* 269
    Tex-Mex Rice, *274,* 275
    Toasted Italian Bread, *11*
    Utica Greens, *14,* 15
    Waldorf Salad, *34,* 35
    Waldorf Salad with Dried Cherries and Pecans, *35*
    Waldorf Salad with Red Grapes and Almonds, *35*
    White Rice, *120,* 121
    Wild Rice Dressing, *270,* 271

Slaw, Carolina Red, *130,* 131
Smoky Kansas City Barbecue Beans, *212,* 213
Snow, used in recipes, *75*
Sonker, Carolina Sweet Potato, *168,* 169
Soups
    Cheddar Beer, Wisconsin, *190,* 191
    Green Bay Booyah, *192,* 193
    Knoephla, *194,* 195
    Navy Bean, Senate, *92,* 93
    Pittsburgh Wedding, *32,* 33
    see also Chowder; Stews
Sour Cream
    –Dill Sauce, *17*
    substituting yogurt for, *283*
South Carolina Shrimp Boil, *118,* 119
South Carolina Shrimp Burgers, *114,* 115
Southern-Style Green Beans, *122,* 123
Spiedies, Chicken, *4,* 5
St. Louis Gooey Butter Cake, *230,* 231
Steak de Burgo, *200,* 201
Stews
    Carne Adovada, *260,* 261
    Hollywood Chili, *262,* 263
    Joe Booker, *30,* 31
    Kentucky Burgoo, *94,* 95
    Mulligan, *256,* 257
    Pork, New Mexican (Posole), *258,* 259
Sticky Rolls, Orange, Tick Tock, *284,* 285
Strawberries
    Harvey House Chocolate Puffs, *286,* 287
Stuffing, Cornflake, *276,* 277
Sugar, confectioners'
    dusting with, *283*
    making your own, *283*
Summer Blueberry Crumble, *72,* 73
Swedish Pancakes, *220,* 221
Sweet Potato(es)
    Biscuits, *146,* 147
    and Cayenne, Corn Chowder with, *29*
    choosing, *147*
    Sonker, Carolina, *168,* 169
Swiss cheese
    The Best Reuben Sandwiches, *180,* 181
    Football Sandwiches, *82,* 83
    Monte Cristo Sandwiches, *242,* 243
    Pastrami and Swiss Football Sandwiches, *83*

T

Taquitos, Crispy Beef, *236,* 237
Tartar Sauce, *114,* 115
Texas Blueberry Cobbler, *292,* 293
Texas Caviar, *268,* 269
Texas Chicken-Fried Steak, *254,* 255
Tex-Mex Rice, *274,* 275
Thoroughbred Pie, *162,* 163
Tick Tock Orange Sticky Rolls, *284,* 285
Toasted Italian Bread, 11
Tomato(es)
    Barberton Hot Sauce, 197
    Caramel, *128,* 129
    Chicken Riggies, *12,* 13
    Country Captain Chicken, *100,* 101
    Gravy, Pork Chops with, *106,* 107
    Green, Fried, *126,* 127
    Green Bay Booyah, *192,* 193
    Lowcountry Red Rice, *132,* 133
    Maque Choux, *90,* 91
    Maque Choux with Shrimp, 91
    New England Bar Pizza, *18,* 19
    peeling, 129
    Perfect Shrimp Jambalaya, *116,* 117
    Pico de Gallo, *240,* 241
    Prosperity Sandwiches, *178,* 179
    Rhode Island Red Clam Chowder, *24,* 25
    Shrimp Étouffée, *120,* 121
    Tex-Mex Rice, *274,* 275
Tortillas
    Crispy Beef Taquitos, *236,* 237
    King Ranch Casserole, *266,* 267
Turkey
    Monte Cristo Sandwiches, *242,* 243
    Prosperity Sandwiches, *178,* 179
Turnips
    Cider-Glazed Root Vegetables, *36,* 37
    Cider-Glazed Root Vegetables with Pomegranate and
        Cilantro, 37
    Mulligan Stew, *256,* 257
    prepping, 37

U

Utica Greens, *14,* 15

V

Vegetables
    Root, Cider-Glazed, *36,* 37
    Root, Cider-Glazed, with Pomegranate and Cilantro, 37
    see also specific vegetables
Vermouth, as wine substitute, 201

W

Waldorf Salad, *34,* 35
    Curried, with Green Grapes and Peanuts, 35
    with Dried Cherries and Pecans, 35
    with Red Grapes and Almonds, 35
Walnuts
    Thoroughbred Pie, *162,* 163
    Waldorf Salad, *34,* 35
Wellesley Fudge Cake, *62,* 63
West Virginia Pepperoni Rolls, *84,* 85
Whipped Cream, Bourbon, *156,* 157
White Rice, *120,* 121
Wild Rice
    Dressing, *270,* 271
    Dressing, Dried Fruit and Nut, 271
    Dressing, Leek and Mushroom, 271
Wine, substituting vermouth for, 201
Wisconsin Cheddar Beer Soup, *190,* 191
Wisconsin Grilled Brats and Beer, *188,* 189
Wood chips, soaking, 247

Y

Yeast, about, 223
Yogurt, as substitute for sour cream, 283